Creating AI Synergy Through Business Technology Transformation

Balaji Sundaramurthy
Al Zahra College for Women, Oman

Padmalosani Dayalan
University of Technology and Applied Sciences, Oman

A volume in the Advances in
Business Information Systems
and Analytics (ABISA) Book
Series

Published in the United States of America by
    IGI Global
    Engineering Science Reference (an imprint of IGI Global)
    701 E. Chocolate Avenue
    Hershey PA, USA 17033
    Tel: 717-533-8845
    Fax: 717-533-8661
    E-mail: cust@igi-global.com
    Web site: http://www.igi-global.com

Library of Congress Cataloging-in-Publication Data

CIP DATA PENDING

ISBN: 9798369341872
eISBN: 9798369341889

British Cataloguing in Publication Data
A Cataloguing in Publication record for this book is available from the British Library.

All work contributed to this book is new, previously-unpublished material.
The views expressed in this book are those of the authors, but not necessarily of the publisher.

For electronic access to this publication, please contact: eresources@igi-global.com.

Table of Contents

Chapter 1
Advanced Banking Solutions for Industry 5.0: From Industry's Perspective 1

Naveen Kumar C. M., Jain College, Bengaluru, India
Santosh Reddy Addula, University of the Cumberlands, USA
R. Seranmadevi, Christ University, Bangalore, India
Amit Kumar Tyagi, National Institute of Fashion Technology, New
        Delhi, India

Chapter 2
Exploring the Implementation and Challenges of AI-Based Fraud Detection
Systems in Financial Institutions: A Review 25

Padmalosani Dayalan, University of Technology and Applied Sciences,
        Ibra, Oman
Balaji Sundaramurthy, Al Zahra College for Women, Muscat, Oman

Chapter 3
AI-Powered Business Evolution: Transformative Strategies for Success of
Evolving Industries 39

Yashodhan Karulkar, Mukesh Patel School of Technology Management
        and Engineering, India
Arshi Shah, Mukesh Patel School of Technology Managemet and
        Engineering, India
Rishab Naik, Mukesh Patel School of Technology Management and
        Engineering, India

Detailed Table of Contents

Chapter 1
Advanced Banking Solutions for Industry 5.0: From Industry's Perspective 1
> *Naveen Kumar C. M., Jain College, Bengaluru, India*
> *Santosh Reddy Addula, University of the Cumberlands, USA*
> *R. Seranmadevi, Christ University, Bangalore, India*
> *Amit Kumar Tyagi, National Institute of Fashion Technology, New*
>   *Delhi, India*

As industries move towards the fourth industrial revolution, commonly referred to as Industry 4.0, the banking sector stands at a critical juncture. With the advent of advanced technologies like artificial intelligence, blockchain, and the internet of things, coupled with the rise of data-driven decision-making, the banking industry is on the top of transitioning towards Industry 5.0. This chapter explores the evolving landscape of banking solutions through the lens of industry stakeholders, shedding light on the opportunities and challenges presented by this paradigm shift. From the industry's perspective, advanced banking solutions offer a myriad of benefits, ranging from enhanced operational efficiency and cost reduction to improved customer experiences and competitive differentiation. By leveraging technologies such as robotic process automation and predictive analytics, banks can streamline their processes, automate routine tasks, and extract actionable insights from vast datasets.

Global financial systems' stability and integrity are seriously threatened by financial fraud. Financial institutions have been using artificial intelligence (AI) and machine learning (ML) technology more and more to improve their fraud detection skills in response to changing fraud schemes and growing complexity. The efficiency of AI-based fraud detection systems in identifying financial crimes and reducing risks, however, is still up for discussion and close examination. The purpose of this qualitative study is to investigate the application of AI-based fraud detection systems in financial institutions, as well as the associated problems. To gather information from important parties involved in the deployment and application of AI-based fraud detection systems in financial institutions, qualitative research techniques such as focus groups and semi-structured interviews will be used.

This chapter, as per the authors, examines the multidimensional function of artificial intelligence (AI) in many industries, focusing on its strategic integration for organizational success, decision-making improvement, and data management efficiency. The chapter examines how AI-driven solutions are altering old processes and catalyzing innovation in the logistics, aeronautics, agriculture and the banking industry. In logistics, AI enables predictive analytics and route optimization, resulting in better supply chain management and operational efficiency. AI in aeronautics improves safety measures, optimizes fuel usage, and revolutionizes flight operations. In addition, the use of AI in agriculture provides farmers with precision farming techniques which allow optimized resource allocation and higher crop yields. Finally, AI in the banking industry streamlines operations, enhances customer experience, and enables data-driven decision making for personalized services and fraud detection.

    M Kiran Kumar, CMS Business School, JAIN University, Bangalore,
        India
    V. Srinidhi, Community Institute of Management Studies, Bengaluru,
        India
    B. S. Shamanth, Surana Evening College, Bengaluru, India
    Amit Kumar Tyagi, National Institute of Fashion Technology, New
        Delhi, India

In today's rapidly changing world/digital landscape, the banking sector is undergoing a profound transformation driven by cutting-edge technologies. This chapter examines the convergence of smart banking with innovative technologies and explores its implications for using sustainability within the financial ecosystem. Modern smart banking leverages a constellation of technologies, including artificial intelligence, machine learning, big data analytics, and blockchain, to revolutionize traditional banking processes and deliver enhanced value to customers. By harnessing these technologies, banks can offer personalized financial services, automate routine tasks, and optimize decision-making processes, thereby improving operational efficiency and customer experiences.

    Akhil Manuel, Christ University, India
    Senthil Kumar Arumugam, Christ University, India

Given the influence of artificial intelligence (AI) on various sectors of the economy, its impact on the internal auditing sector is causing increased attention from the academic and professional communities. This book chapter investigates how AI is revolutionizing internal audit and its implications for the future of internal audit. By examining numerous literature sources and developments from various perspectives, this book chapter conducted a comprehensive analysis of how AI is applied in various processes of internal auditing. In the current data-reliant business society, AI's capacity to handle vast datasets and perform complex analyses plays an important role. The use of AI in internal auditing enhances efficiency, increases accuracy, and improves risk management. However, in the process, audit procedures fundamentally change. This book chapter concludes that while AI will significantly change the internal auditing process, it will not replace human auditors. AI will alter auditing jobs by requiring auditors to learn additional technology.

Chapter 6
    Shalini Swami, G.L. Bajaj Institute of Technology and Management,
       Greater Noida, India
    Pushpa Singh, G.L. Bajaj Institute of Technology and Management,
       Greater Noida, India
    Bhawna Singh, G.L. Bajaj Institute of Technology and Management,
       Greater Noida, India

Augmented reality (AR), computer vision (CV), and deep learning (DL) techniques enable a machine or application to enhance the e-commerce sectors. An integrated approach of AR and CV maximizes the visual information and interaction of the product in the digital environment. This chapter explores the synergistic effect that exists between AR and CV in the e-commerce sector, analyzing the applications and user experiences. It captures how these technologies revolutionize the interaction of consumers with products and an online shopping experience, giving them personalized online journeys, product recommendation, virtual-try-on, try-before-buy, and image-based product search. Furthermore, the chapter highlights that deep learning (DL) techniques such as CNN, GNN, and RNN revolutionized the e-commerce sector when integrated with AR and CV.

Chapter 7
    Revenio C. Jalagat, Al-Zahra College for Women, Oman

This chapter highlights how crucial it is to explore the use of AI applications in businesses nowadays, analyze how AI is being utilized to drive digital transformation, and what that means for the business environment going forward. Additionally, it evaluates the advantages and difficulties of AI as it relates to corporate technology change. Data were collected and analyzed from different scholarly sources, such as books, articles, and websites. Study findings claimed that the application of AI has grown significantly across a range of sectors, including manufacturing, telecommunications, healthcare, banking, education, retail, and e-commerce. Simplifying procedures, facilitating better decision-making, and increasing productivity are just a few of the ways artificial intelligence (AI) is thought to have significantly improved company operations. By leveraging AI's full potential, businesses can rise to a more advantageous position in the market, foster creativity, and innovation, increase productivity, and provide better customer experiences.

Chapter 8
    Annie Issac, Christ University, Bangalore, India
    R. Seranmadevi, Christ University, Bangalore, India

Financial literacy, a cornerstone for stability and empowerment in today's economic landscape, is set to be revolutionized. Finfluencers, individuals with significant financial acumen and a robust digital platform presence, are shaping audiences' financial attitudes and behaviors. This study introduces a conceptual framework based on the decomposed theory of planned behavior (DTPB) that holds the potential to transform how we understand and implement financial education. The unique aspect of this framework is its incorporation of Finfluencers as critical influencers in adopting AI chatbots for financial education. For instance, the model can predict the likelihood of a Finfluencer endorsing an AI chatbot for financial education based on their attitudes, subjective norms, and perceived behavioral control. Despite the widespread use of DTPB across various disciplines, a research gap exists in understanding the determinants of intention and behavior concerning adopting AI chatbots for financial education.

Chapter 9
    Tharaya Said AlHarthi, UTAS Ibra, Oman

In the age of digital technologies and transformation, artificial intelligence (AI) has emerged as essential technology to be integrated into various business activities and practices. The integration of AI into human resource management (HRM) practices has a profound and transformative shift in the way organizations approach workforce management. This technological evolution has not only revolutionized traditional HR methods, but has also introduced novel efficiencies, reshaping the landscape of talent acquisition, employee engagement, and overall organizational effectiveness. In this era of rapid technological advancement, understanding the multifaceted impact of AI on HRM is essential for businesses aiming to stay competitive, foster a more responsive workforce and build its capabilities. By reviewing the existing literature, this chapter offers a systematic analysis to gain insights on the impact of AI on various HRM practices. In addition, it aims to explore how AI technologies assist organizations to tackle numerous challenges associated with HRM.

Chapter 10

K. R. Pundareeka Vittala, ICFAI Foundation for Higher Education, Bangalore, India

J. Nagarathnamma, Presidency College (Autonomous), Bengaluru, India

N. Chidambaram, CHRIST University, Bengaluru, India

Amit Kumar Tyagi, National Institute of Fashion Technology, New Delhi, India

The advent of Industry 5.0 ushers in a new era of manufacturing characterized by unprecedented levels of connectivity, automation, and intelligence. This paradigm shift extends beyond the factory floor, permeating into the realm of financial services, particularly banking. Smart banking, empowered by cutting-edge technologies such as artificial intelligence, blockchain, and the Internet of Things, promises to revolutionize traditional banking practices, offering customers personalized and seamless financial experiences. This paper explores the opportunities and challenges presented by the integration of smart banking within the broader landscape of Industry 5.0. Opportunities include enhanced customer engagement, operational efficiency gains, and the democratization of financial services. However, challenges such as cybersecurity threats, regulatory compliance, and the digital divide must be addressed to fully realize the potential of smart financial services.

Chapter 11

J. Gayathri, Saveetha School of Law, India

J. Yazhini, Saveetha School of Law, India

Artificial intelligence (A.I.) is a multidisciplinary field aimed at automating tasks that currently need human intelligence. Computerized medical diagnosticians and systems that automatically tailor hardware to specific user requirements are examples of recent AI accomplishments. A.I. has spawned a slew of important technical concepts that unify these disparate fields. The search is made complex because of the need to determine the relevance of information and because of the frequent occurrence of uncertain and ambiguous data. Heuristics provide the A.I. system with a mechanism for the focusing its attention and controlling its searching processes. A total number of respondents 206 samples in the age group 18-35 years were selected randomly and forwarded the analyzed question online randomly through a convenient sampling method. The use of SPSS software to analyze and present the data collected from the frequency Graphs,chi-square tests.

In the face of global environmental challenges, the integration of futuristic technologies has emerged as a pivotal factor in the pursuit of a sustainable future. This paper explores the multifaceted contributions of advanced technologies towards building and maintaining a sustainable environment. By examining the intersection of innovation and environmental stewardship, we delve into the transformative potential of futuristic technologies across various sectors. The advent of artificial intelligence, Internet of Things (IoT), renewable energy, and advanced materials has paved the way for a paradigm shift in environmental sustainability. AI-driven predictive models enable precise resource management, optimizing energy consumption, and minimizing waste. The IoT facilitates real-time monitoring and control of environmental parameters, offering a data-driven approach to conservation efforts. Additionally, renewable energy technologies play a crucial role in reducing dependence on fossil fuels, mitigating climate change impacts.

The research delves into the dual-edged nature of AI in business, highlighting both its potential for creating new opportunities and its role in displacing existing jobs. It examines case studies where AI has led to significant changes in workforce requirements and explores the legal framework's response to these changes. Key areas of concern include the protection of displaced workers, the evolution of employment contracts, and the need for regulatory updates to address the challenges posed by automation. Additionally, the study assesses the effectiveness of current labor laws in safeguarding worker interests amidst rapid technological advancements. It proposes potential legal reforms and policy measures aimed at ensuring a balanced approach to AI integration, where technological progress does not come at the expense of worker rights and job security.

Chapter 14

Vimuktha Evangeleen Salis, Global Academy of Technology, India
Sharmila Chidravalli, Global Academy of Technology, India

In our rapidly evolving landscape, the realm of big data has gained prominence across sectors like healthcare, finance, and e-commerce. However, deciphering the vast amounts of generated data presents a significant challenge. Visualization techniques prove invaluable in making sense of this data, but traditional methods fall short. Enter cloud-based visualization platforms and algorithms, offering scalable and cost-effective solutions to tackle big data visualization challenges. This chapter embarks on a survey, comparing these platforms and algorithms based on their unique features, capabilities, and limitations. The literature review underscores the role of cloud computing in addressing the complexities of big data visualization. Methodologically, the authors employ criteria such as scalability, performance, cost-effectiveness, and user-friendliness to select and evaluate platforms and algorithms.

To unravel the complex facets of optimal equilibrium between professional commitments and personal life, this research delves into the intricacies of work-life balance dynamics, employing machine learning to predict factors influencing equilibrium. A stacking-ensemble method utilizes the mutual complementary effects of the base models to improve the performance with better generalization of the model. ML algorithms including gradient boosting algorithm, ridge regression, lasso regression, huber regression, sgd regressor, support vector regressor (SVR), k neighbours regressor, kernel ridge regressor, RANSAC regressor, K means boosting algorithm, and generalized additive model (GAM) were trained meticulously. Fine-tuning the performance of random forest performance having R2 value of 0.9353, the lowest using the stacking ensemble to 0.9999 was performed. The base model combinations encompass a wide array of techniques with random forest as meta learner gave is a notable improvement in its prediction performance.

Foreword

In the transformative age of artificial intelligence (AI), businesses stand at the threshold of unprecedented opportunities and challenges. The integration of AI into business operations is not merely a technological upgrade; it represents a profound shift in how organizations think, operate, and compete. This book, *Creating AI Synergy Through Business Technology Transformation*, aims to illuminate this journey, offering insights, strategies, and real-world examples to guide businesses through the complex landscape of AI adoption and integration.

The idea for this book emerged from a deep-seated belief in the transformative potential of AI when synergized with business technology. Over the years, I have witnessed firsthand the revolutionary impact of AI in various industries, from finance to healthcare, and its potential to drive efficiency, innovation, and growth. However, the path to harnessing AI's full potential is fraught with challenges, requiring a nuanced understanding of both technology and business dynamics.

Creating AI Synergy Through Business Technology Transformation is designed to serve as a comprehensive guide for business leaders, technology enthusiasts, and students alike. It delves into the theoretical underpinnings of AI, explores practical applications, and addresses the ethical and strategic considerations crucial for successful implementation. The goal is to empower readers with the knowledge and tools needed to navigate the AI-driven future with confidence and foresight.

As we stand on the cusp of this exciting frontier, I invite you to explore the myriad possibilities that AI brings to the table. This book is not just about understanding AI; it is about envisioning the future of business through the lens of AI-powered transformation. Let us embark on this journey together, fostering a synergy that will redefine the business landscape and create lasting value.

Preface

In today's rapidly evolving business landscape, the intersection of artificial intelligence (AI) and technological transformation has become a critical juncture for innovation and success. As editors of *Creating AI Synergy Through Business Technology Transformation*, we are thrilled to present this comprehensive exploration of how cutting-edge technologies and strategic business initiatives can intersect to create powerful synergies that drive organizational excellence.

This book delves into the dynamic realm where AI meets business transformation, offering a thorough examination of how organizations can harness the power of AI to enhance various aspects of their operations. In an increasingly interconnected global economy, integrating AI and disruptive technologies is no longer a mere competitive advantage—it is essential for long-term success. Through a blend of insightful research, practical case studies, and forward-thinking ideas, we aim to showcase AI's transformational potential in shaping the future of business.

From optimizing operational efficiency to elevating customer experiences, the strategic use of AI and digital transformation holds the potential to revolutionize industries and redefine organizational capabilities. This book seeks to explore the strategic nexus between AI and business technology transformation, providing readers with the knowledge and tools necessary to integrate AI into their business strategies seamlessly. By doing so, we highlight the importance of fostering synergy across different business domains and demonstrate how AI can serve as a unifying force that enhances productivity, collaboration, and communication throughout an organization.

Our target audience encompasses a diverse group of stakeholders, including business leaders and executives, technology professionals, innovation and strategy teams, entrepreneurs and start-up leaders, business consultants and analysts, academia and researchers, policymakers and regulators, and students. We believe that the insights and practical guidance provided in this book will be valuable across various organizational structures and industries, fostering a holistic understanding of the strategic integration of AI within the broader context of business technology transformation.

The book covers a wide range of topics essential for both business and information technology professionals, including:

Business:

- Strategic Integration of AI in Business
- AI in Decision-Making Processes
- Predictive Analytics and Business Intelligence
- AI Innovation in Product Development
- Digital Transformation through AI
- AI and Supply Chain Management
- AI in Finance and Banking

Information Technology:

- AI in IT Infrastructure Management
- Cybersecurity and AI
- AI in Software Engineering and Development
- Project Management in the Age of AI
- AI in Cloud Computing
- Cognitive Computing for Data Analysis

We hope this book serves as a valuable resource for those seeking to understand and navigate the complexities of AI and business technology transformation. By embracing the synergy between these domains, organizations can unlock new possibilities and achieve sustained success in an ever-changing world.

Chapter 1: Advanced Banking Solutions for Industry 5.0 - From Industry's Perspective

As industries transition towards the fourth industrial revolution, known as Industry 4.0, the banking sector finds itself at a pivotal crossroads. With advanced technologies such as artificial intelligence, blockchain, and the Internet of Things gaining prominence, coupled with the rise of data driven decision-making, the banking industry is on the brink of evolving into Industry 5.0. This chapter delves into the rapidly changing landscape of banking solutions from the viewpoint of industry stakeholders, highlighting the myriad of opportunities and challenges that come with this paradigm shift. Industry stakeholders see advanced banking solutions as avenues for enhanced operational efficiency, cost reduction, improved customer experiences, and competitive differentiation. The chapter explores how technologies like robotic process automation and predictive analytics can streamline processes, automate routine tasks, and extract actionable insights from vast datasets, driving the future of banking.

Chapter 2: Exploring the Implementation and Challenges of AI-Based Fraud Detection Systems in Financial Institutions - A Review

Financial fraud poses a significant threat to the stability and integrity of global financial systems. In response to evolving fraud schemes and increasing complexity, financial institutions are increasingly deploying artificial intelligence (AI) and machine learning (ML) technologies to enhance their fraud detection capabilities. This chapter provides a qualitative analysis of the application of AI-based fraud detection systems in financial institutions, focusing on their effectiveness in identifying financial crimes and mitigating risks. Using qualitative research methods such as focus groups and semi-structured interviews with key stakeholders, the chapter uncovers the implementation challenges and operational impacts of these advanced systems. The study aims to provide a comprehensive understanding of the benefits and limitations of AI-based fraud detection systems in the financial sector.

Chapter 3: AI-Powered Business Evolution - Transformative Strategies for Success of Evolving Industries

This chapter explores the multifaceted role of artificial intelligence (AI) across various industries, emphasizing its strategic integration for achieving organizational success, enhancing decision-making processes, and improving data management efficiency. The authors examine how AI-driven solutions are transforming traditional processes and fostering innovation in sectors such as logistics, aeronautics, agriculture, and banking. In logistics, AI enables predictive analytics and route optimization, improving supply chain management and operational efficiency. AI in aeronautics enhances safety, optimizes fuel usage, and revolutionizes flight operations. In agriculture, AI facilitates precision farming techniques, optimizing resource allocation and increasing crop yields. In the banking sector, AI streamlines operations, enhances customer experiences, and supports data-driven decision-making for personalized services and fraud detection.

Chapter 4: Modern Smart Banking with Cutting-Edge Technologies - A Sustainable Banking and Financial World

In today's rapidly changing digital landscape, the banking sector is undergoing profound transformation driven by cutting-edge technologies. This chapter examines the convergence of smart banking with innovative technologies and explores their implications for sustainability within the financial ecosystem. Modern smart banking leverages technologies such as artificial intelligence, machine learning, big data analytics, and blockchain to revolutionize traditional banking processes and deliver enhanced value to customers. By harnessing these technologies, banks can offer personalized financial services, automate routine tasks, and optimize decision-making processes, thereby improving operational efficiency and customer experiences. The chapter provides insights into how these advancements contribute to creating a sustainable and forward-thinking financial world.

Chapter 5: Harnessing Artificial Intelligence in Internal Auditing - Implementation, Impact, and Innovation

Artificial intelligence (AI) is having a significant impact on the internal auditing sector, drawing increased attention from both academic and professional communities. This chapter investigates how AI is revolutionizing internal audit processes and its implications for the future of internal auditing. Through a comprehensive analysis of various literature sources and developments, the chapter explores AI's application in different aspects of internal auditing. AI's ability to handle vast datasets and perform complex analyses enhances efficiency, accuracy, and risk management in the auditing process. However, the integration of AI also fundamentally changes audit procedures, requiring auditors to acquire new technological skills. The chapter concludes that while AI will significantly alter the internal auditing landscape, it will complement rather than replace human auditors, emphasizing the need for continuous learning and adaptation.

Chapter 6: Revolutionizing E-commerce - The Synergy of Computer Vision and Augmented Reality

Augmented reality (AR), computer vision (CV), and deep learning (DL) are transforming the e-commerce sector by enhancing the interaction between consumers and digital products. This chapter explores the synergistic effects of AR and CV in e-commerce, analyzing their applications and impact on user experiences. The integration of these technologies maximizes visual information and interaction, offering consumers personalized online journeys, product recommendations, virtual try-on experiences, and image-based product searches. The chapter highlights how deep learning techniques such as convolutional neural networks (CNN), graph neural networks (GNN), and recurrent neural networks (RNN) revolutionize e-commerce when combined with AR and CV, creating a more immersive and efficient shopping experience.

Chapter 7: Business Technology Transformation - Perspectives on AI Synergy

This chapter underscores the critical importance of exploring AI applications in businesses today and examines how AI is driving digital transformation across various sectors. By analyzing data from scholarly sources, the chapter evaluates the advantages and challenges associated with AI in corporate technology change. The findings indicate that AI's application has grown significantly in industries such as manufacturing, telecommunications, healthcare, banking, education, retail, and e-commerce. AI simplifies procedures, facilitates better decision-making, and increases productivity, thereby enhancing overall business operations. The chapter argues that leveraging AI's full potential can position businesses more advantageously in the market, fostering creativity, innovation, and superior customer experiences.

Chapter 8: Revolutionizing Financial Literacy Through Exploring Finfluencers' Intentions in Chatbot-Driven Financial Information Dissemination

Financial literacy is crucial for economic stability and empowerment, and this chapter explores how it can be revolutionized through the influence of Finfluencers—individuals with significant financial acumen and digital presence. The chapter introduces a conceptual framework based on the Decomposed Theory of Planned Behavior (DTPB), integrating Finfluencers as key influencers in adopting AI chatbots for financial education. The framework predicts the likelihood of Finfluencers endorsing AI chatbots based on their attitudes, subjective norms, and perceived behavioral control. Despite the widespread application of DTPB, there is a research gap in understanding the determinants of intention and behavior concerning AI chatbot adoption for financial education, which this chapter aims to address.

Chapter 9: The Effect of AI on HRM Practices

The integration of artificial intelligence (AI) into human resource management (HRM) practices is bringing about a profound transformation in workforce management. This chapter explores how AI revolutionizes traditional HR methods, introducing efficiencies that reshape talent acquisition, employee engagement, and organizational effectiveness. In the era of rapid technological advancement, understanding the multifaceted impact of AI on HRM is essential for businesses to remain competitive, foster a responsive workforce, and build capabilities. By reviewing existing literature, the chapter provides a systematic analysis of AI's impact on various HRM practices and explores how AI technologies help organizations tackle HRM challenges, enhancing overall efficiency and effectiveness.

Chapter 10: Smart Financial Services Through Smart Banking in the Era of Industry 5.0 - Opportunities and Challenges

Industry 5.0 introduces a new era of manufacturing characterized by high levels of connectivity, automation, and intelligence, extending its influence beyond the factory floor into financial services. This chapter explores the integration of smart banking within the broader Industry 5.0 landscape, highlighting the opportunities and challenges it presents. Smart banking, powered by technologies such as artificial intelligence, blockchain, and the Internet of Things, promises to revolutionize traditional banking practices, offering personalized and seamless financial experiences. Opportunities include enhanced customer engagement, operational efficiency, and democratized financial services. However, challenges such as cybersecurity threats, regulatory compliance, and the digital divide must be addressed to fully harness the potential of smart financial services.

Chapter 11: An Analytical Study on Emerging Growth of Artificial Intelligence in India

This chapter delves into the advancements in artificial intelligence (AI) with a focus on its applications in automated medical diagnostics and hardware customization tailored to user needs. It highlights the complexity of information retrieval in AI due to uncertain and ambiguous data, and how heuristics aid in refining search processes and focusing system attention. The chapter also presents an empirical analysis using SPSS software to examine data collected from 206 respondents aged 18-35, using frequency graphs and chi-square tests to interpret the findings.

Chapter 12: The Role of Futuristic Technologies in Building Sustainable Environment

This chapter investigates how advanced technologies are shaping the future of environmental sustainability, emphasizing their transformative impact on various sectors. It explores the roles of artificial intelligence, the Internet of Things (IoT), renewable energy, and advanced materials in enhancing environmental steward-ship and optimizing resource management. By analyzing how these technologies contribute to precise resource management, real-time environmental monitoring, and reduced reliance on fossil fuels, the chapter highlights their potential to drive a sustainable paradigm shift.

Chapter 13: The Impact of AI Integration on Workforce Dynamics Legal Challenges and Labour Law Implications in the Era of Business Technology Transformation

This chapter explores the complex impact of artificial intelligence (AI) on the business world, focusing on its dual role in creating new opportunities and displacing existing jobs. Through case studies, it examines the shifts in workforce requirements driven by AI and the legal responses to these changes, including protections for displaced workers and the evolution of employment contracts. The chapter also assesses the effectiveness of current labor laws in addressing these challenges and proposes legal reforms and policy measures to ensure that AI integration advances without undermining worker rights and job security.

Chapter 14: Cloud-Based Visualization Techniques for Big Data A Survey of Platforms and Algorithms

The chapter authors address the growing importance of big data across various sectors and the significant challenges associated with visualizing vast datasets. It reviews the limitations of traditional visualization methods and explores how cloud-based platforms and algorithms offer scalable and cost-effective solutions. By comparing these modern tools based on scalability, performance, cost, and user-friendliness, the chapter highlights their role in effectively managing and interpreting complex big data.

Chapter 15: Decoding Work-Life Balance Conundrum – A Meta - Learning Prediction Approach

This chapter explores the application of machine learning to enhance the under-standing of work-life balance dynamics, focusing on achieving an optimal equilibrium between professional and personal commitments. By employing a stacking-ensemble method, which combines multiple base models to improve prediction accuracy, the research demonstrates significant improvements in performance, notably refining the Random Forest model from an R^2 value of 0.9353 to 0.9999. Through the meticulous training and fine-tuning of various ML algorithms, including Gradient Boosting and

Support Vector Regressor, the chapter highlights how advanced machine learning techniques can effectively predict and optimize work-life balance factors.

In concluding *Creating AI Synergy Through Business Technology Transformation*, we reflect on the transformative potential of artificial intelligence (AI) across various sectors and its profound impact on modern business practices. This comprehensive exploration underscores that the integration of AI is not merely an option but a necessity for organizations aiming to achieve sustained success and innovation in today's dynamic environment.

Throughout the chapters, our esteemed contributors have delved into the myriad ways AI and advanced technologies are reshaping industries, from banking and financial services to e-commerce, internal auditing, and human resource management. Each chapter offers a unique perspective on the strategic application of AI, presenting both opportunities and challenges that businesses must navigate to fully leverage these transformative tools.

The journey begins with an examination of advanced banking solutions in the context of Industry 5.0, where technologies such as AI, blockchain, and the Internet of Things are poised to revolutionize banking operations. Moving forward, the focus shifts to the critical role of AI in fraud detection, highlighting its potential to safeguard financial institutions against evolving threats. The exploration of AI-powered business evolution further emphasizes the transformative strategies that can drive success across diverse industries.

In the realm of smart banking, the convergence of cutting-edge technologies fosters a sustainable financial ecosystem, enhancing operational efficiency and customer experiences. The application of AI in internal auditing showcases how these tools can revolutionize audit processes, emphasizing the importance of human auditors in complementing AI's capabilities. The synergy between computer vision and augmented reality in e-commerce reveals how these technologies enhance consumer interactions and shopping experiences.

As we delve into the broader implications of AI in business technology transformation, the perspectives on AI synergy provide invaluable insights into how businesses can harness AI to drive digital transformation, streamline processes, and foster innovation. The revolutionary potential of AI in financial literacy through chatbot-driven dissemination and the profound impact on human resource management practices highlight the diverse applications of AI in fostering organizational growth and efficiency.

Finally, the exploration of smart financial services within the context of Industry 5.0 brings the discussion full circle, emphasizing the need to address challenges such as cybersecurity, regulatory compliance, and the digital divide to fully realize the benefits of these advanced technologies.

As editors, we hope this book serves as a valuable resource for a diverse audience, including business leaders, technology professionals, researchers, and students. The insights and practical guidance provided herein aim to empower organizations to navigate the complexities of AI integration, fostering a holistic understanding of the strategic nexus between AI and business technology transformation. By embracing this synergy, businesses can unlock new possibilities, drive innovation, and achieve sustained success in an ever-evolving global economy.

Balaji Sundaramurthy
Al Zahra College for Women, Oman

Padmalosani Dayalan
University of Technology and Applied Sciences Ibra, Oman

Creating AI Synergy Through Business Technology Transformation

Creating AI Synergy Through Business Technology Transformation has been a journey of collaboration, dedication, and support from many individuals and organizations.

First and foremost, we would like to express my deepest gratitude to IGI publishing for the opportunity provided.

We are immensely grateful to Al Zahra College for Women and University of Technology and Applied Sciences, Ibra, for providing the academic environment and resources necessary to embark on this venture.

A big thanks to the authors who trusted in our work and contributed the research work. Your insightful contributions have been invaluable in providing a comprehensive and multifaceted view of AI and business technology transformation.

We are deeply indebted to the peer reviewers whose constructive critiques have helped shape and refine the manuscript. Your meticulous reviews and suggestions have been invaluable.

A heartfelt thanks to the numerous industry experts and practitioners who shared their valuable experiences and insights. The real-world perspectives have been instrumental in bridging the gap between theory and practice.

To the publishers and editorial team, thank you for your professionalism and commitment to bringing this book to life. Your expertise in guiding the manuscript through the publication process has been greatly appreciated.

Finally, we would like to extend our gratitude to all the readers and future professionals who will engage with this book. It is our hope that this work will provide you with the insights and tools necessary to harness the power of AI in transforming business technology.

Thank you all for your support and contributions to this endeavor.

Balaji Sundaramurthy,

Al Zahra College for Women, Oman

Padmalosani Dayalan,

University of Technology and Applied Sciences Ibra, Oman

Introduction

In today's rapidly evolving business landscape, the intersection of artificial intelligence (AI) and technological transformation has become a critical axis for innovation and sustained success. *Creating AI Synergy Through Business Technology Transformation* explores this dynamic realm, where cutting-edge technologies and strategic business initiatives converge. The book offers a comprehensive analysis of how organizations can harness the power of AI to generate synergy across various facets of their operations.

As businesses navigate the complexities of an increasingly interconnected global economy, the integration of AI and disruptive technologies has transitioned from being a competitive edge to an essential component for long-term viability. This book showcases AI's transformative potential in shaping the future of business through a blend of rigorous research, practical case studies, and forward-thinking perspectives. By optimizing operational efficiency and enhancing customer experiences, the strategic application of AI and digital transformation can revolutionize industries and expand the horizons of what organizations can achieve.

The purpose of this book is to examine the strategic convergence of artificial intelligence (AI) and business technology transformation, offering insights into how these elements can synergize to foster innovation and long-term success. Readers will gain the knowledge and tools needed to incorporate AI into their business strategies effectively, ensuring that these initiatives align seamlessly with the overall goals of their organizations. This alignment will highlight the importance of fostering synergy across various business domains and demonstrate how AI can serve as a cohesive force, enhancing productivity, collaboration, and communication throughout the enterprise.

Target Audience

The target audience for this book includes:

- Business leaders and executives
- Technology professionals
- Innovation and strategy teams
- Entrepreneurs and start-up leaders
- Business consultants and analysts
- Academics and researchers
- Policymakers and regulators
- Students

By providing valuable insights and practical guidance, this book aims to foster a comprehensive understanding of the strategic integration of AI within the broader context of business technology transformation. The content is designed to be applicable across diverse organizational structures and industries, promoting a holistic approach to the strategic incorporation of AI.

Key Topics

Business

- Strategic Integration of AI in Business
- AI in Decision-Making Processes
- Predictive Analytics and Business Intelligence
- AI Innovation in Product Development
- Digital Transformation through AI
- AI and Supply Chain Management
- AI in Finance and Banking

Information Technology

- AI in IT Infrastructure Management
- Cybersecurity and AI
- AI in Software Engineering and Development
- Project Management in the Age of AI
- AI in Cloud Computing
- Cognitive Computing for Data Analysis

Through this exploration, *Creating AI Synergy Through Business Technology Transformation* aims to provide readers with a roadmap for leveraging AI to drive business success. The insights and strategies discussed in this book will equip organizations with the tools necessary to thrive in an era defined by technological advancements and AI-driven innovation.

Balaji Sundaramurthy

Al Zahra College for Women, Oman

Padmalosani Dayalan

University of Technology and Applied Sciences Ibra, Oman

Chapter 1
Advanced Banking Solutions for Industry 5.0:
From Industry's Perspective

Naveen Kumar C. M.
Jain College, Bengaluru, India

Santosh Reddy Addula
(iD) https://orcid.org/0009-0000-3286-8224
University of the Cumberlands, USA

R. Seranmadevi
Christ University, Bangalore, India

Amit Kumar Tyagi
(iD) https://orcid.org/0000-0003-2657-8700
National Institute of Fashion Technology, New Delhi, India

ABSTRACT

As industries move towards the fourth industrial revolution, commonly referred to as Industry 4.0, the banking sector stands at a critical juncture. With the advent of advanced technologies like artificial intelligence, blockchain, and the internet of things, coupled with the rise of data-driven decision-making, the banking industry is on the top of transitioning towards Industry 5.0. This chapter explores the evolving landscape of banking solutions through the lens of industry stakeholders, shedding light on the opportunities and challenges presented by this paradigm shift. From the industry's perspective, advanced banking solutions offer a myriad of benefits, ranging from enhanced operational efficiency and cost reduction to improved cus-

DOI: 10.4018/979-8-3693-4187-2.ch001

tomer experiences and competitive differentiation. By leveraging technologies such as robotic process automation and predictive analytics, banks can streamline their processes, automate routine tasks, and extract actionable insights from vast datasets.

INTRODUCTION TO INDUSTRY 5.0 AND SMART BANKING SOLUTIONS

In the ever-evolving landscape of industry, we stand at the edge of a new era: Industry 5.0. Building upon the advancements of its predecessors, Industry 5.0 represents a major shift characterized by the fusion of digital technologies with human-centric principles. At its core lies a profound convergence of innovation, where the lines between physical and digital realms blur, giving rise to unprecedented opportunities and challenges. As industries embark on this transformative journey, banking institutions find themselves at the forefront of change, poised to redefine their role in facilitating the needs of Industry 5.0 (Smith, J., & Johnson, R., 2021). In this dynamic environment, the demand for smart banking solutions has never been more pronounced.

Smart banking solutions use the power of emerging technologies to deliver personalized, efficient, and secure financial services tailored to the unique requirements of Industry 5.0. From artificial intelligence and machine learning to blockchain and Internet of Things (IoT), these solutions use a different cutting-edge tool to drive innovation and enhance customer experiences. In this section, we discuss about the essence of Industry 5.0 and discuss the transformative potential of smart banking solutions in shaping its trajectory. We examine the key drivers propelling this convergence, the challenges that lie ahead, and the opportunities that await those ready to use change.

Importance of Advanced Banking Solutions in Today's Era

In today's era, characterized by rapid technological advancement and evolving consumer demands, the importance of advanced banking solutions cannot be overstated. These solutions play an important role in meeting the ever-growing expectations of customers, driving operational efficiency, and using innovation across the financial sector. Here are several key reasons why advanced banking solutions (Chen, L., & Wang, H., 2020) are important in today's landscape (in compare to Industry 4.0, refer figure 1):

- Enhanced Customer Experience: Advanced banking solutions use technologies like artificial intelligence, data analytics, and mobile applications to deliver personalized and continuous experiences to customers. From intuitive digital interfaces to proactive financial advice, these solutions empower customers with greater control over their finances, leading to higher satisfaction and loyalty.

- Improved Efficiency and Productivity: Automation and digitization are central to advanced banking solutions, streamlining routine tasks, reducing manual errors, and accelerating processes. By automating back-office operations, banks can allocate resources more efficiently, enabling employees to focus on higher-value tasks that require human expertise. This results in increased productivity and cost savings for financial institutions.

- Enhanced Security and Compliance: With the rising threat of cybercrime and stringent regulatory requirements, security is an essential issue for banks and their customers. Advanced banking solutions incorporate robust security measures like biometric authentication, encryption, and fraud detection algorithms to safeguard sensitive financial information and mitigate risks. Additionally, these solutions facilitate compliance with regulatory standards, ensuring adherence to industry guidelines and safeguarding against potential penalties.

- Data-driven Insights and Decision Making: Advanced banking solutions use the power of big data and analytics to derive actionable insights from large volumes of customer data. By analyzing spending patterns, transaction histories, and demographic information, banks can gain valuable insights into customer behavior, preferences, and needs. These insights enable banks to tailor their products and services more effectively, anticipate customer needs, and make data-driven decisions to drive business growth.

- Innovation and Competitive Advantage: In today's competitive landscape, differentiation is key to staying ahead of the curve. Advanced banking solutions enable banks to innovate rapidly, introducing new products, services, and features that resonate with customers and set them apart from competitors. Whether it's adopting emerging technologies like blockchain for secure transactions or using artificial intelligence for personalized financial advice, innovation powered by advanced banking solutions is essential for maintaining a competitive edge in the market.

Figure 1. Highlights of Industry 5.0 over Industry 4.0

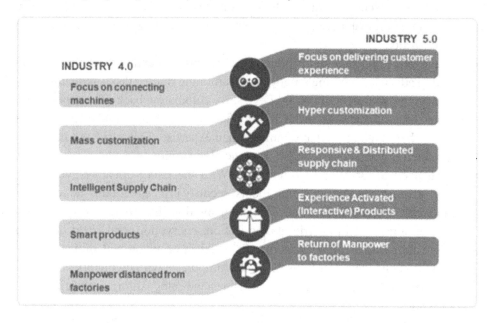

- Financial Inclusion and Accessibility: Advanced banking solutions have the potential to bridge the gap between the banked and unbanked populations, using financial inclusion and accessibility. By providing mobile banking services, digital wallets, and alternative payment methods, banks can extend their reach to underserved communities and provide them with access to essential financial services. This not only expands the customer base for banks but also promotes economic empowerment and social inclusion.

In summary, advanced banking solutions are indispensable in today's era due to their ability to enhance customer experiences, drive efficiency and productivity, ensure security and compliance, derive actionable insights, use innovation, and promote financial inclusion. As technology continues to evolve and customer expectations evolve, the role of advanced banking solutions will only become more useful in shaping the future of the financial industry.

Organization of the Work

This chapter is summarized in 10 sections.

EVOLUTION OF BANKING IN INDUSTRY 5.0

The evolution of banking in Industry 5.0 represents a profound convergence of digital technologies and human-centric principles, reshaping the way financial institutions operate and interact with customers (Patel, A., & Gupta, M., 2019). Here's a breakdown of how banking has evolved within the context of Industry 5.0 (refer figure 2):

Industry 1.0 (Mechanization):

- Banking in the early stages of industrialization was primarily characterized by manual processes and paper-based transactions.
- The advent of mechanization introduced innovations like typewriters and adding machines, streamlining basic banking operations.

Industry 2.0 (Mass Production):

- The rise of mass production during the second industrial revolution saw banking services becoming more standardized and accessible.
- Introduction of automated processes, like check processing machines and early computer systems, laid the foundation for modern banking infrastructure.

Industry 3.0 (Automation):

- The third industrial revolution brought about the widespread adoption of computers and digital technologies in banking.
- Automated teller machines (ATMs), electronic funds transfers, and online banking platforms revolutionized how customers access and manage their finances.
- Banks began using data analytics to improve risk management, marketing strategies, and customer service.

Industry 4.0 (Digitalization):

- Industry 4.0 marked the era of digital transformation, characterized by the integration of cyber-physical systems, IoT, and artificial intelligence.
- Banking services became increasingly digitized, with the rapid growth of mobile banking apps, contactless payments, and robo-advisors.
- The emergence of fintech startups and digital disruptors challenged traditional banking models, prompting incumbents to innovate and adapt to changing consumer preferences.

Industry 5.0 (Human-Centric Innovation):

- Industry 5.0 represents a shift towards human-centric innovation, where technology is used to empower human creativity, collaboration, and well-being.
- In the banking sector, Industry 5.0 entails a focus on delivering personalized and empathetic customer experiences, enabled by advanced technologies like artificial intelligence and machine learning.
- Banks are using data-driven insights to tailor products and services to individual customer needs, providing personalized financial advice, and predictive analytics to enhance decision-making.
- Customer-centric design principles are driving the development of intuitive user interfaces, empathetic chatbots, and virtual assistants, using deeper engagement and trust between banks and customers.

Not that collaboration between banks and industries is essential in Industry 5.0, with financial institutions playing an important role in supporting the digital transformation and innovation initiatives of businesses across various sectors.

Figure 2. Industry 5.0 revolutions

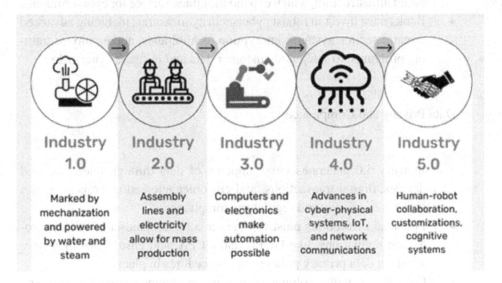

In general, the evolution of banking in Industry 5.0 signifies a departure from traditional transactional models towards a more holistic approach centered around customer-centricity, innovation, and collaboration (Kumar, R., & Singh, P., 2018). By using human-centric principles and using the power of advanced technologies, banks can position themselves as trusted partners in the era of Industry 5.0, driving sustainable growth and prosperity for businesses and individuals alike.

IMPACT OF INDUSTRY 5.0 ON BANKING CHALLENGES

Industry 5.0 brings a change of transformative opportunities for the banking sector, but it also presents a unique set of challenges that financial institutions must navigate rather than industry 4.0 (Wang, Y., & Li, W., 2021). Here are some of the key challenges that banks face in adapting to Industry 5.0:

Cybersecurity Risks:

- With the increasing digitization of banking services and the interconnectedness of systems, cybersecurity threats become more sophisticated and prevalent.

- Industry 5.0 introduces new attack vectors, like IoT devices and cloud-based infrastructure, which expand the attack surface for cybercriminals.
- Banks must invest in robust cybersecurity measures, including advanced threat detection systems, encryption technologies, and employee training programs, to safeguard customer data and mitigate cyber risks.

Data Privacy and Compliance:

- Industry 5.0 generates large amounts of data through interconnected devices, digital transactions, and customer interactions, raising issues about data privacy and regulatory compliance.
- Financial institutions must navigate a complex landscape of data protection regulations, like GDPR and CCPA, and ensure that they have stringent data privacy policies and procedures in place.
- Compliance with evolving regulatory requirements requires ongoing monitoring and adaptation of banking systems and processes, adding complexity and cost to operations.

Customer Expectations and Experience:

- Industry 5.0 uses a culture of instant gratification and personalized experiences, driven by advancements in technology and consumer empowerment.
- Banks face the challenge of meeting heightened customer expectations for continuous, intuitive, and personalized banking experiences across multiple channels and touchpoints.
- To remain competitive, financial institutions must invest in customer-centric design, innovative digital solutions, and data-driven insights to deliver superior customer experiences and build long-term loyalty.

Legacy Infrastructure and Technology:

- Many banks still rely on outdated legacy systems and infrastructure, which hinder agility, innovation, and scalability in the era of Industry 5.0.
- Modernizing legacy systems requires major investment in technology upgrades, migration to cloud-based platforms, and integration with emerging technologies like artificial intelligence and blockchain.
- Legacy systems pose operational risks, including system downtime, data silos, and limited interoperability, which can impede banks' ability to adapt to changing market dynamics and customer demands.

Talent Acquisition and Skills Gap:

- Industry 5.0 demands a workforce equipped with digital skills, data analytics capabilities, and an understanding of emerging technologies.
- Banks face challenges in attracting and retaining top talent with expertise in areas like cybersecurity, data science, software development, and user experience design.
- Note that addressing the skills gap requires investments in employee training and upskilling programs, strategic partnerships with educational institutions, and a culture of continuous learning and innovation within the organization.

In summary, while Industry 5.0 presents exciting opportunities for innovation and growth in the banking sector, it also brings a host of challenges that require proactive management and strategic planning. By addressing cybersecurity risks, ensuring compliance with data privacy regulations, prioritizing customer experience, modernizing infrastructure, and investing in talent development, banks can successfully navigate the complexities of Industry 5.0 and emerge as leaders in the digital economy (Garcia, M., & Martinez, E. (2020), Rahman, M., & Islam, M. (2020)).

OPEN ISSUES AND IMPORTANT CHALLENGES IN THE BANKING SECTOR

In the rapidly evolving landscape of the banking sector, several open issues and important challenges persist, necessitating proactive strategies and innovative solutions. Here are some of the key challenges currently facing the banking industry:

Cybersecurity Threats:

- Cyberattacks continue to face major threat to banks, with hackers targeting sensitive financial data, customer information, and transactional systems.
- Sophisticated cyber threats, including ransomware, phishing attacks, and insider threats, require banks to continuously enhance their cybersecurity defenses and invest in advanced threat detection and prevention technologies.

Data Privacy and Regulatory Compliance:

- The banking sector is subject to a complex web of data protection regulations and compliance requirements, like GDPR, CCPA, PSD2, and KYC/AML regulations.
- Banks must navigate these regulatory frameworks while ensuring the privacy and security of customer data, managing consent mechanisms, and implementing robust data governance practices to mitigate regulatory risks and avoid costly penalties.

Digital Transformation and Legacy Systems:

- Many banks grapple with outdated legacy systems and infrastructure, which hinder their ability to innovate, adapt to changing customer expectations, and compete with agile fintech startups.
- Legacy systems pose challenges in terms of scalability, interoperability, and integration with emerging technologies, necessitating investment in modernization initiatives to drive digital transformation and improve operational efficiency.

Customer Experience and Engagement:

- As customer expectations evolve in the digital age, banks face pressure to deliver continuous, personalized, and omnichannel experiences across various touchpoints, including mobile apps, websites, and branches.
- Banks must use data analytics, artificial intelligence, and customer relationship management (CRM) tools to gain insights into customer preferences, anticipate needs, and enhance engagement throughout the customer journey.

Fintech Disruption and Competitive Landscape:

- The rise of fintech startups and digital disruptors challenges traditional banking models and market dynamics, threatening the market share of incumbent banks.
- Banks must use collaboration and partnerships with fintech firms, use open banking APIs, and innovate at a rapid pace to stay competitive, differentiate their providings, and capture new revenue streams.

Financial Inclusion and Access:

- Despite technological advancements, millions of individuals worldwide remain unbanked or underbanked, lacking access to essential financial services and credit.
- Banks face the challenge of promoting financial inclusion, addressing the needs of underserved populations, and expanding access to banking services through innovative products, digital channels, and partnerships with governments and NGOs.

Sustainability and ESG Issues:

- Environmental, social, and governance (ESG) factors are increasingly shaping investment decisions and user expectations in the banking sector.

- Banks are under pressure to integrate sustainability principles into their business operations, risk management practices, and investment strategies, while balancing financial performance with social and environmental impact.

Hence, addressing these open issues and important challenges requires a holistic approach, combining technological innovation, regulatory compliance, customer-centricity, and strategic partnerships. By proactively addressing these challenges, banks can strengthen their resilience, drive sustainable growth, and remain relevant in an increasingly competitive and complex global marketplace.

FUTURE OPPORTUNITIES FOR ADVANCED BANKING SOLUTIONS

The future holds a multitude of opportunities for advanced banking solutions, driven by technological innovation, changing consumer behavior, and evolving market dynamics (Tan, C., & Lim, H. (2019), Patel, R., & Shah, P., 2018). Here are some key future opportunities for advanced banking solutions:

- Personalized Financial Services: Advanced banking solutions can use artificial intelligence and machine learning algorithms to analyze large amount of customer data and deliver personalized financial advice, product recommendations, and service offerings tailored to individual needs and preferences.
- Predictive Analytics and Risk Management: Advanced analytics tools can enable banks to anticipate market trends, identify emerging risks, and optimize decision-making processes in areas like credit risk assessment, fraud detection, and investment management, enhancing overall risk management practices and financial stability.
- Open Banking and Platform Ecosystems: Open banking initiatives and APIs (Application Programming Interfaces) present opportunities for banks to collaborate with third-party developers, fintech startups, and other ecosystem partners to create innovative financial products, services, and customer experiences, using greater competition, innovation, and customer choice in the market.
- Blockchain and Distributed Ledger Technology (DLT): Blockchain and DLT solutions provide opportunities for banks to streamline cross-border payments, trade finance, and supply chain finance processes, reducing transaction costs, enhancing transparency, and improving efficiency in global finan-

cial transactions (Zhang, H., & Li, J. (2021), Tyagi et al., (2021), (2022), (2023) and (2024)).

Digital Identity and Authentication:

- Advanced banking solutions can use biometric authentication, digital identity verification, and blockchain-based identity management systems to enhance security, combat identity theft, and streamline customer onboarding and authentication processes in a digital-first environment.

Smart Contracts and Decentralized Finance (DeFi):

- Smart contract platforms and decentralized finance (DeFi) protocols present opportunities for banks to discuss new business models, automate financial transactions, and provide innovative financial products and services, like decentralized lending, automated investment strategies, and tokenized assets (Dutta, S., & Jain, S. (2019), Tyagi et al., (2021), (2022), (2023) and (2024)).
- Embedded Finance and Internet of Things (IoT): Advanced banking solutions can integrate with IoT devices, smart appliances, and connected vehicles to enable continuous, frictionless financial transactions, like automated payments, subscription services, and personalized provides embedded within the customer's everyday experiences.
- Regtech and Compliance Solutions: Advanced banking solutions can use regulatory technology (Regtech) tools, artificial intelligence, and machine learning algorithms to automate compliance processes, monitor regulatory changes, and ensure adherence to complex regulatory requirements, reducing compliance costs and mitigating regulatory risks.
- Sustainable Finance and ESG Integration: Advanced banking solutions can support sustainability goals and environmental, social, and governance (ESG) principles by providing sustainable finance products, green bonds, impact investing opportunities, and ESG scoring and reporting tools to help customers make informed investment decisions and achieve positive social and environmental outcomes.

Hence, by using these future opportunities and using advanced banking solutions, banks can drive innovation, enhance customer experiences, and create sustainable value in an increasingly digital and interconnected financial ecosystem.

TECHNOLOGICAL ADVANCEMENTS, MARKET TRENDS AND CONSUMER EXPECTATIONS FOR SMART BANKING IN NEAR FUTURE

In the near future, smart banking is facing huge transformation driven by technological advancements, evolving market trends, and changing consumer expectations (Wong, L., & Tan, K. (2020), Li, W., & Zhang, Y. (2018), and Kim, Y., & Park, J. (2021)). Here's a look at some of the key factors shaping the future of smart banking:

Technological Advancements:

- Artificial Intelligence (AI) and Machine Learning: AI-powered chatbots and virtual assistants will become more sophisticated, providing personalized financial advice, answering customer queries, and automating routine tasks.
- Data Analytics: Advanced analytics tools will enable banks to derive actionable insights from large amounts of customer data, driving personalized product recommendations, risk management strategies, and marketing campaigns.
- Blockchain and Distributed Ledger Technology (DLT): Blockchain and DLT solutions will revolutionize cross-border payments, trade finance, and supply chain finance, enhancing transparency, security, and efficiency in financial transactions.
- Internet of Things (IoT): Integration with IoT devices will enable smart banking solutions to provide context-aware services, like automated bill payments, personalized provides based on real-time spending patterns, and home insurance premiums based on IoT sensor data.

Market Trends:

- Open Banking and API Economy: Open banking initiatives and APIs will use collaboration between banks, fintech startups, and third-party developers, enabling the creation of innovative financial products, services, and customer experiences.
- Embedded Finance: Embedded finance solutions will integrate banking services into non-financial platforms and applications, like e-commerce

websites, ride-sharing apps, and social media platforms, providing continuous and frictionless financial transactions.

- Digital Payments and Contactless Technology: The shift towards digital payments and contactless technology will accelerate, driven by consumer preferences for convenience, speed, and security, leading to increased adoption of mobile wallets, contactless cards, and peer-to-peer payment apps.
- Sustainability and ESG Integration: Consumers will demand more sustainable and socially responsible banking options, driving the adoption of green finance products, ESG investing, and transparent reporting on environmental and social impact metrics.

Consumer Expectations:

- Personalization and Customization: Consumers will expect personalized and customized banking experiences tailored to their individual needs, preferences, and life stages, with proactive recommendations and targeted provides based on their financial goals and behaviors.
- Continuous Omni-channel Experiences: Consumers will look continuous and consistent banking experiences across multiple channels and touchpoints, including mobile apps, websites, social media platforms, chatbots, and physical branches, with the ability to switch between channels continuously.
- Security and Trust: Consumers will prioritize security, privacy, and trust when choosing banking providers, expecting robust cybersecurity measures, transparent data practices, and proactive communication about security incidents and breaches.
- Instant Gratification and Convenience: Consumers will value speed, simplicity, and convenience in banking services, expecting instant account access, real-time transactions, and frictionless onboarding processes with minimal paperwork and authentication requirements.

In summary, the future of smart banking will be characterized by advanced technologies, collaborative ecosystems, personalized experiences, and consumer-centric innovation, driven by the convergence of technological advancements, market trends, and evolving consumer expectations. By using these trends and using smart banking solutions, banks can stay ahead of the curve, drive customer engagement, and create value in the digital economy.

SMART BANKING SOLUTIONS IN INDUSTRY 5.0 THROUGH CUTTING EDGE TECHNOLOGIES

In Industry 5.0, smart banking solutions are poised to use cutting-edge technologies to revolutionize the way financial services are delivered and experienced (Sharma, S., & Kumar, A. (2019), Tyagi et al., (2021) (2022) (2023), and (2024)). Here are some of the key cutting-edge technologies driving innovation in smart banking solutions:

Artificial Intelligence (AI) and Machine Learning (ML):

- AI and ML algorithms enable smart banking solutions to analyze large amount of data, predict customer behavior, and personalize financial services.
- Chatbots and virtual assistants powered by AI provide real-time customer support, answer queries, and assist with transactions, enhancing customer engagement and satisfaction.

Blockchain and Distributed Ledger Technology (DLT):

- Blockchain technology facilitates secure and transparent peer-to-peer transactions, reducing the need for intermediaries and streamlining processes like cross-border payments and trade finance.
- Smart contracts executed on blockchain networks automate contractual agreements, enabling faster settlement times and reducing operational costs for banks and their customers.

Internet of Things (IoT):

- IoT devices connected to smart banking solutions enable contextual banking experiences based on real-time data from sensors and devices.
- Wearable devices, smart home appliances, and connected cars can initiate financial transactions, trigger alerts, and provide insights into consumer behavior, allowing banks to provide personalized services and targeted provides.

Biometric Authentication and Security:

- Biometric authentication methods like facial recognition, fingerprint scanning, and voice recognition enhance security and streamline authentication processes for accessing banking services.
- Behavioral biometrics analyze patterns in user behavior to detect anomalies and prevent fraudulent activities, providing an additional layer of security in smart banking solutions.

Robotic Process Automation (RPA):

- RPA automates repetitive tasks and processes in banking operations, like account reconciliation, loan processing, and compliance reporting, improving efficiency and reducing errors.
- Virtual workforce robots perform tasks with speed and accuracy, freeing up human employees to focus on higher-value activities that require human judgment and creativity.
- Big Data Analytics and Predictive Analytics:
- Big data analytics tools process and analyze large volumes of structured and unstructured data to derive actionable insights into customer behavior, market trends, and risk management.
- Predictive analytics algorithms forecast future outcomes and trends, enabling banks to anticipate customer needs, identify potential risks, and make data-driven decisions to drive business growth.

Augmented Reality (AR) and Virtual Reality (VR):

- AR and VR technologies create immersive banking experiences, allowing customers to visualize financial data, discuss investment opportunities, and interact with virtual banking environments.
- Virtual branch tours, virtual reality investment portfolios, and augmented reality budgeting tools enhance engagement and education, providing innovative ways for customers to manage their finances.

Hence, by using these cutting-edge technologies, smart banking solutions in Industry 5.0 can deliver personalized, efficient, and secure financial services that meet the evolving needs of customers and drive sustainable growth for banks and financial institutions.

REGULATORY FRAMEWORKS FOR INDUSTRY 5.0 FOR SMART BANKING

As Industry 5.0 evolves, regulatory frameworks play an important role in shaping the development and deployment of smart banking solutions. These frameworks aim to ensure consumer protection, data privacy, financial stability, and compliance with legal requirements in the rapidly changing landscape of banking and finance. Here are some key regulatory issues for Industry 5.0 smart banking:

Data Protection and Privacy Regulations:

- Regulations like the General Data Protection Regulation (GDPR) in the European Union and the California Consumer Privacy Act (CCPA) in the United States impose strict requirements on how banks collect, store, process, and protect customer data.
- Banks must implement robust data privacy measures, obtain explicit consent for data processing, and provide transparency regarding the use of personal information in smart banking solutions.

Cybersecurity Standards and Guidelines:

- Regulatory bodies issue cybersecurity standards and guidelines to safeguard banking systems and customer data from cyber threats.
- Banks are required to implement cybersecurity controls, conduct regular risk assessments, and develop incident response plans to mitigate the impact of cyberattacks on smart banking solutions.

Financial Services Regulations:

- Existing financial services regulations, like the Basel III framework for banking supervision and the Payment Services Directive (PSD2) in Europe, govern the operation of banks and financial institutions.
- Regulators may need to adapt these regulations to accommodate new technologies and business models introduced by smart banking solutions, like open banking APIs, digital identity verification, and blockchain-based transactions.

Consumer Protection Laws:

- Consumer protection laws aim to safeguard the rights and interests of banking customers, ensuring fair treatment, transparency, and accountability in financial transactions.
- Regulators may introduce new regulations or guidelines specific to smart banking solutions to address issues like algorithmic bias, discriminatory practices, and unfair treatment of consumers in automated decision-making processes.

Regulatory Sandboxes and Innovation Hubs:

- Regulators may establish regulatory sandboxes and innovation hubs to facilitate experimentation and testing of innovative smart banking solutions in a controlled environment.
- These initiatives enable banks and fintech startups to collaborate with regulators, identify regulatory challenges, and propose solutions to regulatory barriers encountered in the development and deployment of smart banking technologies.

Cross-Border Regulatory Harmonization:

- As smart banking solutions operate across national borders, regulators need to harmonize regulatory requirements and standards to ensure consistency, interoperability, and legal certainty for cross-border transactions.

- International cooperation and collaboration among regulatory bodies are essential to address regulatory gaps and promote regulatory convergence in the global banking industry.

In summary, regulatory frameworks for Industry 5.0 smart banking must strike a balance between using innovation and ensuring safety, security, and trust in financial services. Regulators need to adopt a forward-thinking approach that accommodates technological advancements while safeguarding consumer rights and maintaining the integrity and stability of the financial system.

FUTURE DEVELOPMENTS IN INDUSTRY 5.0 FOR SMART BANKING

In the realm of smart banking within Industry 5.0, several future developments are poised to reshape the landscape of financial services. These developments will be driven by advancements in technology, changing consumer behavior, and evolving market dynamics. Here are some key future developments to watch for:

Hyper-Personalized Customer Experiences:

- Future smart banking solutions will use artificial intelligence and machine learning algorithms to deliver hyper-personalized customer experiences.
- Banks will use data analytics to anticipate individual customer needs, preferences, and life events, providing tailored financial products, services, and advice in real-time.

Intelligent Automation and Robotic Process Automation (RPA):

- Intelligent automation powered by AI and RPA will streamline banking processes, automate routine tasks, and enhance operational efficiency.
- Smart banking solutions will deploy virtual workforce robots to perform tasks like account reconciliation, fraud detection, and compliance reporting with speed and accuracy.

Predictive Analytics and Proactive Financial Management:

- Predictive analytics tools will enable banks to forecast future financial trends, identify potential risks, and provide proactive financial management solutions to customers.
- Smart banking solutions will provide predictive insights into budgeting, savings goals, investment opportunities, and debt management, empowering customers to make informed financial decisions.

Augmented Reality (AR) and Virtual Reality (VR) Banking Experiences:

- AR and VR technologies will create immersive banking experiences, allowing customers to visualize financial data, discuss virtual banking environments, and interact with digital financial advisors.
- Smart banking solutions will provide virtual reality investment portfolios, augmented reality budgeting tools, and virtual branch tours to enhance customer engagement and education.

Decentralized Finance (DeFi) and Tokenization:

- Decentralized finance (DeFi) platforms and tokenization of assets will democratize access to financial services, enabling peer-to-peer lending, automated investment strategies, and tokenized securities trading.
- Smart banking solutions will integrate with DeFi protocols, blockchain networks, and digital asset exchanges to provide innovative financial products and services, like decentralized lending and tokenized assets.

Digital Identity and Self-Sovereign Identity (SSI):

- Digital identity solutions and self-sovereign identity (SSI) platforms will enable secure and portable identity verification for banking transactions.

- Smart banking solutions will use biometric authentication, blockchain-based identity management, and zero-knowledge proofs to enhance security, privacy, and convenience in digital banking.
- Embedded Finance and Open Banking Ecosystems:
- Embedded finance solutions will integrate banking services into non-financial platforms and applications, providing continuous and frictionless financial transactions.
- Open banking ecosystems will use collaboration between banks, fintech startups, and third-party developers, driving innovation, competition, and interoperability in the banking industry.

In summary, the future of smart banking in Industry 5.0 holds immense potential for innovation, disruption, and customer empowerment. By using these future developments, banks can stay ahead of the curve, deliver value-added services, and create meaningful experiences that resonate with customers in the digital age.

CONCLUSION

As we move towards the landscape of Industry 5.0, it is evident that advanced banking solutions play an important role in shaping the future of industries worldwide. Through this exploration, we have uncovered the transformative potential of technologies like artificial intelligence, blockchain, and big data analytics in revolutionizing banking services tailored to the needs of Industry 5.0. Our analysis underscores the importance of agility and adaptability in banking institutions, as they must continually innovate to meet the evolving demands of Industry 5.0. Future collaboration between banks and industries emerges as a cornerstone for success, using synergies that drive efficiency, transparency, and sustainability. Furthermore, we have highlighted the importance of cybersecurity in safeguarding the integrity of advanced banking solutions, highlighting the important need for robust measures to protect against emerging threats. In near future, the journey towards Industry 5.0 promises unprecedented opportunities for banks and industries alike. By using innovation, using collaboration, and prioritizing security, banking institutions can position themselves as catalysts for progress in the era of Industry 5.0, driving sustainable growth and prosperity for generations to come.

REFERENCES

Ajanthaa Lakkshmanan, R. (2024). Engineering Applications of Artificial Intelligence. *Enhancing Medical Imaging with Emerging Technologies*. IGI Global- DOI:10.4018/979-8-3693-5261-8.ch010

Chen, L., & Wang, H. (2020). Next-Generation Banking Services: Advanced Solutions for Industry 5.0. *International Journal of Banking and Finance*, 15(3), 278–295. DOI:10.1002/ijbf.1234

Dutta, S., & Jain, S. (2019). Advanced Banking Solutions in the Industry 5.0 Era: Challenges and Strategies. *Journal of Financial Innovation*, 24(4), 367–382. DOI: 10.1080/20430795.2019.1657299

Garcia, M., & Martinez, E. (2020). Advanced Banking Solutions in the Industry 5.0 Context: Challenges and Perspectives. *Journal of Financial Innovation*, 9(3), 321–336.

Kim, Y., & Park, J. (2021). Innovative Banking Solutions for Industry 5.0: Advanced Practices and Technologies. *Journal of Financial Services Innovation*, 8(1), 45–60.

Kumar, R., & Singh, P. (2018). Advanced Banking Solutions for the Industry 5.0 Era: Challenges and Opportunities. *Journal of Financial Technology*, 22(4), 356–372. DOI:10.1002/jft.567

Li, W., & Zhang, Y. (2018). The Future of Banking in the Industry 5.0 Era: Advanced Solutions and Innovations. *Journal of Financial Innovation*, 21(3), 278–295.

Patel, A., & Gupta, M. (2019). The Role of Industry 5.0 in Shaping Advanced Banking Solutions. *Journal of Banking & Finance*, 6(1), 45–60.

Patel, R., & Shah, P. (2018). Next-Generation Banking: Advanced Solutions for Industry 5.0. *Journal of Banking & Finance*, 25(3), 267–282.

Pundareeka Vittala, K. R., Kiran Kumar, M., & Seranmadevi, R. (2024). *Artificial Intelligence-Internet of Things Integration for Smart Marketing: Challenges and Opportunities. Advancing Software Engineering Through AI, Federated Learning, and Large Language Models*. IGI Global. DOI:10.4018/979-8-3693-3502-4.ch019

Rahman, M., & Islam, M. (2020). Industry 5.0 and Advanced Banking Solutions: A Comparative Study. *International Journal of Banking and Finance*, 17(1), 89–104. DOI:10.1002/ijbf.456

Sharma, S., & Kumar, A. (2019). Advanced Banking Solutions for Industry 5.0: Challenges and Strategies. *Journal of Financial Technology*, 10(2), 145–160.

Shrikant Tiwari, R. (2024). Position of Blockchain: Internet of Things-Based Education 4.0 in Industry 5.0 – A Discussion of Issues and Challenges. Architecture and Technological Advancements of Education 4.0. IGI Global., DOI:10.4018/978-1-6684-9285-7.ch013

Smith, J., & Johnson, R. (2021). Industry 5.0 and Advanced Banking Solutions: A Perspective from the Financial Sector. *Journal of Financial Innovation*, 8(2), 145–160. DOI:10.1080/21657358.2021.1890456

Tan, C., & Lim, H. (2019). Innovative Banking Solutions for Industry 5.0: Advanced Approaches and Strategies. *Journal of Financial Services Innovation*, 14(2), 178–193. DOI:10.1080/20430795.2019.1578311

Tyagi, A. (2024). Engineering Applications of Blockchain in This Smart Era. *Enhancing Medical Imaging with Emerging Technologies*. IGI Global. DOI:10.4018/979-8-3693-5261-8.ch011

Tyagi, A. K. (Ed.). (2021). *Multimedia and Sensory Input for Augmented, Mixed, and Virtual Reality*. IGI Global. DOI:10.4018/978-1-7998-4703-8

Tyagi, A. (2024). The Position of Digital Society, Healthcare 5.0, and Consumer 5.0 in the Era of Industry 5.0. Advancing Software Engineering Through AI, Federated Learning, and Large Language Models. IGI Global. DOI:10.4018/979-8-3693-3502-4.ch017

Wang, Y., & Li, W. (2021). Industry 5.0 and the Future of Banking: Advanced Solutions for Sustainable Finance. *International Journal of Sustainable Finance*, 12(2), 189–204. DOI:10.1080/20430795.2020.1857290

Wong, L., & Tan, K. (2020). Advanced Banking Solutions for Industry 5.0: A Perspective from the Banking Sector. *Journal of Financial Services Innovation*, 15(2), 189–204.

Zhang, H., & Li, J. (2021). Industry 5.0 and Advanced Banking Solutions: Using Cutting-Edge Technologies. *Journal of Financial Technology*, 7(2), 156–171. DOI:10.1016/j.jft.2020.102456

Chapter 2
Exploring the Implementation and Challenges of AI–Based Fraud Detection Systems in Financial Institutions:
A Review

Padmalosani Dayalan

https://orcid.org/0000-0002-1191-3919

University of Technology and Applied Sciences, Ibra, Oman

Balaji Sundaramurthy

Al Zahra College for Women, Muscat, Oman

ABSTRACT

Global financial systems' stability and integrity are seriously threatened by financial fraud. Financial institutions have been using artificial intelligence (AI) and machine learning (ML) technology more and more to improve their fraud detection skills in response to changing fraud schemes and growing complexity. The efficiency of AI-based fraud detection systems in identifying financial crimes and reducing risks, however, is still up for discussion and close examination. The purpose of this qualitative study is to investigate the application of AI-based fraud detection systems in financial institutions, as well as the associated problems. To gather information from important parties involved in the deployment and application of AI-based fraud detection systems in financial institutions, qualitative research techniques such as focus groups and semi-structured interviews will be used.

DOI: 10.4018/979-8-3693-4187-2.ch002

INTRODUCTION

Fraud detection has always been a significant concern for financial institutions. With the rise in digital transactions, the complexity and volume of fraudulent activities have increased. Traditional fraud detection methods are often inadequate to handle the sophisticated nature of modern fraud schemes. AI-based systems offer a promising solution by leveraging machine learning algorithms and data analytics to detect and prevent fraudulent activities in real-time. This paper reviews the implementation strategies, benefits, and challenges associated with AI-based fraud detection systems in financial institutions. Fraud detection in financial institutions involves identifying and preventing fraudulent activities, such as identity theft, phishing, and unauthorized transactions. Traditional methods of fraud detection rely on manual review and rule-based systems, which can be time-consuming and prone to errors. AI-based fraud detection systems, on the other hand, leverage machine learning algorithms to analyze large datasets and identify patterns indicative of fraudulent behavior.

METHODOLOGY

This paper is based on a comprehensive literature review of scholarly articles, industry reports, and case studies related to AI-based fraud detection in financial institutions. The sources were selected based on their relevance, credibility, and publication date, ensuring a thorough and up-to-date analysis of the subject matter.

Implementation of AI-Based Fraud Detection Systems

AI Techniques in Fraud Detection

Machine Learning (ML): The Analytical Vanguard

At the heart of AI fraud detection lies machine learning, a powerful tool that learns from historical data to uncover patterns and anomalies indicative of fraud. Using supervised learning algorithms—like decision trees, support vector machines, and neural networks—ML systems classify transactions as either fraudulent or legitimate. These algorithms are trained on labeled datasets where past transactions have been marked as either fraudulent or not, allowing the system to recognize and flag suspicious activities with remarkable accuracy (Ngai et al., 2011).

Machine learning models play a pivotal role in fraud detection, showcasing impressive accuracy rates across various techniques:

- **Support Vector Machines (SVM)**: SVM models have demonstrated robust performance, often achieving accuracy rates exceeding 90% in controlled experiments (MDPI).
- **Artificial Neural Networks (ANN)**: ANNs are widely adopted in fraud detection, offering accuracy rates typically ranging from 85% to 95%, depending on the dataset and implementation specifics (MDPI)
- **Random Forests**: Known for their robustness, Random Forest algorithms commonly attain around 90% accuracy in detecting fraudulent activities.

Neural Networks: The Brain Behind the Operation

Inspired by the intricate workings of the human brain, neural networks excel at identifying complex patterns within data. This makes them exceptionally suitable for detecting sophisticated fraud schemes that might elude simpler systems. A specialized branch of neural networks, known as deep learning, has shown immense promise. By processing vast amounts of transaction data, deep learning enhances the precision of fraud detection systems, making them more adept at spotting even the most subtle signs of fraud (Bishop, 1995).

Natural Language Processing (NLP): The Linguistic Sentinel

In the realm of fraud detection, NLP techniques play a crucial role in analyzing text data to uncover fraudulent communication patterns. For instance, NLP can scrutinize the content of emails and messages to identify phishing attempts and other malicious activities. By understanding the nuances of human language, NLP provides an additional layer of security, ensuring that fraudulent communications are detected and neutralized before they can cause harm (Jurafsky & Martin, 2009).

Anomaly Detection: The Guardian of Normalcy

Anomaly detection techniques are pivotal in identifying deviations from normal behavior that may signal fraudulent activity. Employing unsupervised learning methods such as clustering and principal component analysis, these techniques detect outliers in transaction data. By highlighting transactions that deviate from established patterns, anomaly detection systems can pinpoint potential fraud with remarkable efficiency, ensuring that suspicious activities are swiftly addressed (Chandola et al., 2009).

Integration Into Financial Systems

The integration of artificial intelligence (AI) into financial institutions is a multi-faceted process that involves several critical steps:

Data Collection

The initial phase involves gathering extensive data from a wide range of sources. These sources may include transaction records, customer profiles, and historical fraud cases. The comprehensive collection of this data is vital for training AI models that are both accurate and effective. By leveraging a diverse dataset, the models can learn to identify subtle patterns and anomalies that may indicate fraudulent activities.

Data Preprocessing

Once data is collected, it must be cleaned and transformed to ensure its suitability for analysis. This preprocessing phase is crucial and involves several tasks. Handling missing values is essential to prevent biases in the model. Normalizing data ensures that numerical values are on a similar scale, which enhances the performance of machine learning algorithms. Additionally, converting categorical variables into numerical formats is necessary, as most machine learning models require numerical input. These steps collectively contribute to the creation of a robust dataset that is ready for effective machine learning model training.

Model Training

With a clean and well-prepared dataset, the next step is to train machine learning models using historical data. This training process enables the models to recognize patterns indicative of fraudulent behavior. Techniques such as cross-validation are employed to assess the model's performance on different subsets of data, ensuring its reliability and robustness. Hyperparameter tuning is also conducted to optimize the model's parameters, thereby enhancing its predictive accuracy and generalizability to new, unseen data.

Real-time Monitoring: The final step involves deploying the trained models to monitor transactions in real-time. This deployment is facilitated by setting up a real-time data pipeline that continuously feeds transaction data into the AI model. The model then evaluates each transaction, assessing the likelihood of fraud based on the patterns it has learned during training. Suspicious activities are flagged for further investigation. This real-time monitoring capability is crucial for promptly identifying and mitigating fraudulent transactions, thereby protecting the financial institution and its customers from potential losses (Ghosh & Reilly, 1994).

Case Studies

JPMorgan Chase

JPMorgan Chase has taken a significant leap in enhancing its fraud detection capabilities by implementing advanced AI-driven systems. These sophisticated systems are designed to monitor and analyze transaction data continuously and in real-time. By utilizing machine learning algorithms, the system can identify unusual patterns that may indicate fraudulent activity. Once these anomalies are detected, the system promptly alerts the fraud prevention team, enabling them to take swift action. This proactive approach has considerably improved JPMorgan Chase's ability to detect and prevent fraud, leading to a notable reduction in financial losses. Furthermore, it has strengthened customer trust by ensuring a safer and more secure transaction environment (JPMorgan Chase, 2018).

PayPal

PayPal has harnessed the power of artificial intelligence and machine learning to manage and scrutinize millions of transactions daily. Their comprehensive system employs both supervised and unsupervised learning techniques to identify fraudulent activities. Supervised learning allows the system to recognize known fraud patterns based on historical data, while unsupervised learning is adept at detecting new and evolving fraud schemes that have not been previously encountered. This dual-approach strategy ensures that PayPal can effectively mitigate fraud risks by addressing both established and emerging threats. As a result, PayPal has achieved a significant reduction in fraud losses, reinforcing their commitment to providing a secure platform for their users (Levy, 2017)

Benefits of AI-Based Fraud Detection Systems

Enhanced Accuracy

Artificial Intelligence (AI) systems excel at processing vast quantities of data and uncovering intricate patterns that often elude traditional detection methods. This advanced capability results in a significantly higher level of accuracy in identifying fraudulent activities. Numerous studies support this, demonstrating that AI models can markedly reduce false negatives, thereby ensuring that a greater number of fraudulent actions are detected and addressed (Bhattacharyya et al., 2011). This precision is pivotal for financial institutions striving to maintain the integrity of their operations and protect their clients' assets.

Real-Time Detection

One of the most profound advantages of AI in fraud detection is its ability to monitor and identify fraudulent transactions in real time. This immediacy allows for prompt intervention, thereby mitigating potential losses. The capability for real-time detection is essential in minimizing the impact of fraud, as it empowers financial institutions to act swiftly and prevent significant damage before it occurs (Dal Pozzolo et al., 2015). By leveraging AI, organizations can enhance their responsive measures, ensuring a robust defense against fraudulent activities.

Cost Efficiency

AI-based fraud detection systems offer substantial cost savings by automating the detection process. This automation reduces the need for extensive manual reviews and investigations, which are often time-consuming and resource intensive. With AI systems streamlining the detection process, human analysts can be allocated to more complex cases that necessitate detailed scrutiny and expert judgment (Barker et al., 2019). Consequently, financial institutions can optimize their resource allocation, achieving greater efficiency and cost-effectiveness in their fraud prevention efforts.

Adaptability

The adaptability of AI systems is a critical advantage in the battle against fraud. These systems are designed to continuously learn and adjust to new fraud patterns, enhancing their effectiveness over time. This capability is particularly vital given the ever-evolving nature of fraudulent schemes. Machine learning models can be frequently updated with new data, ensuring that they maintain a high level of detection accuracy and remain responsive to emerging threats (Chandola et al., 2009). This continuous improvement cycle ensures that AI-based systems remain at the forefront of fraud detection technology, providing robust and dynamic protection against fraudulent activities.

Challenges in Implementing AI-based Fraud Detection Systems

Data Quality and Availability

The efficacy of AI-based fraud detection systems is intricately tied to the quality and availability of the data they utilize. High-quality, complete, and accurate data is paramount for making reliable predictions and ensuring the system's overall reliability. Inaccurate or incomplete data can result in erroneous predictions, thereby undermining the system's trustworthiness. Financial institutions must prioritize substantial investments in robust data collection and preprocessing mechanisms to guarantee data quality. This involves implementing comprehensive strategies for data validation, cleansing, and enrichment to ensure that the input data is both accurate and relevant (Zhang & Zhou, 2004).

Privacy Concerns

The deployment of AI systems necessitates the use of vast amounts of data, which invariably raises significant privacy concerns. Financial institutions are obligated to adhere to stringent data protection regulations, such as the General Data Protection Regulation (GDPR). These regulations impose strict guidelines on data usage and mandate the protection of individuals' privacy rights. Balancing the requirement for comprehensive data to enhance AI system performance with the imperative to uphold privacy standards presents a considerable challenge. Institutions must establish robust data governance frameworks and implement privacy-enhancing technologies to navigate this delicate balance effectively (Goodman & Flaxman, 2017).

Integration With Legacy Systems

Integrating advanced AI systems with pre-existing legacy systems poses a formidable challenge, often requiring substantial investment in both technology and infrastructure. Legacy systems, which may be outdated or incompatible with contemporary AI technologies, necessitate significant upgrades or even complete replacements. This integration process can be both costly and time-consuming, involving extensive changes to the IT infrastructure, retraining of staff, and potential disruptions to business operations. Financial institutions must meticulously plan and execute these integrations to ensure seamless interoperability and to leverage the full potential of AI technologies (Ransbotham et al., 2017).

False Positives

One of the critical challenges faced by AI-based fraud detection systems is the generation of false positives, where legitimate transactions are incorrectly flagged as fraudulent. Such occurrences can significantly inconvenience customers and erode their trust in the financial institution. Mitigating false positives requires the careful calibration of AI models and the incorporation of additional contextual data to refine decision-making processes. This involves continuously monitoring and adjusting the models to enhance their accuracy and reliability while ensuring that legitimate transactions are processed smoothly (Dal Pozzolo et al., 2015).

Ethical and Bias Issues

AI systems have the potential to inadvertently perpetuate biases present in the training data, leading to unfair treatment of certain demographic groups. Ensuring fairness and mitigating bias in AI models is crucial to prevent discrimination and uphold ethical standards. Financial institutions must conduct regular audits of their AI systems to identify and address any biases. This entails making necessary adjustments to both the models and the datasets used for training to ensure that the AI systems operate equitably and do not favor or disadvantage any group. Maintaining these ethical standards is essential for the credibility and integrity of AI-based fraud detection systems (Barocas & Selbst, 2016).

As financial institutions increasingly prioritize the implementation of automated fraud detection systems, they face a number of key challenges (Alarfaj et al., 2022). One of the primary challenges is the need for rapid response times, as fraudulent transactions must be identified and blocked quickly to minimize losses. Additionally, financial institutions must balance the cost-sensitivity of these systems with the need for robust and accurate fraud detection capabilities.

The use of machine learning (ML) and deep learning (DL) algorithms has emerged as a promising approach to address these challenges (Alarfaj et al., 2022). These algorithms can be trained on historical transaction data to build predictive models that can accurately differentiate between fraudulent and legitimate transactions in real-time. However, the effective deployment of these techniques requires careful attention to data preprocessing and feature engineering to ensure the models can effectively extract relevant signals from the available data. (Vivek et al., 2022)

Another key challenge is the need to preserve the privacy and security of sensitive financial data. Training robust fraud detection models requires access to a wide range of transactional and account data across multiple institutions. However, the sharing of such data must be carefully managed to protect customer privacy and comply with regulatory requirements. To address these challenges, recent research has explored the use of privacy-preserving techniques such as federated learning, which allows models to be trained across distributed datasets without exposing the underlying data (Zhang et al., 2023).

FUTURE DIRECTIONS

Explainable AI

The advancement of explainable AI systems is a crucial step forward in the realm of artificial intelligence, particularly in terms of fostering trust and ensuring adherence to regulatory standards. Explainability refers to the capacity of AI systems to elucidate their decision-making processes in a manner that is comprehensible to humans. This transparency is indispensable for stakeholders who require a clear understanding of how decisions are formulated, which, in turn, is vital for ensuring accountability and transparency within AI operations. As Doshi-Velez and Kim (2017) articulate, the ability to demystify the inner workings of AI can significantly bolster stakeholder confidence and facilitate compliance with stringent regulatory requirements.

Advanced Anomaly Detection

The refinement of anomaly detection techniques stands as a pivotal aspect in enhancing the efficacy of AI-based systems, particularly in the domain of fraud detection. Anomaly detection involves identifying deviations from a norm, which is essential in pinpointing fraudulent activities. By developing more sophisticated algorithms and exploring hybrid approaches that amalgamate multiple techniques, the ability to detect subtle and evolving fraud patterns can be markedly improved. Chandola et al. (2009) highlights the importance of continuous research and innovation in this area to achieve higher detection rates and more robust fraud prevention mechanisms.

Collaborative Efforts

The battle against fraud can be significantly fortified through collaborative efforts among financial institutions. By sharing data and best practices, these institutions can collectively enhance their capabilities to detect and prevent fraudulent activities. Industry-wide cooperation and data sharing create a synergistic effect, amplifying the overall effectiveness of fraud detection systems. As Ngai et al. (2011) suggest, such collaborative initiatives can lead to a more resilient financial ecosystem where all participants benefit from shared knowledge and resources.

Enhanced Regulatory Frameworks

The dynamic landscape of AI-based systems necessitates the continual evolution of regulatory frameworks to address their unique challenges. Developing updated guidelines and standards is critical to ensuring the responsible and ethical use of AI technologies. Regulators must strike a balance between fostering innovation and mitigating potential risks, such as bias and lack of transparency. Goodman and Flaxman (2017) emphasize the need for well-crafted regulatory frameworks that not only promote technological advancement but also safeguard against the inherent risks associated with AI. By doing so, regulators can ensure that AI systems are deployed in a manner that is both innovative and conscientious, thereby protecting the interests of all stakeholders involved.

CONCLUSION

Artificial Intelligence (AI) has undeniably revolutionized fraud detection in financial institutions, offering a robust solution to an age-old problem. This review has delved into the various aspects of implementing AI-based fraud detection systems, highlighting their potential to enhance security, efficiency, and accuracy. The integration of machine learning algorithms, neural networks, and other AI technologies has empowered financial institutions to detect and prevent fraudulent activities with unprecedented precision.

However, the journey towards seamless AI implementation is fraught with challenges. Data privacy concerns, the need for large volumes of high-quality data, potential biases within AI models, and the ever-evolving nature of fraud tactics pose significant hurdles. Additionally, the high costs associated with developing and maintaining advanced AI systems can be prohibitive for smaller institutions. Regulatory compliance and the necessity for continuous monitoring and updating of AI systems further complicate the landscape.

Despite these challenges, the benefits of AI in fraud detection are substantial. Financial institutions that successfully navigate the complexities of AI integration stand to gain a competitive edge, safeguarding not only their assets but also their reputation and customer trust. Collaboration between financial entities, technology providers, and regulatory bodies is crucial to addressing the challenges and maximizing the potential of AI-based fraud detection systems.

In conclusion, while the path to fully leveraging AI in fraud detection is complex and challenging, the potential rewards make it a worthy endeavor. Continuous research and development, coupled with a proactive approach to overcoming obstacles, will be essential in harnessing the full power of AI to combat fraud in the financial sector. As technology evolves, so too must the strategies and systems we employ, ensuring that financial institutions remain one step ahead of fraudsters in this ongoing battle.

REFERENCES

Alarfaj, F. K., Malik, I., Khan, H. U., Almusallam, N., Ramzan, M., & Ahmed, M. (2022). Credit card fraud detection using state-of-the-art machine learning and deep learning algorithms. *IEEE Access : Practical Innovations, Open Solutions*, 10, 39700–39715. DOI:10.1109/ACCESS.2022.3166891

Ali, A., Abd Razak, S., Othman, S. H., Eisa, T. A. E., Al-Dhaqm, A., Nasser, M., Elhassan, T., Elshafie, H., & Saif, A.MDPI. (2022). Financial fraud detection based on machine learning: A systematic literature review. *Applied Sciences (Basel, Switzerland)*, 12(19), 9637. DOI:10.3390/app12199637

Barker, K., D'Amato, V., & Di Lorenzo, E. (2019). Artificial intelligence in fraud management: Challenges and opportunities. *Journal of Financial Crime*, 26(4), 1015–1027.

Barocas, S., & Selbst, A. D. (2016). Big data's disparate impact. *California Law Review*, 104(3), 671–732.

Bhattacharyya, S., Jha, S., Tharakunnel, K., & Westland, J. C. (2011). Data mining for credit card fraud: A comparative study. *Decision Support Systems*, 50(3), 602–613. DOI:10.1016/j.dss.2010.08.008

Bishop, C. M. (1995). *Neural networks for pattern recognition*. Oxford University Press. DOI:10.1093/oso/9780198538493.001.0001

Chandola, V., Banerjee, A., & Kumar, V. (2009). Anomaly detection: A survey. *ACM Computing Surveys*, 41(3), 1–58. DOI:10.1145/1541880.1541882

Dal Pozzolo, A., Boracchi, G., Caelen, O., Alippi, C., & Bontempi, G. (2015). Credit card fraud detection: A realistic modeling and a novel learning strategy. *IEEE Transactions on Neural Networks and Learning Systems*, 29(8), 3784–3797. DOI:10.1109/TNNLS.2017.2736643 PMID:28920909

Doshi-Velez, F., & Kim, B. (2017). Towards a rigorous science of interpretable machine learning. *arXiv preprint arXiv:1702.08608*.

Ghosh, S., & Reilly, D. L. (1994). Credit card fraud detection with a neural network. *Proceedings of the 27th Hawaii International Conference on System Sciences, (vol.3*, pp. 621-630]. IEEE. DOI:10.1109/HICSS.1994.323314

Goodman, B., & Flaxman, S. (2017). European Union regulations on algorithmic decision-making and a "right to explanation.". *AI Magazine*, 38(3), 50–57. DOI:10.1609/aimag.v38i3.2741

HyperVerge. (2024, February 5). *How to Leverage AI to Prevent Fraud: A Deep Dive for Financial Institutions*. HyperVerge. https://hyperverge.co/blog/ai-fraud -prevention/ (2020, March 10).

JPMorgan Chase. (2018). *How AI is transforming fraud detection at JPMorgan Chase*. JP Morgan Chase. https://www.jpmorganchase.com

Jurafsky, D., & Martin, J. H. (2009). *Speech and language processing*. Pearson.

Levy, S. (2017). How PayPal beats the bad guys with AI. *Wired*. https://www.wired .com

Ngai, E. W. T., Hu, Y., Wong, Y. H., Chen, Y., & Sun, X. (2011). The application of data mining techniques in financial fraud detection: A classification framework and an academic review of literature. *Decision Support Systems*, 50(3), 559–569. DOI:10.1016/j.dss.2010.08.006

Ransbotham, S., Kiron, D., Gerbert, P., & Reeves, M. (2017). Reshaping business with artificial intelligence. *MIT Sloan Management Review*, 59(1), 1–17.

Vivek, K., Radhakrishnan, R., Sandeep, S., & Ramesh, M. (2022). Credit card fraud detection using machine learning algorithms. *Journal of Financial Crime*, 29(4), 1247–1262. DOI:10.1108/JFC-03-2022-0048

Zhang, C., Li, S., Xia, J., Wang, W., Yan, F., & Liu, Y. (2023). Privacy-preserving federated learning for financial data security. *Journal of Financial Data Science*, 10(2), 120–135. DOI:10.1016/j.jfds.2023.04.007

Zhang, H., & Zhou, Z. (2004). *MLDM 2004: Advances in data mining*. Springer.

Chapter 3
AI–Powered Business Evolution:
Transformative Strategies for Success of Evolving Industries

Yashodhan Karulkar
https://orcid.org/0000-0002-0991-3565
Mukesh Patel School of Technology Management and Engineering, India

Arshi Shah
https://orcid.org/0009-0008-5489-8748
Mukesh Patel School of Technology Managemet and Engineering, India

Rishab Naik
Mukesh Patel School of Technology Management and Engineering, India

ABSTRACT

This chapter, as per the authors, examines the multidimensional function of artificial intelligence (AI) in many industries, focusing on its strategic integration for organizational success, decision-making improvement, and data management efficiency. The chapter examines how AI-driven solutions are altering old processes and catalyzing innovation in the logistics, aeronautics, agriculture and the banking industry. In logistics, AI enables predictive analytics and route optimization, resulting in better supply chain management and operational efficiency. AI in aeronautics improves safety measures, optimizes fuel usage, and revolutionizes flight operations. In addition, the use of AI in agriculture provides farmers with precision farming techniques which allow optimized resource allocation and higher crop yields. Finally, AI in the banking industry streamlines operations, enhances customer experience, and enables data-driven decision making for personalized services and fraud detection.

DOI: 10.4018/979-8-3693-4187-2.ch003

INTRODUCTION

Businesses can see significant benefits in critical areas by incorporating artificial intelligence (AI), potentially transforming their operations. The use of Artificial Intelligence allows companies to gather valuable information, make intelligent decisions and compete more effectively. Predictive Analytics, a subset of Artificial Intelligence, could transform how organizations anticipate future trends and potential risks enabling them to plan ahead for more effective resource allocation. Businesses can predict possible outcomes, keep pace with the curve, reduce risks and take advantage of new opportunities through analyzing past data and identifying patterns. The use of AI to automate repetitive tasks, reduce errors, and save time can increase operational efficiency, resulting in improved productivity and product quality while reducing costs. This section provides an in-depth review of the current literature about AI and the alignment of information technology with business strategy. It introduces the key definitions of fundamental concepts as viewed by different authors in these areas.

Background and Literature of Artificial Intelligence

Since the 1950's, the field of AI has evolved with two main approaches: human centered and rationalist. Human-Centered approaches involve hypothesis and experimental validation, contributing to empirical science (Bellman, 1978; Haugeland, 1985; Kurzweil, 1990; Rich & Knight, 1991). Rationalist approaches, on the other hand, combine engineering and mathematics (Charniak & McDermott, 1985; Luger & Stubblefield, 1993; Schalkoff, 1990; Winston, 1970).

AI is a field focused on developing software and hardware capable of executing actions that require cognition. From rationalist approaches, AI encompasses techniques that enable machines to simulate human behavior to achieve the best results, particularly in uncertain scenarios.

In the early stages of AI development, the primary obstacle has been (and continues to be) the ability to execute tasks that come naturally to humans but are challenging to articulate using mathematical principles (Abramson, Braverman, & Sebestyen, 1963; Goodfellow, Bengio, & Courville, 2016).

The challenge of explaining this type of task through predefined rules demonstrated the need for AI techniques to be able to identify patterns in data and acquire knowledge autonomously (Abramson et al., 1963; Goodfellow et al., 2016; Michie, 1968; Solomonoff, 1985). This capability is known as machine learning (Goodfellow et al., 2016), empowering computer- based applications to automatically recognize patterns in data and perform tasks without explicit programming (Murphy, 2012). As a result, the field of AI has evolved beyond simply following rules predefined by humans to simulate human behavior and make decisions (as in classical AI algorithms), now also striving to replicate human learning.

With the advent of machine learning algorithms, the advancement of AI has necessitated the ability to translate learned knowledge into accurate predictions. This demand has led to the evolution of representation learning approaches, where features are converted into a valuable intermediate representation carrying essential information (Bengio, Courville, & Vincent, 2013; Witten & Frank, 2016).

In order to effectively express complex concepts, deep learning techniques are essential.

Deep learning enables the representation of the world through a hierarchy of concepts, allowing for diverse levels of abstraction. This approach involves the use of multiple processing layers to learn and define concepts in relation to simpler ones (Goodfellow et al., 2016; LeCun, Bengio, & Hinton, 2015). Remember that deep learning is a form of representation learning, utilized in various machine learning approaches, which itself is a subset of AI. One key distinction between AI disciplines is the diminishing reliance on humans to establish rules or define features to represent a problem as we move to inner layers from the AI layer.

Consider the problem of recommending products to a customer on an e-commerce platform. A classic AI algorithm would involve implementing a program based on a rule such as: if the customer has made a purchase, then recommend the products most frequently purchased by them. Classic AI algorithms are constructed using hand-designed programs that contain rules defined by a domain expert (Goodfellow et al., 2016).

When a customer who has never made a purchase on the platform is considered, the current rule fails. One potential solution is to leverage the customer's age to make recommendations based on product categories. These features, such as age and product category, are defined by humans. Additional rules can be established by human specialists based on historical purchase data. However, as the platform's product range and customer base grow, defining these rules becomes increasingly challenging. Therefore, training a machine learning model based on historical data using these features could be a viable alternative. Classic machine learning algorithms require human-designed features, which the algorithm uses to identify patterns and acquire knowledge (Murphy, 2012).

In the realm of product recommendations, customer age is just one piece of the puzzle. In real-world scenarios, additional customer features are often crucial. One widely used approach involves clustering customers using representation learning algorithms. Unlike traditional machine learning, representation learning algorithms kickstart the learning process, offering the ability to glean insights from human-inputted features and map out valuable connections (Goodfellow et al., 2016).

When it comes to customer clustering, representation learning models have the amazing ability to determine a client's cluster without prior human knowledge. However, in real-world scenarios with numerous features, the model's accuracy can be enhanced by using initial human-defined features to map more abstract features, which is a capability of deep learning algorithms. Deep learning algorithms, a subset of representation learning, only require simple features defined by humans. From these simple features, they can define more abstract features through additional layers of learning, resulting in a feature mapping process. The "deep" in deep learning refers to these additional layers of learning (Goodfellow et al., 2016; LeCun et al., 2015).

Figure 1. Diagram that represents the relationship between AI, ML, representation learning, and DL

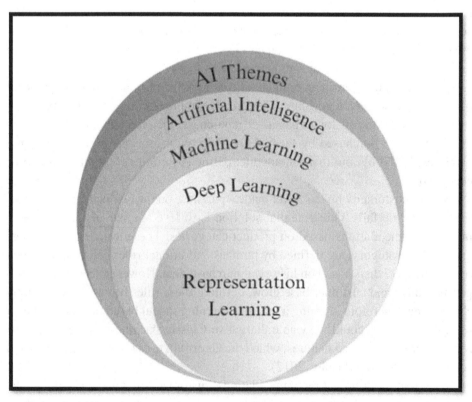

(Source: Created by authors)

AI in Organizations

In the context of organizations, the initial stages of AI research emerged in the 1960s, focusing on facilitating decision-making processes (Buchanan & O'Connell, 2006). During this time, AI primarily addressed problems that could be represented using mathematical formulas (McCarthy & Hayes, 1981; Siklóssy, 1970). Remember that AI has been an integral part of the business world since the 1980s. Many companies have invested significantly in developing and implementing computer vision systems, robotics, expert systems, as well as software and hardware for these purposes (Boden, 1984; Russell & Norvig, 2010). It's worth noting that AI was already being recognized at that time as a strategic tool to enhance organizational competitiveness in a rapidly evolving business environment (Holloway, 1983; Porter & Millar, 1985).

Prior to the year 2000, computer science research in the field of AI primarily focused on developing algorithms to create new approaches or enhance existing ones (Zhuang, Wu, Chen, & Pan, 2017). However, from 2001 onwards, researchers have highlighted that the major challenge for many AI problems lies in the vast volume of data present in very large databases (Russell & Norvig, 2010). As a result, new AI techniques were developed (Brynjolfsson & McAfee, 2017; Zhuang et al., 2017) thanks to advancements in hardware. This technological advancement is attributed to the emergence of big data, characterized by the fusion of technology, methodology, and analytical capacity to search, aggregate, and cross-reference large datasets in order to identify patterns and gain insights (Boyd & Crawford, 2012).

In 2016, the Google DeepMind team showcased the remarkable potential of AI technology with AlphaGo, a computer program that uses deep learning to play the ancient game of Go. Unlike traditional AI, AlphaGo was not programmed with specific moves or rules but instead learned from human experts and through self-play. This approach allowed AlphaGo to challenge and defeat the world champion, Lee Sedol, in a five-game match, showcasing its creativity and ability to generate new insights in Go. This ground-breaking achievement marked a significant advancement in the history of machine learning.

The rapid advancement of AI in recent years can be attributed to three main factors: the abundance of data, enhanced algorithms, and significantly improved computational hardware (Brynjolfsson & McAfee, 2017). This progress has captured the interest of major technology- focused companies, leading to the provision of machine learning infrastructure in the cloud by companies such as Google, Amazon, Microsoft, Salesforce, and IBM. This has made cognitive technologies more accessible and easier to use (Brynjolfsson & Mcafee, 2017; Davenport, 2018; Marr & Ward, 2019; Venkatraman, 2017).

In the modern workplace, AI represents a ground-breaking technology designed to mimic human capabilities, learn independently, and enhance cognitive processes. This powerful tool has the potential to not only support human cognition, but also to take over cognitive tasks entirely (Chakravorti et al., 2019). Overall, AI has the capacity to drive improvements in speed, flexibility, customization, scalability, innovation, and decision-making within organizations (Venkatraman, 2017; Wilson & Daugherty, 2018).

Don't forget the following text: "AI can bring immense value to companies in various business areas, including process automation, data-driven decision-making, customer and employee engagement, as well as the creation and delivery of new products and services (Davenport & Harris, 2017; Davenport & Ronanki, 2018; Davenport, 2018; Lyall, Mercier, & Gstettner, 2018; Mikalef et al., 2019; Ransbotham, Gerbert, Reeves, Kiron, & Spira, 2018; Schrage & Kiron, 2018; Westerman, Bonnet, & McAfee, 2014)."

The Strategic Use of Technology

In today's research landscape, AI tools fall under the umbrella of Information Technology (IT). IT is a multifaceted field that encompasses human, organizational, and administrative aspects, including information systems, data processing, software engineering, and hardware and software (Keen, 1993; Porter & Millar, 1985).

It is crucial to adopt a comprehensive definition of IT that takes into account both technological aspects and considerations related to workflow, personnel, and information. Porter and Millar (1985) propose a broad definition of IT which covers the information generated and utilized by businesses, as well as a diverse range of interconnected and integrated technologies involved in processing this information (Porter & Millar, 1985).

Despite the surge in the digital era, the impact of IT on organizations is not a recent phenomenon. As early as the late 1970s, researchers were already discussing the potential of IT to influence organizational competition (Benjamin, Rockart, Morton, & Wyman, 1983; Henderson & Venkatraman, 1992; Keen, 1991; King, 1978; McFarlan, 1984; Porter, 1979; Laurindo, 2008; Luftman, Lewis, & Oldach, 1993). Some scholars began using the term "strategic use" to describe how IT can shape new business strategies or support existing ones, providing significant value to businesses (Frangou, Wan, Antony, & Kaye, 1998; Henderson & Venkatraman, 1999; Luftman et al., 1993; McFarlan, 1984; Philip, Gopalakrishnan, & Mawalkar, 1995; Porter & Millar, 1985).

Henderson and Venkatraman (1999) propose that aligning business and IT strategies involves a continuous process of adaptation and transformation that encompasses business strategy, IT strategy, organizational infrastructure and processes, as well as IT infrastructure and processes. In this context, strategic IT utilization can empower organizations to stay ahead in a rapidly changing competitive landscape (Laurindo, 2008).

Numerous models, theories, and methodologies have been put forward in the literature, with a focus on aligning IT with business strategy and operations (Gerow et al., 2014).Over time, digital technologies have become essential in shaping business strategies (Bharadwaj et al., 2013; Bughin & Catlin, 2019; Laurindo, 2008; Mattos, Kissimoto, & Laurindo, 2018; Venkatraman, 2017).

STRATEGIC INTEGRATION OF AI IN BUSINESS

The integration of AI and sustainability has become an important force for medium sized organizations, due to the fast-changing business world. Companies can use artificial intelligence technology to tackle challenges of the environment, society and economy in innovative ways by promoting sustainability efforts. It is worth noting that a small percentage of companies are not investing in artificial intelligence, indicating the enormous potential for this technology. With the United States and Western Europe leading the way, more than 30 countries have developed AI strategies. Serbia is leading the way in the Balkan region by establishing its national strategy on artificial intelligence until 2025, which recognizes that it has a crucial role to play in driving economic growth and digital transformation.

Think of a world where data driven strategies underpin every decision that corporations make. It's not just a dream anymore, it's reality! A fundamental change in the way companies operate has taken place as AI is integrated into everyday operations. And guess what? This isn't just a random occurrence, it's a well thought out strategy based on theoretical considerations. In the following sections, we'll explore these perspectives, which form the foundation of the strategic integration of artificial intelligence in terms of sustainability. Get ready to dive deep into this exciting world!

Figure 2. The Convergence of AI Tools and Business Strategy that Simplifies Processes

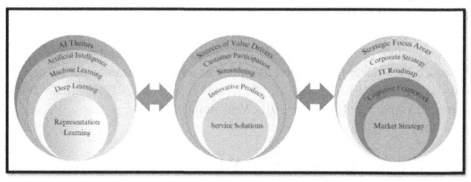

(Source: Created by authors)

CASE STUDY ONE: THE CASE OF FOURKITES (BASED IN CHICAGO, ILLINOIS)

FourKites, the leading supply chain solutions provider named one of Forbes' Next Billion- Dollar Startups, it connects global end-to-end supply chains with the most powerful technology on the planet, helping their customers work better together. Due to the rapid adoption of AI technologies, the logistics sector is experiencing considerable transformation. The need for effective, flexible and data intensive logistics operations is ever more important as the world's supply chains are becoming complex and interconnected. In order to address these challenges, AI provides a powerful set of tools that allow logistics firms to optimize routes, predict demand, perform automated warehouse operations and improve the customer experience. AI is revolutionizing all aspects of the logistics value chain, from predictive analytics and route optimization to warehouse automation and last mile delivery solutions. The introduction sets the stage for exploring a wide range of ways in which artificial intelligence is transforming the logistics sector, enabling new efficiencies and driving innovation to meet the evolving needs of modern trade.

The management of large data sets from different sources, example GPS devices and traffic management systems, which can be overwhelmed by conventional systems, makes it difficult to keep track of them. Delays, inaccuracies and diverse data sources make it hard to track shipments accurately in order to achieve real time visibility across the supply chain. Due to dynamic factors such as traffic conditions and weather, the optimization of routes is a major challenge that complicates efforts to reduce costs and improve delivery time. In addition, resources and scale may be strained and could lead to poor customer experiences if inefficient customer service is provided for tracking shipments and resolving enquires.

In order to address the challenges faced by logistics technology companies such as FourKites, AI offers promising solutions. AI is capable of processing and analyzing large and complicated datasets in an efficient manner, providing vital information and enhancing decision making processes by means of state-of-the-art computer learning algorithms. Predictive analytics powered by AI can enhance real-time visibility by forecasting shipment arrival times, identifying potential delays, and enabling proactive notifications to logistics operators. Dynamic adjustment of transport routes based on current conditions and historical data, optimizing efficiency and reducing costs can be achieved through AI driven route optimization algorithms. Furthermore, AI powered chatbots and virtual assistants can automate routine customer inquiries, providing timely updates and resolutions while alleviating the burden on human customer service agents, thereby enhancing overall customer satisfaction.

DATA MANAGEMENT STRATEGIES

To incorporate AI technologies into their day-to-day operations, companies of all sizes must have the right data management practices that will allow them to operate effectively. In order to ensure that AI is successfully used both inside and outside the company, a well-defined data governance framework, rules and policies are necessary. As the volume of information that companies produce on a daily basis, increases, effective governance is becoming more important. The importance of data management frameworks covering process, policy, standards and metrics is recognized by organizations to guarantee the quality, security and compliance with legal requirements (Svetozar D & Dejan M,2023). The AI context has been analyzed and data governance frameworks have been found to be critical tools for ensuring the protection of human rights, data protection and regulatory compliance. According to current research, a link between data governance frameworks and the use of artificial intelligence is one of the key factors thatneed to be taken into account for an AI adoption index in medium sized and larger companies.

CASE STUDY TWO: THE CASE OF BOEING (BASED IN ARLINGTON, VIRGINIA)

As a leading global aerospace company, Boeing develops, manufactures and services commercial airplanes, defense products and space systems for customers in more than 150 countries. As a top U.S. exporter, the company leverages the talents of a global supplier base to advance economic opportunity, sustainability and community impact. In order to change the way aircrafts are designed, manufactured, operated and maintained, Boeing, a global aerospace manufacturer, has adopted AI technologies. Boeing aims to increase safety, efficiency and sustainability across the entire aerospace lifecycle by applying AI based solutions. Boeing has pioneered new frontiers of aeronautics technology, demonstrating its commitment to leadership and innovation in the world's aviation sector by using cutting edge analytics and autonomous systems. From predictive maintenance of autonomous flight systems, AI is reshaping the future of aerospace at Boeing. In order to minimize interruptions and ensure timely delivery of components and streamlining operations, Boeing faces a number of challenges in the aerospace industry. These include including ensuring highest quality and safety standards for aircraft production. Other challenges include predicting problems with airplane maintenance as well as optimizing its extensive supply chain.

In order to address these challenges faced by Boeing, Artificial Intelligence provided Promising solutions. In order to detect anomalies at the actual time of manufacturing, AI helped analyze huge amounts of production data through sophisticated analytics and machine learning algorithms in order to ensure a high level of quality and safety for aircraft making that met industry standards. Predictive maintenance systems, which use artificial intelligence to predict component failures and schedule repairs ahead of time, allowed for preventive maintenance plans that minimize unplanned breakdowns. By anticipating demand, optimizing inventory levels and identifying potential bottlenecks to ensure timely delivery of components, AI driven optimization algorithms made supply chain operations more efficient. By optimizing flight paths, cutting pilot workload and automation of routine tasks, autonomous flight systems with AI enhance aircraft performance, fuel efficiency as well as safety.

COGNITIVE DECISION MAKING

Human beings are innately capable of making decisions, but in some cases, they can have significant consequences. Researchers are developing computer technology that enables human capabilities to be improved and extended in order to increase the quality of their decisions. This objective has been met in a variety of fields, e.g. finance, health care, marketing, trade, management and control as well as cyber security, thanks to the introduction of artificial intelligence. Intelligent decision support systems are designed to replicate human reasoning skills and, in order to be able to make reasoned decisions, employ AI tools for learning, remembering, planning or analyzing.

AI tools can scan and select relevant information from a wide variety of data sources, including an analytical tool for unstructured data, develop general solutions to rule sets and probabilities that could influence decisions as well as identify connections between different resources which may affect the choice. Tools such as Artificial Neural Networks, Fuzzy Logic, Intelligence Agents, Agent Teams, Case-Based Reasoning, Evolutionary Computing, and probabilistic reasoning, when combined with decision support systems, can help a decision – maker asses and select alternatives (Gloria Phillips-Wren, April 2012). These systems have particular value whenfaced with complicated problems, including uncertainty and high numbers of data which are not determinable.

The decision-making process is an important part of every organization, and numerous scholars who create Decision Support Systems (DSS) readily accept H. Simon's approach, as seen in Figure 3. This paradigm is broken down into four stages: cognition, design, decision- making, and issue comprehension. During the design phase, they identify requirements, develop a model, and investigate various solutions. During the selecting phase, a choice or decision is made, and the decision-maker follows through on it and learns during the implementation phase.

Figure 3. The process described by H. Simon for decision making

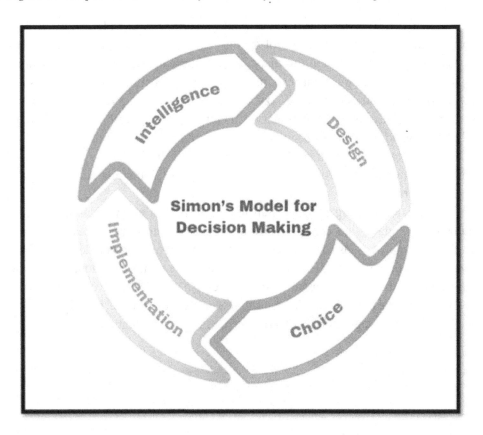

The procedure is typically carried out in a sequential manner, with feedback loops taking place in between each stage. Judgments are classified as ordered, unorganized, or partially coordinated based on the degree of confidence in the resolution and depiction of the problem. Decisions that are structured have a predetermined solution, while there is no agreement on the approach for unstructured judgments. However, these two classifications can also be applied to semi-structured judgments that may be depicted by data-driven analytical models.

Technology can be used to provide assistance in decision-making by identifying and selecting relevant inputs, choosing appropriate data, aligning models with specific conditions, presenting outcomes to decision makers, or helping them understand their achievements. Although the Decision-Making Process involves input, processing, and output stages, decision makers are still considered vital members of a larger system.

The scope of Decision Support has expanded lately and now includes a wider range of technological assistance, including systems that handle Business Intelligence and Analytics, as well as those that lack specific features related to decision making. Analytics and BI techniques are capable of tackling complex issues involving extensive data, such as that provided by the Big Data Network. Artificial Intelligence techniques are often utilized to solve these demanding problems. By combining AI with decision support methods, intelligent guidance systems can be developed that are closely aligned with the user's decision-making style and the decision problem. These systems could be deeply embedded in the work environment to provide better support to users.

CASE STUDY THREE: THE CASE OF JOHN DEERE (BASED IN MOLINE, ILLINOIS)

Deere & Company, doing business as John Deere, is an American corporation that manufactures agricultural machinery, heavy equipment, forestry machinery, diesel engines, drivetrains used in heavy equipment, and lawn care equipment. By adopting AI innovations that will improve all stages of agriculture, John Deere has revolutionized the conventional farming processes, productivity, sustainability and efficiency. The commitment of John Deere to the use of artificial intelligence has led to groundbreaking technological developments, such as autonomous tractors with embedded attachments that incorporate an AI drone for spraying and precision weed management systems, which are shaping the future of agriculture. This is an initial step in exploring how John Deere uses artificial intelligence to help farmers, optimize crop management and make sustainable agricultural practices more effective through different means.

Challenges such as labor shortages, wastefulness of resources and sustainability in the environment, have been faced by the agricultural industry for many years. In traditional farming methods, there was often a heavy reliance on manual labor that led to increased costs and limited capacity. In addition, the excessive use of fertilizers and pesticides has contributed to soil degradation, water pollution as well as biodiversity loss which is a major concern for sustainable development. In addition, the risks to crop yields and food security are constantly threatened by unpredictable weather patterns and pests that threaten farmers' livelihoods.

By using advanced technologies such as artificial intelligence, John Deere has redefined the agricultural practice. John Deere has eliminated reliance on unskilled labor, increased operational efficiency and scale through the development of its own machinery and precision agriculture solutions. Precise application of inputs and minimizing resource waste can be achieved by integrating AI algorithms into machines. Moreover, farmers are being provided with real-time information on weather patterns, pest detection and crop monitoring through AI powered systems which can mitigate risks or optimize yields. In modern farming operations, John Deere's innovative use of AI supports sustainability, durability and productivity.

HARMONIZING AI WITH BUSINESS PROCESS MANAGEMENT: ELEVATING INNOVATION

Business Process Management (BPM) software is becoming increasingly popular among businesses due to its ability to reduce paperwork and optimize resource utilization. This software helps organizations improve their business outcomes by providing a systematic approach to process optimization, access to key metrics, and enhancing user usability. By using BPM software, organizations can streamline their operations, make them more efficient and achieve their business goals more easily.

Business Process Management (BPM) Software has the potential to revolutionize the way organizations operate. The processes can identify patterns and make choices that humans cannot or may not be able to perform, using machine learning in conjunction with BPM software. Through this combination, businesses can make better decisions and more effective use of their data by making it easier to analyze them. There are many advantages to using machine learning in BPM software, including increasing productivity, reducing costs and improving accuracy. The following abstract model (Figure 2) illustrates how AI will be integrated into BPM software to create a brighter future for businesses all over the world.

Figure 4. Integration of AI into BPM

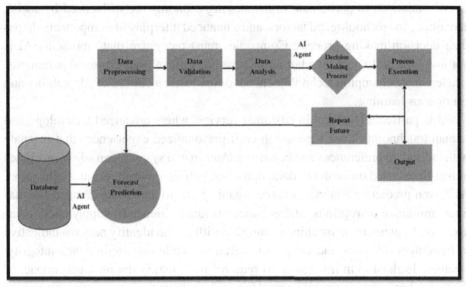

(Adapted from "AI Integration in Business Process Management",IEEE, 2019 International Conference) (CREBUS)

UNVEILING THE SIGNIFICANCE OF AI IN BUSINESS TRANSFORMATION

Artificial Intelligence (AI) is revolutionizing the business landscape, offering enormous potential for revenue growth and strategic leadership. However, there is a significant gap between companies that have embraced AI and those that have not. To bridge this gap, it is essential for managers to understand the advantages of AI. AI can help personalize customer interactions based on factors such as location, gender, time, and trends, leading to increased customer satisfaction and retention. It also enables customer service departments to manage requests more effectively and improve satisfaction levels by combining AI with traditional methods. AI can benefit various areas of business operations, including data analysis process optimization, supply chain management, and production reform. It can automate tasks, enhance efficiency, and improve fraud detection while ensuring data integrity.

Strategic leadership during the AI era requires identifying individuals with the knowledge, experience, and confidence to tackle complex challenges. These challenges require innovative solutions that adapt to the ever-changing business landscape. One of the most critical topics in recent times is the sharing economy, and studies have focused on understanding its drivers from the user's perspective. Users' intentions to participate in the sharing economy are influenced by social, economic, and technological factors, and a nuanced interplay of components shapes their decision-making process. Companies must recognize that embracing AI is not just a technological leap but a fundamental shift in organizational paradigms. Leaders must champion technological adoption, foster a culture of adaptability and continuous learning.

AI is particularly useful in customer service, where advanced technology and human touchpoints work together to craft personalized experiences that resonate with individual preferences and behaviors. Automated systems can adjust processes in real-time based on evolving data, optimizing efficiency and resource allocation. AI-driven predictive analytics enable organizations to anticipate demand fluctuations, minimize disruptions, and enhance overall resilience in supply chain management. Implementing machine leaning algorithms can identify patterns indicative of fraudulent activities and safeguard operations while maintaining data integrity. Strategic leadership in the age of AI requires recognizing the profound impact of the technologies on the organizational fabric. The sharing economy presents unique challenges and opportunities, and understanding the drivers from the user's perspective is crucial for companies seeking to tap into this market.

Addressing components such as pleasure, network externalities, perceived quality, cost savings, and efficiency can enhance user engagement and contribute to the sustained growth of businesses operating in this space. The integration of AI and the dynamics of the sharing economy represent pivotal points of transformation for businesses, strategic leaders must navigate these shifts with agility, recognizing the broader implications beyond technological advancements. By embracing a holistic approach that combines technological innovation, cultural adaptation, and a keen understanding of user dynamics, businesses can position themselves for sustained success in the evolving landscape.

ADVANTAGES AND CHALLENGES OF LEVERAGING AI

Artificial intelligence (AI) is a rapidly growing field that involves the creation of intelligent machines that are capable of performing tasks that typically require human intelligence. AI has brought about numerous advantages, including increased efficiency and time management in everyday life. This has resulted in a more efficient and fast-paced environment for employees and customers leading to significant savings in time and money. Moreover, AI has revolutionized how we process vast amounts of data, allowing for higher-quality research and data access like never before. AI machines can process data without getting tired, leading to fewer mistakes and errors in companies worldwide.

Despite these benefits, AI also has its downsides. One of the major drawbacks is that the cost of repair, installation, and frequent upgrades is high. Although AI machines are built to think like humans, they do not possess emotions or moral values, and they lack judgment skills. Performing the same function repeatedly can lead to wear and tear on the machine. Thinking outside the box is crucial to success, but AI machines do not have the same level of creativity as humans. This implies that they will have difficulty in developing new and innovative ideas. While AI is a source of employment opportunities, it also leads to the loss of jobs in sectors where human labor requirements have been reduced. There are many benefits and drawbacks to artificial intelligence. As advantages and disadvantages of AI to ensure that we can create a world where artificial intelligence and human intelligence work together to achieve optimal results.

Advantages of AI

There are many advantages (Ku. Chhaya A. Khanzode, Dr. Ravindra D. Sarode, 2020) to AI integration with different sectors, which can be seen in their ability to improve efficiency, simplify operations and give valuable information on decisions. The ability to significantly increase productivity through automation of redundant tasks, which enables businesses to allocate their staff for more challenging and strategic activities is one of the most important advantages of (AI) Driven Automation. This will not only save time, but also reduce the likelihood of error, which will ultimately lead to improved operational efficiency and profitability. In addition, AI has excelled in the analysis of data and pattern recognition. In order to gain important insights and trends that can't be easily seen by an analyst, it may process large amounts of data. Productivity is further enhanced by the continuous operation of an artificial intelligence system, thus ensuring uninterrupted service without interruption or disruption. In addition, AI algorithms perform tasks that range from prediction modelling to customer service interaction at a level of accuracy and precision which minimizes errors and improves reliability. As AI reduces the need for human labor in resource intensive tasks, these benefits contribute to reducing costs.

Disadvantages of AI

The integration of AI also presents significant challenges and potential drawbacks that must be carefully addressed. The most significant disadvantages to be addressed on a careful basis are mentioned further. Job displacement is one of the main concerns, given that automation by artificial intelligence might cause unemployment in some sectors and require retraining and redeployment for workers concerned (Flor Maria Lorena et. al, 2022). In addition, AI algorithms may be exposed to biases in training data, which may lead to unfair or discriminatory results and raise ethical concerns. Another limitation is the lack of ability to tackle novel or foreseen situations without predefinedrules or guidelines. Dependency on data quality and quantity is also critical, as biased or incomplete data can lead to inaccurate predictions or decisions. Additionally, security risks associated with AI systems, such as vulnerabilities to hacking and malicious use, necessitate robust protection measures to safeguard sensitive information and prevent potential breaches. Furthermore, the high initial costs of implementing AI technologies,including infrastructure, training and maintenance, may pose financial barriers for some organizations. Addressing these challenges requires careful consideration of ethical, social and economic implications, along with ongoing efforts to mitigate risks and maximize the benefits of AI integration. This includes regularly reviewing and updating training data to minimize bias, investing in security measures, and providing training opportunities for affected workers. In doing so, organizations can take advantage of the benefits from artificial intelligence and mitigate potential risks in a way that ensures equal opportunity for all.

1. **Decision support:** Certain AI technologies require a human expert in the problem domain to form a hypothesis and choose relevant features. However, the concern of job displacement may discourage humans from offering valuable information for creating AI models. In many cases, cognitive AI technologies do not enable humans to comprehend and justify their behavior.
2. **Customer and employee engagement:** Anticipated significant shifts in the workforce leading to potential job cuts, alongside the prevailing skepticism surrounding the accuracy and reliability of AI-generated decisions, suggestions, and reactions.
3. **Automation:** Ensuring a successful digital business strategy requires leveraging AI for automation benefits. Developing capabilities that incorporate business rules is vital to harness automation and gain a competitive edge.
4. **High Costs:** Developing a machine capable of simulating human intelligence is a significant challenge. It demands considerable time, resources, and financial investment. Additionally, AI systems must be regularly updated with the latest hardware and software to meet evolving demands, adding to the overall cost.
5. **Encouraging Human Complacency:** The growing use of AI for a wide range of tasks may contribute to human complacency. As AI assumes more duties, individuals may be less motivated to enhance their skills and knowledge, relying excessively on technology (Ahmad, S.F., Han, H., Alam, M.M. et al., 2023). This overreliance can erode critical thinking and problem-solving abilities, as people

may turn to AI solutions without questioning their effectiveness or considering other options. Ultimately, this could result in a workforce that is less capable and less adaptable to new challenges, stifling human potential and creativity.

6. **Job Displacement:** The rapid advancement of AI and automation technologies presents a considerable threat to employment, particularly in fields that rely on repetitive and routine tasks. Automation is increasingly replacing jobs in manufacturing, retail, customer service, and even certain professional domains like legal research or medical diagnostics. While AI can lead to the creation of new job opportunities, the transition period can be challenging, necessitating the retraining and upskilling of many workers. If not managed properly, widespread job displacement can have serious economic and social repercussions, leading to higher unemployment rates and increased social inequality.

Figure 5. Disadvantages of AI

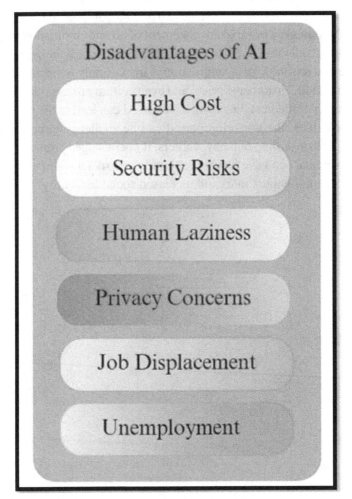

(Source: Created by Authors)

CASE STUDY FOUR: COMPANIES REVOLUTIONIZING PERSONALIZED BANKING WITH AI

Customers have become accustomed to expecting their financial institutions to provide them with continuous, personalized banking services at all times in the age of competency. Consumers are expecting real time access to their own financial data, and they want the convenience of getting it by simply clicking on a button. Fortunately, institutions are able to meet these requirements now that artificial intelligence is available. The personalized baking industry is currently confronted with several challenges. One of the most pressing issues is the need to meet increasingly high customer expectations. Additionally, banks must find ways to handle vast amounts of data efficiently while keeping operational costs under control. Furthermore, these institutions must contend with competition from fintech startups, as well as navigate through stringent regulatory requirements. Addressing these challenges will be crucial for banks to continue providing personalized services to their customers while staying competitive in the market.

Kasisto: - The pioneering organization behind KAI, a realtime functional chatbot that allows customers to receive prompt and effective answers to their inquiries, is Kasisto, a New York City based company. This is not just a benefit to the customer, who will be given timely and efficient answers to their questions but a revolutionary change. This not only benefits the customers, but also gives them a number of advantages when they are seeking information. Kasisto has an extensive client base of financial institutions worldwide, including J.P. Morgan, The Development Bank of Singapore, Emirates NBD Bank, Standard Chartered, and Absa Group Limited, among others.

Abe AI: - Abe AI, based in Orlando, is renowned for its virtual assistant capabilities through technology such as Amazon Alexa, Google Home, and other mobile and web devices. Abe AI offers a diverse range of services to its customers, from processing bills to comprehensive financial management and forecasting.

Trim: - Trim, a San Francisco based company, has developed a ground-breaking tool with the primary goal of helping customers save money. Trim's app can analyze customer spending across multiple accounts and identify areas where they are spending excessively. According to Trim, they have saved their users over $40 million since the establishment of the company. Trim has also gained recognition from reputable sources like The New York Times, NBC News, Good Morning America, Fortune Magazine, ABC News, and many others.

THE ROLE OF ARTIFICIAL INTELLIGENCE IN PREVENTING MALICIOUS INTRUSIONS

There are both opportunities and challenges in the growing use of Artificial Intelligence for Cyber Security. On one hand, by improving threat detection, automated response actions, and human capabilities, AI technologies have shown significant potential to strengthen cybersecurity defenses. AI powered systems can quickly identify patterns which indicate cyber threats more accurately than traditional methods by analyzing large amounts of data in real time. In addition, machine learning algorithms are capable of adapting and evolving in response to emerging threats that allow proactive defense measures against new vectors of attack. Routine security tasks can also be automated by AI, freeing up human resources to address more complex cybersecurity challenges.

Artificial Neural Networks (ANN) is a prominent technique that has emerged from the field of artificial intelligence. ANNs are models of statistical learning, which imitate the structure and functions of a person's brain. In environments where the rules or algorithms for solving problems are difficult to describe, or not known at all, these models can be of particular use in teaching and solving problems. However, since the behavior of the ANN system is not known, they are considered to be undefinable black box models. ANNs have proved to be effective in addressing all stages of the cyber kill chain. They can be integrated with security systems to monitor network traffic and detect malicious attacks in advance of the actual attack.

That's a good goal for cybersecurity, because it allows for the prevention of cyber-attacks before they happen. ANN's can be effectively used to learn from past network activities and attacks in order to prevent future attacks from occurring. This approach is consistent with the principle of perimeter defense, which aims at protecting against potential attacks. Conventional techniques have limitations in the area of cyber defense, as they are dependent on security professionals' expertise. Manual patter definition is a time-consuming process that can also result in misses' threats. However, Artificial Neural Networks (ANN's) have emerged as a promising solution to overcome these limitations. ANNs are able to automatically learn from the previous data transmitted over the network and identify patterns which describe both normal and abnormal network operations. The ability to learn and adapt in real time provides the ANN with a significant advantage over traditional techniques, which makes it an important tool for cyber defense.

Figure 6. Integration of AI in Security

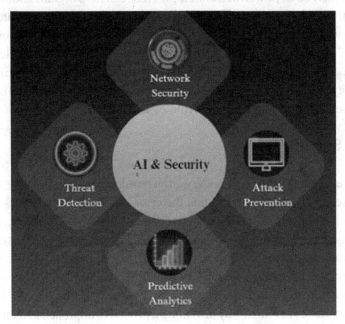

(Source: Created by Authors)

Threat Hunting

The way cyber security professionals search for and react to threats has been transformed by AI. It enabled dynamic behavioral analysis, enabling organizations to detect anomalies in real time, thanks to its unparalleled ability to process vast amounts of data and quickly detect patterns. Organizations will be able to efficiently manage an ever-evolving threat landscape and secure the digital environment for themselves and their clients through a proactive approach, enabling them to anticipate and prevent cyber-attacks before they happen, moving from reactive security frameworks into more robust comprehensive and proactive cybersecurity frameworks with artificial intelligence.

Vulnerability Management

Cyber security threats are evolving faster than ever before in today's digital world, making it difficult for organizations to keep up with the pace of change. The existing reactive approach to vulnerability management has not been enough, and organizations are now looking at proactive and predictive approaches for the protection of their systems and information. Artificial Intelligence (AI) and Machine Learning (ML) have emerged as powerful technologies that can help organizations detect and respond to threats before they can cause damage. AI and ML can help prevent zero-day attacks while protecting against possible breaches through continuous analysis of user and event behavior, enabling organizations to build a complete defense mechanism. This new approach to vulnerability management is revolutionizing the cybersecurity industry, and organizations that embrace it can stay ahead of the curve and keep their systems and data safe from cyber threats.

Network Security

The development of AI technology in network security is a game changer. It empowers security teams to streamline the creation of security policies and gain a comprehensive understanding of the network topography (Aickelin, U., & Das, S). By analyzing massive datasets, AI supports the development of precise security policies and simplifies the interpretation of network traffic patterns. This optimization facilitates greater efficiency, freeing up valuable resources and allowing security teams to focus on strategic aspects of network security. Furthermore, it enhances protection against cyber threats by providing a proactive approach to identifying and mitigating potential risks. Overall AI's integration in network security is a significant step forward in safeguarding digital assets against cyberattacks.

CASE STUDY FIVE: THE CASE OF JP MORGAN CHASE (BASED IN NEW YORK)

JP Morgan Chase and Co., the world's largest financial firm based in New York City, has long been associated with innovation in banking. The company has modernized its operations in order to increase efficiency and improve the customer experience, using cutting edge technologies such as AI. JP Morgan Chase continues to lead the way when it comes to shaping the future of financial services, demonstrating its commitment to innovation and excellence in a constantly changing digital landscape with AI at the heart of its initiatives. JP Morgan Chase intends to remain at the forefront of banking innovation, driving sustainable growth and delivering value for its clients around the world by using AI.

Historically, the banking sector has faced difficulties such as inefficient manual procedures, legacy systems and burdensome regulatory compliance requirements. Delays, errors and increased operating costs are the result of cumbersome processes that affect efficiency and customer service. There was often a lack of interoperability and scale in legacy systems, which hindered innovation and dynamism. In addition, major resources and expertise were needed for effective management of the regulatory compliance requirements, which also further strained operating efficiency and increased risk of breaches.

By applying state of the art technology and innovation strategies, JPMorgan Chase has dealt with these traditional problems. The Bank has automated manual processes, streamlined operations and reduced costs through its digital transformation initiatives. For example, in order to analyze legal documents and extract key data points and clauses revolutionizing the review of commercial credit agreements, JPMorgan Chase introduced a "chatbot" technology called Contract Intelligence. This AI-driven solution drastically reduces the time required for manual review, from 360,000 hours to mere seconds, enhancing operational efficiency and scalability. JP Morgan Chase has also been able to modernize its legacy systems, improve interoperability and scale while promoting innovation through investment in modern technology infrastructure and cloud solutions. In order to increase regulatory compliance efforts, facilitate active risk management and ensure compliance with legal requirements, the Bank has also put in place advanced Analytics and Artificial Intelligence solutions. JP Morgan Chase has positioned itself as a leader in overcoming traditional banking industry challenges by adopting technology and innovation, driving efficiency, adaptability and compliance excellence.

FUTURE TRENDS AND EMERGING TECHNOLOGIES IN AI

The landscape of businesses and industries is being shaped by future and emerging technologies in AI, which are driving innovation, efficiency, and transformation (Allioui, Hanane et. Al) i n AI is a dynamic field with several key developments that are expected to have a significant impact on how it is used in the years to come. These developments range from advancements in deep learning to emergence of ethical AI frameworks. In this exploration, we will take a closer look at these trends and technologies.

Advancements in Deep Learning

The field of deep learning (Buczak, A. L., & Guven, E), branch of artificial intelligence that stimulates the functions of the human brain through neural networks, is rapidly advancing. One prominent trend in this field is the development of more intricate and efficient neural network architectures. Transformers, which are a type of neural network architecture, have achieved widespread recognition for their effectiveness in performing natural language processing tasks. These advancements facilitate better understanding of complex data sets and enable more precise predictions and decision-making.

Reinforcement Learning

Increased adoption of reinforcement learning, a machine learning branch where an agent learns to make decisions by receiving feedback from an environment, is being observed. This approach is particularly useful in sequential decision-making scenarios, such as autonomous vehicles, robotics, and game playing. Reinforcement learning has potential to solve complex problems in dynamic environments as algorithms become more scalable and sophisticated.

Natural Language Processing (NLP) Advancements

The advancement of Natural Language Processing (NLP), which enables machines to comprehend and produce human language, is progressing rapidly. Recent developments in models such as OpenAI's GPT (Generative Pre-trained Transformative) series are pushing the boundaries of language comprehension and production. These models are particularly good at tasks like creating text, translating language and analysing sentiment. As NLP models Become more capable and accessible, they have far reaching implications for a wide range of industries, from customer service to content creation.

AI Automation and Augmentation

Industries are being transformed through the use of AI-Powered automation. This has resulted in the optimization of repetitive tasks, increased productivity, and the development of new capabilities. Robotic Process Automation (RPA) technologies, for instance, are being utilized to automate tedious tasks across different business processes, thus allowing human resources to focus on more strategic activities. In addition, AI-driven augmentation is becoming a more common place, where machines work alongside humans to complement their skills rather than replacing them. This approach enhances human capabilities in areas such as decision-making, creativity and problem-solving.

Edge AI and Federated Learning

The utilization of edge computing, which refers to processing data in closer proximity to its source, is gaining popularity in combination with artificial intelligence. Edge AI allows for instant decision-making and lessens the delay by executing computations on devices or at the edge of the network, instead of relying solely on centralized cloud servers. Federated Learning, a decentralized Technique for training machine learning models across multiple devices or edges nodes without exchanging raw data, is an emerging trend in privacy-preserving AI. It permits collaboratives model training while maintaining user privacy, making it suitable for use in healthcare, finance and IoT applications.

Explainable AI (XAI)

With AI systems being utilized more often in crucial areas like healthcare, finance, and criminal justice, it has become increasingly important to ensure transparency and accountability. The goal of explainable AI (XAI) is to make AI algorithms and decisions comprehensible to humans. XAI achieves this by offering explanations for model predictions and decisions, which in turn promotes trust, simplifies regulatory compliance, and enables stakeholders to identify and address biases and errors.

AI Ethics and Responsibilities AI Practices

Society is increasingly aware of the impact of AI, leading to a greater emphasis on the ethical implications of AI technologies. Ethical AI practices include the consideration of fairness, transparency, accountability and privacy. To align with ethical principles and societal values, companies are investing in ethical AI frameworks, carrying out AI impact assessments, and establishing AI ethics boards for their AI initiatives.

Quantum Computing and AI

Quantum Computing is a groundbreaking technology that harnesses quantum mechanical phenomena to perform computations. Its potential for accelerating AI research and applications is enormous. Quantum algorithms have the ability to solve specific AI tasks exponentially faster than classical computers, unlocking new horizons in optimization, machine learning, and cryptography. Although quantum computing is still in its early stages, it holds the promise of transforming the AI landscape in the long term.

CONCLUSION

- The widespread integration of Artificial Intelligence (AI) has undeniably proven to be transformative across various industries, revolutionizing traditional practices and unlocking new avenues for innovation and growth. From optimizing supply chains and enhancing safety measures to improving agricultural productivity and transforming decision- making processes, AI-driven solutions have significantly impacted strategic success and data management. As industries continue to embrace AI technologies, the potential for further advancements and efficiencies is immense. To maximize the benefits of AI integration, it is crucial for organizations to invest in continuous research and development, foster a culture of innovation, and ensure ethical implementation of AI technologies. Embracing AI not only presents opportunities for operational enhancements but also contributes to sustainable growth and competitive advantage in the rapidly evolving business landscape.

The increasing prevalence of AI technologies in business has sparked significant interest due to their demonstrated potential for creating competitive advantages. This chapter aims to explore the correlation between AI usage and transformative business strategy through a comprehensive literature review. The study also introduces a conceptual framework (Figure 2) that elucidates the dynamic relationship between AI technologies and business strategy in terms of creating business value. These findings offer valuable insights for both theoretical understanding and practical management, paving the way for the development of new management practices and theoretical contributions. From a managerial standpoint, the proposed framework can serve as a valuable tool for guiding decision-making and reshaping organizational culture, urging the adoption of new managerial models. Furthermore, highlighting the connection between AI and business strategy can facilitate informed decision- making among executives, enabling them to harness the full potential of AI technologies while being well-versed in the associated opportunities, challenges, and benefits for their organizations.

- **Review Questions: -**
- Describe regulatory measures do you believe are necessary to ensure the responsible use of AI technologies in commercial context?
- Evaluate tactics or techniques you believe are essential for firms looking to maximize the benefits of AI adoption while minimizing associated risks?
- Understand how is it that AI addresses the difficulties faced by the banking industry?

REFERENCES

Abramson, N., Braverman, D., & Sebestyen, G. (1963). Pattern recognition and machine learning. *IEEE Transactions on Information Theory*, 9(4), 257–261. DOI:10.1109/TIT.1963.1057854

Ahmadi, S. (2024). A Comprehensive Study on Integration of Big Data and AI in Financial Industry and Its Effect on Present and Future Opportunities. *International Journal of Current Science Research and Review*, 07(1).

Aickelin, U., & Das, S. (2011). *Artificial intelligence for security*. Springer Science & Business Media.

Allioui, H. (2023). *Unleashing the Potential of AI: Investigating Cutting-Edge Technologies That Are Transforming Businesses.*

Allioui, H. (2023). Unleashing the Potential of AI: Investigating Cutting-Edge Technologies That Are Transforming Businesses.

Ambati, L. (2022). *Factors Influencing the Adoption of Artificial Intelligence in Organizations – From an Employee's Perspective*. AIS Electronic Library (AISeL).

Anna, N. E., Novian, R. M., & Ismail, N. (2023, October). Enhancing Virtual Instruction: Leveraging AI Applications for Success. *Library Hi Tech News*, 9. DOI:10.1108/LHTN-09-2023-0175

Bellman, R. E. (1978). *An introduction to Artificial Intelligence: Can computers think?* Boyd & Fraser Publishing Company.

Bengio, Y., Courville, A., & Vincent, P. (2013). Representation learning: A review and new perspectives. *IEEE Transactions on Pattern Analysis and Machine Intelligence*, 35(8), 1798–1828. DOI:10.1109/TPAMI.2013.50 PMID:23787338

Bharadwaj, A., El Sawy, O. A., Pavlou, P. A., & Venkatraman, N. (2013). Digital business strategy: Toward a next generation of insights. MIS Quarterly: Management. *Information Systems*, 37(2), 471–482.

Boden, M. A. (1984). Impacts of artificial intelligence. *Futures*, 16(1), 60–70. DOI:10.1016/0016-3287(84)90007-7

Boyd, D., & Crawford, K. (2012). Critical questions for big data: Provocations for a cultural, technological, and scholarly phenomenon. *Information Communication and Society*, 15(5), 662–679. DOI:10.1080/1369118X.2012.678878

Brynjolfsson, E., & Mcafee, A. N. (2017). Artificial intelligence, for real. *Harvard Business Review*.

Buchanan, L., & O'Connell, A. (2006). Brief history of decision making. *Harvard Business Review*, 84(1), 32–41. PMID:16447367

Buczak, A. L., & Guven, E. (2016). A survey of data mining and machine learning methods for cyber security intrusion detection. *IEEE Communications Surveys and Tutorials*, 18(2), 1153–1176. DOI:10.1109/COMST.2015.2494502

Bundy, A., Young, R. M., Burstall, R. M., & Weir, S. (1978). *Artificial intelligence: An introductory course*. Edinburgh Univ. Press.

Campbell, C. (2020). From Data to Action: How Marketers Can Leverage AI. *Business Horizons*, (vol. 227–243).

Chakravorti, B., Bhalla, A., & Chaturvedi, R. S. (2019). Which countries ate leading the data economy? *Harvard Business Review*.

Charniak, E., & McDermott, D. (1985). Introduction to artificial intelligence. Boston, EUA: Addison-Wesley.

Davenport, T., & Harris, J. (2017). *Competing on analytics: Updated, with a new introduction: The new science of winning*. Harvard Business Review Press.

Davenport, T. H., & Ronanki, R. (2018). Artificial intelligence for the real world. *Harvard Business Review*, 108–116.

De Fátima Soares Borges, A. (2021, April). The Strategic Use of Artificial Intelligence in the Digital Era: Systematic Literature Review and Future Research Directions. *International Journal of Information Management*, 102225, 1.

Echeberría, A. (2022). AI Integration in the Digital Transformation Strategy. Springer eBooks.

Garcia, A. (2023). *Data-Driven Decision Making: Leveraging Analytics and AI for Strategic Advantage*.

Gerow, J. E., Grover, V., Thatcher, J., & Roth, P. L. (2014). Looking toward the future of it–Business strategic alignment through the past: A meta-analysis. MIS Quarterly: Management. *Information Systems*, 38(4), 1159–1185.

Goodfellow, I., Bengio, Y., & Courville, A. (2016). *Deep learning MIT press*.

Hassabis, D., Suleyman, M., & Legg, S. (2017). *DeepMind's work in 2016: A round-up*. DeepMind.

Haugeland, J. (1985). *Artificial Intelligence: The very idea*. MIT Press.

Henderson, J. C., & Venkatraman, N. (1999). Strategic alignment: Leveraging Information Technology for transforming organizations. *IBM Systems Journal*, 38(2), 472–484. DOI:10.1147/SJ.1999.5387096

Holloway, C. (1983). Strategic management and artificial intelligence. *Long Range Planning*, 16(5), 89–93. DOI:10.1016/0024-6301(83)90082-1

Janković, S., & Curovic, D. M. (2023, October). Strategic Integration of Artificial Intelligence for Sustainable Businesses: Implications for Data Management and Human User Engagement in the Digital Era. *Sustainability (Basel)*, 15208(21, 24), 15208. DOI:10.3390/su152115208

Janković, S., & Curovic, D. M. (2023, October). Strategic Integration of Artificial Intelligence for Sustainable Businesses: Implications for Data Management and Human User Engagement in the Digital Era. *Sustainability (Basel)*, 15(21), 15208–15208. DOI:10.3390/su152115208

Kaur, R., Gabrijelčič, D., & Klobučar, T. (2023, September). Artificial Intelligence for Cybersecurity: Literature Review and Future Research Directions. *Information Fusion*, 101804, 1. DOI:10.1016/j.inffus.2023.101804

Kulkov, I. (2021, August). The Role of Artificial Intelligence in Business Transformation: A Case of Pharmaceutical Companies. *Technology in Society*, 101629, 1. DOI:10.1016/j.techsoc.2021.101629

Kumar, S. (2023). Artificial Intelligence. *Journal of Computers Mechanical and Management, 31–42*(3).

Kurzweil, R. (1990). *The age of intelligent machines*. MIT Press.

Laurindo, F. J. (2008). *Information technology: Planning and strategy management*. Atlas.

Ledro, C., Nosella, A., & Dalla Pozza, I. (2023, December). Integration of AI in CRM: Challenges and Guidelines. *Journal of Open Innovation*, 100151(4), 1. DOI:10.1016/j.joitmc.2023.100151

Lei, H. (2023). *Artificial Intelligence—A New Knowledge and Decision-Making Paradigm*. Springer eBooks.

Luger, G. F., & Stubblefield, W. A. (1993). *Instructor's manual for Artificial Intelligence: Structures and strategies for complex problem solving*. São Francisco, EUA: Benjamin Cummings.

Lyall, A., Mercier, P., & Gstettner, S. (2018). The death of supply chain management. *Harvard Business Review*, 1–4.

Maramganti, K. (2019). *Role of Artificial Intelligence in Business Transformation.* Research Gate.

Marr, B., & Ward, M. (2019). *Artificial Intelligence in practice: How 50 successful companies used artificial intelligence to solve problems.* Hoboken, EUA: Wiley.

Martellini, M., & Rule, S. (2016). *Cybersecurity: The Insights You Need from Harvard Business Review.* Harvard Business Review Press.

McCarthy, J., & Hayes, P. J. (1981). Some philosophical problems from the standpoint of artificial intelligence. *Readings in artificial intelligence.* Morgan Kaufman. DOI:10.1016/B978-0-934613-03-3.50033-7

Michie, D. (1968). "Memo" functions and machine learning. *Nature*, 218(5136), 19–22. DOI:10.1038/218019a0

Mishra, S. (2021). AI Business Model: An Integrative Business Approach. *Journal of Innovation and Entrepreneurship,' 10*(1). Springer Science and Business Media LLC.

Morocho-Cayamcela, M. E., Lee, H., & Lim, W. (2019). Machine learning for 5G/B5G mobile and wireless communications: Potential, limitations, and future directions. *IEEE Access : Practical Innovations, Open Solutions*, 7, 137184–137206. DOI:10.1109/ACCESS.2019.2942390

Nosova, S. (2024). Strategies for Business Cybersecurity Using AI Technologies. *Studies in Computational Intelligence.*

Phillips-Wren, G. (2012, April). AI TOOLS IN DECISION MAKING SUPPORT SYSTEMS: A REVIEW. *International Journal of Artificial Intelligence Tools*, 21(02), 1240005. DOI:10.1142/S0218213012400052

Porter, M. E., & Millar, V. E. (1985). How information gives you competitive advantage. *Harvard Business Review*, 63(4), 149–160.

Ransbotham, S., Gerbert, P., Reeves, M., Kiron, D., & Spira, M. (2018). Artificial intelligence in business gets real. *MIT Sloan Management Review.*

Rich, E., & Knight, K. (1991). *Introduction to artificial networks.* Mac Graw-Hill.

Russell, S. J., & Norvig, P. (2010). *Artificial intelligence: A modern approach. Nova Jersey, EUA.* PrenticeHall.

Russell, S. J., & Norvig, P. (2010). *Artificial intelligence: A modern approach. Nova Jersey, EUA.* PrenticeHall.

Schalkoff, R. J. (1990). *Artificial intelligence engine*. Mac Graw-Hill.

Schrage, M., & Kiron, D. (2018). Leading with next-generation key performance indicators. *MIT Sloan Management Review*, 16.

Silver, D., Huang, A., Maddison, C. J., Guez, A., Sifre, L., Van Den Driessche, G., Schrittwieser, J., Antonoglou, I., Panneershelvam, V., Lanctot, M., Dieleman, S., Grewe, D., Nham, J., Kalchbrenner, N., Sutskever, I., Lillicrap, T., Leach, M., Kavukcuoglu, K., Graepel, T., & Hassabis, D. (2016). Mastering the game of go with deep neural networks and tree search. *Nature*, 529(7587), 484–489. DOI:10.1038/nature16961 PMID:26819042

Silver, D., Schrittwieser, J., Simonyan, K., Antonoglou, I., Huang, A., Guez, A., Hubert, T., Baker, L., Lai, M., Bolton, A., Chen, Y., Lillicrap, T., Hui, F., Sifre, L., van den Driessche, G., Graepel, T., & Hassabis, D. (2017). Mastering the game of Go without human knowledge. *Nature*, 550(7676), 354–359. DOI:10.1038/nature24270 PMID:29052630

Solomonoff, R. J. (1985). The time scale of artificial intelligence: Reflections on social effects. *Human Systems Management*, 5(2), 149–153. DOI:10.3233/HSM-1985-5207

Song, Y., Xue, Y., Li, C., Zhao, X., Liu, S., & Zhuo, X. (2017). *Online cost efficient customer recognition system for retail analytics. in: 2017 IEEE Winter Applications of Computer Vision Workshops*. WACVW.

Svetlana, N. (2022). Artificial Intelligence as a Driver of Business Process Transformation. *Procedia Computer Science*, 276–284.

Venkatraman, V. (2017). *The digital matrix: New rules for business transformation through technology*. EUA: LifeTree Media Ltd.

Wilson, H. J., & Daugherty, P. R. (2018). Collaborative intelligence: Humans and AI are joining forces. *Harvard Business Review*, 96(4), 114–123.

Winston, P. H. (1970). *Learning structural descriptions from examples*. Massachusetts Institute of Technology.

Zhuang, Y. T., Wu, F., Chen, C., & Pan, Y. H. (2017). Challenges and opportunities: From big data to knowledge in AI 2.0. *Frontiers of Information Technology & Electronic Engineering*, 18(1), 3–14. DOI:10.1631/FITEE.1601883

KEY TERMS AND DEFINITIONS

Artificial Intelligence: Artificial intelligence popularly abbreviated as AI refers to computer systems that simulate human intelligence processes. These processes involve learning, reasoning and correction. To perform tasks traditionally carried out by human intelligence carried out by human intelligence, AI systems are designed.

Business Process Management: In order to achieve more effective results, better customer satisfaction, and overall business efficiency, BPM is a systematic approach to improving the organization's processes. In order to align business processes with organizational objectives and targets, BPM involves the design, implementation, monitoring and optimization of these processes.

Cognitive Decision Making: Cognitive Decision Making refers to the process through which people or systems use their cognitive skills to evaluate available information, assess potential options and decide what course of action is best for them.

Data Management: In order to guarantee the accuracy, accessibility, reliability and security of data over their life cycle, data management is a process by which data are acquired, stored, organized and managed. Various activities, such as data collection, storage, integration, transformation, analysis and dissemination, are involved.

Malicious Intrusions: Unauthorized access or penetration into computer systems, networks or digital environments with malicious intent is called malicious intrusions, also known as cyber intrusions or security breaches.

Chapter 4
Modern Smart Banking With Cutting–Edge Technologies:
A Sustainable Banking and Financial World

M Kiran Kumar

https://orcid.org/0000-0003-2084-9418

CMS Business School, JAIN University, Bangalore, India

V. Srinidhi

Community Institute of Management Studies, Bengaluru, India

B. S. Shamanth

Surana Evening College, Bengaluru, India

Amit Kumar Tyagi

https://orcid.org/0000-0003-2657-8700

National Institute of Fashion Technology, New Delhi, India

ABSTRACT

In today's rapidly changing world/digital landscape, the banking sector is undergoing a profound transformation driven by cutting-edge technologies. This chapter examines the convergence of smart banking with innovative technologies and explores its implications for using sustainability within the financial ecosystem. Modern smart banking leverages a constellation of technologies, including artificial intelligence, machine learning, big data analytics, and blockchain, to revolutionize traditional banking processes and deliver enhanced value to customers. By harnessing these

DOI: 10.4018/979-8-3693-4187-2.ch004

technologies, banks can offer personalized financial services, automate routine tasks, and optimize decision-making processes, thereby improving operational efficiency and customer experiences.

INTRODUCTION TO SMART BANKING AND ITS IMPORTANCE IN SUSTAINABLE BANKING PRACTICES

In the ever-evolving landscape of finance, the advent of smart banking represents a transformative shift in how financial services are delivered and consumed. Smart banking uses cutting-edge technologies such as artificial intelligence, blockchain, and the Internet of Things to revolutionize traditional banking practices. This section will discuss about the importance of smart banking within the context of sustainable banking practices, highlighting its potential to drive positive environmental, social, and economic impacts (Smith, J., & Johnson, R. (2021)).

Importance of Smart Banking in Sustainable Banking Practices

Smart banking plays an important role in advancing sustainable banking practices by providing innovative solutions that optimize efficiency, reduce environmental footprint, and promote financial inclusion. Through the integration of advanced analytics and automation, smart banking enables institutions to streamline operations, minimize paper-based processes, and optimize resource utilization, thus contributing to lower carbon emissions and overall environmental sustainability (Chen, L., & Wang, H. (2020)). Moreover, smart banking uses financial inclusion by extending services to underserved populations through digital channels. By using mobile banking apps and online platforms, financial institutions can reach individuals in remote areas and marginalized communities, empowering them with access to essential financial services. This inclusivity not only enhances social equity but also stimulates economic growth and resilience.

Furthermore, smart banking enhances security and risk management through technologies like blockchain, which provide immutable transaction records and robust authentication mechanisms (Patel, A., & Gupta, M. (2019)). By fortifying cybersecurity measures and mitigating fraud risks, smart banking instills trust and confidence in the financial system, thereby safeguarding the interests of users and preserving financial stability.

Additionally, the data-driven nature of smart banking enables personalized and tailored financial services, leading to improved customer experiences and satisfaction. By analyzing large amount of data, financial institutions can gain valuable information about customer preferences, behaviors, and needs, allowing them to provide targeted products and services that meet individual requirements. This customer-centric approach not only strengthens customer relationships but also improves business growth and profitability.

In summary, smart banking represents a major shift towards more sustainable, inclusive, and resilient banking practices. By using the power of technology, financial institutions can drive positive environmental, social, and economic outcomes while delivering enhanced value to customers and society at large. Using smart banking is not only imperative for staying competitive in the digital age but also for contributing to a more sustainable and equitable future.

Evolution of Banking Technologies

The evolution of banking technologies has been a remarkable journey, marked by huge milestones that have transformed the way financial services are delivered, accessed, and managed. This evolution can be traced through several key stages:

- Manual Banking (Pre-Industrial Revolution): Historically, banking transactions were conducted manually, involving physical ledgers, handwritten records, and face-to-face interactions at brick-and-mortar branches. This era was characterized by limited accessibility, lengthy processing times, and a heavy reliance on human labor.
- Mechanical Banking (Late 19th to Early 20th Century): The advent of mechanical devices, such as cash registers and adding machines, revolutionized banking operations, enabling faster and more accurate transaction processing. However, banking remained largely centralized, with limited automation and scalability.
- Electromechanical Banking (Mid-20th Century): The introduction of electromechanical systems, such as early computers and magnetic stripe cards, ushered in a new era of automation and innovation in banking. This period saw the emergence of automated teller machines (ATMs), electronic funds transfer (EFT) systems, and the first online banking services, laying the foundation for digital banking.
- Digital Banking (Late 20th Century to Present): The proliferation of personal computers, the internet, and mobile devices catalyzed the rise of digital banking, enabling customers to access banking services remotely, 24/7. This era witnessed the development of online banking platforms, mobile banking apps, and electronic payment systems, transforming the banking landscape and enhancing convenience, efficiency, and accessibility.
- Smart Banking (21st Century): The latest evolution in banking technologies revolves around the convergence of cutting-edge technologies, such as arti-

ficial intelligence, blockchain, biometrics, and the Internet of Things. Smart banking encompasses advanced analytics, personalized services, real-time insights, and seamless omnichannel experiences, providing unprecedented levels of customization, security, and innovation (Kumar, R., & Singh, P. (2018), Tyagi et al., (2021) (2022) (2023) and (2024)).

- Future Trends (Beyond): Looking ahead, banking technologies are poised to continue evolving rapidly, driven by emerging trends such as open banking, digital currencies, quantum computing, and decentralized finance (DeFi). These developments promise to further reshape the banking landscape, using greater transparency, interoperability, and democratization of financial services.

In summary, the evolution of banking technologies reflects a relentless pursuit of innovation, efficiency, and customer-centricity in the quest to meet the evolving needs and expectations of consumers in an increasingly digital and interconnected world.

Historical Development of Banking Technologies

The historical development of banking technologies is a journey marked by innovation, adaptation, and transformation. We will discuss few key stages in this evolution, as:

- Ancient Times to Middle Ages: The origins of banking can be traced back to ancient civilizations such as Mesopotamia, Egypt, and Greece, where rudimentary financial transactions and record-keeping systems were practiced. In the Middle Ages, European merchants and traders began to use bills of exchange and promissory notes as a means of facilitating international trade and credit.

- Rise of Banking Institutions (Late Middle Ages to Early Modern Period): The 14th and 15th centuries saw the emergence of early banking institutions, such as the Medici Bank in Florence and the Bank of Amsterdam, which provided services such as deposits, loans, and currency exchange. These institutions laid the groundwork for modern banking practices and helped use economic growth and development.

- Industrial Revolution (18th to 19th Century): The Industrial Revolution brought about huge changes in banking technologies and practices. The introduction of steam power, mechanization, and mass production led to the establishment of centralized banks, improved communication networks, and standardized currency systems. Innovations such as the telegraph and the printing press facilitated faster and more efficient banking operations.

- Introduction of Electronic Banking (20th Century): The 20th century witnessed the advent of electronic banking technologies, starting with the introduction of automated teller machines (ATMs) in the 1960s. ATMs revolutionized the way customers access their funds, providing convenience and flexibility beyond traditional branch banking. The development of electronic funds transfer (EFT) systems enabled the electronic processing of transactions, paving the way for online banking and electronic payment systems.
- Digital Revolution (Late 20th Century to Present): The digital revolution of the late 20th century transformed banking technologies on a global scale. The widespread adoption of personal computers, the internet, and mobile devices revolutionized the way banking services are delivered and accessed. Online banking platforms, mobile banking apps, and electronic payment systems became mainstream, providing customers greater convenience, accessibility, and flexibility in managing their finances.
- Emergence of FinTech (21st Century): The 21st century has witnessed the rise of financial technology (FinTech) companies that use cutting-edge technologies such as artificial intelligence, blockchain, and big data analytics to innovate and disrupt traditional banking practices (Wang, Y., & Li, W. (2021), Garcia, M., & Martinez, E. (2020), Tan, C., & Lim, H. (2019)). These companies provide a wide range of services, including peer-to-peer lending, digital wallets, robo-advisors, and crowdfunding platforms, catering to the evolving needs and preferences of modern consumers.

In summary, the historical development of banking technologies reflects a continuous evolution driven by technological advancements, economic forces, and changing consumer behaviors. From ancient civilizations to the digital age, banking technologies have evolved to meet the needs of an increasingly interconnected and technological connected world.

SUSTAINABILITY IN BANKING

Importance of Sustainability in the Financial Sector

The importance of sustainability in the financial sector cannot be overstated, as it plays an important role in using long-term economic prosperity, environmental stewardship, and social well-being. We will include several key reasons here with explaining why sustainability is important in the financial sector:

- Risk Mitigation: Using sustainability practices helps financial institutions mitigate various risks, including environmental, social, and governance (ESG) risks. By incorporating ESG factors into investment decisions and lending practices, institutions can identify and manage risks associated with climate change, resource scarcity, social unrest, regulatory changes, and reputational damage.
- Enhanced Financial Performance: Research indicates that companies with strong sustainability practices tend to outperform their peers financially over the long term. Sustainable investing strategies not only generate competitive returns but also promote resilience and stability in volatile market conditions. By integrating sustainability criteria into investment portfolios, financial institutions can create value for investors while advancing sustainability goals.
- Market Relevance and Competitiveness: Sustainability has become a key driver of consumer and investor preferences, influencing purchasing decisions, brand loyalty, and investment allocations. Financial institutions that demonstrate a commitment to sustainability are more likely to attract and retain customers, investors, and talent. By aligning with sustainability principles, institutions can enhance their market relevance, competitiveness, and reputation in an increasingly socially conscious world.
- Regulatory Compliance: Governments and regulatory bodies are increasingly imposing stricter regulations and disclosure requirements related to sustainability and ESG factors. Financial institutions must adhere to these regulations to mitigate legal and compliance risks, avoid regulatory penalties, and maintain their license to operate. By integrating sustainability issues into their operations and reporting practices, institutions can stay ahead of regulatory developments and ensure compliance with evolving standards.
- Long-Term Value Creation: Sustainability is essential for using long-term value creation and resilience in the financial sector. By investing in sustainable infrastructure, renewable energy, clean technologies, and socially responsible projects, financial institutions can contribute to economic growth, job creation, and community development. Sustainable finance initiatives also help address global challenges such as climate change, poverty alleviation, and social inequality, thereby creating positive impacts for society and future generations.

In summary, sustainability is fundamental to the financial sector's role in driving economic growth, promoting environmental stewardship, and advancing social progress (Rahman, M., & Islam, M. (2020)). By using sustainability principles, financial institutions can mitigate risks, enhance financial performance, maintain market relevance, comply with regulations, and create long-term value for users and society as a whole.

Role of Smart Banking in Promoting Sustainable Practices

Smart banking plays an important role in promoting sustainable practices within the financial sector and beyond. Here's how it is importance, can be discussed as::

- Efficiency and Resource Optimization: Smart banking uses advanced technologies such as artificial intelligence, data analytics, and automation to streamline processes, reduce operational costs, and optimize resource utilization. By digitizing transactions, minimizing paper-based processes, and implementing energy-efficient infrastructure, smart banking helps financial institutions operate more efficiently and sustainably, thereby reducing their carbon footprint and environmental impact.

- Financial Inclusion: Smart banking enhances financial inclusion by using digital channels and innovative technologies to reach underserved populations and remote communities. Mobile banking apps, online platforms, and digital payment systems enable individuals with limited access to traditional banking services to participate in the formal financial system, empowering them with greater financial literacy, access to credit, and economic opportunities (Patel, R., & Shah, P. (2018)).

- Environmental Sustainability: Smart banking promotes environmental sustainability by facilitating paperless transactions, electronic statements, and digital signatures, reducing the consumption of paper and other resources. Moreover, smart banking enables remote banking services, reducing the need for physical branches and commuting, which in turn lowers carbon emissions and contributes to environmental conservation efforts.

- Data-Driven Decision Making: Smart banking uses big data analytics and machine learning algorithms to analyze large amount of data, generate actionable insights, and inform strategic decision-making processes. By using data analytics, financial institutions can identify opportunities for efficiency improvements, risk mitigation, and sustainable investments, aligning their business practices with environmental, social, and governance (ESG) criteria.

- Customer Empowerment: Smart banking empowers customers with greater control over their finances, enabling them to access banking services anytime, anywhere, and on any device. Personalized financial management tools, budgeting apps, and interactive dashboards help customers make informed decisions, manage their savings, and track their environmental footprint. By promoting financial literacy and sustainability awareness among customers, smart banking uses a culture of responsible consumption and environmentally conscious behaviors.

- Risk Management and Resilience: Smart banking strengthens risk management and resilience by enhancing cybersecurity measures, fraud detection systems, and regulatory compliance frameworks. By using blockchain technology, biometric authentication, and secure encryption protocols, financial institutions can protect sensitive data, prevent unauthorized access, and ensure the integrity and trustworthiness of financial transactions, thereby safeguarding against operational, reputational, and systemic risks.

In summary, smart banking plays an important role in promoting sustainable practices by driving efficiency improvements, enhancing financial inclusion, reducing environmental impact, enabling data-driven decision-making, empowering customers, and strengthening risk management and resilience within the financial sector and beyond. By using smart banking solutions, financial institutions can contribute to the transition towards a more sustainable and inclusive future.

ROLE OF CUTTING-EDGE TECHNOLOGIES IN SMART BANKING

Cutting-edge technologies play a fundamental role in shaping the landscape of smart banking, enabling financial institutions to innovate, enhance efficiency, and deliver superior customer experiences (Zhang, H., & Li, J. (2021), Dutta, S., & Jain, S. (2019)). We can discuss that how these technologies contribute to the evolution of smart banking:

- Artificial Intelligence (AI) and Machine Learning (ML): AI and ML algorithms are at the core of smart banking, powering personalized customer interactions, predictive analytics, and automated decision-making processes. AI-driven chatbots provide instant customer support, while ML models analyze large amount of data to detect patterns, detect fraud, and provide tailored financial advice. AI also enables algorithmic trading, risk management, and credit scoring, optimizing investment strategies and lending practices (Tyagi et al., (2021) (2022) (2023) and (2024)).).
- Blockchain Technology: Blockchain technology enhances the security, transparency, and efficiency of smart banking operations by enabling secure and immutable transactions (refer figure 1). Distributed ledger technology (DLT) facilitates real-time settlement, reduces transaction costs, and mitigates the risk of fraud and tampering. Blockchain-based smart contracts automate con-

tractual agreements, enabling seamless execution of transactions without the need for intermediaries, thereby streamlining processes and reducing administrative overhead.

Figure 1. Role of blockchain in finance

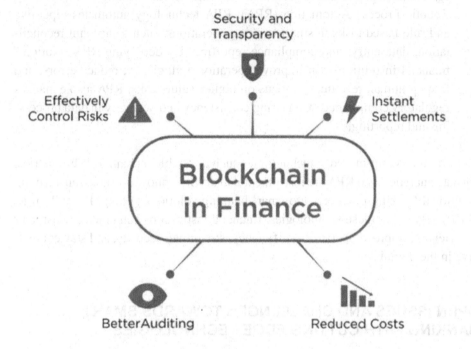

- Internet of Things (IoT): IoT devices, such as wearables, sensors, and connected devices, enable the collection of real-time data and enable innovative banking solutions. IoT-powered banking applications allow customers to make contactless payments, monitor their finances, and manage their accounts remotely. IoT sensors also enable predictive maintenance of ATMs and other banking infrastructure, optimizing performance and reducing downtime.
- Biometrics and Identity Verification: Biometric authentication methods, such as fingerprint scanning, facial recognition, and voice recognition, enhance security and convenience in smart banking applications. Biometric authentication enables frictionless login processes, secures transactions, and prevents unauthorized access to accounts. Moreover, biometric data can be used for identity verification and fraud detection, providing an additional layer of security in digital banking environments.

- Big Data Analytics: Big data analytics tools and techniques enable financial institutions to analyze large amount of structured and unstructured data to gain actionable insights into customer behavior, market trends, and risk factors. By using big data analytics, banks can personalize product offerings, optimize marketing campaigns, and identify opportunities for revenue growth. Moreover, predictive analytics models help anticipate customer needs, manage credit risk, and detect fraudulent activities in real-time.
- Robotic Process Automation (RPA): RPA technology automates repetitive and rule-based tasks in smart banking operations, such as account reconciliation, data entry, and compliance reporting. By deploying RPA solutions, financial institutions can improve operational efficiency, reduce errors, and free up human resources to focus on higher-value tasks. RPA also enhances regulatory compliance by ensuring consistency and accuracy in data processing and reporting.

In summary, cutting-edge technologies such as AI, blockchain, IoT, biometrics, big data analytics, and RPA are instrumental in driving innovation and transforming traditional banking practices into smart banking solutions (Wong, L., & Tan, K. (2020)). By using these technologies, financial institutions can enhance customer experiences, improve operational efficiency, strengthen security, and stay competitive in the digital age.

OPEN ISSUES AND CHALLENGES TOWARDS SMART BANKING WITH CUTTING EDGE TECHNOLOGIES

While smart banking with cutting-edge technologies provides several benefits, several open issues and challenges need to be addressed to realize its full potential. Hence, here are some key areas of issue, as:

- Cybersecurity and Data Privacy: As smart banking relies heavily on digital platforms and interconnected systems, cybersecurity threats and data breaches face huge risks. Financial institutions must implement robust cybersecurity measures, encryption protocols, and authentication mechanisms to protect sensitive customer data and prevent unauthorized access. Moreover, ensuring compliance with data privacy regulations such as GDPR and CCPA is important to maintaining customer trust and regulatory compliance.
- Ethical and Bias Issues: AI and machine learning algorithms used in smart banking applications may inadvertently perpetuate biases or discriminatory practices if not properly designed and monitored. Financial institutions must

ensure transparency, fairness, and accountability in algorithmic decision-making processes to mitigate ethical risks and avoid unintended consequences. Additionally, addressing issues related to algorithmic transparency, explainability, and bias detection is essential to building trust and confidence in AI-driven banking solutions.

- Digital Divide and Accessibility: While smart banking provides convenience and flexibility, there remains a digital divide between populations with access to digital technologies and those without. Ensuring equitable access to smart banking services for underserved communities, elderly individuals, and people with disabilities is essential to promoting financial inclusion and reducing digital exclusion. Financial institutions must develop user-friendly interfaces, provide digital literacy programs, and provide alternative channels for accessing banking services to bridge the digital divide.

- Regulatory Compliance and Legal Frameworks: The rapid pace of technological innovation in smart banking poses challenges for regulatory bodies and policymakers in keeping pace with emerging trends and ensuring regulatory compliance. Financial regulations and legal frameworks must be updated to address the unique risks and complexities associated with smart banking technologies, such as blockchain, AI, and IoT.

- Interoperability and Standardization: The growth of diverse technologies and platforms in smart banking ecosystems may lead to interoperability challenges and fragmentation, hindering seamless integration and data exchange between systems. Standardization efforts, interoperability protocols, and open banking initiatives are needed to promote collaboration, compatibility, and interoperability among different banking systems, applications, and devices. Moreover, ensuring data portability and customer control over their personal data is essential to using competition and innovation in smart banking markets.

- Resilience and Continuity Planning: Smart banking systems are susceptible to disruptions from technological failures, cyberattacks, natural disasters, and other unforeseen events. Financial institutions must develop robust resilience strategies, business continuity plans, and disaster recovery mechanisms to ensure the uninterrupted provision of banking services and the protection of customer assets. Redundancy measures, failover mechanisms, and real-time monitoring systems are essential for maintaining operational resilience and minimizing service disruptions in smart banking environments.

Hence, addressing these open issues and challenges requires collaborative efforts from financial institutions, technology providers, regulators, and other users to use trust, innovation, and sustainability in the evolution of smart banking with cutting-edge technologies.

FUTURE RESEARCH OPPORTUNITIES TOWARDS SMART BANKING SOLUTIONS WITH CUTTING EDGE TECHNOLOGIES

Future research opportunities towards smart banking solutions with cutting-edge technologies abound, providing avenues for innovation, optimization, and advancement (Li, W., & Zhang, Y. (2018)). Here few/ some potential areas for future research work can be discussed as:

- AI-Powered Personalization: Further research is needed to enhance the capabilities of AI-driven personalization in smart banking solutions. Investigating advanced machine learning algorithms, natural language processing techniques, and predictive analytics models can help develop more accurate and context-aware recommendations tailored to individual customer preferences, behaviors, and financial goals (refer figure 2).

Figure 2. Smart banking with AI based solutions

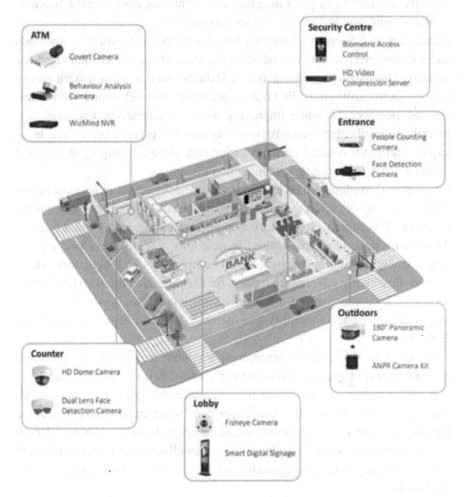

- Blockchain Applications: Research into blockchain technology can discuss new applications and use cases in smart banking beyond cryptocurrency transactions. Areas of interest include decentralized finance (DeFi), asset tokenization, supply chain finance, and digital identity management. Investigating scalability, interoperability, and regulatory implications of blockchain solutions can pave the way for broader adoption and integration into mainstream banking operations.
- IoT Integration: Research opportunities exist in discussing the potential of IoT integration in smart banking applications. Investigating use cases such as smart contracts for automated insurance claims processing, real-time as-

set tracking for supply chain finance, and sensor-based risk management for property insurance can yield insights into optimizing operational efficiency, reducing risks, and enhancing customer experiences.

- Biometrics and Security: Research into biometric authentication methods and security mechanisms can advance the state-of-the-art in smart banking security. Discussing new biometric modalities, such as vein pattern recognition, electrocardiogram (ECG) authentication, and behavioral biometrics, can enhance security while improving user convenience and accessibility. Investigating robustness against spoofing attacks, privacy-preserving techniques, and multi-modal biometric fusion can address emerging threats and vulnerabilities in biometric authentication systems.

- Regulatory Compliance and Governance: Research opportunities exist in discussing regulatory challenges and governance frameworks for smart banking solutions. Investigating regulatory compliance requirements for AI-driven decision-making, blockchain-based transactions, and IoT data privacy can help financial institutions navigate legal complexities and regulatory uncertainties. Discussing governance models for decentralized finance (DeFi) platforms, smart contracts, and tokenized assets can address governance challenges and ensure accountability, transparency, and trust in emerging banking technologies.

- Customer Experience and Engagement: Research into enhancing customer experience and engagement in smart banking solutions can drive innovation and differentiation. Investigating user interface design, conversational AI, and augmented reality (AR) experiences can create immersive and intuitive banking experiences. Discussing gamification techniques, behavioral economics principles, and personalized financial wellness programs can promote financial literacy, incentivize positive behaviors, and use long-term customer relationships.

In summary, by addressing these research opportunities, academia, industry, and regulatory bodies can collaborate to unlock the full potential of smart banking solutions with cutting-edge technologies, driving innovation, sustainability, and inclusivity in the future of banking (Kim, Y., & Park, J. (2021), Sharma, S., & Kumar, A. (2019)).

CASE STUDIES TOWARDS SMART BANKING SOLUTIONS WITH CUTTING EDGE TECHNOLOGIES

We will discuss few case studies of smart banking solutions using cutting-edge technologies:

AI-Powered Chatbots for Customer Service:
Bank of America's virtual assistant, Erica: Bank of America introduced Erica, an AI-powered virtual assistant that provides personalized financial guidance and assistance to customers through the bank's mobile app. Erica uses natural language processing (NLP) and machine learning algorithms to understand customer inquiries, provide insights into spending patterns, suggest budgeting tips, and facilitate transactions. By using AI, Bank of America aims to enhance customer engagement, improve financial literacy, and streamline banking processes.

Blockchain-Based Cross-Border Payments:
JPMorgan Chase's Interbank Information Network (IIN): JPMorgan Chase developed the Interbank Information Network (IIN), a blockchain-based platform that facilitates cross-border payments and reduces transaction processing times. IIN uses distributed ledger technology (DLT) to enable real-time verification of payment information between participating banks, eliminating delays and inefficiencies associated with traditional correspondent banking networks. By using blockchain, JPMorgan Chase aims to enhance the speed, transparency, and security of cross-border transactions for its clients.

IoT-Enabled Smart ATMs:
Barclays' SmartSpend ATM: Barclays introduced SmartSpend ATMs equipped with IoT sensors and connectivity capabilities to provide personalized recommendations and rewards to customers based on their spending habits. SmartSpend ATMs analyze transaction data in real-time, identify patterns, and provide targeted provides or discounts on products and services from partner merchants. By using IoT technology, Barclays aims to enhance customer engagement, drive loyalty, and provide value-added services through its ATM network.

Biometric Authentication for Enhanced Security:
HSBC's Voice ID Authentication: HSBC implemented Voice ID, a biometric authentication system that uses voice recognition technology to verify customers' identities over the phone. Voice ID analyzes unique vocal characteristics, such as pitch, tone, and cadence, to authenticate customers securely without the need for passwords or security questions. By using biometric authentication, HSBC aims to enhance security, prevent fraud, and improve the customer experience by eliminating the need for cumbersome authentication processes.

Big Data Analytics for Personalized Insights:
Capital One's CreditWise: Capital One's CreditWise is a credit monitoring service that provides customers with personalized insights and recommendations based on their credit profile and financial behavior. CreditWise analyzes data from credit bureaus, transaction history, and spending patterns to provide tailored advice on credit management, debt reduction, and financial planning. By using big data analytics, Capital One aims to empower customers with actionable insights and tools to improve their financial health.

Hence, these case studies discuss about that how smart banking solutions with cutting-edge technologies are transforming traditional banking practices, enhancing customer experiences, and driving innovation in the financial services industry.

EMERGING TECHNOLOGIES AND FUTURE TRENDS IN SMART BANKING

Emerging technologies and future trends in smart banking are shaping the future of financial services, providing innovative solutions to meet the evolving needs of customers and drive industry transformation. Here are some key emerging technologies and trends to watch in smart banking:

- Decentralized Finance (DeFi): DeFi is a rapidly growing sector within smart banking that uses blockchain technology to create decentralized financial systems and applications. DeFi platforms enable peer-to-peer lending, decentralized exchanges, yield farming, and other financial services without the need for traditional intermediaries such as banks. DeFi provides opportunities for financial inclusion, transparency, and innovation but also poses challenges related to regulation, security, and scalability.
- Central Bank Digital Currencies (CBDCs): CBDCs are digital currencies issued by central banks as legal tender, aiming to digitize fiat currencies and modernize payment systems. CBDCs provide benefits such as faster settlement times, lower transaction costs, and increased financial inclusion. Several countries are discussing or piloting CBDC projects, with potential implications for monetary policy, financial stability, and the future of banking.
- Open Banking and APIs: Open banking initiatives promote data sharing and interoperability among financial institutions through open application programming interfaces (APIs). Open banking enables third-party developers to build innovative financial products and services, such as personal finance management apps, payment solutions, and lending platforms. By using col-

laboration and competition, open banking enhances customer choice, convenience, and transparency in banking services.

- Artificial Intelligence (AI) and Machine Learning (ML): AI and ML technologies continue to drive innovation in smart banking, powering personalized
recommendations, fraud detection, risk assessment, and customer service
automation. Advanced AI algorithms analyze large amount of data to identify patterns, predict customer behavior, and optimize banking operations.
AI-driven chatbots, virtual assistants, and robo-advisors enhance customer
experiences, improve operational efficiency, and enable data-driven decision-
making in banking.

- Biometric Authentication and Identity Verification: Biometric authentication
methods, such as fingerprint scanning, facial recognition, and voice recognition, provide secure and convenient ways to verify customers' identities
in smart banking applications. Biometric authentication enhances security,
reduces fraud, and improves user experiences by eliminating the need for
passwords or security questions. Biometric data also enables seamless onboarding processes, account access, and transaction authorization in digital
banking environments.

- Quantum Computing: Quantum computing holds the potential to revolutionize smart banking by enabling faster processing speeds, stronger encryption,
and more complex simulations and optimizations. Quantum computers can
solve complex mathematical problems and cryptographic algorithms that are
infeasible for classical computers, enhancing security, risk management, and
data analysis capabilities in banking. While quantum computing is still in its
early stages, it presents exciting opportunities for future innovation and disruption in smart banking.

Hence, these emerging technologies and future trends are driving major shifts
in the banking industry, using innovation, competition, and digital transformation.
Financial institutions that use these technologies and adapt to changing customer
expectations will be well-positioned to thrive in the future of smart banking.

AN OPEN DISCUSSION ON SMART BANKING
SOLUTIONS WITH CUTTING EDGE TECHNOLOGIES

Today's smart banking represents the convergence of innovative technologies
such as artificial intelligence, blockchain, Internet of Things (IoT), and biometrics
to revolutionize traditional banking practices. Here are some key points to consider:

- Enhanced Customer Experience: Smart banking solutions use cutting-edge technologies to provide personalized, convenient, and seamless customer experiences. AI-powered chatbots and virtual assistants provide instant support and guidance to customers, while mobile banking apps and online platforms enable anytime, anywhere access to banking services. Biometric authentication methods enhance security and streamline authentication processes, improving user experiences.
- Data-Driven Insights: Advanced analytics and machine learning algorithms enable financial institutions to analyze large amount of data to gain actionable insights into customer behavior, market trends, and risk factors. By using big data analytics, banks can personalize product offerings, optimize marketing campaigns, and detect fraudulent activities in real-time. Predictive analytics models help anticipate customer needs, manage credit risk, and identify opportunities for revenue growth.
- Blockchain for Security and Transparency: Blockchain technology provides secure, transparent, and immutable transaction records, reducing the risk of fraud and enhancing trust in banking systems. Smart contracts automate contractual agreements, enabling seamless execution of transactions without the need for intermediaries. Blockchain-based solutions also facilitate cross-border payments, supply chain finance, and digital identity management, revolutionizing traditional banking practices.
- Internet of Things (IoT) for Connectivity: IoT devices and sensors enable real-time data collection, monitoring, and automation in smart banking applications. IoT-powered banking solutions include smart ATMs, wearable payment devices, and connected banking infrastructure, providing personalized services and insights to customers. IoT also enables predictive maintenance of banking equipment, optimizing performance and reducing downtime.
- Regulatory Compliance and Security: While smart banking solutions provide several benefits, they also raise regulatory compliance and security challenges. Financial institutions must ensure compliance with data privacy regulations such as GDPR and CCPA, implement robust cybersecurity measures, and adhere to industry standards and best practices. Collaboration between regulators, industry users, and technology providers is essential to address regulatory uncertainties and security risks in smart banking.
- Future Opportunities and Challenges: The future of smart banking holds immense promise for innovation, efficiency, and inclusivity. Emerging technologies such as decentralized finance (DeFi), central bank digital currencies (CBDCs), and quantum computing present new opportunities for disruption and transformation in the banking industry. However, challenges related to

cybersecurity, data privacy, regulatory compliance, and digital divide must be addressed to realize the full potential of smart banking solutions.

In summary, smart banking solutions with cutting-edge technologies are reshaping the banking industry, providing personalized experiences, data-driven insights, and secure transactions. By using innovation and collaboration, financial institutions can use these technologies to drive digital transformation, enhance customer value, and stay competitive in the evolving landscape of smart banking.

CONCLUSION

The integration of cutting-edge technologies into modern smart banking represents a major step towards building a sustainable banking and financial world. Through innovations like AI-driven customer service, blockchain-enabled security, and IoT-powered transactions, financial institutions can enhance efficiency, security, and accessibility while reducing costs and environmental impact. Furthermore, smart banking uses financial inclusion by reaching underserved communities and promoting economic empowerment. By using data analytics, banks can provide personalized services tailored to individual needs, thereby using stronger customer relationships and loyalty. However, to ensure the sustainability of this digital transformation, it's important to address cybersecurity challenges, privacy issues, and ethical implications. Collaborative efforts between regulators, industry users, and technology providers are essential to establish robust frameworks and standards that safeguard both users and the integrity of the financial system. Modern smart banking holds huge promise in creating a more resilient, inclusive, and environmentally aware financial ecosystem, poised to meet the evolving needs of society while advancing towards a sustainable future.

REFERENCES

Chen, L., & Wang, H. (2020). Building a Sustainable Financial World: Smart Banking Innovations and Technologies. *Sustainable Development Journal*, 15(3), 278–295. DOI:10.1002/sd.2076

Dutta, S., & Jain, S. (2019). Innovations in Sustainable Banking: Smart Banking Initiatives with Cutting-Edge Technologies. *Sustainable Finance Review*, 24(4), 367–382. DOI:10.1080/20430795.2019.1657299

Garcia, M., & Martinez, E. (2020). Innovative Solutions for Sustainable Banking: Smart Banking Technologies and Cutting-Edge Practices. *International Journal of Sustainable Banking*, 9(3), 321–336.

Kim, Y., & Park, J. (2021). Sustainable Financial Systems: Smart Banking Practices and Cutting-Edge Technologies. *Journal of Sustainable Banking and Finance*, 8(1), 45–60.

Kumar, R., & Singh, P. (2018). Sustainable Smart Banking: Using Cutting-Edge Technologies for Financial Inclusion. *Sustainable Development Review*, 22(4), 356–372. DOI:10.1002/sdr.2047

Li, W., & Zhang, Y. (2018). Driving Sustainability through Smart Banking: Emerging Technologies and Innovations. *Sustainable Development Review*, 21(3), 278–295.

Patel, A., & Gupta, M. (2019). Smart Banking for Sustainable Finance: A Review of Cutting-Edge Technologies and Practices. *Journal of Sustainable Banking and Finance*, 6(1), 45–60.

Patel, R., & Shah, P. (2018). Towards Sustainable Finance: Smart Banking Solutions and Cutting-Edge Technologies. *International Journal of Sustainable Development*, 25(3), 267–282.

Pundareeka Vittala, K. R., Kiran Kumar, M., & Seranmadevi, R. (2024). Artificial Intelligence-Internet of Things Integration for Smart Marketing: Challenges and Opportunities. Advancing Software Engineering Through AI, Federated Learning, and Large Language Models. IGI Global. DOI:10.4018/979-8-3693-3502-4.ch019

Rahman, M., & Islam, M. (2020). Promoting Financial Inclusion and Sustainability: Smart Banking Approaches with Cutting-Edge Technologies. *Sustainable Development Journal*, 17(1), 89–104. DOI:10.1002/sd.2036

Sharma, S., & Kumar, A. (2019). Transforming Banking for Sustainability: Smart Banking Solutions with Cutting-Edge Technologies. *International Journal of Sustainable Banking*, 10(2), 145–160.

Shrikant Tiwari, R. (2024). Ravinder Reddy, Amit Kumar Tyagi, Position of Blockchain: Internet of Things-Based Education 4.0 in Industry 5.0 – A Discussion of Issues and Challenges. Architecture and Technological Advancements of Education 4.0. IGI Global. DOI:10.4018/978-1-6684-9285-7.ch013

Smith, J., & Johnson, R. (2021). Towards Sustainable Smart Banking: Integrating Cutting-Edge Technologies for a Green Financial World. *Journal of Sustainable Finance*, 8(2), 145–160. DOI:10.1080/20430795.2021.1890456

Tan, C., & Lim, H. (2019). Using Sustainable Financial Systems: The Evolution of Smart Banking with Cutting-Edge Technologies. *Journal of Sustainable Finance & Investment*, 14(2), 178–193. DOI:10.1080/20430795.2019.1578311

Wang, Y., & Li, W. (2021). Towards a Sustainable Financial Ecosystem: The Role of Smart Banking and Cutting-Edge Technologies. *Journal of Sustainable Business and Finance*, 12(2), 189–204. DOI:10.1080/20430795.2020.1857290

Wong, L., & Tan, K. (2020). Towards a Green Financial World: Smart Banking Strategies with Cutting-Edge Technologies. *Journal of Sustainable Finance and Banking*, 15(2), 189–204.

Zhang, H., & Li, J. (2021). Smart Banking for a Sustainable Future: Using Cutting-Edge Technologies for Financial Resilience. *Journal of Sustainable Financial Innovation*, 7(2), 156–171.

Chapter 5
Harnessing Artificial Intelligence in Internal Auditing:
Implementation, Impact, and Innovation

Akhil Manuel
https://orcid.org/0000-0002-4066-2485
Christ University, India

Senthil Kumar Arumugam
https://orcid.org/0000-0002-5081-9183
Christ University, India

ABSTRACT

Given the influence of artificial intelligence (AI) on various sectors of the economy, its impact on the internal auditing sector is causing increased attention from the academic and professional communities. This book chapter investigates how AI is revolutionizing internal audit and its implications for the future of internal audit. By examining numerous literature sources and developments from various perspectives, this book chapter conducted a comprehensive analysis of how AI is applied in various processes of internal auditing. In the current data-reliant business society, AI's capacity to handle vast datasets and perform complex analyses plays an important role. The use of AI in internal auditing enhances efficiency, increases accuracy, and improves risk management. However, in the process, audit procedures fundamentally change. This book chapter concludes that while AI will significantly change the internal auditing process, it will not replace human auditors. AI will alter auditing jobs by requiring auditors to learn additional technology.

DOI: 10.4018/979-8-3693-4187-2.ch005

INTRODUCTION

The landscape of internal auditing is undergoing a transformative evolution driven by the rapid advancements in Artificial Intelligence (AI). As organizations navigate the complexities of modern business environments, the need for more efficient, effective, and insightful auditing processes has become paramount. "Harnessing Artificial Intelligence in Internal Auditing: Implementation, Impact, and Innovation" delves into the multifaceted role of AI in reshaping internal audit functions, offering a comprehensive examination of how AI technologies can be integrated, the profound impacts they have on audit processes, and the innovative advancements they bring to the field. Internal auditing traditionally functions as a critical administrative tool, ensuring compliance with established protocols, safeguarding against financial discrepancies, and promoting operational integrity. However, the conventional methods of internal auditing are often labor-intensive, time-consuming, and limited in their ability to provide real-time insights. The advent of AI introduces a paradigm shift, offering the potential to automate routine tasks, enhance analytical capabilities, and provide predictive insights that were previously unattainable.

Technological innovations have significantly changed traditional techniques in the dynamic field of auditing. The notion of agile auditing, originally derived from software development, has gained popularity among auditors. It emphasizes the importance of flexibility and reactivity. At the same time, AI has emerged as a powerful force ready to transform the accounting and assurance professions profoundly. Integrating AI in auditing addresses the daunting task of effectively handling and processing vast amounts of data. AI improves productivity and accuracy by automating repetitive operations like data entry and complicated analysis. This modernization enhances both the precision of audits and the speed of the process, resulting in higher audit results. One of the most remarkable features of AI in audit software is its significant capacity to extract more profound insights from complex data sets. This feature enables the detection of meaningful patterns and trends that enhance the dependability of audit reports.

Moreover, AI plays a crucial role in identifying and preventing fraudulent activities. It thoroughly analyzes transactions and notifies auditors of possible inconsistencies, allowing them to address indications of financial malfeasance promptly. AI audit technologies improve the integrity and compliance of financial reporting by providing detailed reports on suspicious actions. AI greatly enhances risk assessment techniques. It enables auditors to perform sophisticated analysis of a client's data, identifying specific areas that need further scrutiny. By strategically allocating resources, the efficiency of audits is maximized, resulting in more focused and impactful audit engagements. Incorporating advanced technology in the accounting industry will lead to a future of auditing marked by increased accuracy, productivity, and reliability. A recent study examining the influence of AI on the quality and efficiency of audits highlights these key factors. The research analyzed comprehensive resumes of more than 310,000 employees from the 36 top audit companies, emphasizing the connection between investments in AI and the effectiveness of audits. The findings revealed that for every one-standard-deviation rise in recent AI investments, there was a 5.0% decrease in the probability of audit restatements and a 0.9% decrease in audit fees. Several global initiatives are being experimented with today, and the largest accounting firms EY, Deloitte, KPMG, and PwC are spending tens of millions of dollars on AI to gain the opportunity to conduct cheaper and high-quality audits than their competitors. For example, KPMG recently began testing the ability of IBM Watson's high-end deep learning systems to investigate credit files for a commercial mortgage loan portfolio in a bank. Deloitte signed an agreement with Kiva systems and now uses AI to check contracts, leases, and accounts (Sun & Vasarhelyi, 2017). PWC uses Halo, machine learning technology, to investigate journal entries and cites areas of concern (Dickey et al., 2019). The World Economic Forum predicted that 30% of corporate audits would be AI by 2025 and the field of auditing is in for a significant change (World Economic Forum, 2015).

Implementation of AI in Internal Auditing

The implementation of AI in internal auditing involves several strategic steps, beginning with the identification of areas where AI can add the most value. This includes automating repetitive tasks such as data entry, transaction testing, and compliance checks, which frees up auditors to focus on more complex and judgment-intensive activities. Machine learning algorithms can analyze vast amounts of data quickly and accurately, identifying patterns and anomalies that may indicate potential risks or areas of concern. Organizations must invest in the appropriate AI tools and technologies that align with their specific auditing needs. This involves not only selecting the right software but also ensuring that the necessary infrastructure and data governance frameworks are in place.

Data quality is crucial for AI to function effectively, requiring robust data management practices to ensure accuracy and reliability. Training and change management are also critical components of AI implementation. Internal auditors need to develop new skills to work effectively with AI tools, including understanding how to interpret AI-generated insights and integrating these insights into their audit processes. Change management strategies are essential to address resistance and ensure that the transition to AI-enhanced auditing is smooth and accepted by all stakeholders.

Impact of AI on Audit Processes

The impact of AI on audit processes is profound, fundamentally altering how audits are conducted and the value they deliver. One of the most significant benefits of AI is the ability to perform continuous auditing. Unlike traditional audits, which are periodic and retrospective, AI enables real-time monitoring and analysis of financial transactions and operational activities. This allows for immediate identification of anomalies and potential issues, facilitating timely interventions and reducing the risk of significant financial losses or compliance breaches. AI-driven analytics enhance the depth and breadth of audit insights. Machine learning models can sift through large datasets to identify trends, correlations, and outliers that might be missed by human auditors. These advanced analytics provide a more comprehensive view of the organization's risk landscape, enabling auditors to focus on high-risk areas and make more informed recommendations.

Fraud detection is another area where AI has a substantial impact. Traditional fraud detection methods often rely on sampling and manual review, which can be both inefficient and ineffective. AI algorithms can analyze entire datasets, detecting subtle patterns and behaviors indicative of fraudulent activity. This enhances the auditor's ability to detect and prevent fraud, protecting the organization's financial integrity.

Innovation in Internal Auditing Through AI

AI is driving innovation in internal auditing by enabling new approaches and methodologies that were previously unimaginable. Predictive analytics is one such innovation, where AI models forecast potential risks and issues based on historical data and current trends. This proactive approach allows organizations to mitigate risks before they materialize, significantly enhancing risk management capabilities. Natural language processing (NLP) is another innovative application of AI in auditing. NLP can analyze unstructured data, such as emails, contracts, and meeting minutes, extracting relevant information and identifying potential compliance issues or risks. This expands the scope of internal audits beyond structured financial data, providing a more holistic view of the organization's operations and risk environment. AI also facilitates greater collaboration and knowledge sharing within the auditing function. Advanced AI platforms can integrate with other enterprise systems, providing a centralized repository of audit findings, insights, and recommendations.

This enhances communication and coordination among audit teams, fostering a more cohesive and effective auditing process.

The integration of AI into internal auditing represents a significant advancement in the field, offering substantial benefits in terms of efficiency, accuracy, and insight. By automating routine tasks, enhancing analytical capabilities, and enabling real-time monitoring, AI transforms internal auditing into a more proactive, strategic, and impactful function. As organizations continue to embrace AI technologies, the role of internal auditors will evolve, requiring new skills and approaches to leverage these tools effectively. "Harnessing Artificial Intelligence in Internal Auditing: Implementation, Impact, and Innovation" explores these themes in depth, providing a roadmap for organizations seeking to navigate this transformative landscape and harness the full potential of AI in their auditing practices.

LITERATURE REVIEW

Internal audit is a vital administrative tool that ensures organizational operations run smoothly by enforcing adherence to established instructions and preventing embezzlement. It plays a key role in maintaining operational integrity and efficiency. The internal audit function is a critical service department within an organization, aiding management in fulfilling its responsibilities. Internal audits prepare the organization for potential official audits, providing the readiness and experience needed to handle them effectively. Additionally, they help the organization view audits as a routine aspect of implementing and developing a Quality Management System (Morris et al., 2009). Thus the importance of internal auditing lies in its role as an administrative tool that drives the progression and improvement of the organization's operations. The world has undergone rapid changes across many fields due to the industrial and scientific revolutions. Technical and scientific advancements have significantly impacted individuals and society, both positively and negatively. The industrial revolution led to the development of AI, now integral to modern life. AI has fostered growth in various domains, including science, humanities, economics, and social sciences.

The rapid integration of AI into the field of internal auditing is reshaping the landscape of this discipline. This literature review consolidates various scholarly sources to examine the impact of AI on the efficiency, accuracy, and strategic implementation of internal audit processes. Digital transformation is a multifaceted and a challenging developmental trajectory involving the exclusive extent of corporate resources – human, technological, existing and financial-organizational, and physical (Stark, 2020). A growing number of procedures previously performed on paper are being digitized. From this, more data are being generated within various businesses

(Reinsel et al, 2018). Nowadays, there are cloud-based systems that are more and more cheap and easy to use; these new technologies are based on an analytical applications, AI, Big Data, Internet of Things, robotics, and so on . Technology, however, does nothing by itself, it is necessary to know the environment in which digital transformation is included; it is a change in the organization, culture and business (Stark, 2020).

AI's impact on risk assessment and fraud detection is particularly notable. There is no doubt that AI integration in supplementary health plans is significant. This tool has the capacity to help identify financial irregularities, find outliers, and identify patterns that would not have been evident without the AI tool. The working of AI algorithms is such that they would be able to monitor the financial transaction every few seconds every day and quickly identify potential fraud or error. Through this process, the audit process would be faster, efficient, and shall provide prompt information to the stakeholders (Patel et al., 2023). Internal audit contributes to the achievement of confidence in financial statements, the prevention of fraud and manipulation, and the reduction of risks, so there must be an artificially intelligent system that helps the internal auditor to provide excellent audit services (Altaee, 2023). Future AI systems will continuously manage data and alert internal auditors within the IAF about the status of transmitted and stored data, as well as potential fraud and related disclosures (Berrydunn, 2020). The AI's ability to understand and perform tasks faster than humans will pose significant challenges in developing innovative methods for planning and testing controls to evaluate the effectiveness of AI systems (Seethamraju & Hecimovic, 2022). Introducing AI into internal audit tasks can significantly enhance the audit process by automating routine tasks, thus making the process faster and more efficient. This allows internal auditors to focus on more complex tasks, such as analyzing business processes, identifying associated risks and controls, anticipating fraud detection, and monitoring anomalies in real-time. By leveraging AI, internal auditors can improve their skills and effectiveness in these areas, leading to more thorough and proactive audit outcomes (Couceiro et al., 2020).

Future AI technologies can provide a significant competitive advantage. One of the main benefits of AI is its ease of deployment and the ability to be reprogrammed to work for extended periods without fatigue or boredom. However, a disadvantage of AI is that machines can only perform tasks they are specifically designed or programmed to do. When faced with tasks outside their programming, they may crash or produce irrelevant outputs, posing a serious drawback. Additionally, creating, rebuilding, and repairing AI systems can be very costly and time-consuming (Bhosale et al., 2020).Internal audit should leverage AI for its cognitive capabilities, which typically require human intelligence. This translates into augmenting or replacing human thinking in a natural and intuitive way. By using AI, internal audit can provide assurance for companies, helping them distinguish truth from lies, with a focus on ethics. The aim is to enhance internal control, risk management, and governance (Carata et al., 2018). The internal audit control system can be defined as a process that ensures the operational, financial, and compliance efficiency and effectiveness of a company. The integration of neural networks has improved the assessment of audit risk by incorporating AI, leading to shorter audit completion times and better recommendations from auditors. Friedlob and Schleifer (1999) highlighted that internal auditors should focus on advancing fuzzy logic to detect uncertainties in daily operations. Shim and Rice (1988) emphasized that AI, particularly expert systems, will play a crucial role in the efficient and effective preparation of internal and external financial reports, thus enhancing audit planning and internal control functions.

This review suggests that AI profoundly enhances internal auditing by improving efficiency, accuracy, and proactive risk management. However, the successful adoption of AI technologies also necessitates addressing ethical issues, ensuring transparency in AI processes, and adapting training programs to equip auditors with necessary technological skills.

OBJECTIVE

In this regard, the following chapter seeks to comprehensively analyze the various ways in which AI impacts an internal audit operation and businesses at large. The research will reveal the extent to which a business can benefit from the implementation of such technology and how it can enhance generalized performance through nuanced contributions.

RESEARCH QUESTION

The primary research question this study addresses is: What impact does AI have on the internal audit function and overall business performance? Through a comprehensive analysis, the study seeks to provide valuable insights for organizations looking to leverage AI to optimize their internal audit functions and drive overall business success.

METHODOLOGY

This study is descriptive in nature. It applies to reviewing and synthesizing existing literature including secondary data sources. It involves a thorough review of the available literature, and empirical studies form part of an academic database, books, journals, reports, and relevant websites. With the help of secondary data sources, this study seeks to aggregate and analyze insights about the role and effectuality of AI in modern accounting practice to get a comprehensive overview of the effect of AI on efficiency, accuracy, and strategic decision-making in accounting.

RESULTS AND DISCUSSION

How is AI Used in Audit?

The incorporation of AI into accounting and auditing significantly enhances the efficacy and scope of audit processes. Machine learning programs, proficient in analyzing extensive financial datasets, quickly identify anomalies such as duplicate payments and signs of fraudulent activities. Additionally, AI extends its capabilities to "read" and interpret data from contracts and internal notes, delivering critical insights during the analysis of financial statements. This thorough review and analysis by AI not only identifies existing issues but also reveals new opportunities. Below are several key applications of AI in the auditing process:

1. **Data Analytics:** AI excels in processing and analyzing large volumes of both structured and unstructured data rapidly. Internal auditors use AI-driven data analytics to detect patterns, anomalies, and trends that might indicate areas of risk, inefficiency, or malpractice. This allows auditors to be more proactive in addressing potential issues before they escalate.
2. **Continuous Auditing:** AI facilitates continuous auditing by automating the routine tasks of data collection and analysis. This enables real-time monitoring and reporting of an organization's financial status and operations, allowing internal auditors to provide timely insights and enhance decision-making processes. Continuous auditing also helps in maintaining compliance with regulatory standards and internal policies.
3. **Fraud Detection:** AI algorithms are particularly effective at identifying irregular transactions and patterns that may suggest fraudulent activity. By analyzing transaction data, AI can flag unusual activities based on historical data and predictive behaviors, enabling auditors to investigate and respond to potential fraud more swiftly.

4. **Natural Language Processing (NLP):** NLP is a branch of AI that helps computers understand, interpret, and manipulate human language. In internal auditing, NLP is used to analyze textual data from various sources like emails, contracts, and business documents. This helps auditors extract relevant information, understand contractual obligations, and ensure compliance with laws and regulations.

5. **Risk Assessment and Management:** AI enhances risk assessment by analyzing vast amounts of data to identify potential risks and trends within an organization. It provides auditors with insights into areas that require attention, helping to prioritize audit activities based on the risk profile derived from AI analyses. Additionally, AI can help simulate different risk scenarios and predict their potential impacts on the organization.

6. **Predictive Analytics:** Predictive analytics powered by AI can forecast future trends and behaviors based on historical data analysis. In internal auditing, this capability allows auditors to anticipate potential areas of concern, assess the likelihood of risks, and advise management on preventive measures.

7. **Enhancing Audit Quality:** AI tools improve the quality of audits by providing more accurate and comprehensive analyses. They help in verifying the accuracy of financial statements and ensure that the data reflects true and fair views of the organization's financial condition.

8. **Resource Allocation:** AI can optimize audit planning by suggesting the best allocation of resources based on the complexity and risk involved in different audit areas. This leads to more efficient audits, as resources are concentrated where they are most needed.

9. **Documentation and Reporting:** AI streamlines documentation by automating the generation of audit reports and other necessary documents. This not only speeds up the process but also reduces the likelihood of human error in report preparation.

10. **Machine Learning:** Machine learning, a subset of AI, involves systems that improve their performance over time without being explicitly programmed. In internal auditing, machine learning algorithms learn from past audits to enhance future audits. They can refine audit strategies, improve risk models, and deliver more accurate predictions and recommendations.

Tools like Chat GPT play a crucial role in developing foundational audit programs. By leveraging AI, auditors can devise customized audit programs that align precisely with the specific scope and objectives of each engagement, thus enhancing the planning process and overall audit efficiency. Despite AI's increasing influence, it remains a relatively new technology in the auditing field. Continuous development and refinement of AI tools are underway, with major auditing firms actively exploring their implementation. Some firms have started using machine learning technology, including Chabot's on websites to handle basic inquiries. An increase in the use of AI in audit processes is anticipated over the next decade. However, the transition to fully AI-driven audits will be gradual. The indispensable human element in auditing remains vital and the synergy between human expertise and AI-driven efficiencies is expected to result in more comprehensive and effective audits.

Benefits of Using AI in Audits

The integration of AI-enabled tools in auditing processes yields substantial benefits, notably enhancing efficiency and precision. Computer algorithms are adept at processing vast quantities of data and text rapidly, which markedly diminishes the likelihood of human errors. By assigning repetitive tasks such as spread sheet reviews, data digitization, and dataset comparisons to AI, auditors are freed to engage in more in-depth analyses based on insights provided by AI. Here are specific advantages of incorporating AI into audit processes:

1. **Increased Efficiency:** AI automates routine and time-consuming tasks such as data collection, data entry, and initial analysis, which traditionally take up a significant portion of the auditors' time. This automation allows internal auditors to focus more on complex, judgment-intensive aspects of the audit, such as risk assessment and strategic planning, ultimately speeding up the entire audit process.
2. **Enhanced Accuracy:** AI tools are capable of processing large volumes of data with a high degree of accuracy. They minimize human errors that can occur due to fatigue or oversight, especially when dealing with repetitive tasks. The precision of AI systems ensures that the data used in audits is reliable, improving the overall quality of audit findings and reports.
3. **Improved Detection of Anomalies and Fraud:** AI excels in identifying patterns and anomalies that might be difficult for human auditors to detect. Machine learning algorithms can analyze transactional data and flag activities that deviate from the norm, which could indicate potential fraud or compliance issues. This capability not only enhances the effectiveness of the audit but also helps in mitigating risks proactively.
4. **Advanced Data Analytics:** AI enables the handling of both structured and unstructured data, providing deeper insights through advanced analytics. This includes predictive analytics, which helps forecast future trends and potential risk areas, and prescriptive analytics, which can suggest possible actions to take based on the data analyzed. Such analytics empower auditors to make informed decisions and provide more strategic advice to the organization.

5. **Continuous Auditing:** AI facilitates continuous monitoring and auditing of systems and transactions. This on-going process allows for real-time risk assessment and quicker responses to issues as they arise, rather than waiting for periodic audit cycles. Continuous auditing helps maintain a consistently high level of oversight, which is particularly beneficial in dynamic and fast-paced business environments.

6. **Better Risk Management:** With AI, auditors can achieve a more comprehensive risk assessment process. AI systems can process vast amounts of historical and transactional data to identify risk patterns and emerging risks. This capability enables auditors to focus on high-risk areas, ensuring that resources are allocated effectively and risks are managed more proactively.

7. **Resource Optimization:** AI can optimize the allocation of human and financial resources within the audit function by identifying the key areas that require human intervention and automating the rest. This leads to a more efficient use of auditor time and skills, which can be directed towards tasks that add more value to the organization.

8. **Consistency in Audits:** AI systems follow a consistent methodology when processing data and performing analyses, which helps in maintaining the consistency of audits across different departments and geographic locations. This consistency is crucial for organizations that need to ensure compliance with various regulatory standards and internal policies.

9. **Enhanced Decision Making:** AI's ability to provide quick and accurate data analysis supports better decision-making at all levels of the organization. The insights generated by AI can help senior management understand complex scenarios and make strategic decisions that align with the company's risk appetite and objectives.

10. **Skill Development:** The adoption of AI in internal audits encourages auditors to acquire new skills in data science and analytics, which are increasingly important in the modern digital economy. This skill development not only enhances the auditors' capabilities but also adds value to the organization's talent pool.

In summary, AI significantly enriches the internal audit function by boosting efficiency, accuracy, and the strategic value of audit activities. As AI technology continues to evolve, its integration into auditing is expected to deepen, offering even more profound benefits and transforming the audit process in ways that were previously unimaginable.

Risk of AI in Internal Audit

The integration of AI in internal auditing offers numerous benefits, such as increased efficiency, enhanced accuracy, and improved risk assessment capabilities. However, the adoption of AI also introduces several risks that organizations must carefully manage. Here are some of the key risks associated with using AI in internal audits:

1. **Data Privacy and Security Risks**: AI systems require access to vast amounts of data, raising significant concerns about data privacy and security. The potential for data breaches or unauthorized access to sensitive information can lead to serious compliance and reputational issues for organizations.
2. **Dependence on Data Quality**: AI's effectiveness is heavily reliant on the quality of data it processes. Inaccurate, incomplete, or biased data can lead to erroneous AI conclusions, potentially compromising the audit's integrity. Ensuring data quality is paramount to prevent the propagation of errors throughout the auditing process.
3. **Lack of Transparency (Black Box Issue)**: Many AI systems operate as "black boxes," where the decision-making process is not transparent. This lack of transparency can make it difficult for auditors and stakeholders to understand how conclusions are derived, leading to challenges in validating and trusting AI-generated findings.
4. **Regulatory Compliance Risks**: As AI technologies evolve rapidly, regulatory frameworks often struggle to keep pace. This lag can result in uncertainties about compliance with existing laws, including those related to financial reporting and audit standards. Organizations must navigate these uncertainties to avoid potential legal penalties.
5. **Skill Gaps and Training Needs**: The effective implementation of AI in internal auditing requires auditors to possess a new set of skills, including proficiency in data science and AI technology. The current skill gaps in many audit teams may hinder the effective deployment and management of AI tools, necessitating significant investments in training and development.
6. **Over-reliance on AI**: There is a risk that auditors may become overly reliant on AI tools, potentially neglecting their professional judgment. Such over-reliance can lead to a degradation of critical thinking and analytical skills, which are essential in scenarios where AI may not provide sufficient insights.
7. **Ethical Concerns**: AI systems can unintentionally perpetuate existing biases present in the data they analyze. These biases can lead to discriminatory practices or unfair outcomes, raising ethical concerns about the impartiality of AI-driven audits.

8. **Integration Challenges**: Integrating AI systems with existing IT infrastructures and audit processes can be complex and costly. Technical incompatibilities and resistance to change within organizations can further complicate these integration efforts.

9. **Increased Complexity of Audits**: As AI enables deeper and more complex data analysis, the scope and complexity of audits may increase. This can make audits more challenging to manage and extend the time required to conduct them effectively.

10. **Job Displacement Fears**: The automation of routine tasks by AI may lead to fears of job displacement among auditing professionals. While AI is likely to shift the nature of auditing work rather than replace it entirely, managing the transition and addressing these concerns is crucial for maintaining staff morale and productivity.

In summary, while AI presents significant opportunities to enhance internal auditing, it also introduces a range of risks that must be managed thoughtfully. Organizations adopting AI in their audit processes need to develop robust strategies to address these risks, ensuring that AI technologies are used ethically, effectively, and in a manner that complements human expertise.

Effects of Implementation of AI in Internal Auditing

From the discussion, it is evident that the adoption of AI is indispensable for modern organizations, despite the emergence of certain challenges associated with disruptive technologies. To navigate these challenges, comprehensive measures including the development and implementation of ethical guidelines, cybersecurity laws, and AI-specific regulations are crucial. These policies must be established at both national and international levels to standardize the use of cognitive technologies effectively. The advent of AI in the workplace raises significant ethical considerations and fears of job displacement. While the automation of routine tasks might lead to job losses in some areas, it also creates opportunities for new types of employment. The World Economic Forum (WEF) forecasts that the implementation of AI and automation could result in a net increase of 58 million jobs, with a significant portion requiring high-level skills. This transformation mirrors historical shifts in the accounting field, such as the transition from manual bookkeeping to computerized systems, which initially spurred fears of unemployment but ultimately led to job growth and the evolution of roles within the sector. For instance, the introduction of software like Intuit in 1983 and Microsoft Excel in 1985 did not lead to the demise of bookkeeping jobs as feared; instead, the sector experienced a 75% growth over the following decade. Today, AI is set to transform manual bookkeeping roles, shifting the focus of professionals towards more strategic tasks that leverage their expertise in new ways. This shift indicates a transition from traditional job roles to more dynamic, hybrid positions that may involve freelance work and less traditional employment structures, potentially impacting organizational compliance and human resource responsibilities.

Moreover, leading accounting firms such as Ernst & Young, PricewaterhouseCoopers, and Deloitte Touche Tohmatsu Limited are actively integrating AI technologies to enhance efficiency and service quality. These developments suggest a trend toward more sophisticated, AI-enhanced processes that not only streamline operations but also require a new cadre of professionals equipped with both accounting knowledge and technological proficiency. In conclusion, while AI introduces challenges such as ethical dilemmas, potential job displacement, and the need for new laws and standards, it also offers substantial opportunities for growth and innovation in the accounting field. Organizations and professionals must adapt to these changes by embracing new technologies and preparing for the evolving demands of the global market. This will involve significant adjustments in professional training and development, policy formulation, and strategic planning to fully leverage the benefits of AI while mitigating its risks.

Future Trends and Predictions in AI for Internal Auditing

The future of internal auditing is poised for significant transformation, driven by the rapid advancement and integration of emerging AI technologies. As we look forward to the next decade, several key trends and predictions emerge, indicating how AI will continue to evolve and shape the auditing profession. One of the most promising areas of development is the integration of advanced machine learning algorithms and deep learning models. These technologies will enable even more sophisticated data analysis, allowing auditors to uncover hidden patterns, predict future risks, and provide deeper insights into financial and operational data. Emerging AI technologies such as reinforcement learning and unsupervised learning are set to revolutionize how internal audits are conducted. Reinforcement learning, which involves training AI systems through trial and error, can enhance the decision-making capabilities of AI tools, leading to more effective risk assessment and management strategies. Unsupervised learning, which allows AI to identify patterns in data without pre-labeled outcomes, will be crucial for anomaly detection and fraud prevention, providing auditors with the ability to detect previously unnoticed irregularities in vast datasets.

Natural language processing (NLP) is another area where significant advancements are expected. NLP technologies are becoming increasingly sophisticated, enabling AI systems to understand and interpret unstructured data such as emails, contracts, and social media interactions. This capability will allow auditors to perform more comprehensive analyses of an organization's communications and documents, identifying potential compliance issues and risks that would be difficult to detect using traditional methods. The ability to analyze sentiment and tone in communication can also provide insights into organizational culture and employee behavior, further enhancing the scope of internal audits. The integration of AI with blockchain technology represents another future trend with profound implications for internal auditing. Blockchain's decentralized and immutable ledger system, combined with AI's analytical capabilities, can provide unprecedented levels of transparency and security in financial transactions. This integration will facilitate real-time auditing, where transactions are continuously monitored and verified, reducing the need for periodic audits and enhancing the accuracy and reliability of financial reporting.

As AI technologies evolve, we can also expect the rise of autonomous auditing systems. These systems, powered by AI and robotic process automation (RPA), will be capable of conducting end-to-end audits with minimal human intervention. Autonomous auditing systems will handle everything from data collection and analysis to reporting and compliance checks, significantly reducing the time and effort required for internal audits. While human auditors will still play a crucial role in overseeing these systems and making judgment-based decisions, their focus will shift towards more strategic and high-value tasks. The next decade will also see a greater emphasis on ethical AI in auditing. As AI systems become more integral to audit processes, ensuring their transparency, fairness, and accountability will be paramount. Organizations will need to implement robust governance frameworks to oversee the ethical use of AI, addressing issues such as bias, data privacy, and the accountability of AI-driven decisions. Auditors will play a key role in evaluating and validating the ethical considerations of AI applications, ensuring that they comply with regulatory standards and organizational values.

AI's impact on the auditing profession will extend beyond technological advancements to include changes in the skill sets required for auditors. The demand for auditors with expertise in data science, machine learning, and AI will continue to grow. Training and professional development programs will need to evolve to equip auditors with the necessary skills to leverage AI technologies effectively. Additionally, interdisciplinary collaboration between auditors, data scientists, and IT professionals will become increasingly important to harness the full potential of AI in auditing. Predicting how AI might evolve within the auditing profession over the next decade, it is clear that AI will not only enhance the efficiency and effectiveness of audits but also transform the role of auditors. Auditors will transition from being traditional compliance checkers to becoming strategic advisors who provide deeper insights into organizational risks and opportunities. AI will enable auditors to move from a reactive to a proactive approach, identifying potential issues before they escalate and advising management on mitigating strategies.

Furthermore, the adoption of AI in auditing will drive innovation in audit methodologies and frameworks. Traditional audit frameworks, which are often rigid and linear, will be replaced by more dynamic and flexible approaches that can adapt to the rapidly changing business environment. AI-driven continuous auditing and monitoring systems will become the norm, providing organizations with real-time assurance and enabling them to respond swiftly to emerging risks. Thus, the future of internal auditing will be profoundly shaped by the on-going advancements in AI technologies. From enhanced data analysis and anomaly detection to autonomous auditing systems and ethical AI considerations, the next decade promises significant innovations that will transform the auditing profession. Organizations that embrace these technologies and invest in developing the necessary skills and governance frameworks will be well-positioned to reap the benefits of AI-enhanced auditing, achieving greater transparency, efficiency, and strategic value in their audit processes. As AI continues to evolve, it will undoubtedly unlock new possibilities and drive the auditing profession towards a more intelligent, proactive, and impactful future.

CONCLUSION

The implementation of AI in internal auditing is a transformative development that promises substantial improvements in how audits are conducted, in terms of both efficiency and effectiveness. As AI technologies continue to evolve, they offer new possibilities for enhancing audit processes, delivering better insights, and facilitating a more proactive approach to risk management and compliance. Implementation of AI in internal auditing has been driven by the need for faster and more accurate audits. AI enables auditors to automate routine tasks, such as data entry and transaction testing, which frees up time to focus on more complex aspects of the auditing process. This shift not only increases the productivity of internal auditors but also enhances their ability to delve deeper into analytical reviews and strategic issues that require human judgment and expertise. The impact of AI on internal auditing has been profound. AI-driven data analytics tools have improved the precision of audits by enabling the handling of large volumes of data more efficiently and accurately. These tools facilitate enhanced anomaly detection, fraud prevention, and risk assessment, providing auditors with the capability to uncover insights that were previously difficult or impossible to obtain. Moreover, the integration of continuous auditing techniques, powered by AI, allows for real-time monitoring and assessment of an organization's financial health, leading to quicker responses to potential issues. However, the use of AI also introduces new challenges and responsibilities. Ethical considerations, data privacy concerns, and the need for transparency in AI's decision-making processes are critical issues that need addressing. Auditors must ensure that AI systems are used responsibly and that they comply with regulatory standards and ethical guidelines. Additionally, there is a growing need for auditors to acquire new skills related to data science and AI technologies to remain effective in their roles.

Innovation in AI is continuously reshaping the landscape of internal auditing. Future developments are likely to focus on further enhancing AI's analytical capabilities, improving the integration of AI tools with existing audit software, and exploring new areas where AI can add value. As AI technology becomes more sophisticated, its potential to revolutionize internal auditing becomes increasingly apparent, suggesting a future where AI and human expertise are intertwined more seamlessly. In conclusion, the harnessing of AI in internal auditing represents a significant advancement with the potential to greatly enhance audit quality, efficiency, and strategic insight. Organizations that successfully integrate AI into their auditing processes are likely to achieve substantial benefits, including improved accuracy, enhanced risk management, and greater overall audit effectiveness. Moving forward, it is crucial for the auditing profession to embrace these changes, adapt to new technologies, and address the challenges that come with AI implementation to fully realize its benefits and ensure the integrity and reliability of audit practices.

LIMITATIONS AND FUTURE DIRECTIONS OF THE STUDY

This The study faces several limitations due to its reliance on secondary data sources, which may not fully capture the latest advancements or provide real-time, context-specific insights. The quality and biases of the existing literature can affect the comprehensiveness and accuracy of the findings, and the varied methodologies and contexts of the reviewed studies pose challenges for synthesis and generalization. Another limitation is the contextual variability of the secondary sources reviewed, which may originate from diverse contexts such as different countries, industries, and organizational sizes. This variability makes it challenging to generalize the findings universally, as the impact of AI on internal auditing can differ significantly based on these contextual factors. Additionally, ethical and legal considerations, as well as practical implementation challenges, may be underexplored.

To overcome these limitations, future research should incorporate primary data collection methods such as surveys, interviews, and case studies with organizations actively using AI in internal auditing. This approach would provide real-time, context-specific insights and practical examples, enhancing the relevance and applicability of the findings. Conducting longitudinal studies would help track the impact of AI over time, providing a better understanding of the long-term benefits and challenges associated with its implementation in internal auditing. Focusing on specific industries, regions, or types of organizations can provide more detailed and relevant insights. Comparative studies across different contexts can highlight unique challenges and best practices, offering a more nuanced understanding of AI's impact. Future research should delve deeper into the ethical and legal implications of using AI in internal auditing, developing guidelines and frameworks to ensure responsible and compliant use of AI technologies. Keeping pace with rapid technological advancements, future studies should continually update and review the latest AI tools and applications in internal auditing to provide up-to-date insights. Investigating the interaction between AI and human auditors, including the impact on job roles, required skills, and the potential for human-AI collaboration, would provide a comprehensive view of AI's role in transforming internal auditing practices.

REFERENCES

Altaee, O. Z. I. (2023). The Role of Artificial Intelligence in Improving the Quality of Internal Audit: An Exploratory Study in Some Iraqi Banks. *Regional Studies Journal, 17*(55).

Berrydunn. (2020). *Artificial Intelligence and the Future of Internal Audit*. Berrydunn. https://www.berrydunn.com/news-detail/artificial-intelligence-and-the-future -of-internal-audit

Bhosale, S., Pujari, V., & Multani, Z. (2020). *Advantages And Disadvantages Of Artificial Intellegence.*

Carata , M. (2018). *Alina, Cerasela, S., & Gabriela, G.* Internal Audit Role in Artificial Intelligence.

Couceiro, B., Pedrosa, I., & Marini, A. (2020). State of the Art of Artificial Intelligence in Internal Audit context. *2020 15th Iberian Conference on Information Systems and Technologies (CISTI)*. IEEE. DOI:10.23919/CISTI49556.2020.9140863

Dickey, G., Blanke, S., & Seaton, L. (2019). Machine Learning in auditing: Current and future applications. *TheCPA Journal*, 89(6), 16–21.

Friedlob, G. T., & Schleifer, L. L. F. (1999). Fuzzy logic: Application for audit risk and uncertainty. *Managerial Auditing Journal*, 14(3), 127–137. DOI:10.1108/02686909910259103

. Morris, G. D., McKay, S., & Oates, A. (2009). Audit. *Finance Director's Handbook*, 1–126. DOI:10.1016/B978-0-7506-8701-0.00001-1

Patel, R., Khan, F., Silva, B., & Shaturaev, J. (2023, August 8). *Unleashing the Potential of Artificial Intelligence in Auditing: A Comprehensive Exploration of its Multifaceted Impact*. Mpra.ub.uni-Muenchen.de. https://mpra.ub.uni-muenchen .de/119616/

Reis, J., Amorim, M., Melão, N., & Matos, P. (2018). Digital Transformation: A Literature Review and Guidelines for Future Research. *Advances in Intelligent Systems and Computing*, 745, 411–421. DOI:10.1007/978-3-319-77703-0_41

Seethamraju, R., & Hecimovic, A. (2022). Adoption of artificial intelligence in auditing: An exploratory study. *Australian Journal of Management*, 48(4), 031289622211084. DOI:10.1177/03128962221108440

Shim, J. K., & Rice, J. S. (1988). Expert Systems Applications To Managerial Accounting. *Journal of Systems Management*, 39(6).

Stark, J. (2020) Digital Transformation Industry- Continiuing Change. Cham: Springer. Teichert Roman(2019). *Digital Transformation Maturity: A systematic Review of Literature*. Acta Universitatis Agriculturae et Silviculturate Mendelianae Brunensis.

Sun, T., & Vasarhelyi, M. A. (2017). Deep Learning and the Future of Auditing: How an Evolving Technology Could Transform Analysis and Improve Judgment. *The CPA Journal*, 87(6).

World Economic Forum. (2015). *Deep Shift: Technology Tipping Points and Social Impact*. WEF. at:http://www3.weforum.org/docs/ WEF_GAC15_Technological_ Tipping_ Points_ report_2015.pdf

Chapter 6
Revolutionizing E–Commerce:
The Synergy of Computer Vision and Augmented Reality

Shalini Swami
https://orcid.org/0009-0008-7429-2655

G.L. Bajaj Institute of Technology and Management, Greater Noida, India

Pushpa Singh
https://orcid.org/0000-0001-9796-3978

G.L. Bajaj Institute of Technology and Management, Greater Noida, India

Bhawna Singh
https://orcid.org/0000-0002-6179-7100

G.L. Bajaj Institute of Technology and Management, Greater Noida, India

ABSTRACT

Augmented reality (AR), computer vision (CV), and deep learning (DL) techniques enable a machine or application to enhance the e-commerce sectors. An integrated approach of AR and CV maximizes the visual information and interaction of the product in the digital environment. This chapter explores the synergistic effect that exists between AR and CV in the e-commerce sector, analyzing the applications and user experiences. It captures how these technologies revolutionize the interaction of consumers with products and an online shopping experience, giving them personalized online journeys, product recommendation, virtual-try-on, try-before-buy, and image-based product search. Furthermore, the chapter highlights that deep learning (DL) techniques such as CNN, GNN, and RNN revolutionized the e-commerce sector when integrated with AR and CV.

DOI: 10.4018/979-8-3693-4187-2.ch006

INTRODUCTION

In today's digitally driven world, advanced and rapidly transforming the e-commerce sector. Computer vision (CV), augmented reality (AR) and virtual reality (VR)become a new era technologies offering customers an enriched, personalized, customized purchasing experience.Weinstein(2018) defined, CV makes possible for computers to understand important aspects of a picture or video feed for tasks like recognizing products or searching for pictures on e-commerce sites. CV, when combined with other technologies such as AR and Deep learning revolutionizes the online shopping sector. Online shopping sector is full of images, image classification and its recognition. To enhance the online shopping services of e-commerce, AR is combined with CV to detect objects in the real world as depicted in figure 1.

Figure 1. Integration of augmented reality and computer vision

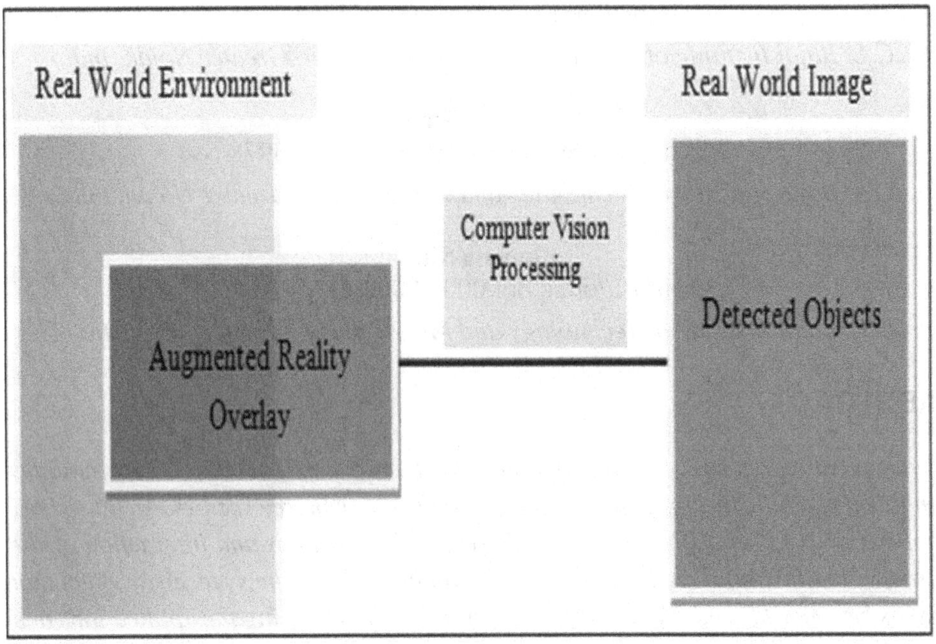

Furthermore, Deep learning (DL) algorithms/techniques help to improve AR and CV. DL allows for object detection and recognition, and the outcomes of these make effective communication between real-world and virtual objects possible. All three technologies: AR, CV and DL step into a revolutionizing e-commerce to make effective shopping experiences possible with immersive AR features through merchandise recognition.The rapid growth in e-commerce increases during COVID pandemic, this make online business more important for B2C business online (Киш, 2020).

At the time of pandemic there are lots of crises, but e-commerce sector was getting benefit during the period of Covid-19 (Singh & Agrawal, 2021). Mnyakin(2020) revealed by analyzing 190 global e-commerce sites that technology like Artificial Intelligence (AI); AR has significant positive impact on e-commerce sales.AR applications such as virtual try-on, personalized shopping experiences, visualization of product,interactive product manuals etc improve the user experience and potential decrease the return rate. Chatbots and product recommendation system are some applications of AI and ML help the customer in real time query, to make decision to purchase the product.

The need of interactive product description and images are important for e-commerce. ML learning is used to analyze data from big online store to improve customer interaction with the product. The system used deep learning and CV to analyze images at different stages and make a proper decision to increase product sale and user engagement (Chaudhuri 2018). E-commerce had undergone a revolution since 2016 from manual to automatic system. AI significantlyled to synergy between user and technology. The aim of these technologies to provide personalized experience in online shopping by facilitate with various features like customized content for visualize content. AI provides virtual assistance at real-time, visualization of product; try before use and many more that show the revolution in ecommerce. Amazon and Netflix are the best examples that show the impact of AI technologies increase sales and customer satisfaction (Thandekkattu et al., 2022).The major contribution of the chapteris to discuss the following points:

Role of CV and AR in E-commerce.
Deep learning techniques (DLT) used in e-commerce with CV.

Rest of chapter is structured as follows. Section 2 is related work, section 3 discusses about role of AR, CV with DLT in the e-commerce. Section 4 presents the result and discussion part while section 5 concludes the chapter.

RELATED WORK

Use of technologies makes a revolutionary change in every field in the digital world. Techniques that impact e-commerce are CV and AR. Gundimeda (2019) explored the need for high quality of meta-data in online business. They proposed an automatic method to extract meta-data from unstructured data by using natural language processing(NLP), CV traditional algorithms and ML to enhanced image quality to improve product information and product search in online stores.CV used to automate functioning in fashion industry like man-made drawing and feature extraction etc. Author used line extraction and thinning algorithms to convert the drawing into digital format and detect details like colors, patterns etc. By using ML and DL for efficient feature extraction to avoid redundancy to increase marketing efforts (Donati, Iotti & Prati 2019).To enhance search in e-commerce FashionSearch-Net introduced for detailed search using query images and attributes. Proposed work has the ability to discover relevant regions and merge with attributes to get features extracted from the specific area for search (Ak & Kassim, 2019).

Authors (Yang & Liu 2021) explored the integration of CV in e-commerce to enhance the customer engagement and customer satisfaction, additionally also focusing on the evaluation of CV in main tasks like image processing, detection, classification and segmentation. The paper also highlights the key tasks of CV in e-commerce applications like search, content supervision, intelligent system, tracking system. Lastly, the paper also provides how CV positively impacts on various conditions of e-commerce.

He et al. (2017) presented relevance of AR by enduing the system with the ability to perceive and comprehend the environment in a manner similar to human beings. It implies a number of key techniques: Image Recognition: It is used to detect objects, places, people, and writing, and so on in the AR environment. Depth Sensing: It basically uses sensors in determining the distance between objects and the AR device, a process of recognizing the location of virtual objects in the real world. Edge Detection: This helps in recognizing the shapes and outlines of objects in the visual field. Pattern Recognition: This enables the system to recognize as well as.

Author (Li & Barmaki 2019) highlights the latest research advances on ACM Symposium on Eye Tracking research & applications (ETRA) 2019 and several recent representative paper works. AR, a field combining CV and graphics, has applications in gaming, entertainment, education, and healthcare. It has been around for almost fifty years but has only recently become interesting due to the success of the deep learning models in a variety of AR applications, allowing for the birth of new AR technologies.

Modern AR from application and technical views with discussing main AR applications and promising ML works for AR systems (Minaee et al., 2022) and provides comprehensive review of AR in retailing and also identify and discuss features of AR, applications used in online retail systems for both consumers and retailers. Additionally, explained the difference between AR and virtual reality (VR), and evaluates the types of application used in online web-based, in-store, and mobile apps (Caboni et al., 2019). The research explained that implementation of AR with online shopping outperforms in consumer responses. The main advantage of integrating AR in online shopping facilitates online "try-before-you-buy" experience, which positively impacts customers for online purchase (Smink et al., 2020). Discussed the growth and utilization of AR in e-commerce, and also explained its acceptance and potential revenue. It emphasizes AR's applications across various industries and its transformative impact on the shopping experience. However, there is a lack of detailed analysis, ethical review, and a comparison with other technologies. Additionally, it fails to notice the impact on supply chain logistics. They analyzed the impact of AR in e-commerce, comparing it with web-based product presentations. The research explained how AR enhances consumer attention and ease, while web-based presentations are considered more useful(Garg et al., 2021). To find the impact of AR in real author intention to use e-commerce using AR technology, focusing on the case of IKEA Place app to find the answers of questions about the impact of AR on online shopping confidence and convenience, sociodemographic factors, operating systems, organization familiarity, purchase attractiveness, ease of purchase and utilities by using mixed methodology in the form of questionnaire (Alves & Luís Reis et al., 2020).

To explore how 3D e-commerce, which combine with AR and VR can help to overcome the traditional e-commerce and how it can improve consumer satisfaction. It outlines the issues with the current VR shopping system, proposes a new VR shopping approach integrating e-commerce into open-world games, and discusses the benefits and challenges of 3D e-commerce, including the requirement for improved peripherals and software development (Billewar et al., 2022). Paper suggests a novel approach to enhance e-commerce user experience using AR and Transient Chaotic Neural Networks (TCNN). Proposed marker less tracking system which relies on image sequences to show the object in dimension. This innovative experiment helps in showcasing the object to improve the user experience on e-commerce Nandhini et al.(2022). Investigated how different display and interaction systems in the virtual environment can influence the shopping experience of the product. The study compared a shopping experience on a desktop computer (DVR) and a shopping experience in IVR (Ricci et al., 2023). Research investigates the impact of AR on consumer buying behavior in the Indian e-commerce sector. Using a quantitative approach with 300 participants, the study reveals a positive influence of AR on perceived usefulness, ease of use, enjoyment, and purchase intention. Besides these advantages, problem like privacy, technical issues, and lack of knowledge were noted. Author suggests improving noted issues to enhance AR experiences that help to make trust and satisfaction in the Indian online market (Gupta et al., 2023).

Lalonde (2018) explained about how deep learning helps to solve CV tasks for augmented reality 6-DOF and illumination tasks. The proposed method used deep neural networks for 6-DOF by taking two input images: a rendered image of an object and their predicted pose and observed image of the object at current timestamp. For illumination the author used convolution neural network (CNN). Sheikh et al.,

(2019) proposed SFnet (size and fit network), this method is used to predict size and fit for users and articles in ecommerce. Technique combined with content-based filtering to learn hidden features of customers and articles. This method uses split input neural networks that use random user and article features to predict size and fit score for each pair that help to reduce return cost. Sembium et al., (2018). Another novel approach used to reduce return in online shopping author used Bayesian logit and probit regression models with ordinal categories divided in 3 sizes. Bayesian also helps in handling noise in the data and handling larger datasets. The deep siamese architecture (Sharma & Vishvakarma, 2019) proposed with Deep (CNN). Its ability to capture fine-grained image similarities makes it versatile for applications in image analysis and similarity detection across different domains.

Xu (2024) study explores how integrating DL, semantic web, and knowledge graphs enhances augmented reality functions, providing dynamic and personalized information in real-time interactions between physical and digital worlds. Table 1 shows the outcome of the previous research papers.

Table 1. Outcome of the previous research

Ref.	Technology & Approach	Purpose&Limitation
Gundimeda, 2019	CV, ML, NLP and OCR	To find meta data from unstructured data
Donati et al., 2019	CV used for line extraction and thinning and CNN for final feature extraction	To convert pen paper images to vectorization image. ADIDAS data set used
Ak&Kassim, 2019	CV and AlexNeta developed CNN	For visual search
Sembiumet al.,2018	ML- Bayesian logit and probit regression, mean-field variation inference and ploy-gamma-augmentation to approximate posterior distribution.	Model depends on purchase and return data, which may be incomplete, contain noise. Not added other sources that help in size recommendations
Lalonde, 2018	Deep learning: Proposed 6-DOF object tracking and illumination estimation used DNN and CNN.	Method required high computational, quality of data required and not easy to edit due to deep learning models.
Sharma &Vishvakarma, 2019	Deep CNN with Siamese architecture	Need to assess its generalization, scalability, and comparison against other models.
Caboni &Hagberg 2019	AR	Focuses more on the technological aspects of AR and less on user experiences. Try before you buy
Sheikh et al. 2019	Deep Learning: Proposed SFnet (size and fit network) to predict size and fit for user and article in e-commerce	Neural network is used with content based filtering to learn hidden features of customer and article.Split-input neural network is used in this model. Method required high computation

continued on following page

120

Table 1. Continued

Ref.	Technology & Approach	Purpose&Limitation
Smink et al. 2020	AR: Compare to find the impact of AR apps and non-AR apps.	Mainly focus on two type of applications make-up as spatial presence and virtual furniture in user surrounding.
Garg et al. 2021	AR: Integration of AR in E-com for utilizing, marketing, and overcome physical limitations.	No discussion for ethical and privacy issues using AR in E-com
Alves et al. 2020	AR: Conceptual model for IKEA Place evaluation based on technology acceptance model (TAM) and other models	Focusing on single AR app and product category. Small and biased sample.
Kowalczuket al. 2021	Deep learning: Transient Chaotic Neural Networks (TCNN)	Specific technologies (Vuforia, Unity3D, C#, Wikitude) might pose limitations in terms of compatibility, accessibility, or integration with other existing e-commerce systems
Fincato et al. [8] (2022)	Deep learning	Model created transform, dress, and wrap First two for geometric view. Generative network used for virtual try. Only designed for upper body.
(Nandhini et al. 2022)	AR: proposes a consumer response model to check the impact of AR T and TCNN	Focus on specific products (furniture and sunglasses) Lack of generalization
(Xu et al. 2024)	Deep learning: Integrating DL, semantic web, knowledge graphs	Complexity of implementation, security concern and performance issues

From the past research we find that CV and AR help to enhance the e-commerce activity. These technologies increase the customer engagement and enhance the product visualization. CV and AR significantly increase customer engagement in various ways personalized shopping by analyzing past data and providing preferences to provide personal recommendations. AR with CV helps to visualize these recommendation products. Virtual try on AR technology buy before you try in products such as clothing, accessories etc. Additionally, CV helps to detect accurate size, shape and facial features to provide recommendations that help to build confidence to purchase virtually.

CV enhances product visualization by analyzing and identifying product images and AR overlay the product information, rating, reviews on the products that help to increase the engagement and also make help in purchase decisions. Demonstration of products with AR and CV, for example the use instructions provide the way to scan and pay, applying makeup, accessories, and arrangement of furniture in your space. CV helps in virtual assistance to clear the doubts before buying in real time. Overall, CV and AR significantly revolutionize e-commerce by providing creative solutions to enhance customer experiences, promote sales, and well organized operations.

Role of CV and AR in E-Commerce

Deep learning combined with AR and CV helps customers to overlay virtual information to real recommendation, world. Image based product recommendation, product visualization and virtual try-on, enhanced product information, product searching are certain applications that are provided by the AR, and CV. Deep learning methods enhance the role of CV and AR. DL methods such as CNN, generative neural network, graph neural networks, and recurrent neural network with their different variations helps to enhance the e-commerce features (Singh, Singh, & Gupta, 2020). In this section we explain the role and use of CV and AR in various e-commerce applications with DL algorithms.

Product Recommendation System

In virtual world when a customer visits on e-commerce platform to find and explore product. How visual search and recommendation suggest similar products. When a customer visits an online shop and wants to search desired dress CV provide an option for visual search by visual catalog for the product or customer can upload their desired image to search similar product. Figure 2 makes understanding how CV and DL models help a customer in searching their desired product and form their past data also recommend the suggestion. For example if a customer wishes to search a particular dress/attire then customer simply search it by submitting the images of the dress in the system. Following steps are performed to recommend the similar dress to the customer.

Preprocessing

A set of product images from the dataset as input. Preprocessing phase applies necessary action to transform and prepare for feature extraction. The process prepares the images for feature extraction.

Feature Extraction

Feature extraction depends on various factors such as the types of the input data and image, availability of labeled and unlabeled data and resources. Various DL models such as CNN, RNN, GNN are used and all are depending on the factors of feature extraction.

In E-commerce CV are used for images and video processing to create recommendation systems. CNN work on supervised learning used various algorithms to classify the images and video by using regression and loss function.CNN are a class of DL algorithm and used for image recognition and image classification. CNN helps to analyze deep association with different set and help to tag them and trained the data (Rong et al., 2021). As per the past research shows CNN and ResNet-50 are better approach for image based search (Kumar et al., 2023). Deep CNN: Type of CNN with large numbers of layers it is mainly used to detect complex object detection and patterns. Neural network: are inspired by human brain neurons. They are interconnected to each other called neurons and work on different layers by using weight computation. In e-commerce it helps in pattern matching, image classification, NLP and segmentation etc. There are various variations are used AR with transient chaotic neural networks based on chaos theorem, this method used to find not changeable features extracted first, is used to define global feature matching (Nandhini et al., 2022).

Generative neural network is a well-known DL algorithm used to generate new training data with the same statistics. It provides a virtual try on feature in ecommerce (Kumar, 2018). All the methods are used to convert preprocessed images to vector images.

After getting vector images, we apply ML classifiers, to find the similar product use nearest neighbor (Addagarla & Amalanathan, 2020). Additionally previous research also used unsupervised methods for the recommendation system K-Mediod, Agglomerative, Brich, and the Gaussian Mixture Model (GMM) (Addagarla & Amalanathan, 2021). The use of this model to train for similar products for search visual query.

Recommendation Engine

The output generated by the system for the corresponding product in the visual representation. This system helps the customer to provide each and every possible detail about the product and helps to increase the customer satisfaction in online shopping. Additionally, this system used metadata to elaborate more options and provide personalized recommendation systems on the basis of past browsing history, feedbacks, their buying patterns and other details to refine the recommendation results.

Figure 2. Product recommendation system

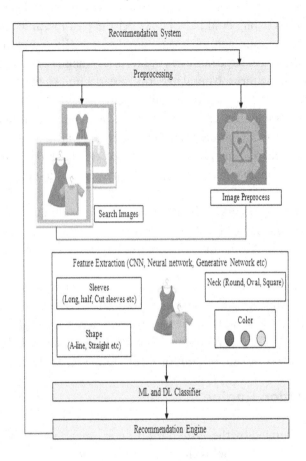

PRODUCT VISUALIZATION AND VIRTUAL TRY-ON IN AR

In this section we explain how AR works for Product visualization and virtual-try-on to facilitate e-commerce.AR permits the customers to view the product in the virtual form before making a purchase. We have taken an example of furniture visualization to explore the functionality of AR in e-commerce depicted as shown in figure 3. Customer can view how particular furniture will be fitted in their home.

For this customer may have submit images of his drawing room or any other room where he wishes to have the desired furniture.

AR and CV are both emerging technologies that revolutionize e-commerce in various way. Using the DL algorithm enhances the working of AR and CV. DL models help to analyze the data to boost sales and decision strategies for buyer and seller. AR offers the product to feel in the customer's real world as a virtual try on feature.

Figure 3. Augmented reality working in e-commerce

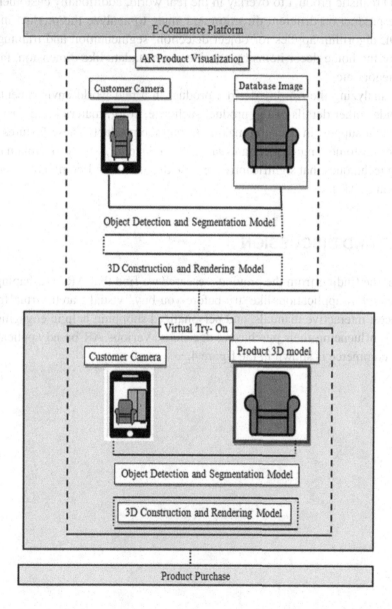

On e-commerce platforms, furniture items need to enhance customer experience by including AR features to help the buyer to visualize the product in a real environment. Additionally, e-commerce also provides virtual try on features.

The customer opens an app or web to visualize the product through its own camera. App having features to scan the real environment where customers want to fit their furniture. Customers are able to browse the visual product catalog. The object detection and segmentation model use algorithm (RCNN, YOLO etc)the input from camera to identify area (Mishraet al., 2021).DL model reconstruct and render 3D realistic product to overlay in the real world, additionally customer can move the product on different direction and angle to analyze the product in real world. DL algorithm applies for object detection, segmentation and training the dataset for the home decor items by considering metadata like dimension, fabric, color, category etc.

After analyzing the overlay desired product in a real world environment, the app provides other details of the product such size, color, material and customer feedback that support in decision making to buy the product. These features help to enhance customer engagement and satisfaction. Overall, we try to explain these emerging techniques that significantly increase the growth in Ecommerce industry (Alves et al., 2020).

RESULT AND DISCUSSION

As per the finding from the previous research we find that AR is reshaping the e-commerce with applications like "try-before-you-buy," visual search, virtual try-on experiences, interactive manuals, and personalized shopping help in engaging the users and influencing their purchasing decisions. Various AR based applications for the e-commerce is shown in the figure 4.

Figure 4. Applications used in E-commerce

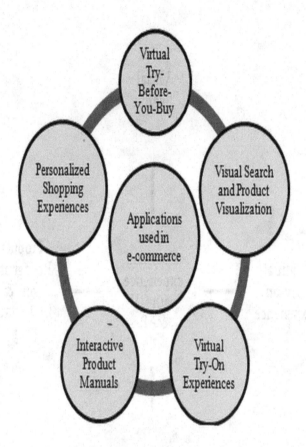

CV enhanced the online shopping experience for the user in many ways like visual search, product recognition; Interactive and Immersive experiences and Virtual Try-On experiences are highlighted in figure 5.

Figure 5. Shopping experience with AR and CV

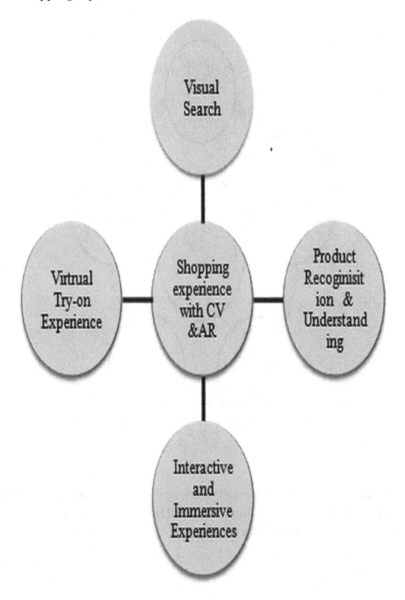

As per our analysis of table 1 we find that the deep CNN, generative network, RNN, are some DL based techniques. The use of DL techniques with AR are useful in predicting size of users, virtual try-on experience, try before buy, image recognition for the similar search product as depicted in the figure 6.

Figure 6. DLT used in e-commerce with AR

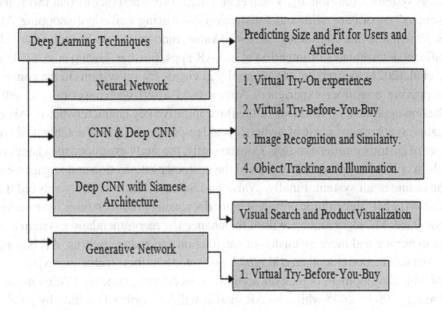

DL techniques used directly or indirectly in e-commerce with AR. These techniques play a significant role in e-commerce in various ways such as recommendation system, fit and size, try-on-experience and visual search and many more. These findings indicate a rapid development in the CV and AR, providing new perspectives for online shopping.

Further, integration of CV and AR enhances the customer engagement in E-commerce. As long as the potential users are on an e-commerce site, there will be higher chances of purchasing. AR and CV maximize the customer engagement and foster a relationship between product and brand. It always increases the chances of the customer in the future to buy something.

IMPACT OF AI, CV, AND AR IN RETAIL SECTOR

It has been recently discovered that CV and AR have had a major impact on customer engagement and satisfaction in the retail sector. These are important findings that help to understand consumer behavior in e-commerce, as they are based on various theoretical frameworks and methodologies. Another analysis explained by Fan et al. (2020), that intelligent retail technology such as human machine interaction and intelligent systems help to enhance customer engagement. The Authors used Stimulus-Organism-Response framework and structural equation modeling; they found that these technologies are very important to increase the customer engagement in smart systems. Additionally, Voicu et al. (2023) examined factors that influence consumers' experience with and satisfaction after using makeup e-shopping AR apps. Concluded that confidence fit, social value, innovativeness, perceived are all significant determinants of intention to use AR apps. Further, Huang et al. (2019), Jung et al. (2021) focused on AR especially in virtual try-on systems in the context of improving consumer experience. Author used a self determination and self-evaluation approach, on the basis of the three intuitive key characteristics of AR is modality, synchronous sense of ownership and re-processes ability, notably positive impact of customer understanding. Consequently, the study examined the changing trends in online shopping; AR improved the customer satisfaction and engagement in the online retail system. Finally, Walsh and Schaarschmidt (2023) analyzed the utilization of ML algorithmic preferences for decreasing product returns in an online marketplace. ML algorithms are used to enhance the recommendation system that helps in buying and increase customer satisfaction and reduce returns. AR beyond customer satisfaction (Jonathan et al., 2024) presented how these technologies promote sustainable development objectives around the world governments. Global market will reach $190 by 2025 while the AR market will be worth $97 billion by 2028.

The use of AI optimized resource utilization, reducing waste as well as improving maintenance practices. All these studies basically show that intelligent technologies and AR are transforming retail engagement. They offer useful advice for marketing managers who want to improve customer experiences, have sustainable business practices, and produce better products for today's internet-based consumers.

CONCLUSION

This chapter aim to know about the emerging technologies such as AR, CV and DL in the e-commerce sector. Chapter focuses on product recommendation and product virtualization like how user interacts with product and their experiences. Related research analyzes the papers and makes an understanding about the CV and AR in e-commerce. Implementing DL techniques such as CNN, GNN and RNN offers an efficient way to analyze e-commerce and enhance the user experiences. Overall, AR, CV with DL techniques are reshaping the e-commerce sector and offers more immersive, interactive, and personalized shopping experiences such as virtual-try-on, buy-before-try, desired search of product for consumers. In future we explore case studies, methods to enhance the understanding about CV and AR in ecommerce and explore ML bases applications and how it helps in the field of CV and AR.

REFERENCES

Addagarla, S. K., & Amalanathan, A. (2020a). Probabilistic unsupervised machine learning approach for a similar image recommender system for E-commerce. *Symmetry*, 12(11), 1783. DOI:10.3390/sym12111783

Addagarla, S. K., & Amalanathan, A. (2021b). e-SimNet: A visual similar product recommender system for E-commerce. *Indonesian Journal of Electrical Engineering and Computer Science*, 22(1), 563–570. DOI:10.11591/ijeecs.v22.i1.pp563-570

Ak, K. E., Kassim, A. A., Lim, J. H., & Tham, J. Y. (2018). Learning attribute representations with localization for flexible fashion search. *Proceedings of the IEEE conference on computer vision and pattern recognition* (pp. 7708-7717). IEEE. DOI:10.1109/CVPR.2018.00804

Alves, C., & Luís Reis, J. (2020). The intention to use e-commerce using augmented reality-the case of IKEA place. In *Information Technology and Systems: Proceedings of ICITS 2020* (pp. 114-123). Springer International Publishing. DOI:10.1007/978-3-030-40690-5_12

Bazaki, E., &Wanick, V. (2019). *Unlocking the potential of the salesperson in the virtual fitting room: Enhancing the online retail experience for fashion brands.*

Behgounia, F., & Zohuri, B. (2020). Machine learning driven an e-commerce. [IJCSIS]. *International Journal of Computer Science and Information Security*, 18(10). DOI:10.5281/zenodo.4252454

Billewar, S. R., Jadhav, K., Sriram, V. P., Arun, D. A., Mohd Abdul, S., Gulati, K., & Bhasin, D. N. K. K. (2022). The rise of 3D E-Commerce: The online shopping gets real with virtual reality and augmented reality during COVID-19. *World Journal of Engineering*, 19(2), 244–253. DOI:10.1108/WJE-06-2021-0338

Caboni, F., & Hagberg, J. (2019). Augmented reality in retailing: A review of features, applications and value. *International Journal of Retail & Distribution Management*, 47(11), 1125–1140. DOI:10.1108/IJRDM-12-2018-0263

Chaudhuri, A., Messina, P., Kokkula, S., Subramanian, A., Krishnan, A., Gandhi, S., & Kandaswamy, V. (2018). A smart system for selection of optimal product images in e-commerce. In *2018 IEEE International Conference on Big Data (Big Data)* (pp. 1728-1736). IEEE. DOI:10.1109/BigData.2018.8622259

Donati, L., Iotti, E., & Prati, A. (2019). Computer Vision for Supporting Fashion Creative Processes. In Hassaballah, M., & Hosny, K. (Eds.), *Recent Advances in Computer Vision. Studies in Computational Intelligence* (Vol. 804). Springer. DOI:10.1007/978-3-030-03000-1_1

Fan, X., Ning, N., & Deng, N. (2020). The impact of the quality of intelligent experience on smart retail engagement. *Marketing Intelligence & Planning*, 38(7), 877–891. DOI:10.1108/MIP-09-2019-0439

Fincato, M., Cornia, M., Landi, F., Cesari, F., & Cucchiara, R. (2022). Transform, warp, and dress: A new transformation-guided model for virtual try-on. [TOMM]. *ACM Transactions on Multimedia Computing Communications and Applications*, 18(2), 1–24. DOI:10.1145/3491226

Garg, N., Pareek, A., Lale, A., & Charya, S. J. (2021). Evolution in E-Commerce with Augmented Reality. In *IOP Conference Series: Materials Science and Engineering, 1012(1), 012041.* IOP Publishing. DOI:10.1088/1757-899X/1012/1/012041

Gundimeda, V., Murali, R. S., Joseph, R., & Naresh Babu, N. T. (2019). An automated computer vision system for extraction of retail food product metadata. In *First International Conference on Artificial Intelligence and Cognitive Computing: AICC 2018* (pp. 199-216). Springer Singapore. DOI:10.1007/978-981-13-1580-0_20

Gupta, S. S., Ghosal, I., & Ghosh, R. (2023). How does Augmented Reality (AR) impact on Consumer buying behavior? A Study in Indian E commerce Industry. [EEL]. *European Economic Letters*, 13(4), 700–707.

He, J., Han, P., Liu, H., Men, S., Ju, L., Zhen, P., & Wang, T. (2017, December). The research and application of the augmented reality technology. *In 2017 IEEE 2nd Information Technology, Networking, Electronic and Automation Control Conference* (ITNEC) (pp. 496-501). IEEE. DOI:10.1109/ITNEC.2017.8284781

Huang, T. L., Mathews, S., & Chou, C. Y. (2019). Enhancing online rapport experience via augmented reality. *Journal of Services Marketing*, 33(7), 851–865. DOI:10.1108/JSM-12-2018-0366

Jonathan, H., Magd, H., & Khan, S. A. (2024). Artificial Intelligence and Augmented Reality: A Business Fortune to Sustainability in the Digital Age. In *Navigating the Digital Landscape: Understanding Customer Behaviour in the Online World* (pp. 85-105). Emerald Publishing Limited. DOI:10.1108/978-1-83549-272-720241005

Jung, T. H., Bae, S., Moorhouse, N., & Kwon, O. (2021). The impact of user perceptions of AR on purchase intention of location-based AR navigation systems. *Journal of Retailing and Consumer Services*, 61, 102575. DOI:10.1016/j.jretconser.2021.102575

Киш, Л. М. (2020). Adaptation of b2c e-commerce to the conditions of the COVID-19 pandemic. *East European Scientific Journal*, *12*(64), 14-19.

Kowalczuk, P., Siepmann, C., & Adler, J. (2021). Cognitive, affective, and behavioral consumer responses to augmented reality in e-commerce: A comparative study. *Journal of Business Research*, 124, 357–373. DOI:10.1016/j.jbusres.2020.10.050

Kumar, A., Biswas, A., & Sanyal, S. (2018). Ecommerce gan: A generative adversarial network for e-commerce. *arXiv preprint arXiv:1801.03244*.

Kumar, B., Singh, A. K., & Banerjee, P. (2023, June). A deep learning approach for product recommendation using resnet-50 cnn model. In *2023 International Conference on Sustainable Computing and Smart Systems (ICSCSS)* (pp. 604-610). IEEE. DOI:10.1109/ICSCSS57650.2023.10169441

Lalonde, J. F. (2018, July). Deep learning for augmented reality. In *2018 17th workshop on information optics (WIO)* (pp. 1-3). IEEE. DOI:10.1109/WIO.2018.8643463

Lampropoulos, G., Keramopoulos, E., & Diamantaras, K. (2020). Enhancing the functionality of augmented reality using deep learning, semantic web and knowledge graphs: A review. *Visual Informatics*, 4(1), 32–42. DOI:10.1016/j.visinf.2020.01.001

Li, J., &Barmaki, R. (2019). *Trends in virtual and augmented reality research: a review of latest eye tracking research papers and beyond.*

Minaee, S., Liang, X., & Yan, S. (2022). *Modern augmented reality: Applications, trends, and future directions.* arXiv preprint arXiv:2202.09450.

Mishra, S., Hashmi, K. A., Pagani, A., Liwicki, M., Stricker, D., & Afzal, M. Z. (2021). Towards robust object detection in floor plan images: A data augmentation approach. *Applied Sciences (Basel, Switzerland)*, 11(23), 11174. DOI:10.3390/app112311174

Mnyakin, M. (2020). Investigating the Impacts of AR, AI, and Website Optimization on Ecommerce Sales Growth. *ResearchBerg Review of Science and Technology*, 3(1), 116–130.

Nandhini, P., Hariprabha, S., Abirami, S., Jaseenash, R., & Kaviyaraj, R. (2022). Design and Development of an Augmented Reality E-Commerce 3D models. *In 2022 3rd International Conference on Smart Electronics and Communication COSEC)*, (pp. 127-132). IEEE. DOI:10.1109/ICOSEC54921.2022.9952109

Ricci, M., Evangelista, A., Di Roma, A., & Fiorentino, M. (2023). Immersive and desktop virtual reality in virtual fashion stores: A comparison between shopping experiences. *Virtual Reality (Waltham Cross)*, 27(3), 1–16. DOI:10.1007/s10055-023-00806-y PMID:37360805

Rong, L., Weibai, Z., & Debo, H. (2021) Sentiment Analysis of Ecommerce Product Review Data Based on Deep Learning. *2021 IEEE 4th Advanced Information Management, Communicates, Electronic and Automation Control Conference (IMCEC)*. IEEE. DOI:10.1109/IMCEC51613.2021.9482223

Sembium, V., Rastogi, R., Tekumalla, L., & Saroop, A. (2018, April). Bayesian models for product size recommendations. In *Proceedings of the 2018 world wide web conference* (pp. 679-687). ACM. DOI:10.1145/3178876.3186149

Sharma, R., & Vishvakarma, A. (2019). Retrieving similar e-commerce images using deep learning. *arXiv preprint arXiv:1901.03546.*

Sheikh, A. S., Guigourès, R., Koriagin, E., Ho, Y. K., Shirvany, R., Vollgraf, R., & Bergmann, U. (2019, September). A deep learning system for predicting size and fit in fashion e-commerce. In *Proceedings of the 13th ACM conference on recommender systems* (pp. 110-118). ACM. DOI:10.1145/3298689.3347006

Singh, N., Singh, P., & Gupta, M. (2020). An inclusive survey on machine learning for CRM: A paradigm shift. *Decision (Washington, D.C.)*, 47(4), 447–457. DOI:10.1007/s40622-020-00261-7

Singh, P., & Agrawal, R. (2022). Modelling and prediction of COVID-19 to measure the impact of lockdown on organisation in India. *International Journal of Indian Culture and Business Management*, 26(2), 259–275. DOI:10.1504/IJICBM.2022.123593

Smink, A. R., Van Reijmersdal, E. A., Van Noort, G., & Neijens, P. C. (2020). Shopping in augmented reality: The effects of spatial presence, personalization and intrusiveness on app and brand responses. *Journal of Business Research*, 118, 474–485. DOI:10.1016/j.jbusres.2020.07.018

Thandekkattu, S. G., & Kalaiarasi, M. (2022). Customer-Centric E-commerce Implementing Artificial Intelligence for Better Sales and Service. *Reddy, A.B., Kiranmayee, B., Mukkamala, R.R., Srujan Raju, K. (eds) Proceedings of Second International Conference on Advances in Computer Engineering and Communication Systems. Algorithms for Intelligent Systems.* Springer, Singapore. DOI:10.1007/978-981-16-7389-4_14

Voicu, M. C., Sîrghi, N., & Toth, D. M. M. (2023). Consumers' experience and satisfaction using augmented reality apps in E-shopping: New empirical evidence. *Applied Sciences (Basel, Switzerland)*, 13(17), 9596. DOI:10.3390/app13179596

Walsh, G., & Schaarschmidt, M. (2023). *Taking Advantage of Algorithmic Preference to Reduce Product Returns in E-Commerce.* AISEL. https://aisel.aisnet.org/icis2023/emobilecomm/emobilecomm/3

Weinstein, B. G. (2018). A computer vision for animal ecology. *Journal of Animal Ecology*, 87(3), 533–545. DOI:10.1111/1365-2656.12780 PMID:29111567

Xu, X. Y., Jia, Q. D., & Tayyab, S. M. U. (2024). Exploring the stimulating role of augmented reality features in E- commerce: A three-staged hybrid approach. *Journal of Retailing and Consumer Services*, 77, 103682. DOI:10.1016/j.jretconser.2023.103682

Yang, C., & Liu, Z. (2021, August). Application of computer vision in electronic commerce. In *Journal of Physics: Conference Series* (*Vol. 1992*, No. 2, p. 022134). IOP Publishing. DOI:10.1088/1742-6596/1992/2/022134

Chapter 7
Business Technology Transformation:
Perspectives on AI Synergy

Revenio C. Jalagat
https://orcid.org/0000-0002-8878-3825
Al-Zahra College for Women, Oman

ABSTRACT

This chapter highlights how crucial it is to explore the use of AI applications in businesses nowadays, analyze how AI is being utilized to drive digital transformation, and what that means for the business environment going forward. Additionally, it evaluates the advantages and difficulties of AI as it relates to corporate technology change. Data were collected and analyzed from different scholarly sources, such as books, articles, and websites. Study findings claimed that the application of AI has grown significantly across a range of sectors, including manufacturing, telecommunications, healthcare, banking, education, retail, and e-commerce. Simplifying procedures, facilitating better decision-making, and increasing productivity are just a few of the ways artificial intelligence (AI) is thought to have significantly improved company operations. By leveraging AI's full potential, businesses can rise to a more advantageous position in the market, foster creativity, and innovation, increase productivity, and provide better customer experiences.

INTRODUCTION

Technological advances have paved the way in changing the way businesses operate and with the emergence of Artificial Intelligence (AI), it has captured global attention as a disruptive power reshaping the business environment by contributing

DOI: 10.4018/979-8-3693-4187-2.ch007

unmatched opportunities for creativity and innovation. According to Davenport (2018), businesses that integrate AI into their operations have experienced a technological revolution by transforming conventional business methods and industry standards into modern AI-generated operational outcomes. Businesses from various sectors have realized the importance of adopting AI technologies to become operationally efficient, enhance processes for making decisions, and achieve competitive advantage in the marketplace.

Tracing back the evolution of AI, prominent personalities like John McCarthy and Alan Turing formulated the theoretical foundation for Artificial Intelligence. The concept of machines emulating human intelligence was exhibited in the vision of Turing and matched with McCarthy's introduction of the term "AI," which in turn developed into a technological revolution (Ekmekci et al., 2020). Later in 1990, there was a resurgence of technological advancement with the growth of machine learning algorithms. Yet, 2010 demonstrated the paradigm shift with the introduction of big data, wherein deep learning is a subgroup of machine learning, serving as the impetus for AI's emergence. Innovation extends to natural language processing, autonomous approaches, and picture identification. According to Manyika et al. (2017), AI has become an integral part of daily living, and it encompasses applications in smart home systems, autonomous vehicles, and healthcare diagnostics. Hence, the influence of AI in business operations in terms of efficiency has been reflected in streamlining automation in the routine tasks found in customer service, manufacturing, logistics, etc.

Furthermore, Chen et al. (2012) stressed that AI-driven analytics became a foundation for companies that are looking for implementable insights from massive datasets. Notably, the utilization of AI algorithms, for instance, enhanced businesses to achieve well-informed decisions encompassing from market trends to customer behavior showcasing its ability to comprehend and respond to the needs of consumers resulting in an interactive approach between the organizations and their customers. Loureiro et al. (2021) emphasized that businesses' interaction with customers can be shown by utilizing chatbots, virtual assistants, and personalized recommendations for a better customer experience and satisfaction. Hence, this chapter emphasizes the importance of examining the current state of AI applications in businesses to facilitate an analysis of the implementation of AI towards digital transformation and future implications for the business environment. It also assesses the AI benefits and challenges in the transition into business technology transformation. The chapter is organized into the following topics: Introduction; the current state of AI application in business; artificial intelligence and digital transformation; digital transformation in the business sector; business technology transformation through generative AI; opportunities on AI and business technology transformation; challenges on AI and business technology transformation; future implications of AI synergy and digital transformation; and conclusion and recommendations.

THE CURRENT STATE OF AI APPLICATIONS IN BUSINESSES

The global market of AI is forecasted to attain $1.81 trillion by 2030 according to Grand View Research Inc., 2024). The revenues experienced an upward trend from 2018 to 2025 (Fig. 1) in the global setting. The data indicates that artificial intelligence has caught the attention of the global market as evidence of rapid digital transformation in businesses regardless of its type and business formation.

Figure 1. Global artificial intelligence software market revenue

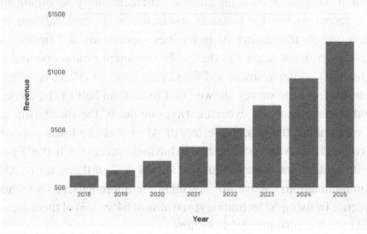

(Exploding Topics, 2024).

Furthermore, the average global revenues from 2018-2025 have reached $53 billion with the highest revenues expected to reach $126 billion in 2025. Moreover, the average growth rate from 2018-2025 accounted for 38.86% which can be considered a high growth ratio. Based on the data provided, Table 1 shows the annual global revenues of AI software from 2018-2025.

Table 1. AI Software Market's Global Annual Revenue (2018 to 2025) (Grand View Research, 2024)

Year	Revenue
2018	$10.1 billion
2019*	$14.69 billion
2020*	$22.59 billion
2021*	$34.87 billion
2022*	$51.27 billion
2023*	$70.94 billion
2024*	$94.41 billion
2025*	$126 billion

Companies implement artificial intelligence in several ways to save time and cost while attaining efficiency in business operations. Across businesses and sectors, the potential of AI application is undeniable with technology becoming a precious resource. A recent survey for instance conducted by Forbes Advisor to around 600 business owners integrating AI in business operations and findings revealed that there is a significant impact in the fields of content production and customer support (chatbots), cybersecurity, and fraud management (Haan & Watts, 2023). Summary result from the survey showed that more than half of the owners utilize AI for fraud management and cybersecurity; one out of the four business owners expressed views about the potential effect of AI on website traffic; about 97% of the owners agreed that AI is instrumental to business success; ChatGPT is useful to write website content and other languages; almost 46% of them utilize AI to make internal communications; above 40% of them are apprehensive on technological overdependence by using AI technology; and almost 64% (2/3) of them are confident that AI will enhance customer relationships.

Relative to the current state of AI implementation is examining how businesses utilize artificial intelligence. Companies and organizations employ AI with the intent of transforming their operations into a better position and a greater degree of improvement if perfection is far-reaching. Forbes Advisor survey results also revealed that the use of AI covers a wide range of fields in descending order which include customer service; cybersecurity; fraud management, customer relationship management, digital personal assistants, inventory management, content production, product recommendations, accounting, supply chain operations, recruitment and talent sourcing, and audience segmentation (Haan & Watts, 2023).

An AI expert and professor from Harvard University named Mark Esposito expressed his views on the technological empowerment of businesses by addressing some of the biggest challenges currently faced by modern companies and firms. The introduction of various AI models enables businesses to discover potentials and possibilities to apply machine learning in their operations. Utilizing AI has been implemented in production and manufacturing but now expanded to include the service industries and sectors having the same approach and methodologies. For example, modern marketers use digital interfaces related to the availability of technologies so that AI enables companies to perform interfaces with customers, marketing campaigns, customer profiling, and algorithmic governance.

According to the Center for the Fourth Industrial Revolution. (2024), the fourth industrial revolution network (C4IR Network) which comprised 18 centers aimed at changing the business landscape of businesses and industries through enhancing technology management using the network. The C4IR network endeavors to adopt common standards for utilizing the latest technologies and implement them more collaboratively and flexibly starting with local industries. The rise of social innovators has paved the way for these technological advancements by using new ways of delivering services encompassing the fields of microfinance, resource management, smart healthcare, and evidence of the increasing importance of digital working methods (Word Economic Forum, 2022). For social innovators, adopting and implementing the fourth industrial revolution are important for businesses not only to be sustainable but also to ensure that businesses are not left behind competition, and transform into modern industries with technological transformation from the usual traditional industries.

Verhoef et al. (2021) stressed that three major external forces have driven the need for digital transformation. Firstly, the evolution of the World Wide Web (www) has spread worldwide leading to the development of technologies such as smartphones, cloud computing, broadband, speech recognition, Web 2.0, online payments, SEO, and cryptocurrencies, and the popularization of e-commerce. Second, the degree of competition has significantly increased with the advent of recent technologies changing the retail sales landscape from conventional into modern technologically aided retail entrusted to young digital companies. Thirdly, the behaviors of customers significantly changed in congruence with the development of new technologies and according to market data, a considerable shift from conventional to online shopping has been experienced by retailers and digital touchpoints essentially served a critical role in the consumers' buying patterns which led to the blend of both offline and online sales.

In the study of Saarikko et al. (2020), they found that the digital infrastructure has expanded from back-office servers to technology-influenced operations with the customers increasing utilization of mobile technologies, smart sensors, cloud computing, miniaturization, and middleware. For instance, developing new prospects for products and services by businesses through the utilization of the Internet of Things (IoT) that can identify, collect, process, and transmit significant data in real-time. Through IoT, operating activities can be digitalized, analyzed, and monetized as well as allowing the formation of situational, desirable, smart, and cost-effective products and services. Moreover, data collected from existing goods and products enable marketers to monitor efficiently the product status and provide after-sale service while analyzing data from various sources, interrelated products, streams, and processes that can be investigated to acknowledge behaviors and patterns wherein using algorithms can decide on process optimization and service provisions.

Sestino et al. (2020) feature how the IoT and big data transform management and marketing strategies via digitalization, symbolizing a recent development for business competitiveness through Industry 4.0. This new concept has transformed daily activities and, the manner, in which firms and organizations run and operate. In other words, integrating the industry 4.0 methodologies in their business activities to survive amid intense competition, thus, signaling them to change production methods, and management activities. An example is the application of the reengineering method which can be a suitable approach originating in the IT sector and expanded to the business sector redesigning main business methods to increase operational efficiency. While various methods and approaches are available in applying digital business transformation processes, businesses need to select a route that will enable them to build business strategies that will lead to sustainability and generate more revenues.

ARTIFICIAL INTELLIGENCE (AI) AND DIGITAL TRANSFORMATION

The relationship between AI and digital transformation has become a critical component in modeling the recent business setting. With the fast pace of technological development, companies take into consideration leveraging AI to maximize benefits in their operations, obtain valuable perspectives from data usage, and provide matchless services to clientele. In the aspect of business processes, AI developed synergy that has contributed to the change in business perspectives enabling businesses to reshape business strategies, customer exchanges, and value propositions in the midst of digital transformation. Daly (2023) stressed that the convergence between AI and digital transformation provides a lot of opportunities including increased productivity, streamlined operations, increased consumer exchanges, and new innovative business prototypes. AI, one of the latest definitions from the Association for Advancement of Artificial Intelligence (2014, p.5) referred to AI as mechanisms underlying thought and intelligent behavior and their embodiment in machines. In other words, AI can mimic human thinking or do similar tasks that humans perform. When linked with digital transformation, the term digital transformation refers to the incorporation of digital technologies in all business fields by changing how companies and firms are managed and delivering customer value. It is a comprehensive approach that operates not only based on digitalization but also on changes in the organizational functions, competencies, processes, and business strategies and models to leverage the blend of using digital technologies applications. Changing business landscape is one of the driving forces of digital transformation along with other factors such as efficiency, customer satisfaction, competitive advantage, and others.

One of the essential areas that businesses should take into consideration is business processes. The synergy of AI and business processes is important as businesses need to continue with innovative ideas while ensuring the efficiency of their operations. The concept of business technology transformation allows businesses to paradigm operational change, increase productivity, streamline operations, and enhance informed decision-making. The next section explains how AI is utilized in operations, decision-making, and productivity as enumerated:

AI and Operations Simplification

AI has already been known for its ability to streamline operations to achieve efficient operations and dexterity. AI eliminates time-consuming and repetitive work assignments through automation, reduces human errors, and enables human resources to skip tasks that AI can perform and focus on creative and strategic functions. As an example, workers' tasks can be reduced by allowing AI-aided bots and automation to perform customer inquiries, manage basic administrative assignments, and process data. Furthermore, AI is capable of processing and evaluating huge quantities of information that allows companies to improve their supply chain, enhance resource distribution, and estimate demands with precision, thus, increasing overall efficiency in operations.

AI-Powered Decision-Making

Integrating AI into the processes of making decisions is considered a remarkable transformation in achieving business strategic and well-informed decisions. Daly (2023) considered AI as a catalyst for attaining strategic decisions. The ability of AI to process voluminous datasets enables user organizations to formulate perspectives, acknowledge trends, and forecast patterns that help decision-makers decide based on data analytics. The use of predictive analytics and data-driven insights as examples provides companies with a better understanding of consumer preferences, emerging risks, market dynamics, risk management, and strategic planning. It also brings real-time ideas by using the AI-enhanced decision-making mechanisms to help organizations provide prompt feedback to customer needs and changing market dynamics, hence, sustaining competitive advantage.

Enhancing Productivity Through AI

Undeniably, AI has proven to improve productivity and it has become pivotal to an organization's productive operations. Automating the works and tasks made the operations easier and faster as well as optimizing the flows of tasks or workflows. In other words, job assignments that do not require high thinking abilities are performed by automated AI technology such that employees can focus on creative, strategic, and high-value tasks that AI cannot perform. Integral to the capability of AI rests on assisting project management, resource allocation, project, and other tasks prioritization, minimizing bottlenecks, and maximizing workflows. Furthermore, AI's adaptability mechanisms enable continuous improvement and process optimization that leads to incremental productivity enrichment over time.

Digital Transformation in the Business Sector

Banking Sector Transformation

Artificial intelligence becomes essential for banks to increase efficiency, security, and customer satisfaction. Financial institutions such as banks maximize their potential in operations, provide customization in terms of service offerings, and mitigate risks. Banks recently employed virtual assistants and AI-powered chatbots to cater to routinary inquiries from clients thus, reducing reliance on human agents and at the same time performing complicated tasks (Nambiar et al., 2020). In addition, the use of AI algorithms in office processes including transaction monitoring, data entry, fraud detection, large-volume processing enhances banks' operations and accurate service (Liao et al., 2019). Through machine learning model applications, suspicious transactions are discovered, and fraudulent activities are potentially flagged for further examination (Mendelson, 2019). According to Cai et al. (2020), banks have utilized AI-driven bibliometric authentication systems that improve security by validating the identities of clients using voice authentication technology or facial recognition. Machine learning also evaluates the borrowers' creditworthiness by assessing their spending patterns, financial history, and others. And AI-enhanced predictive analytics aided banks predict market fluctuations and maximize investment schemes to reduce cases of losses (Cai et al., 2020).

Manufacturing Sector Transformation

The use of AI in the manufacturing sector is evident and encompasses a wide range of applications. Marr (2021) posited that AI technologies implemented in the manufacturing sector include quality control, supply chain management, predictive maintenance, and robotics automation. Predictive maintenance, for instance, leverages machine learning algorithms to evaluate anticipated failures, minimize downtime, reduce maintenance costs, and examine equipment data (Luo et al., 2020. On the other hand, quality control procedures empowered by AI-enhanced image identification systems can acknowledge defects with higher precision and speed comparable to human assessment (Jia et al., 2019). Furthermore, Sarkis et al. (2021) explained that AI-empowered supply chain management devices enhance inventory levels, augment logistics, and improve demand forecasting leading to cost savings and enhanced operational efficiency. Lee et al. (2019) also stressed that AI-enhanced robotics automation empowers manufacturers to attain higher levels of accuracy in manufacturing operations, improve productivity, and reduce repetitive tasks by automation.

Educational Sector Transformation

In the education sector, the AI-enhanced adaptive learning system enabled personalized learning capabilities by evaluating the student information, granting customized content and suggestions anchored on personal learning requirements (Koedinger et al., 2012). AI practically increases student interactions, enhances learning outputs, and develops AI-driven tutoring mechanisms that leverage machine learning algorithms and natural language processing to offer customized responses and assistance to students, modeling face-to-face tutoring encounters (VanLehn, 2011). Martin (2020) postulated that automation is also a remarkable transformation in using the AI-aided system as it automates for example student, enrollment, scheduling, grading, teaching loads, and workloads, and in enhancing operational efficiency and effectiveness. Chatbots driven by AI technologies manage regular queries, supplementing human resources for more complicated assignments.

Retail and E-commerce sector Transformation

Central to retail and e-commerce is how to enhance customer satisfaction and experience. AI can revolutionize retail and e-commerce by providing a better customer experience by analyzing consumer preferences, providing purchase history, and speedy browsing mechanisms to offer customized product suggestions. The study conducted by Cremonesi et al. (2011), features the quality of using collaborative filtering strategies in augmenting customer satisfaction and accuracy of the strategy deployment. The results of which enable retailers to reduce stockouts, minimize the excessive cost of inventory, and raise inventory levels. Fildes et al. (2019) supported the above findings by displaying the effectiveness of demand forecasting models powered by AI in enhancing efficient inventory management and retailers' profitability. Findings in the study of He et al. (2017) also highlight cost-effective and efficient AI-powered chatbots in enhancing services to customers and achieving higher satisfaction levels for e-commerce and retail operations.

Telecommunication Sector Transformation

Like the other sectors, the implementation of AI is comprised of varied domains and dimensions encompassing optimization to customer service, network management, and marketing. One of the main applications of AI in the telecommunication industry is using AI algorithms where voluminous data are analyzed to maximize network operation, detect possible operational failures, and allocate resources dynamically for improved efficiency and reliability (Cisco, 2021). As an example, anomalies in network infrastructure can be discovered using AI-aided predictive maintenance and proactively reconcile problems before they accelerate, lessening downtime and service interruptions. In addition, cooperation between AI technology experts, providers, and telecommunication firms can elevate innovation and transformation industry-wide and by empowering synergies and resource sharing, different stakeholders can transform challenges into opportunities through collaborative efforts and maximize the full potential of AI in the telecommunication industry (ABI Research, 2020).

Healthcare Sector Transformation

The use of AI has extended to the healthcare sector and the so-called AI-powered diagnostic tools have exhibited accuracy in discovering several medical illnesses. As evidence, the IBM Watson for Oncology evaluates the data of patients and recommends individualized medication plans according to patients' records and extensive medical literature. On the same note, Google's DeepMind has established algorithms that foretell the possibility of acute kidney problems or injury 48 hours in advance, thereby helping healthcare professionals in early interference (Tomasev et al., 2019). Moreover, AI hastens drug detection procedures by evaluating huge datasets to recognize drug candidates and forecast their efficiency. Aliper et al. (2016) asserted that the use of AI assists the computer-generated testing of compounds, minimizing the time spent and cost related to conventional laboratory tests. The AI-powered prognostic analytics improve resource allotment, forecasting patient admissions, and enhancing inventory management (Liu et al., 2019).

Business Technology Transformation Through Generative AI

One of the popular subsets of AI is Generative Artificial Intelligence (Generative AI). This innovative and highly adaptable technology can elevate digital transformation and provide substantial commercial value to different sectors and industries in their operations. Restructuring businesses to integrate AI drives them to achieve digital transformation. The introduction of Generative AI has gone through many trials, however; it steadily produced promising outcomes (Singh, 2024). In better understanding Generative AI, as a subset of AI, this technology can produce several types of content such as audio, texts, images, and video sequences. Due to the application of advanced deep learning techniques such the variational autoencoders and generative adversarial networks, the generative AI can analyze large datasets and identify structures and patterns in creating new and unique contents that mimic humans. The transformation continues to evolve across a wide range of industries from customized content making to healthcare developments. Hence, generative AI appears as a transformative agent that promotes digital transformation and cultivates unequaled efficiency and creativity.

Fast-tracking digital transformation, the essentiality of understanding the technological advancements through generative AI is critical to the success of every business operation. The knowledge of the different generative AI tools helps businesses conduct their functions and these tools include but are not limited to stable diffusion, ChatGPT, and GitHub Copilot. Huge investments undertaken in recent years backing the development of deep and machine learning. Driving transformation through generative AI becomes vital to business digital transformation and is expressed in many ways as specified in the next paragraphs:

1. *Content Production*

Generative AI generates automated content in the form of blog posts, producing product descriptions, and crafting social media blogs. As applied in business settings, content building is a time-consuming and resource-intensive undertaking. However, with the use of generative AI, considerable time-savings experienced with a consistent high-quality outcome.

2. *Increased Customization*

The application of generative AI enhances companies to offer highly customized encounters to their clients. For example, generative AI produced personalized product approvals, tailor-made marketing communications, and customized design customer interfaces. The increased level of customization can improve customer loyalty and engagement.

3. *Product Design and Development*

Generative AI can facilitate the designing of products by producing 3D models and samples and it can also assist in maximizing approaches to dealing with customer preferences and feedback. Generative AI can generate faster product development phases.

4. *Eliminate Tasks Repetition*

One of the main capabilities of generative AI is the automation of different job assignments that are used to be traditionally performed and it ranges from chatbot responses to data entry. Because of automation, human resources can spend more time on creative and strategic tasks and functions.

5. *Data Escalation*

The essence of applying AI models rests on data and information as its lifeblood. Generative AI creates artificial information to increase current datasets, producing training, and augmenting AI models with ease. This is applicable specifically in companies such as finance and healthcare wherein the security of data and confidentiality are highly upheld, and scarcity of data has become a major concern.

Moreover, the business value of generative AI cannot be underestimated since this technology marks the organizations' business transformation. The potential of adopting generative AI is promising and crucial in delivering the most value that it can contribute to the economy and society at large (Singh, 2024).

Opportunities for AI and Business Technology Transformation

Integrating AI in the operations of businesses promotes technological break-throughs converting conventional business strategies and reshaping company standards (Davenport, 2018). Businesses across industries are applying AI-powered technologies to improve decision-making, operational efficiency and attain competitive advantage over competitors in the marketplace. The enormous benefits offered by implementing AI are evident as it practically increases operational performance and at the same time simplifies processes and tasks (Chui & Malhotra, 2018). In different sectors such as manufacturing firms, the utilization of AI-enhanced robotic systems transformed production levels with higher efficiency, thereby making production faster and attaining a more precise manufacturing operation (Arntz et al., 2016). Furthermore, in attaining efficient operations the use of predictive analytics makes users evaluate vast datasets, predict future developments, and enable well-informed and strategic decisions.

Another opportunity for AI implementation is that it facilitates innovativeness in the production of goods and services. Businesses maximize the utilization of machine learning algorithms to determine the preferences of customers and offer highly personalized product recommendations and customized services (Bughin et al., 2017). Top performers in e-commerce businesses such as Amazon utilize AI to offer consumers customized shopping encounters, which contributes to higher loyalty and customer satisfaction.

According to Chatterjee et al. (2022), AI enhances the human workforce and does not replace them. The use of AI helps improve the human worker's capability by making their tasks fast and easier. The utmost benefits gained by employees are a reduction in repetitive work, real-time insights, and facilitated decision-making. The benefits extend to different sectors including law, banking, and medicine wherein examinations are required for vast datasets, in spotting trends, and data-driven recommendations via AI-enhanced tools. According to Bar and Chaudhuri (2023), AI-aided technology helps in gaining insights about customer behavior and preferences as it examines the huge amount of consumer information which includes purchase history, browsing mechanisms, customer feedback, and social media encounters. Machine learning algorithms enable users to understand the customers' needs, wants, and likes.

Challenges to AI and Business Technology Transformation

Undeniably, the implementation of AI has provided enormous benefits in line with the business technology transformation. However, it also faced challenges and limitations that impact operations and one of the increasing challenges is ethical considerations. According to Floridi et al. (2018), ethical challenges related to AI have increased due to its impact on human decisions and human lives. Biases generated by AI algorithms are inadvertently sourced from historical data attributed to ethical issues and need cautious surveillance to avoid discriminatory results (Barocas & Selbst, 2016). Moreover, the negative implications of automating routine tasks for employees have been emphasized considering job displacement, requiring upskilling and reskilling initiatives to train them for the tasks that match AI technologies (Bessen, 2019). Other ethical concerns rest on the possibility of misuse, copyright issues, deepfake creation, and implementation of less impactful policies and guidelines.

Privacy and security are paramount challenges with the implementation of AI technology as it can cause security and privacy risks, intentionally or unintentionally because of data algorithms or mechanisms to gather, keep, or process information. Risks in security and privacy can negatively impact integrity, confidentiality, and insights, and can result in compromises to employees, stakeholders, and customers. Unattended risks may result in violating legal, ethical, and social expectations and standards that further lead to penalties, liability, and losses. Crucial challenges are also prevalent in human dignity and autonomy. The AI implementation can affect human dignity and independence because it diminishes the value of respect, worth, well-being, freedom, and empowerment of employees, customers, and stakeholders. When human dignity ceases because of the AI replacement, reputation, credibility, and trust also cease.

In the aspect of technical and organizational challenges in AI implementation, common challenges comprise the lack of skills, lack of culture, lack of data, and lack of infrastructure. The lack of skills hindered the effective deployment of AI because AI skills are the instrument of successful AI. To have a skilled workforce is expensive, competitive, scarce, and talent shortages. Furthermore, AI skills can be complicated, changing, specialized, and need endless learning and upgrading intended for AI users and professionals. Secondly, the lack of culture is another challenge which means without a sufficient, positive, and supportive environment. Culture is an enforcer of AI and if not embraced, resulted in a cultural barrier. Culture can be challenging, cynical, and fearsome, building obstacles or tensions for AI transformation. It can also be firm, ordered, or maintained, which can prevent AI innovation and cooperation.

The lack of data is another hindrance to implementing AI. Without enough quality and relevant data, AI cannot operate effectively and efficiently. The scarcity of data, inconsistency, inaccuracy, fragmented, and incompleteness restrict AI capabilities and outputs. Moreover, data can become regulated, sensitive, confidential, posturing ethical, legal, and security challenges for utilizing AI and sharing it. Finally, a lack of infrastructure, or without sufficient, secure, and robust infrastructure. When infrastructure is not supported, results in inadequacy, incompatibility, vulnerability, and outdated, thus limiting AI reliability and performance. IT infrastructure can be complicated, costly, and regulated, facing technical, financial, and legal challenges for AI maintenance and deployment.

Future Implications of AI Synergy and Digital Transformation

The technological revolution is experienced with the emergence of AI, and it shows a progressing trend. As it is beginning to be applied in almost all industries, the various elements of AI collaborated to shift from traditional to modern methods of operations in business empowerment, learning, and communications. This paradigm shift brought people into a new age of technological synergy leading to remarkable growth in technological utilization. Mari (2024) has outlined the future landscape of technology and industries' emphasis on "AI-to-AI" methodology can be applied in the healthcare sector. The emphasis on its application is presented in detail in the succeeding paragraphs.

Healthcare Market Intensification. An AI system has a huge potential to transmit information across different healthcare mediums ranging from electronic health records (HER) to diagnostic devices. As an example, the patient's information can be evaluated with EHR by interacting with the other AI specialist in imaging, allowing a thorough and speedy diagnosis by healthcare specialists. The AI-to-AI interactions can maximize the management of patients by cooperating with other service providers wherein one AI can make schedules, while the other can supervise medication management, enabling a synchronized method in handling patient care. Furthermore, AI can personalize treatment plans whereby one AI can evaluate generic information while the other AI investigates recent medical studies, and the third AI monitors the patient's feedback on the medication which leads to the overall provision of highly customized treatment to patients.

Research and Development (R&D) Focus. In the healthcare industry, research and development rests on the Pharmaceutical Companies. The role of AI systems in the process is to collaborate with the different AIs to hasten the discovery of medicine. One AI analyzes biological data to recognize possible drug targets and the other AI replicates drug exchanges. AI can reimagine clinical trials, for example, one AI can outline trial procedures based on historical information while the other AI can supervise experimental data in real-time, acknowledging patterns or problems at earlier stages. In other words, different AI devices estimate the success ratio of varied research platforms, thus helping companies distribute resources more effectively to many desirable projects and activities.

Optimizing Procedure Focus. Vital to the operation in the healthcare industry is supply chain management. The role of AI systems lies in their ability to forecast demands for inventory, supervise logistics, and order processing automation. The AIs execute the process by interacting with vendor systems, making sure that optimum levels of inventories are met and processed on time. AI designed in prognosis can connect with those specialized in medication planning. For instance, an AI-empowered device analyzes medical photos like CT scans and MRIs and communicates the results to the other AI system focused on medication plans, ascertaining a speedy and smooth transition from prognosis to treatment. Furthermore, an AI system utilized in examining biochemical reactions can cooperate with another AI system that evaluates clinical trial data, hence fastening the recognition of probable drug entrants and heightening medical testing designs. It facilitates the acceleration of time to market for the latest medicines. On one hand, AI in telehealth podiums can closely operate with A-powered distant patient monitoring machines. In terms of data security, a specialized AI with clinical AI functions provides constant protection of patient data including real-time censoring of any information anomalies or breaches and ascertaining fulfillment with rules and regulations such as the Health Insurance Portability and Accountability Act (HIPAA) or General Data Protection Regulation (GDPR).

Ethical and Practical Implications. One of the aspects that needs greater consideration is the ethical and practical implications of AI systems. AI systems communicate effectively when standardized data formats and procedures are adequately maintained. Over and across the healthcare sector, sensible data of patients should be secured. Through the AI systems, encrypted and protected communication mediums are useful in complying with the governing principles like HIPAA in the United States or GDPR in Europe. AI systems operate in a vast quantity of sensible patient information and these data are private and confidential with which AI-powered technology can interact while keeping its confidentiality and privacy. AI systems also enable addressing risks of unauthorized access and data breaches when it is shifted from one system to another. In addition, AI algorithms can get and strengthen biases in instructing information. Exchanges between AI systems can hypothetically proliferate these biases throughout various mediums, leading to inequitable schemes.

The future potentials of AI sustainability and harnessing its uses, optimizing the implementation of AI should be given preference, especially in harnessing various strategies, and maximizing capabilities to maintain and sustain a competitive edge in the long run. These are comprised of (1) Data-driven culture which means that AI algorithms take charge in enabling decision making; (2) Human-AI collaboration where companies must emphasize the promotion of synergies between the AI systems and human intelligence rather than thinking of AI as a substitute to human performance (Borges et al., 2021); (3) Constant learning and adaptation that focuses on AIs potential to develop quickly themes that allow firms for constant updates and recent developments. It enhances continuous learning and examination of promising technological developments for application and competitive advantage; (4) Agility and adaptability which means that the establishment of company structure is essential for attaining adaptability and agility, a structure that can quickly accommodate the changing market dynamics and effectively incorporate AI technologies. Companies progress to a higher position in the marketplace by taking advantage of AIs' full potential, supporting creativity and innovation, enhancing efficiency, and offering superior consumer encounters in the future by implementing these approaches (Mari, 2024).

Artificial Intelligence (AI) has emerged as a highly promising alternative for businesses looking to fully utilize its potential, thanks to the rapid advancement of futuristic technologies. Before deciding to construct AI, software and considering the bigger picture, the organization must consider the project's scope as well as the specific need or issue it addresses. Additionally, the AI ought to easily mesh with the business procedures of the organization. AI implementations are typically more expensive than creating standard software and mobile app solutions. As a result, the business should spend on hiring a group of knowledgeable data scientists, ML specialists, and AI developers.

CONCLUSION AND RECOMMENDATIONS

The business environment has progressed with the emergence of artificial intelligence that transformed how businesses and organizations manage and their performance. The technological revolution has paved the way in building a pathway wherein efficiency, innovation, and value creation are the central considerations in reshaping the business landscape. The AI synergy through business technology transformation practically aided businesses in areas where convergence explained how transformation can be implemented by changing the organization's decision-making, and management, and yield better outcomes utilizing AI-powered mechanisms that operate beyond attaining productivity and efficiency but redefining and revolution-izing the manner how value is developed, offered, and delivered to stakeholders. The chapter outlines the topics including the importance of examining the current state of AI applications in businesses to facilitate an analysis of the implementation of AI towards digital transformation and future implications to the business environ-ment. It also assesses the AI benefits and challenges in the transition into business technology transformation. The chapter is organized into the following topics: Introduction; the current state of AI application in business; artificial intelligence and digital transformation; digital transformation in the business sector; business technology transformation through generative AI; opportunities on AI and business technology transformation; challenges on AI and business technology transformation; and future implications of AI synergy and digital transformation.

Taking into consideration the global market revenue of AI software, the average global revenues from 2018-2025 have reached $53 billion with the highest revenues expected to reach $126 billion in 2025. Moreover, the average growth rate from

2018-2025 accounted for 38.86% which can be considered a high growth ratio. Moreover, AI utilization has expanded tremendously encompassing various industries such as healthcare, banking, education, retail and e-commerce, manufacturing, tele-communications, etc. Considered a major contribution of AI in business operations includes but is not limited to simplifying operations, enhancing decision-making, and improving productivity. Specifically, using generative AI as one of a system under AI systems has transformed businesses digitally as it aids companies in the delivery of content production, product customization, development of product designs, elimination of job redundancy, and data escalation.

To navigate the complexities of the modern corporate environment and adapt to its ongoing evolutions, artificial intelligence (AI) and business processes work well together. This presents both new potential and problems in the areas of customer experiences, data management, and analysis. By utilizing AI, businesses may predict a future characterized by ground-breaking and sustainable growth, investigate deeper synergies, get beyond implementation roadblocks, and realize the enormous potential in real-world applications and upcoming advances in digital transformation for businesses. However, AI has its share of challenges that consist of ethical issues and implications, AI biases, possible job-employee job displacements, privacy and security, human dignity, and autonomy, etc. Weighing its advantages and disadvantages will be left to the businesses who decide their business operations. Companies progress to a higher position in the marketplace by taking advantage of AIs' full potential, supporting creativity and innovation, enhancing efficiency, and offering superior consumer encounters in the future by implementing these approaches. The AI-to-AI mechanisms have been seen to be a potential endeavor that works for any business operation though it was first emphasized in the healthcare sector, it is indicative of its applicability to the different sectors.

Lastly, one of the main contributions of this chapter is that it provides scenarios of how digital transformation has been implemented in various industries with their accompanying outcomes. It also outlines the emphasis on business technology transformation utilizing AI synergy by taking into consideration explaining the re-lationship between AI and digital transformation in business operations. Using AI, businesses can predict a future characterized by ground-breaking and sustainable growth, deeper synergy exploration, successful implementation of solutions, and realization of the enormous potential in real-world applications and future innova-tions in corporate digital transformation.

REFERENCES

Aliper, A., Plis, S., Artemov, A., Ulloa, A., Mamoshina, P., & Zhavoronkov, A. (2016). Deep learning applications for predicting pharmacological properties of drugs and drug repurposing using transcriptomic data. *Molecular Pharmaceutics*, 13(7), 2524–2530. DOI:10.1021/acs.molpharmaceut.6b00248 PMID:27200455

Arntz, M., Gregory, T., & Zierahn, U. (2016). The Risk of Automation for Jobs in OECD Countries: A Comparative Analysis. *OECD Social, Employment, and Migration Working Papers*. OECD Publishing Association for Advancement of Artificial Intelligence. https://aaai.org/

Bar, A. K., & Chaudhuri, A. K. (2023). Emotica.AI - a customer feedback system using AI. *International Research Journal on Advanced Science Hub*, 5(03), 103–110. DOI:10.47392/irjash.2023.019

Barocas, S., & Selbst, A. D. (2016). Big Data's Disparate Impact. *California Law Review*, 104(3), 671–732.

Bessen, J. E. (2019). AI and Jobs: The Role of Demand. *NBER Working Paper*, (24235).

Borges, A. F. S., Laurindo, F. J. B., Spínola, M. M., Gonçalves, R. F., & Mattos, C. A. (2021). The strategic use of artificial intelligence in the Digital Era: Systematic Literature Review and Future Research Directions. *International Journal of Information Management*, 57, 102225. DOI:10.1016/j.ijinfomgt.2020.102225

Bughin, J., Hazan, E., Ramaswamy, S., Chui, M., Allas, T., Dahlström, P., & Henke, N. (2017). *Artificial Intelligence: The Next Digital Frontier?* McKinsey Global Institute.

Cai, K., Zhu, Y., & Cao, J. (2020). The Application of Artificial Intelligence in the Banking Sector. In *2020 IEEE 3rd International Conference on Information Systems and Computer Aided Education (ICISCAE)* (pp. 439-442). IEEE.

Center for the Fourth Industrial Revolution. (2024). *We are a global platform focused on inclusive technology governance and responsible digital transformation*. WeForum. https://centres.weforum.org/centre-for-the-fourth-industrial-revolution/about

Chatterjee, S., Khorana, S., & Kizgin, H. (2022). Harnessing the potential of artificial intelligence to foster citizens' satisfaction: An empirical study on India. *Government Information Quarterly*, 39(4), 101621. DOI:10.1016/j.giq.2021.101621

Chen, M., Chiang, R. H., & Storey, V. C. (2012). Business Intelligence and Analytics: From Big Data to Big Impact. *Management Information Systems Quarterly*, 36(4), 1165–1188. DOI:10.2307/41703503

Chui, M., & Malhotra, S. (2018). *AI adoption advances, but foundational barriers remain*. McKinsey and company.

Cisco. (2021). *How AI is Transforming the Telecommunications Industry*. CISCO. https://www.cisco.com/c/en/us/products/collateral/se/internet-of-things/white-paper -c11-744544.html

Cremonesi, P., Koren, Y., & Turrin, R. (2011). Performance of recommender algorithms on top-on recommendation tasks. [TIST]. *ACM Transactions on Intelligent Systems and Technology*, 2(3), 1–17. DOI:10.1145/2870627

Daly, S. (2023). Intelligence in Business Digital Transformation. *Newer Tech*. https://www.neweratech.com/us/blog/role-of-artificial-intelligence-business-digital -transformation/

Davenport, T. H. (2018). *The AI advantage: How to put the artificial intelligence revolution to work*. MIT Press. DOI:10.7551/mitpress/11781.001.0001

Ekmekci, P. E., & Arda, B. (2020). History of Artificial Intelligence. In: *Artificial Intelligence and Bioethics*. Springer, Cham. DOI:10.1007/978-3-030-52448-7_1

Fildes, R., Goodwin, P., & Lawrence, M. (2019). The state of demand forecasting technology: Results of a global survey of forecasting practitioners. *International Journal of Forecasting*, 35(1), 103–114.

Floridi, L., Cowls, J., Beltrametti, M., Chatila, R., Chazerand, P., Dignum, V., & Engel, C. (2018). AI4People—an ethical framework for a good AI society: Opportunities, risks, principles, and recommendations. *Minds and Machines*, 28(4), 689–707. DOI:10.1007/s11023-018-9482-5 PMID:30930541

Haan, K., & Watts, R. (2023). How Businesses are using artificial intelligence in 2024. *Forbes*. https://www.forbes.com/advisor/business/software/ai-in-business/

He, J., Liu, Y., Song, M., He, H., & Jiang, T. (2017). *Learning to respond with deep neural networks for retrieval-based human-computer conversation system*. arXiv *preprintarXiv*:1709.00023.

Jia, F., Chen, J., Wu, T., & He, L. (2019). A Review of Artificial Intelligence Applications in the Manufacturing Sector. *IEEE Access : Practical Innovations, Open Solutions*, 7, 114490–114499.

Koedinger, K. R., Corbett, A. T., & Perfetti, C. (2012). The Knowledge-Learning-Instruction Framework: Bridging the Science-Practice Chasm to Enhance Robust Student Learning. *Cognitive Science*, 36(5), 757–798. DOI:10.1111/j.1551-6709.2012.01245.x PMID:22486653

Lee, J., Bagheri, B., & Kao, H. (2019). A Cyber-Physical Systems architecture for Industry 4.0 based manufacturing systems. *Manufacturing Letters*, 21, 64–69.

Liao, S. H., Chu, P. H., & Hsiao, P. Y. (2019). Data mining techniques and applications–A decade review from 2000 to 2011. *Expert Systems with Applications*, 39(12), 11303–11311. DOI:10.1016/j.eswa.2012.02.063

Liu, X., Chen, Q., Tsai, C. W., Gao, W., & Zhang, A. (2019). Integrating blockchain for data sharing and collaboration in mobile healthcare applications. *IEEE Access : Practical Innovations, Open Solutions*, 7, 36592–36606.

Loureiro, S. M. C., Guerreiro, J., & Tussyadiah, I. (2021). Artificial intelligence in business: State of the art and future research agenda. *Journal of Business Research*, 129, 911–926. DOI:10.1016/j.jbusres.2020.11.001

Luo, S., Xu, L., Xu, X., Zeng, Y., & Liu, Y. (2020). A Survey of Artificial Intelligence Applications in Smart Manufacturing. *Journal of Manufacturing Systems*, 56, 333–349.

Manyika, J., Lund, S., Chui, M., Bughin, J., Woetzel, J., Batra, P., & Sanghvi, S. (2017). Jobs lost; jobs gained: Workforce transitions in a time of automation. *McKinsey Global Institute*, 150(1), 1–148.

Mari, L. (2024). *AI Synergy – How AI collaborations are shaping the future*. Digital Health Global. https://www.digitalhealthglobal.com/ai-synergy-how-ai-collaborations-are-shaping-the-future/

Marr, B. (2021). How AI Is Revolutionizing Manufacturing In 2021. *Forbes*. https://www.forbes.com/sites/bernardmarr/2021/02/15/how-ai-is-revolutionizing-manufacturing-in-2021/?sh=3c3c64a65f3b

Martin, F. (2020). The Role of Artificial Intelligence in the Transformation of Higher Education. *EDUCAUSE Review*.

Mendelson, D. N. (2019). Applying AI in Banking, Investments, and Personal Finance. *California Management Review*, 61(4), 91–115.

Nambiar, R., Varma, V., & Chakraborty, T. (2020). AI in Banking: A Review of the Applications and Opportunities. In *International Conference on Intelligent Data Communication Technologies and Internet of Things* (pp. 381-390). Springer, Cham.

Saarikko, T., Westergren, U. H., & Blomquist, T. (2020). Digital transformation: Five recommendations for the digitally conscious firm. *Business Horizons*, 63(6), 825–839. DOI:10.1016/j.bushor.2020.07.005

Sarkis, J., Cohen, M. J., Dewick, P., & Schröder, P. (2021). Artificial intelligence and supply chain sustainability: A systematic review and agenda for future research. *Computers & Industrial Engineering*, 152, 107057.

Sestino, A., Prete, M. I., Piper, L., & Guido, G. (2020). Internet of Things and Big Data as enablers for business digitalization strategies. *Technovation*, 98, 102173. DOI:10.1016/j.technovation.2020.102173

Singh, S. (2024). *Generative AI: Accelerating Digital Transformation & Business Value. United States Artificial Intelligence Institute*. USAII. https://www.usaii.org/ai-insights/generative-ai-accelerating-digital-transformation-business-value

Tomašev, N., Glorot, X., Rae, J. W., Zielinski, M., Askham, H., Saraiva, A., & Ravuri, S. (2019). A clinically applicable approach to continuous prediction of future acute kidney injury. *Nature*, 572(7767), 116–119. DOI:10.1038/s41586-019-1390-1 PMID:31367026

VanLehn, K. (2011). The Relative Effectiveness of Human Tutoring, Intelligent Tutoring Systems, and Other Tutoring Systems. *Educational Psychologist*, 46(4), 197–221. DOI:10.1080/00461520.2011.611369

Verhoef, P. C., Broekhuizen, T., Bart, V., Bhattacharya, A., Qi Dong, J., Fabian, N., & Haenlein, M. (2021). Digital transformation: A multidisciplinary reflection and research agenda. *Journal of Business Research*, 122, 889–901. DOI:10.1016/j.jbusres.2019.09.022

World Economic Forum. (2022). *How digital tech can turbo-charge the social economy*. WEF. https://www.weforum.org/agenda/2022/05/how-digital-tech-turbo-charge-social-enterprises/

Chapter 8
Revolutionizing Financial Literacy Through Exploring Finfluencers' Intentions in Chatbot–Driven Financial Information Dissemination

Annie Issac
https://orcid.org/0000-0003-3921-2900
Christ University, Bangalore, India

R. Seranmadevi
Christ University, Bangalore, India

ABSTRACT

Financial literacy, a cornerstone for stability and empowerment in today's economic landscape, is set to be revolutionized. Finfluencers, individuals with significant financial acumen and a robust digital platform presence, are shaping audiences' financial attitudes and behaviors. This study introduces a conceptual framework based on the decomposed theory of planned behavior (DTPB) that holds the potential to transform how we understand and implement financial education. The unique aspect of this framework is its incorporation of Finfluencers as critical influencers in adopting AI chatbots for financial education. For instance, the model can predict the likelihood of a Finfluencer endorsing an AI chatbot for financial education based

DOI: 10.4018/979-8-3693-4187-2.ch008

on their attitudes, subjective norms, and perceived behavioral control. Despite the widespread use of DTPB across various disciplines, a research gap exists in understanding the determinants of intention and behavior concerning adopting AI chatbots for financial education.

INTRODUCTION

The dawn of the twenty-first century marks a pivotal juncture characterized by the seismic impact of the COVID-19 pandemic, delineating a clear demarcation between the pre-COVID and post-COVID epochs. As societies navigate this new landscape, technology has emerged as a cornerstone of resilience and adaptation, driving unprecedented transformations across global economies (Srisathan & Naruetharadhol, 2022). This accelerated adoption of advanced technologies, such as artificial intelligence (AI) and deep intelligence, signifies a profound shift towards a tech-centric civilization. This shift is characterized by the increasing integration of technology into various aspects of our lives, from healthcare and education to business operations. It is poised for remarkable progress and innovation. (McKinsey Global Surveys, 2021: A Year in Review, 2021)) report that the pandemic accelerated digital adoption by three to four years, significantly influencing healthcare, education, and business operations. AI-driven solutions like predictive analytics and telemedicine proved instrumental in managing the pandemic's challenges, optimizing resource allocation, and enhancing patient care (Chalutz Ben-Gal, 2023). In education, digital learning platforms ensure that students can continue their education despite school closures, highlighting the potential of technology to bridge gaps in access and quality of education (Dhawan, 2020). Likewise, AI in business facilitated process automation, improved decision-making, and enhanced customer service through innovations like chatbots and virtual assistants (Pendy, 2023). The pandemic underscored the critical need for resilient technological solutions, prompting increased investments in digital tools and innovations across industries to bolster operational continuity and adaptability (Brynjolfsson et al., 2020).

Concurrently, the pervasive influence of social media continues to permeate the fabric of contemporary existence, manifesting in multifaceted domains ranging from communication and information dissemination to entertainment, marketing, e-commerce, and virtual interactions. Social media platforms have become indispensable tools for real-time communication and engagement, facilitating global connectivity and community-building during periods of social distancing (Cinelli et al., 2020). The integration of AI and social media analytics has further amplified the impact of digital platforms, enabling businesses to personalize customer interactions, target specific demographics, and measure campaign effectiveness with unprecedented granularity. This transformative period highlights the necessity and potential of technology to drive societal resilience, economic recovery, and future growth in a post-pandemic world.

The COVID-19 pandemic has also brought financial wellness to the forefront, as many individuals have been exposed to economic downturns and financial insecurity (Anand et al., 2021). This exposure has highlighted the detrimental effects of financial illiteracy, exacerbating issues such as inadequate retirement savings, debt accumulation, and lack of insurance coverage (Naidu, 2017). A study by the (National Endowment for Financial Education and the Council for Economic Education Financial Education Policy Convening Initiative, 2021) found that 70% of Americans reported increased financial stress due to the pandemic, underscoring the urgent need for improved financial literacy. The Organization for Economic Co-operation and Development (OECD, 2011) defines financial literacy as skills, knowledge, attitudes, and behaviors necessary for sound financial decision-making and overall well-being. Financial literacy is essential for empowering individuals to make informed financial decisions, effectively manage risks, and plan for their future financial well-being (Prihartanti et al., 2022). However, despite its significance, formal education systems in many developing nations often struggle to promote financial literacy adequately, thus contributing to continued financial instability (Muliana et al., 2023).

In response to these needs and challenges in financial education, the rise of "finfluencers" – individuals who wield significant influence on social media platforms, focusing primarily on personal finance, investment strategies, and financial literacy – has emerged as a notable trend (Singh & Sarva, 2024). These finfluencers play a crucial role in sharing valuable insights, recommendations, and personal experiences to educate and empower their audience to make informed financial decisions, thus democratizing financial literacy and influencing consumer financial behavior through engaging content and real-time updates. Their influence is not just in disseminating financial knowledge but also in making complex financial concepts more understandable and relatable to their audience. According to a survey by The Financial Brand (2022), 65% of millennials and Gen Z follow at least one finfluencer on social media, indicating the significant impact these influencers have on younger generations. This influence is significant in the digital age, where traditional financial education methods may struggle to engage audiences effectively due to limited attention spans and prevalent information overload (Setiawan et al., 2022).

Integrating AI chatbots within financial literacy marks a significant stride forward, leveraging advancements in artificial intelligence and natural language processing. Recent years have witnessed remarkable progress in the development of chatbots, driven by advancements in artificial intelligence and natural language processing technologies (Gatzioufa & Saprikis, 2022). Chatbots, also known as artificial intelligence (AI) agents, can be characterized as "software entities facilitating automated communication through the application of natural language processing," (Farazouli et al., 2024). By leveraging machine learning algorithms, these AI agents enable real-time responses to financial inquiries, personalized budgeting advice, and tailored investment recommendations, thereby democratizing access to financial knowledge for individuals who may lack traditional avenues for financial counseling. Their ability to analyze user data ensures that advice is customized to individual financial circumstances, enhancing the relevance and effectiveness of financial guidance compared to conventional one-size-fits-all approaches.

Moreover, AI chatbots enhance financial literacy's accessibility, particularly in underserved communities and developing regions where traditional financial education resources are scarce. Accessible via smartphones and digital devices, AI chatbots bridge educational gaps by delivering financial knowledge remotely. This technological accessibility promotes financial inclusion globally and empowers users with the skills and confidence to navigate their financial futures effectively. As AI chatbots evolve, their role in making financial education engaging and understandable through interactive interfaces and personalized content delivery methods underscores their potential to transform how financial literacy is disseminated and embraced in the digital age.

The successful implementation of AI chatbots in financial education hinges significantly on the intentions and strategies of finfluencers tasked with leveraging this technology to disseminate financial knowledge. The integration of AI chatbots by finfluencers represents a critical yet underexplored area within influencer marketing and financial education, underscoring the pivotal role of finfluencers in shaping the future of financial education. While significant attention has been directed toward understanding the role of finfluencers in disseminating financial knowledge, more studies are needed to unravel the intricate web of factors influencing finfluencers' intentions toward adopting AI chatbots. Existing research has primarily focused on exploring finfluencers' attitudes and beliefs within the context of traditional financial education methods, overlooking the potential impact of AI chatbots on their strategies and practices.

By adapting and refining "The Decomposed Theory of Planned Behavior (DTPB) Model" to this context, research can significantly stride in understanding the nuances of technology adoption within the dynamic realm of finfluencer-led financial education initiatives. This study does not merely fill a research gap; it serves as a beacon, illuminating pathways for stakeholders navigating the ever-evolving landscape of influencer-driven financial literacy campaigns. Its meticulous examination of finfluencers' adoption intentions offers actionable insights that transcend individual strategies, empowering policymakers, administrators, and educators alike to craft policies and initiatives that harness the full potential of AI chatbots in fostering financial literacy. Furthermore, exploring the practical implications of integrating AI technology in financial education initiatives can contribute to broader discussions on innovation in education and inform transformative advancements in how financial literacy is disseminated and embraced in the digital age. Thus, this study sets the stage for future empirical research to test the proposed conceptual model and further elucidate the dynamics of AI chatbot adoption among finfluencers.

LITERATURE REVIEW

Evolution and Definitions of Financial Literacy

Financial literacy is recognized globally as a vital life skill essential for individual empowerment and fostering financial well-being at both personal and societal levels. (G20, 2021). The term "financial literacy" was first introduced by the Jumpstart Coalition for Personal Financial Literacy in 1997. It is defined as utilizing knowledge and skills effectively to manage financial resources for lifetime financial security (Ameer & Khan, 2020). Researchers have proposed various definitions to capture the multidimensional nature of financial literacy. According to the Organization for Economic Co-operation and Development (OECD), financial literacy includes the knowledge and skills necessary to comprehend risks, capabilities, motivation, and confidence crucial for financial prosperity, as well as the capacity to contribute to the economic vitality of one's business (Stolper & Walter, 2017). Other definitions emphasize the ability to make well-informed financial choices and manage financial resources effectively (Bojuwon et al., 2023). (Huston, 2010) characterized financial literacy as possessing the knowledge, awareness, and practical capability to apply financial understanding in everyday situations. (Marinov, 2023) described it as a multidimensional construct comprising awareness, knowledge, skills, attitudes, and behaviors. (Lusardi and Mitchell, 2014) Defined financial literacy as analyzing economic information and making informed decisions regarding financial planning, wealth accumulation, debt management, and retirement. (U.S. National Strategy for Financial Literacy, 2020) described financial literacy as the abilities, information, and resources that empower individuals to make personalized financial decisions to achieve their objectives.

Need or Importance of Financial Literacy

Financial literacy is crucial for various aspects of individuals' lives, beginning with the need for young people to develop financial knowledge and skills to establish saving habits and prevent financial problems (Mohta & Shunmugasundaram,

2022). Early financial literacy education is essential for economic development, potentially leading to increased wealth, financial security, and economic growth (Amonhaemanon, 2024). Technological advancements have expanded access to financial products, requiring consumers to possess sufficient financial knowledge for informed decision-making. Additionally, regulatory changes emphasize individual responsibility for sound financial management, underscoring the importance of active engagement in personal finance (Bhandare et al., 2021). (Grohmann et al., 2018) found a significant link between financial literacy and inclusion, indicating a positive influence on economic development. Their study, encompassing 119 countries, revealed that financial literacy can enhance economic growth. Furthermore, (Effendi et al., 2021) demonstrated that financial well-being positively influences GDP growth, which is improved by financial literacy components such as financial behavior, attitude, and knowledge.

Financial literacy is vital for sustainable financial well-being and investment behavior. Research has shown that financial literacy strongly and positively correlates with active investment behavior, which may affect wealth accumulation and long-term financial well-being (Lusardi & Mitchell, 2023a). For instance, studies conducted in Japan and Singapore found that financial literacy levels are generally low, yet it significantly impacts investment behavior and financial well-being (Bayram & Palese, 2022; Perdanasari et al., 2019). Moreover, financial education is fundamental to understanding the need to combat climate change, especially among rural populations (S. et al., 2021). Teachers' roles in providing age-appropriate financial literacy materials are crucial for students' future financial management (Perdanasari et al., 2019). Financial literacy is necessary to avoid financial problems and enhance financial behavior and inclusion, contributing to a sustainable financial future (Damayanti et al., 2018).

Determinants of Financial Literacy

Several factors determine the level of financial literacy. Financial education is the primary determinant, as highlighted by the OECD 2020 report, which emphasizes the importance of financial knowledge in enabling individuals to make well-informed financial decisions (OECD/INFE 2020 International Survey of Adult Financial Literacy, 2020). Financial behavior, including budgeting, saving, investing, and borrowing habits, is another crucial determinant (Khalisharani et al., 2022). Socioeconomic factors such as education level, income, age, gender, and cultural background also significantly influence financial literacy levels (Ndou, 2023). Typically, individuals with higher education and income levels exhibit greater financial literacy, while younger individuals and males tend to demonstrate higher literacy levels (Wagner, 2019). Access to financial education and resources, such as formal education and financial advisors, also positively impacts financial literacy levels (Okello. et al., 2020).

Consequences of Financial Illiteracy

Financial illiteracy has profound consequences across various dimensions. It leads to poor financial decision-making, instability, and debt accumulation (Lusardi & Mitchell, 2011). Individuals lacking financial literacy often struggle with budgeting, managing debt responsibly, and planning for long-term financial goals such as retirement, resulting in heightened financial stress and reduced overall well-being (Lusardi & Mitchell, 2023b). Moreover, financial illiteracy exacerbates socioeconomic inequalities, particularly affecting vulnerable groups with limited access to financial education and resources (Sconti & Fernandez, 2023). This can lead to higher exposure to predatory lending practices and financial scams, perpetuating cycles of poverty and financial insecurity (Klapper et al., 2013). At a macroeconomic level, countries with low levels of financial literacy experience slower economic growth and greater financial instability, with individual financial missteps amplifying systemic risks during economic downturns (Dunn, 2023). Addressing financial illiteracy through comprehensive education and policy interventions is crucial for promoting economic development, reducing disparities, and fostering a financially resilient society.

The Influence of Social Media Influencers

In recent years, the global presence of social media has experienced remarkable growth, with internet users worldwide reaching 5.44 billion as of April 2024, constituting approximately 67.1 percent of the global population and 5.07 billion individuals actively engaging with various social media platforms. (DataReportal, 2024). This surge in social media usage underscores its pervasive influence on modern communication and interaction. Concurrently, there has been a notable proliferation of social media influencers who regularly utilize these platforms to express opinions and critiques on various topics, such as lifestyle, health, and beauty, as well as objects like brands, services, and products(Lajnef, 2023). These influencers significantly shape consumer behaviors and preferences by fostering authentic relationships and meaningful engagement(Kaukab et al., 2023). Trust, relatability, and authenticity characterize the symbiotic bond between social media influencers and their followers (Gurrieri et al., 2023). Followers perceive influencers as genuine individuals offering valuable insights and recommendations from personal experiences and expertise, influencing consumer decisions from product purchases to lifestyle choices(Agnihotri et al., 2023).

Emergence of Finfluencers

Social media platforms have revolutionized the dissemination of financial education by providing accessible and interactive channels for individuals to enhance their financial literacy (Shvaher et al., 2021). In this rapidly evolving digital landscape, social media has transitioned from primarily an entertainment platform to a significant financial and investment information source (Singh Khurana, 2023). This shift has given rise to a new category of influencers, known as financial influencers or "finfluencers," who play a pivotal role in shaping financial decisions through promotions or recommendations on social media platforms (Guan, 2022). Finfluencers leverage social media platforms to provide insights, tips, and guidance on personal finance, empowering their followers to make informed financial decisions. They utilize platforms like Instagram, YouTube, and TikTok to disseminate engaging content formats such as videos, blogs, and interactive posts, making complex financial concepts more digestible and relatable.

Challenges and Ethical Considerations in Finfluencer Content

The emergence of finfluencers has significantly contributed to democratizing financial knowledge and enhancing financial literacy among the public. However, concerns regarding transparency, ethics, and the reliability of financial advice on social media have surfaced. Many finfluencers lack formal qualifications in finance, raising questions about the accuracy and credibility of their information. (Parthasarthy, 2023). The potential for conflicts of interest due to lucrative brand partnerships further undermines the integrity of their recommendations. In response, regulatory bodies like the Securities and Exchange Board of India (SEBI) have tightened restrictions and promoted greater transparency and accountability among finfluencers (Tiwari, 2024). Efforts to enhance financial literacy among finfluencers and their followers are underway to ensure a more informed audience. SEBI has raised concerns about finfluencers misleading the audience with unsolicited opinions on investment and stock trading. The regulatory body's consultation paper aims to address this issue, proposing penalization for unregistered entities using the name of SEBI-registered entities and making it mandatory for finfluencers to display their registration number alongside their name and qualifications. The guidelines also clarify that financial advice influencers must possess appropriate credentials, such as a license from the Insurance Regulatory and Development Authority of India (IRDAI) or be a qualified chartered accountant. (Burugula, 2024).

Influence of Finfluencers on Market Dynamics

Recent research on finfluencers, or finance influencers, highlights their growing impact on financial markets and investor behavior. (Vu et al,2022) investigate the dynamics of parasocial relationships between finfluencers and their followers, revealing how these relationships influence satisfaction and behaviors among followers, thereby shaping market sentiment. Similarly, (Oosting, 2022) explores the influence of finfluencers on stock prices, finding that while they promote specific stocks in their content, their actual manipulation capacity over market dynamics is limited, underscoring the complexities of their influence in financial markets.

Role of Finfluencers in Enhancing Financial Literacy

Studies by (Chikhi, 2021) and (Kedvarin Saengchote, 2023) explores the role of social media platforms, particularly Instagram and YouTube, in fostering financial literacy through finfluencer content. Chikhi discusses the broader societal implications of finfluencer content beyond immediate investment decisions, emphasizing its potential to educate diverse audiences on financial matters. Meanwhile, Kedvarin and Saengchote analyze how YouTube finfluencers influence market sentiment, particularly in speculative areas like cryptocurrency, showcasing the power of these influencers in shaping consumer behavior and financial decisions.

Impact of Finfluencer Content on Consumer Behaviour

(van Reijmersdal & Hudders, 2023) Examine the effects of warning videos about investing in shares on young adults, revealing complex outcomes such as altered perceptions of financial security and improved financial decision-making. (Manfredo, 2024) advocates for regulatory measures to enhance transparency and accountability among finfluencers, addressing ethical concerns about their influence on financial decision-making. Additionally, (Ahuja & Grover, 2023) investigate how excessive social media usage impacts Generation Z's investment intentions, highlighting the role of finfluencers in shaping financial attitudes and behaviors among younger demographics.

Consumer Perceptions and Reactions to Finfluencer Content

(de Regt et al., 2023) analyze Instagram content from personal finance influencers, exploring how factors like gender and race moderate perceptions of financial expertise and influence consumer responses to product recommendations. (Canatan et al., 2023) Identify trust-based determinants and financial literacy as significant influencers of viewer attitudes towards online financial content created by finfluencers, illustrating the multifaceted nature of consumer interactions with finfluencer-driven financial advice.

Integration and Capabilities of AI and Chatbots

AI is progressively woven into our daily routines by developing and utilizing intelligent software and hardware, known as intelligent agents, capable of performing various tasks, from mundane chores to complex operations (Adamopoulou & Moussiades, 2020). These intelligent agents, powered by AI, have become integral to modern technology, facilitating automation, decision-making, and problem-solving across diverse domains(S. et al. et al., 2024). Chatbots emerge as notable examples among these AI-driven systems, embodying the fusion of artificial intelligence with human-computer interaction. Chatbots, as AI-powered software applications, can replicate human conversational interactions. Through sophisticated algorithms and Natural Language Processing (NLP) techniques, chatbots can interpret user queries, engage in meaningful conversations, and provide relevant responses, all without human intervention. This capability makes chatbots indispensable in various contexts, from customer service and support to personal assistance and information retrieval. Moreover, chatbots represent a fundamental aspect of intelligent Human-Computer Interaction (HCI), demonstrating how AI technologies can enhance communication between humans and machines (Khanna et al., 2015). Chatbots bridge the gap between users and computer systems by simulating intelligent responses in text or voice interactions, enabling intuitive and user-friendly interactions.

However, despite their numerous advantages, chatbots also present certain limitations that must be addressed. For instance, while chatbots excel at handling routine inquiries and tasks with speed and accuracy, they may struggle with understanding complex queries or nuances in language (Sitthipon et al., 2022). Additionally, chatbots often lack emotional intelligence, limiting their ability to provide empathetic responses or understand the emotional context of user interactions. Furthermore, the widespread adoption of chatbots raises data privacy and security concerns. As chatbots collect and process user data to improve their performance and personalize responses, there is a risk of data breaches or unauthorized access to sensitive information (Labadze et al., 2023). Ensuring robust data protection measures and compliance with privacy regulations is crucial to mitigating these risks and building trust in chatbot systems.

Applications of AI Chatbots in the Financial Sector

Chatbots serve as valuable tools across multiple domains such as education, business and e-commerce, healthcare, and entertainment, with their applications extending even to finance, where they streamline customer interactions and offer personalized financial assistance. The latest comprehensive review on artificial intelligence in finance reveals that numerous research papers utilize AI for predictive purposes, including forecasting stock prices, performance, and volatility, as well as for classification problems and warning systems to detect credit risk and fraud. These applications extend to classifying firms based on qualitative and quantitative data, developing warning systems for identifying unusual transactions, and employing text mining and sentiment analysis for behavioral analysis. Additionally, popular aspects of AI in finance include trading models, algorithmic trading, growing interest in robo-advisory services, and exploring the modeling capabilities of algorithms and traditional machine-learning techniques (Bahoo et al., 2024).

The emergence of chatbots in the finance sector represents the latest disruptive force that has transformed customer interactions. AI chatbots are increasingly utilized in the finance sector to improve efficiency, decision-making, and customer satisfaction (Ghandour,2021). AI chatbots in finance can automate tasks, enhance accessibility, and provide various features to customers (S. Kiruthika et al., 2023). AI chatbots are rapidly transforming the financial sector landscape, expanding their applications beyond banking to encompass insurance, stock trading, and retail finance (Wube et al., 2022). Leveraging natural language processing, artificial intelligence, and machine learning techniques (Kooli, 2023), these chatbots serve as virtual assistants in insurance, facilitating policy inquiries, claims processing, and personalized recommendations based on individual risk profiles (Nuruzzaman & Hussain, 2020). In stock trading, AI chatbots offer real-time market insights, investment advice, and portfolio management assistance, utilizing advanced algorithms to analyze market trends and execute trades on behalf of clients (Pattnaik et al., 2024). Furthermore, in retail finance, these chatbots automate routine tasks and provide round-the-clock support for account inquiries, fund transfers, and bill payments, enhancing accessibility and convenience for customers (Khan & Rabbani, 2020) (Cîmpeanu et al., 2023). As technology advances, AI chatbots will play a pivotal role in driving innovation, efficiency, and customer satisfaction across the financial industry.

THEORETICAL FOUNDATION: DECOMPOSED THEORY OF PLANNED BEHAVIOUR

Technology adoption is selecting technology for use by individuals or organizations(Gangaiamaran & Anil Premraj, 2020). Various models have been proposed to predict intentions toward adopting information technology (IT), including the Diffusion of Innovation Theory, Theory of Reasoned Action, Theory of Planned Behavior (TPB), Social Cognitive Theory, Technical Adoption Model, Unified Theory of Acceptance and Use of Technology, and the Decomposed Theory of Planned Behavior (DTPB)(Lai, 2017). Among these models, TPB and its extension, DTPB, have gained considerable attention for their effectiveness in anticipating technology adoption across diverse domains.

(Taylor & Todd, 1995), introduced DTPB, expanding on the TPB framework to provide a more complex view of behavior. DTPB combines elements of the Innovation Diffusion Theory with the Technology Acceptance Model, offering insights into how individual attitudes influence technology adoption. Rooted in the Theory of Reasoned Action (TRA) by Icek Ajzen and Martin Fishbein and later extended into TPB (Ajzen, 1991), DTPB introduces a nuanced perspective by decomposing key constructs and incorporating additional variables. Unlike TPB, DTPB breaks down constructs into more specific, multidimensional belief structures, allowing for a finer-grained analysis of intention and behavior antecedents, thereby enhancing predictive power and explanatory depth.

Research suggests that DTPB outperforms TPB and other models in predicting technology adoption intentions. For example, Taylor and Todd's study (1995) found that DTPB predicts the intention to use internet-based services better than TPB(Shih & Fang, 2004). Composing critical factors and including normative and control beliefs account for more significant variance in behavioral intention. One of DTPB's strengths lies in its comprehensive nature, incorporating elements from other theoretical models like TAM and Innovation Diffusion Theory. For instance, including compatibility and ease of use factors from TAM enhances DTPB's applicability to technology adoption contexts.

DTPB has been applied across diverse domains, including healthcare, education, mobile commerce, and finance, with promising results (Kanimozhi & Selvarani, 2019). In healthcare, DTPB has been used to understand factors influencing patients' intentions to adopt telemedicine services (Ooi et al., 2024), while in the financial technology (Fintech) sector, the Decomposed Theory of Planned Behavior (DTPB) has been effectively utilized to investigate the factors influencing consumers' adoption of various financial innovations, including mobile payment systems, cryptocurrencies, online banking services, and investment platforms (A. et al., 2023). In the education sector, the Decomposed Theory of Planned Behavior (DTPB) is applied to understand the factors influencing students' and educators' adoption of e-learning technologies and digital educational tools (Chien et al., 2018) (Nyasulu & Dominic Chawinga, 2019). DTPB distinguishes between attitudinal, normative, and control beliefs, each comprising subdivisions, enabling a precise examination of factors shaping behavioral intentions and actions(Durac & Moga, 2023). Attitudinal beliefs encompass perceived usefulness, compatibility, and ease of use, drawing from innovation diffusion theory. Based on interpersonal behavior theory, normative beliefs are divided into peer and superior influences. Control beliefs, rooted in self-efficacy theory, are decomposed into self-efficacy and resource-facilitating conditions. Figure 1 illustrates the Decomposed Theory of Planned Behavior (Ghani et al., 2017).

Figure 1. Decomposed theory of planned behaviour

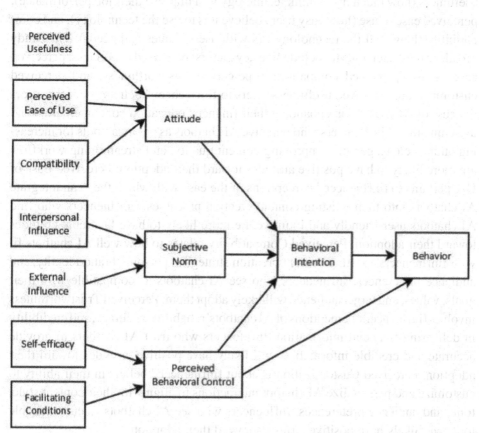

CONCEPTUAL MODEL FOR FINFLUENCERS
TO IMPLEMENT AI CHATBOTS

This study customizes the Decomposed Theory of Planned Behavior (DTPB) framework to include factors unique to finfluencers' intent to use AI chatbots. The model aims to explain finfluencer behavior by investigating the interaction of beliefs, attitudes, intentions, and actual behavior in the context of adopting chatbots for financial education. Using Taylor and Todd's (1995) approach, the essential elements of attitudes, subjective norms, and perceived behavioral control are broadened to better capture the factors influencing individual intentions to accept AI chatbots among finfluencers.

Three main factors influence attitudes towards technology adoption: perceived usefulness (how much users think technology will improve their job performance), perceived ease of use (how easy users believe it is to use the technology), and compatibility (how well the technology fits with users' values and needs). This study broadens these elements to include five key factors: perceived usefulness, perceived ease of use, perceived compatibility, perceived trustworthiness, and perceived customization. Perceived usefulness refers to finfluencers' beliefs about the effectiveness of AI chatbots in enhancing their financial education content creation and dissemination. Finfluencers who perceive AI chatbots as practical tools for increasing audience engagement, improving content quality, and streamlining workflow are more likely to have positive attitudes toward their adoption. Perceived Ease of Use pertains to finfluencers' perceptions of the ease with which they can integrate AI chatbots into their existing content creation processes. Finfluencers who find AI chatbots user-friendly and intuitive are more likely to have favorable attitudes toward their adoption. Perceived Compatibility relates to how well AI chatbots fit with finfluencers' existing content creation strategies, personal brand identity, and audience preferences. Influencers who see AI chatbots as compatible with their goals, values, and target audience will likely adopt them. Perceived Trustworthiness involves finfluencers' perceptions of AI chatbots' reliability, accuracy, and credibility in delivering financial information. Influencers who trust AI chatbots to provide accurate and credible information will likely have positive attitudes toward their adoption. Perceived Customization is about finfluencers' beliefs in their ability to customize and personalize AI chatbot interactions to align with their content style, tone, and audience preferences. Influencers who see AI chatbots as customizable tools will likely have positive attitudes toward their adoption.

Subjective norms encompass two components: peer influence and authority influence, as outlined by (Taylor & Todd, 1995) Subjective norms in this context encompass peer influence, industry trends, and authority influence. Peer Influence means that finfluencers are swayed by the endorsements and recommendations of their peers within the financial education community. Positive endorsements from influential finfluencers who have successfully integrated AI chatbots can enhance perceptions of their credibility and effectiveness, thus influencing adoption intentions. Industry Trends refer to the broader trends and developments in adopting AI chatbots in financial education. Positive indications of AI chatbots' increasing popularity, adoption rates, and success stories within the industry can create a sense of social pressure and legitimacy, encouraging finfluencers to adopt similar technologies to stay competitive and relevant. Authority Influence involves the impact of opinions and insights from thought leaders, financial experts, and technology experts. Endorsements and recommendations from respected figures regarding the benefits and advantages of AI chatbots can bolster finfluencers' confidence in adopting these technologies.

Behavioral control involves self-efficacy and conditions facilitating resources, such as access to capital and technology(Durac & Moga, 2023). Behavioral control in the context of chatbot implementation involves self-efficacy, resource-facilitating conditions, and technology-facilitating conditions. Self-efficacy refers to finfluencers' confidence in navigating and utilizing AI chatbots effectively. Resource-facilitating conditions include access to capital, reliable internet access, and dedicated time for financial learning, which can motivate finfluencers to adopt chatbots. Technology-facilitating conditions pertain to user-friendly interfaces and compatibility.

Figure 2. Conceptual model for finfluencers to implement AI chatbots

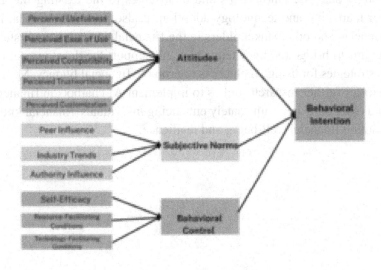

Research Gap

The current state of research into financial influencers (finfluencers) is uncharted territory. This study aims to fill this gap by providing new insights into how finfluencers employ AI chatbots to disseminate financial information. While substantial research exists on influencers across various domains, such as beauty, food, travel, and sports, there is a noticeable lack of understanding of the influencer phenomenon in the financial sector, particularly in adopting AI chatbots for financial literacy.

Despite the growing prominence of finfluencers in shaping financial behaviors and literacy, there is limited academic focus on this niche. Most studies have examined influencers in more visually appealing and lifestyle-oriented industries, leaving the financial sector relatively unexplored. Previous empirical research on chatbot adoption has predominantly concentrated on customer service, banking, insurance, and e-commerce (Gatzioufa & Saprikis, 2022). There is a lack of investigation into how AI chatbots can be integrated into financial education, specifically by finfluencers, who play a crucial role in disseminating financial knowledge and advice to the public.

This study is the first to develop a framework explicitly tailored for using chatbots to enhance financial literacy. By applying the Decomposed Theory of Planned Behavior (DTPB), this research aims to uncover the determinants influencing finfluencers' inclination to incorporate AI chatbots. The primary purpose of this study is to develop a framework for the scope of finfluencers to implement AI chatbots for enhancing financial literacy initiatives in future studies.

This study addresses these gaps and contributes to the existing literature on influencer marketing and technology adoption. It also provides practical insights for finfluencers and other stakeholders in the financial education ecosystem. This research aims to bridge the knowledge gap and support the development of more effective strategies for using AI chatbots to promote financial literacy. Moreover, it seeks to foster further research studies to implement AI chatbots in financial education and other core areas, ultimately enhancing individuals' financial knowledge and promoting financial well-being and resilience.

RESEARCH METHODOLOGY

Objectives

1. To examine the existing literature on financial literacy, finfluencer studies, AI chatbots, and the Decomposed Theory of Planned Behavior (DTPB) to develop a comprehensive model for future studies aimed at adopting AI chatbots for finfluencers.
2. Develop a conceptual framework to elucidate the factors impacting finfluencers' inclination towards integrating chatbots, leveraging the Decomposed Theory of Planned Behavior (DTPB).

Research Problem

A recent study conducted by SEBI found that only 27% of India's population possesses sufficient financial literacy, indicating a significant deficit in financial knowledge and awareness among the majority (Afaqs, 2024). This is particularly concerning given that forecasts indicate India will experience the fastest GDP growth over the next decade. (Majumdar, 2024)However, without the necessary financial literacy, the nation's citizens may not be able to fully capitalize on this substantial economic potential.

The COVID-19 pandemic has catalyzed a significant shift in the financial education landscape, giving rise to a new class of influencers known as "finfluencers."These individuals act as intermediaries, making complex financial concepts more accessible and relatable to the general public, thereby enhancing financial literacy across diverse audiences.

AI chatbots augment finfluencer-driven financial literacy initiatives. They offer personalized interactions, 24/7 accessibility, interactive learning experiences, and data-driven insights, making financial education more engaging and effective. This innovative combination of finfluencers and AI chatbots has the potential to democratize financial education by broadening its reach and impact, making it accessible and engaging for users worldwide.

This study examines the factors influencing the adoption of AI chatbots among finfluencers through an implementation readiness assessment. By integrating the Decomposed Theory of Planned Behavior, this research seeks to fill gaps in the current literature and provide a comprehensive understanding of the determinants driving finfluencers' decisions to adopt AI chatbots. The insights gained from this study will inform the development of strategies to enhance the effectiveness of financial education, ensuring that more individuals can benefit from the economic opportunities presented by India's rapid growth.

Research Design

This study has devised a conceptual framework that centers on Attitudes, Subjective norms, Perceived behavioral control, and their antecedents, specifically tailored to scrutinize the implementation decisions undertaken by finfluencers within the realm of financial education. Grounded in the theoretical framework of the Decomposed Theory of Planned Behavior, this conceptual model serves as a foundation for understanding the dynamics influencing finfluencers' adoption intentions of AI chatbots.

To evaluate the robustness of this framework, further research initiatives are underway, primarily involving collecting data through interviews conducted with finfluencers. Interviews are chosen as the preferred method due to their effectiveness in delving into each participant's nuanced perspectives, experiences, beliefs, and motivations, as highlighted by (P. Gill et al., 2008).

The survey questions utilized in these interviews will be adapted from previous DTPB surveys. They will primarily focus on comprehending the intentions of influencers regarding the implementation of chatbots while also identifying additional antecedents relevant to influencer adoption intention of AI chatbots. The target population for this study consists of financial influencers actively disseminating financial content across various social media platforms.

Qualitative data from participants' open-ended responses will undergo content analysis, employing an analytical approach that categorizes responses based on predefined coding categories derived from initial thematic analysis. The content analysis serves as a valuable technique, enabling the description and inference of aspects related to readiness that significantly influence the adoption decisions of finfluencers.

Theoretical Implications

By integrating the Decomposed Theory of Planned Behavior into the study of chatbot adoption among finfluencers, this research contributes to developing and refining the theoretical framework. It elucidates how attitudes, subjective norms, and perceived behavioral control influence influencers' readiness to adopt AI-driven chatbots for financial content dissemination. Additionally, this research explores the dynamic capabilities of natural language processing and machine learning in shaping practical financial education tools. By incorporating these technological advancements into the theoretical framework, the study offers insights into how AI-driven chatbots can be leveraged to enhance financial literacy initiatives.

Moreover, the study extends the application of DTPB theory to social media influencer studies, highlighting the relevance and applicability of this theoretical framework in understanding influencers' adoption behaviors in emerging digital contexts. By focusing on adopting AI-driven chatbots for financial education purposes, this research contributes to the broader field of financial education research. It underscores the importance of innovative technological solutions in addressing the challenges of financial literacy and consumer engagement in the digital age.

Furthermore, this research contributes to emerging research in finfluencers because finfluencers are the future of the financial world. Regulatory authorities like SEBI and others frame rules and regulations to promote influencers and financial literacy. This research serves as the foundation for advanced studies in various areas related to finfluencers, paving the way for further exploration and understanding of their role in shaping financial education and consumer behavior.

Practical Implications

The practical implications of this conceptual framework extend across various stakeholders within the financial education landscape. For finfluencers, implementing AI-driven chatbots, as outlined in this conceptual framework, presents a remarkable opportunity to enhance their educational outreach and engagement with followers. By integrating chatbots into their content strategy, finfluencers can offer personalized financial guidance, answer queries, and provide real-time support to their audience. Chatbots enable finfluencers to streamline content dissemination and interact with followers more efficiently, strengthening their influence and credibility within the financial education community. Additionally, chatbots empower finfluencers to automate routine tasks and focus on creating high-quality educational content that resonates with their followers.

Followers, or consumers, stand to benefit significantly from the adoption of AI-driven chatbots by finfluencers. Through these chatbots, followers access personalized financial advice, tailored recommendations, and interactive learning experiences. Chatbots offer followers the convenience of 24/7 access to financial education materials, allowing them to learn at their own pace and convenience. This accessibility is particularly beneficial for individuals with busy schedules or limited access to traditional educational resources. Additionally, chatbots can help followers make more informed financial decisions by providing real-time support and guidance based on their unique financial goals and preferences.

Regulatory organizations play a crucial role in promoting the adoption of AI-driven chatbots for financial education. By providing guidance and support to finfluencers, followers, and financial institutions, regulatory organizations can ensure that these technologies comply with relevant regulations and standards. Regulatory organizations can advocate for the inclusion of financial education requirements in school curricula and workplace training programs, further promoting the adoption of chatbots as a means of advancing financial literacy and inclusion. Additionally, regulatory organizations can collaborate with other stakeholders to develop policies and initiatives that support the responsible use of AI-driven chatbots in financial education.

Financial institutions and organizations can leverage AI-driven chatbots to enhance their financial literacy initiatives and consumer engagement efforts. By incorporating chatbots into their educational platforms, financial institutions can provide personalized financial guidance and support to consumers at scale. Chatbots enable financial institutions to streamline the delivery of financial education materials, offer real-time assistance to users seeking information or advice, and collect valuable data on user interactions and preferences. This data can inform the development of tailored educational content and improve the overall effectiveness of financial education efforts.

Fintech companies are well-positioned to develop innovative chatbot solutions that meet the evolving needs of finfluencers, followers, and financial institutions. Fintech companies can create more intelligent and intuitive financial education tools by incorporating advanced natural language processing and machine learning capabilities into their chatbot platforms. These tools can offer personalized recommendations, interactive learning experiences, and real-time support to users, enhancing the overall effectiveness of financial education efforts. Additionally, fintech companies can collaborate with other stakeholders to integrate their chatbot solutions into existing educational platforms, further expanding their reach and impact in the financial education ecosystem.

FUTURE DIRECTION FOR RESEARCHERS

Future research in financial literacy and technology integration offers promising avenues for scholars to explore. Firstly, empirical validation of proposed conceptual frameworks, mainly through qualitative studies among finfluencers, is essential to refine models and identify additional factors relevant to integrating AI chatbots into financial literacy initiatives. Subsequently, quantitative research can explore the adoption of AI-driven chatbots by finfluencers, utilizing established conceptual models to discern influencing factors and assess their impact on financial literacy outcomes through adapted questionnaires.

Further avenues for investigation include understanding followers' intentions to engage with chatbot-driven financial education content, whether through quantitative surveys or experimental studies, to unveil underlying mechanisms of user engagement and behavior change. Comparative studies can be undertaken to assess the effectiveness of chatbot interventions against traditional educational methods or alternative technological solutions, providing valuable insights for practitioners and policymakers. Additionally, exploring moderating and mediating variables such as personalization, trust, and technology acceptance can shed light on their effects on chatbot interventions and financial literacy outcomes.

Cross-cultural studies are also warranted to examine cultural nuances in financial education and chatbot adoption, enabling the development of culturally sensitive solutions for diverse audiences. Longitudinal research is essential to assess the long-term impact of chatbot interventions on financial knowledge, attitudes, and behaviors, elucidating sustained behavior change and educational outcomes over time. Moreover, experimental studies can investigate optimal design features and intervention strategies of chatbots to maximize user engagement, learning outcomes, and retention of financial concepts.

Ethical and privacy considerations surrounding AI-driven chatbots in financial education must also be addressed, including user perceptions of privacy, data security, and regulatory compliance. Collaborative research efforts with stakeholders such as financial institutions, educators, policymakers, and community organizations can facilitate the co-design and implementation of chatbot solutions to tackle real-world challenges and promote financial literacy on a global scale. These avenues of inquiry hold promise for advancing our understanding of the role of technology in enhancing financial literacy and improving financial well-being across diverse populations.

CONCLUSION

Despite the growing acknowledgment of finfluencers' potential impact in reshaping the financial landscape, a substantial research gap persists in understanding their pivotal role. This gap becomes even more critical as regulatory bodies like the Securities and Exchange Board of India (SEBI) actively formulate regulations to enhance transparency in finfluencers' operations and utilize them as valuable resources for financial literacy education. This study, grounded in the Decomposed Theory of Planned Behavior (DTPB), addresses this research gap by developing a theoretical framework to illuminate finfluencers' intentions regarding implementing AI chatbots.

Through an extensive literature review, the author proposes a comprehensive framework incorporating antecedents such as attitude, subjective norms, and perceived behavioral control. While DTPB originated in information systems research, its adaptability to studying consumer behavior in diverse contexts, including financial services, underscores its practicality and relevance. Although the proposed framework remains theoretical and untested empirically, its primary goal is to contribute to the current literature on finfluencers and enhance their capabilities in promoting financial literacy. Acknowledging its limitations, future research endeavors should prioritize empirical validation and incorporate additional variables of interest.

Furthermore, this study transcends theoretical exploration by delving into the empirical investigation through data collection, specifically focusing on evaluating the effectiveness of AI chatbots in augmenting financial literacy through direct engagement with finfluencers. As the world increasingly embraces digitalization, this research delves into the feasibility of integrating AI into financial literacy efforts and explores how technology can facilitate informed financial decision-making. Ultimately, this research contributes to broader initiatives promoting economic empowerment, stability, and enhanced financial literacy by understanding effective strategies for leveraging technology, especially in the post-pandemic era.

REFERENCES

Adamopoulou, E., & Moussiades, L. (2020). An Overview of Chatbot Technology. *IFIP Advances in Information and Communication Technology,* 373–383. DOI:10.1007/978-3-030-49186-4_31

Agnihotri, D., Chaturvedi, P., Kulshreshtha, K., & Tripathi, V. (2023). Investigating the impact of authenticity of social media influencers on followers' purchase behavior: Mediating analysis of parasocial interaction on Instagram. *Asia Pacific Journal of Marketing and Logistics,* 35(10), 2377–2394. DOI:10.1108/APJML-07-2022-0598

Ahuja, S., & Grover, K. (2023). Excessive Use of Social Networking Sites and Intention to Invest in Stock Market among Gen Z: A Parallel Mediation Model. *Journal of Content, Community, and Communication,* 17(9), 63–79. DOI:10.31620/JCCC.06.23/06

Ajzen, I. (1991). The theory of planned behavior. *Organizational Behavior and Human Decision Processes,* 50(2), 179–211. DOI:10.1016/0749-5978(91)90020-T

Ameer, R., & Khan, R. (2020). Financial Socialization, Financial Literacy, and Financial Behavior of Adults in New Zealand. *Financial Counseling and Planning,* 31(2), 313–329. DOI:10.1891/JFCP-18-00042

Amonhaemanon, D. (2024). Financial stress and gambling motivation: The importance of financial literacy. *Review of Behavioral Finance,* 16(2), 248–265. DOI:10.1108/RBF-01-2023-0026

Anand, S., Mishra, K., Verma, V., & Taruna, T. (2021). Financial literacy mediates personal financial health during COVID-19: A structural equation modeling approach. *Emerald Open Research,* 2. DOI:10.1108/EOR-04-2023-0006

Azhar, K. A., Shah, Z., & Ahmed, H. (2023). HOW DO SOCIAL MEDIA INFLUENCERS DRIVE CONSUMER BEHAVIOUR? *Pakistan Journal of International Affairs,* 6(2). DOI:10.52337/pjia.v6i2.943

Bahoo, S., Cucculelli, M., Goga, X., & Mondolo, J. (2024). Artificial intelligence in Finance: A comprehensive review through bibliometric and content analysis. *SN Business & Economics,* 4(2), 23. DOI:10.1007/s43546-023-00618-x

Bayram, A., & Palese, A. (2022). The importance of financial literacy in nursing. *Obzornik Zdravstvene Nege,* 56(2), 100–104. DOI:10.14528/snr.2022.56.2.3166

Bhandare, P. V., Guha, S., Chaudhury, R. H., & Ghosh, C. (2021). Impact of financial literacy models on the financial behavior of individuals: An empirical study on the Indian context. *Strategic Change*, 30(4), 377–387. DOI:10.1002/jsc.2431

Bojuwon, M., Olaleye, B. R., & Ojebode, A. A. (2023). Financial Inclusion and Financial Condition: The Mediating Effect of Financial Self-efficacy and Financial Literacy. *Vision (Basel)*. DOI:10.1177/09722629231166200

Brynjolfsson, E., Horton, J., Ozimek, A., Rock, D., Sharma, G., & Tuye, H.-Y. (2020). NBER Working Paper Series Covid-19 and Remote Work: An Early Look At Us Data. In *NBER Working Paper Series* (Issue June 220). NBER.

Canatan, E. C., Coskun, A., & Toker, A. (2023). ADOPTION ATTITUDE AND CONTINUANCE INTENTION TO ONLINE FINFLUENCER VIDEO USAGE: THE ROLE OF TRUST. *Proceedings of the International Conferences on ICT, Society, and Human Beings 2023, ICT 2023; e-Health 2023, EH 2023; Connected Smart Cities 2023, CSC 2023; and Big Data Analytics, Data Mining and Computational Intelligence 2023, BigDaCI 2023*. IEEE. DOI:10.33965/MCCSIS2023_202305C003

Chalutz Ben-Gal, H. (2023). Artificial intelligence (AI) acceptance in primary care during the coronavirus pandemic: What is the role of patient's gender, age, and health awareness? A two-phase pilot study. *Frontiers in Public Health*, 10, 931225. DOI:10.3389/fpubh.2022.931225 PMID:36699881

Chien, S. P., Wu, H. K., & Wu, P. H. (2018). Teachers' Beliefs About, Attitudes Toward, and Intention to Use Technology-Based Assessments: A Structural Equation Modeling Approach. *Eurasia Journal of Mathematics, Science and Technology Education*, 14(10), 1–17. DOI:10.29333/ejmste/93379

Chikhi, I. (n.d.). *Financial Influencers and Social Media: The Role of Valuable and Financial Influencers and Social Media: The Role of Valuable and Trusted Content in Creating a New Form of Authenticity Trusted Content in Creating a New Form of Authenticity*. Academic Works. https://academicworks.cuny.edu/bb_etds/113Discoveradditionalworksat:https://academicworks.cuny.edu

Cîmpeanu, I.-A., Dragomir, D.-A., & Zota, R. D. (2023). Banking Chatbots: How Artificial Intelligence Helps the Banks. *Proceedings of the International Conference on Business Excellence, 17*(1), 1716–1727. DOI:10.2478/picbe-2023-0153

Cinelli, M., Quattrociocchi, W., Galeazzi, A., Valensise, C. M., Brugnoli, E., Schmidt, A. L., Zola, P., Zollo, F., & Scala, A. (2020). The COVID-19 social media infodemic. *Scientific Reports*, 10(1), 16598. DOI:10.1038/s41598-020-73510-5 PMID:33024152

Damayanti, S. M., Murtaqi, I., & Pradana, H. A. (2018). The Importance of Financial Literacy in a Global Economic Era. *The Business and Management Review, 9*(3).

de Regt, A., Cheng, Z., & Fawaz, R. (2023). Young People Under 'Finfluencer': The Rise of Financial Influencers on Instagram: An Abstract. In *Developments in Marketing Science:Proceedings of the Academy of Marketing Science.* Springer. DOI:10.1007/978-3-031-24687-6_106

Dhawan, S. (2020). Online Learning: A Panacea in the Time of COVID-19 Crisis. *Journal of Educational Technology Systems*, 49(1), 5–22. DOI:10.1177/0047239520934018

Dunn, B. (2023). For financial illiteracy. *Economic and Labour Relations Review*, 34(2), 299–313. DOI:10.1017/elr.2023.8

Durac, L., & Moga, L. M. (2023). Applications of Decomposed Theory of Planned Behaviour in Making Decision to Adopt a Career in Social Entrepreneurship. *European Journal of Interdisciplinary Studies*, 15(1), 16–30. DOI:10.24818/ejis.2023.02

Effendi, K. A., Ichsani, S., Saputera, D., Hertina, D., Wijaya, J. H., & Hendiarto, R. S. (2021). The Importance of Financial Literacy in Preventing Illegal Fintech in MSMEs in Indonesia. *Review of International Geographical Education Online*, 11(6). DOI:10.48047/rigeo.11.06.38

Farazouli, A., Cerratto-Pargman, T., Bolander-Laksov, K., & McGrath, C. (2024). Hello GPT! Goodbye home examination? An exploratory study of AI chatbot's impact on university teachers' assessment practices. *Assessment & Evaluation in Higher Education*, 49(3), 363–375. DOI:10.1080/02602938.2023.2241676

Gangaiamaran, R., & Anil Premraj, J. (2020). Technology adoption in self-access language learning: A review. In *Journal of Critical Reviews* (*Vol. 7*, Issue 4, pp. 642–645). Innovare Academics Sciences Pvt. Ltd. DOI:10.31838/jcr.07.04.119

Gatzioufa, P., & Saprikis, V. (2022). A literature review on users' behavioral intention toward chatbots' adoption. In *Applied Computing and Informatics.* Emerald Group Holdings Ltd. DOI:10.1108/ACI-01-2022-0021

Ghandour, A. (2021). Opportunities and Challenges of Artificial Intelligence in Banking: Systematic Literature Review. *TEM Journal, 10*(4), 1581–1587. https://doi.org/DOI:10.18421/TEM104-12

Ghani, W. S. D. W. A., Khidzir, N. Z., Guan, T. T., & Ismail, M. (2017). Towards Modelling Factors of Intention to Adopt Cloud-Based M-Retail Application among Textile Cyberpreneurs. *Journal of Advances in Information Technology.* DOI:10.12720/jait.8.2.114-120

Gill, P., Stewart, K., Treasure, E., & Chadwick, B. (2008). Methods of data collection in qualitative research: interviews and focus groups. *British Dental Journal 2008 204:6, 204*(6), 291–295. DOI:10.1038/bdj.2008.192

Gill, S. S., Xu, M., Patros, P., Wu, H., Kaur, R., Kaur, K., Fuller, S., Singh, M., Arora, P., Parlikad, A. K., Stankovski, V., Abraham, A., Ghosh, S. K., Lutfiyya, H., Kanhere, S. S., Bahsoon, R., Rana, O., Dustdar, S., Sakellariou, R., & Buyya, R. (2024). Transformative effects of ChatGPT on modern education: Emerging Era of AI Chatbots. *Internet of Things and Cyber-Physical Systems*, 4, 19–23. DOI:10.1016/j.iotcps.2023.06.002

Grohmann, A., Klühs, T., & Menkhoff, L. (2018). Does financial literacy improve financial inclusion? Cross-country evidence. *World Development*, 111, 84–96. DOI:10.1016/j.worlddev.2018.06.020

Guan, S. S. (2022). *FINFLUENCERS AND THE REASONABLE RETAIL INVESTOR*. DISB. https://disb.dc.gov/page/beware-financial-influencers

Gurrieri, L., Drenten, J., & Abidin, C. (2023). Symbiosis or parasitism? A framework for advancing interdisciplinary and socio-cultural perspectives in influencer marketing. In *Journal of Marketing Management* (*Vol. 39*, Issues 11–12, pp. 911–932). Routledge. DOI:10.1080/0267257X.2023.2255053

Huston, S. J. (2010). Measuring Financial Literacy. *The Journal of Consumer Affairs*, 44(2), 296–316. DOI:10.1111/j.1745-6606.2010.01170.x

Kanimozhi, S., & Selvarani, A. (2019). Application of the Decomposed Theory of Planned Behaviour in Technology Adoption: A Review. *International Journal of Research and Analytical Reviews*, 6(2).

Kedvarin, S., & Saengchote, K. (2023). Social Media Finfluencers: Evidence from YouTube and Cryptocurrencies. SSRN *Electronic Journal*. DOI:10.2139/ssrn.4594081

Khalisharani, H., Johan, I. R., & Sabri, M. F. (2022). The Influence of Financial Literacy and Attitude towards Financial Behaviour Amongst Undergraduate Students: A Cross-Country Evidence. *Pertanika Journal of Social Science & Humanities*, 30(2), 449–474. DOI:10.47836/pjssh.30.2.03

Khan, S., & Rabbani, M. R. (2020, November 17). Chatbot as Islamic finance expert (CaIFE): When finance meets artificial intelligence. *ACM International Conference Proceeding Series*. ACM. DOI:10.1145/3440084.3441213

Khanna, A., Pandey, B., Vashishta, K., Kalia, K., Pradeepkumar, B., & Das, T. (2015). A Study of Today's A.I. through Chatbots and Rediscovery of Machine Intelligence. *International Journal of U- and e-Service. Science and Technology*, 8(7), 277–284. DOI:10.14257/ijunesst.2015.8.7.28

Kiruthika, S., Prasanna, V., Santhosh, A., Santhosh, R., & Sri Vignesh, P. (2023). Virtual Bank Assistance: An AI-Based Voice BOT for Better Banking. *International Journal of Advanced Research in Science. Tongxin Jishu*, 196–201. DOI:10.48175/IJARSCT-9194

Klapper, L., Lusardi, A., & Panos, G. A. (2013). Financial literacy and its consequences: Evidence from Russia during the financial crisis. *Journal of Banking & Finance*, 37(10), 3904–3923. DOI:10.1016/j.jbankfin.2013.07.014

Kooli, C. (2023). Chatbots in Education and Research: A Critical Examination of Ethical Implications and Solutions. *Sustainability (Basel)*, 15(7), 5614. DOI:10.3390/su15075614

Kumari, A., & Devi, N. C. (2023). Blockchain technology acceptance by investment professionals: A decomposed TPB model. *Journal of Financial Reporting and Accounting*, 21(1), 45–59. DOI:10.1108/JFRA-12-2021-0466

Kumari, S., & Harikrishnan, A. (2021). Importance of Financial Literacy for Sustainable Future Environment: A Research Among People In Rural Areas With Special Reference To Mandi District, Himachal Pradesh. *International Journal of Engineering. Science and Information Technology*, 1(1), 15–19. Advance online publication. DOI:10.52088/ijesty.v1i1.36

Labadze, L., Grigolia, M., & Machaidze, L. (2023). Role of AI chatbots in education: systematic literature review. In *International Journal of Educational Technology in Higher Education* (Vol. 20, Issue 1). Springer Science and Business Media Deutschland GmbH. DOI:10.1186/s41239-023-00426-1

Lai, P. (2017). The literature review of technology adoption models and theories for the novelty technology. *Journal of Information Systems and Technology Management*, 14(1), 21–38. DOI:10.4301/S1807-17752017000100002

Lajnef, K. (2023). The effect of social media influencers on teenagers Behavior: An empirical study using cognitive map technique. *Current Psychology (New Brunswick, N.J.)*, 42(22), 19364–19377. DOI:10.1007/s12144-023-04273-1 PMID:36742063

Lusardi, A., & Mitchell, O. S. (2011). Financial Literacy and Retirement Preparedness: Evidence and Implications for Financial Education Programs. SSRN *Electronic Journal*. DOI:10.2139/ssrn.957796

Lusardi, A., & Mitchell, O. S. (2014). The economic importance of financial literacy: Theory and evidence. *Journal of Economic Literature*, 52(1), 5–44. DOI:10.1257/jel.52.1.5 PMID:28579637

Lusardi, A., & Mitchell, O. S. (2023a). The Importance of Financial Literacy: Opening a New Field. *The Journal of Economic Perspectives*, 37(4), 137–154. DOI:10.1257/jep.37.4.137

Lusardi, A., & Mitchell, O. S. (2023b). The Importance of Financial Literacy: Opening a New Field. SSRN *Electronic Journal*. DOI:10.2139/ssrn.4420560

Manfredo, T. (2024). How to Make $1 Million in 30 Seconds or Less: The Need for Regulations on Finfluencers. *SSRN*, 84(2). Advance online publication. DOI:10.2139/ssrn.4398463

Marinov, K. M. (2023). Financial Literacy: Determinants and Impact on Financial Behaviour. *Economic Alternatives*, 2023(1), 89–114. DOI:10.37075/EA.2023.1.05

Mohta, A., & Shunmugasundaram, V. (2022). Financial Literacy Among Millennials. *International Journal of Economics and Financial Issues*, 12(2), 61–66. DOI:10.32479/ijefi.12801

Ndou, A. (2023). The relationship between demographic factors and financial literacy. *International Journal of Research in Business and Social Science (2147–4478)*, *12*(1), 155–164. DOI:10.20525/ijrbs.v12i1.2298

Nuruzzaman, M., & Hussain, O. K. (2020). IntelliBot: A Dialogue-based chatbot for the insurance industry. *Knowledge-Based Systems*, 196, 105810. DOI:10.1016/j.knosys.2020.105810

Nyasulu, C., & Dominic Chawinga, W. (2019). Using the decomposed theory of planned behavior to understand university students' adoption of WhatsApp in learning. *E-Learning and Digital Media*, 16(5), 413–429. DOI:10.1177/2042753019835906

Okello Candiya Bongomin, G., Munene, J. C., & Yourougou, P. (2020). Examining the role of financial intermediaries in promoting financial literacy and financial inclusion among people with low incomes in developing countries: Lessons from rural Uganda. *Cogent Economics & Finance*, 8(1), 1761274. DOI:10.1080/23322039.2020.1761274

Ooi, E. C. W., Isa, Z. M., Manaf, M. R. A., Fuad, A. S. A., Ahmad, A., Mustapa, M. N., & Marzuki, N. M. (2024). Factors influencing the intention to use the ICD-11 among medical record officers (MROs) and assistant medical record officers (AMROs) in the Ministry of Health, Malaysia. *Scientific Reports*, 14(1). DOI:10.1038/s41598-024-60439-2 PMID:38688966

Oosting, J. (2022). *Finfluencers and their impact on the Stock Market.*

Pattnaik, D., Ray, S., & Raman, R. (2024). Artificial intelligence and machine learning applications in the financial services industry: A bibliometric review. *Heliyon*, 10(1). DOI:10.1016/j.heliyon.2023.e23492 PMID:38187262

Pendy, B. (2023). Role of AI in Business Management. *Brilliance: Research of Artificial Intelligence*, 3(1), 48–55. DOI:10.47709/brilliance.v3i1.2191

Perdanasari, A., Sudiyanto, S., & Octoria, D. (2019). The Importance of Financial Literacy Knowledge For Elementary School Students In the 21st Century. *Efektor*, 6(1), 26. DOI:10.29407/e.v6i1.12591

Prihartanti, F. W., Murtini, W., & Indriayu, M. (2022). The Need for Financial Literacy Proficiency Level for Generation Z Students at School. *Eduvest - Journal Of Universal Studies, 2*(3). DOI:10.36418/edv.v2i3.383

Shih, Y. Y., & Fang, K. (2004). Using a decomposed theory of planned behavior to study Internet banking in Taiwan. *Internet Research*, 14(3), 213–223. DOI:10.1108/10662240410542643

Shvaher, O. A., Degtyarev, S. I., & Polyakova, L. G. (2021). The effect of social media on financial literacy. *International Journal of Media and Information Literacy*, 6(1). Advance online publication. DOI:10.13187/ijmil.2021.1.211

Singh, S., & Sarva, M. (2024). The Rise of Finfluencers: A Digital Transformation in Investment Advice. In *AABFJ, 18*(3).

Sitthipon, T., Siripipatthanakul, S., Phayaprom, B., Siripipattanakul, S., & Limna, P. (2022). Determinants of Customers' Intention to Use Healthcare Chatbots and Apps in Bangkok, Thailand. In *International Journal of Behavioral Analytics, 2*(2). https://ssrn.com/abstract=4045661

Srisathan, W. A., & Naruetharadhol, P. (2022). A COVID-19 disruption: The great acceleration of digitally planned and transformed behaviors in Thailand. *Technology in Society*. DOI:10.1016/j.techsoc.2022.101912

Stolper, O. A., & Walter, A. (2017). Financial literacy, financial advice, and financial behavior. *Journal of Business Economics*, 87(5), 581–643. DOI:10.1007/s11573-017-0853-9

van Reijmersdal, E. A., & Hudders, L. (2023). How do you become a millionaire in three steps? An experimental study on the persuasive power of financial advice by finfluencers. *Tijdschrift voor Communicatiewetenschap*, 51(3). DOI:10.5117/TCW2023.3.004.REIJ

Vu, V. C., Keating, B., & Wang, S. (n.d.). *Association for Information Systems Association for Information Systems #finfluencers: Understanding the Role of Parasocial Relationships #finfluencers: Understanding the Role of Parasocial Relationships and Psychological Need Support and Psychological Need Support.* AISEL. https://aisel.aisnet.org/acis2022

Wagner, J. (2019). Financial education and financial literacy by income and education groups. *Financial Counseling and Planning*, 30(1), 132–141. DOI:10.1891/1052-3073.30.1.132

Wube, H. D., Esubalew, S. Z., Weldesellasie, F. F., & Debelee, T. G. (2022). Text-Based Chatbot in Financial Sector: A Systematic Literature Review. *Data Science in Finance and Economics*, 2(3), 232–259. DOI:10.3934/DSFE.2022011

Chapter 9
The Effect of AI on HRM Practices

Tharaya Said AlHarthi

UTAS Ibra, Oman

ABSTRACT

In the age of digital technologies and transformation, artificial intelligence (AI) has emerged as essential technology to be integrated into various business activities and practices. The integration of AI into human resource management (HRM) practices has a profound and transformative shift in the way organizations approach workforce management. This technological evolution has not only revolutionized traditional HR methods, but has also introduced novel efficiencies, reshaping the landscape of talent acquisition, employee engagement, and overall organizational effectiveness. In this era of rapid technological advancement, understanding the multifaceted impact of AI on HRM is essential for businesses aiming to stay competitive, foster a more responsive workforce and build its capabilities. By reviewing the existing literature, this chapter offers a systematic analysis to gain insights on the impact of AI on various HRM practices. In addition, it aims to explore how AI technologies assist organizations to tackle numerous challenges associated with HRM.

THE EFFECT OF AI ON HRM PRACTICES

In the age of digital technologies and transformation, Artificial Intelligence (AI) has emerged as essential technology to be integrated into various business activities and practices. The integration of Artificial Intelligence (AI) into Human Resource Management (HRM) practices has a profound and transformative shift in the way organizations approach workforce management. This technological evolution has not only revolutionized traditional HR methods but has also introduced novel efficiencies,

DOI: 10.4018/979-8-3693-4187-2.ch009

reshaping the landscape of talent acquisition, employee engagement, and overall organizational effectiveness. In this era of rapid technological advancement, understanding the multifaceted impact of AI on HRM is essential for businesses aiming to stay competitive, foster a more responsive workforce and build its capabilities. By reviewing the existing literature, this chapter offers a systematic analysis to gain insights on the impact of AI on various HRM practices. In addition, it aims to explore how AI technologies assist organizations to tackle numerous challenges associated with HRM. The impact of AI on various HRM practices including recruitment and talent acquisition, sourcing and matching, performance management and HR analytics and reporting, are explained. In conclusion, human resource management practices focused on AI have a great potential to enhance employee performance, talent development, learning and development, and employee retention, while also helping to minimize employee turnover. Hence, organizations, regardless of their size, are recommended to adapt to AI technologies and deploy robust strategies to boost up their HR functions.

INTRODUCTION

Nowadays, emerging technologies are changing how businesses handle their various activities, and one big change is the use of Artificial Intelligence (AI). This technological change can be viewed as a smart system that can mimic humans' abilities, like thinking and learning in a much faster rate. In fact, AI in recent years is being adopted more and more in different domains and notably many organizations around the globe have realized the importance of deploying AI solutions in their processes.

Prior to addressing its impact on organizations and understanding its applicability to different areas and practices, it is important to shed a light on what Artificial Intelligence is and what it entails.

Artificial intelligence has gained more attention in the recent years as it encompasses many areas and as it is predicted to significantly affect our everyday life and to transform nearly every business. In order to understand this concept, it is important first to look into two terms "Artificial" and "Intelligence" separately. With regards to artificial, it is used a notion to refer to something which is not occurring naturally rather is produced by human (Mikalef & Gupta, 2021). On the other hand, the word intelligence used to refer to "the ability to acquire and apply knowledge and skills". It is also used to describe the involvement and use of mental abilities, e.g., learning, understanding and reasoning (Lichtenthaler, 2019). When both terms are combined, it is worthy to mentioned that several definition for AI have been proposed. According to a definition provided by Kolbjørnsrud et al. (2017), AI is used to refer to "computers and applications that sense, comprehend, act, and learn". This definition is similar to those of Demlehner and Laumer (2020) who defined AI as "a computer system having the ability to percept, learn, judge, or plan without being explicitly programmed to follow predetermined rules or action sequences throughout the whole process.". A most recent and broad definition of AI has been given by Wang et al. (2019) who described AI as "a broad concept that captures the intelligent behavior of the machine"

Throughout this present chapter, the broad definition suggested by (Afiouni, 2019) to describe AI is followed. According to Afiouni (2019) as a term is to refer to the use of machines/computers abilities to "perform tasks that usually need natural human intelligence".

Despite few researchers argued that AI has limited applicability in HRM processes (Chitrao et al., 2022) and that availability of these technologies is not very well known to recruiters, many other researchers believed that it has the potential to shape the future of HRM practices (Pan & Froese, 2023); (Vedapradha et al., 2023), Ekuma, K. (2023) and hence becomes a phenomenon of interest for HR professionals and practitioners. (Agarwal et al., 2023). A more intriguing fact in the literature is that AI-based applications are regarded as one of the most advance development in HRM technologies.

Although it is still in the infancy stage and has a limited applicability to tech focused and innovative firms (Albert, 2019), the use of AI in the field of HRM has witnessed a rapid growth (Pan & Froese, 2023) (Davenport et al., 2020). And the impact of the digitization, in particular AI, on different HR functions has becomes a phenomenon of interest for HR professionals and practitioners (Pandita, 2019) The presence of Artificial Intelligence (AI) effect on human resource represents a paradigm shift on various HR practices from planning, recruiting talents to retention. By all means, this has not only transformed traditional human resources practices but has certainly offered both opportunities as well as concerns in multifaceted ways for HR professionals.

Indeed, literature indicates many reasons contributing to keenness among organizations to integrate AI technologies into their processes and functions. For instance, AI technologies have the potential to make HR tasks faster than before. Also, these technologies ensure more accurate HR processes and better alignment with organizational goals. For instance, with the help of AI tools, organizations spend less time to scan resumes and quickly identify the best suitable candidate. The secret behind this is the use of algorithms as a main enabler to save time and efforts and undoubtedly reduce cost per hire.

The use of AI powered tools help HR departments to make things work better and faster. For this reason, many practitioners believe that AI has a significant impact in HR functions as it can help with tasks like hiring new employees or assessing the performance of the existing employees.

As mentioned above, literature indicates various HR key areas affected by the adoption of AI. However, the following part of this paper moves on to describe in greater detail four HR areas revolutionized by the advent of AI. The areas are: (1) recruitment and talent acquisition, (2) candidates sourcing and matching, (3) performance management and (4) HR analytics and reporting. However, before proceeding to discuss how AI affect HR practices, it deems necessary to offer the readers with a general overview about the history of AI.

HISTORY OF ARTIFICIAL INTELLIGENCE

This sections intends to provide a general overview about the history of AI. Unlike what many people think about AI as a new phenomenon, AI technologies has been "traced back to philosophy, fiction and imagination" (Buchanan, 2006). According to Cordeschi R. (2007)., the origin of AI can be traced back to the Dartmouth Summer Research Project on AI before 1960, where a group of researchers were formulated the term "Artificial Intelligence" with the objective of imitating human intelligence into machines. In his book (*brief history of artificial intelligence: what it is, where we are, and where we are going*), Wooldridge (2021) attributed the emergence, spread and growth of AI to three reasons: genuine scientific breakthroughs, access to more powerful and cheap computer capabilities and the availability of big data. According to the author, AI has evolved significantly over the decades, with ongoing advancements shaping its current state and future prospects. In recent years, these technologies have witnessed a huge explosion in its capability affecting almost every individual and transforming nearly every industry and activities including HR functions. Having briefly traced back the history of AI, the section that follows review the literature related to the theoretical frameworks and models underpinning the adoption and use of AI in different organizational areas including HR activities.

THEORETICAL FRAMEWORKS UNDERPINNING AI ADOPTION IN ORGANIZATIONAL CONTEXT

Several studies investigating the adoption of artificial intelligence (AI) in organizational contexts used various theoretical frameworks to explore AI adoption in organizational settings. One of the most popular framework commonly used is the Technology-Organization-Environment (TOE) framework, which explores how technological features, organizational factors (including structure and culture), and external environmental factors influence AI adoption. For instance, Al Hadwer, A., Tavana, M., Gillis, D., & Rezania, D. (2021) draw on TOE framework by Tornatzky and Fleischer (1990) which focuses on the organizational factors that affect the adoption process. In addition to TOE framework, there has been a great deal of research on Technology Acceptance Model (TAM) to understand the adoption of AI in organization. This model has been widely used to study the adoption process of technologies in organizations as well as by individuals.

In the context of human resource management (HRM), researchers often employ specific theoretical frameworks to understand the adoption of emerging technologies including AI technologies within organizational context. For instance, Hmoud (2021) used TAM to investigate HR roles and the attitude of HR practitioners towards the adoption of AI-based solutions. In addition to the TOE framework, Institutional Theory, and Diffusion of Innovations theory, researchers also draw on other theoretical perspectives to explore AI adoption in organizational settings. The Resource-Based View (RBV) explores how internal resources of an organization and its other capabilities, such as knowledge assets and technology infrastructure, shape its ability to new innovations including AI technologies. Another key framework is the Resource-Based View (RBV), which emphasizes on how human capital (knowledge and skills) organizational capabilities can be well-utilized to effectively adopt and integrate AI. Additionally, HRM researchers also draw on Institutional Theory to examine how organizational norms and pressures from external sources affect HR practices (e.g., workforce planning and skill development) related to AI adoption. Similarly, the Psychological Contract Theory was employed to see how AI adoption affects the implicit expectations and mutual obligations between an organization and its employees.

In addition to the above mentioned theoretical framework to explore the drivers of adopting AI technologies in organizational contexts, Mariani et al. (2023) presented other theoretical lenses used by researchers to address the adoption and implementation of AI technologies in organization. This includes: diffusion of innovation theory and technological innovation systems (TIS).

These diverse theoretical lenses offer better understandings of the multifaceted factors and drivers influencing AI adoption decisions, intentions as well as implementation strategies across various organizational contexts. These frameworks, theories and models provide HR professionals with better insights into addressing and managing the human side of AI adoption, aligning technology implementation with organizational culture, employee motivation, and well-being. This alignment covers and affected HR areas and functions. The section below describes the impact of AI in one of the main HR area, recruitment and talent acquisition.

(1) Recruitment and Talent Acquisition (TA)

Recruitment and talent acquisition are integral functions of HR that have been directly influenced by technological advancement (Hmoud & Laszlo, 2019). They are seen as a top priority for many HR leaders and professionals due to their significant contribution to drive organizational success and growth. But, to achieve organizational success and growth, organizations need to compete with others for hiring and acquiring qualified talents. When it comes to certain areas of recruitment process in which AI tools are adopted, a recent study by (Albert, 2019) has identified 11 areas across recruitment process where AI are utilized.

As data-driven technologies continue to unfold, the competition to attract and retain talents has become more intensified today than ever before. As a result, AI tools "constitute a force that will intensify" (Black & van Esch, 2021) and drive the competition sparking the race between organizations to incorporate these cutting-edge technologies. AI enhances recruitment by assisting managers to gain access to highly skilled individuals (Meshram, 2023) and also by introducing innovative ways to personnel management, boosting overall organizational performance (Khaled et al., 2023; Hemalatha et al., 2021). Therefore, AI applications emerge extensively to transform the landscape of HR and to increase the value of human capital and reducing the switching cost of talents in various organizations (Pillai & Sivathanu, 2020). It is one of the crucial activities where the impact of AI is highly noticed as compared to other HR processes (Ramesh & Das, 2022).

As the talent pool become more divers due to globalization, AI solutions are instrumental in leveraging the benefits and optimizing talent acquisition. They support organizations to identify and select the appropriate resources to take the right organizational roles (Bashynska et al, 2023). They also enable recruiters to eliminate human bias and favoritism that normally featured conventional recruitment methods. AI tools allow recruiters to fairly screen candidates resume and "neutralize human mistakes and bias" (Hmoud & Laszlo, 2019).

A substantial body of literature has proven a great impact as well as a positive attitude of HR leaders towards AI technologies adoption in talent acquisition. It is worth noting that a recent study by (Hmoud & Várallyai, 2021) indicates that HR leaders have a positive belief towards adopting AI solutions in talent acquisition. AI Tools like applicant tracking system (ATS) has shown a remarkable role to streamline the hiring process. They play a central role in enabling HR professionals to quickly analyze job applicants' documents, assess job candidates and accurately predict job-fit.

These applications have increased the efficiency of recruitments and talent acquisition and enhanced its accuracy. In addition, it has resulted in more easy and much smoother process when compared to how the process was done traditionally.

According to a study by, it has been reported that slightly more than 4% of HR managers prefer to use traditional methods in talent acquisition compared to more than 95% who were inclined to use AI technologies. In addition, AI tools were found useful in talent identification paving the way to successful attraction and acquisition of talents. (Massoud et al., 2024). Furthermore, the use of AI has shown a remarkable impact in enhancing employee experience as hence positively affecting retention rate. Beside the above, AI enabled HR professional to quickly identify top talents and easily acquire them by allowing the analysis of massive amount of data. It also helps HR managers to ensure more efficient recruitment particularly in the process of choosing the best talents. For example, Natural Language Processing (NLP), an AI tool, helps organizations to adjust talent strategies with their broader goals. In other words, organizations tend to stay competitive and remain agile as they are able to anticipate their future workforce needs through the help of AI.

There are many AI tools that are adopted by organizations to enhance talent acquisition. For instance, IBM uses an in-house AI tool named, IBM Watson Recruitment, to support the giant tech company initiative in talent acquisition. This tool enables IBM to streamline the hiring process by effectively analyze applicants' documents in order to identify qualified talents. Integrating these tools has positively contributed to improve quality of candidates besides saving the time and effort required for candidate initial evaluations.

In conclusion, it is believed that AI technologies will facilitate talents access forcing recruiters to employ strong retention strategies to retain their talents. The following section moves on to describe in details how AI technologies influence business in candidate matching and sourcing.

(2) Candidate Matching and Sourcing

Candidate matching and sourcing is identified as one of the HR areas that AI has most impacted. It is a smart recruiting software that uses semantic search algorithm to match job applicants with the right jobs. AI has revolutionized candidate matching by not only using keywords but rather analyze job descriptions and candidate profiles to ensure a high level of accuracy. It also enables HR professional to explore vast datasets identifying patterns that provide insights to select the most qualified candidates to perform specific tasks or to take up certain roles in their organizations. (Nyathani, 2022). In other words, these intelligent tools assist organizations to quickly and perfectly match candidates based on the job needs and candidate attributes. Hence, it shortens and optimizes the sourcing process minimizing time and reducing cost per hire.

Compared to traditional screening process, quality, speed and accuracy are three main outcomes that recruiters gain out of using AI powered candidate matching software. Many companies adopt a skills-based recruiting approach. For instance, HireVue, a human resource management company, employed AI-powered chatbots to send screening questions and cognitive ability tests to potential candidates. The company also uses a 24/7 hiring assistant to assist candidates unlocking their potential by matching their skills with listed job opportunities using AI conversational assistant.

AI powered candidate matching tools use a variety of data sources including social media and both employers and employees' data to match right individuals with the suitable jobs. Also, AI technologies can be used to upskill and develop talents to align them to the jobs requirements.

There are many AI applications that help recruiters with reviewing and matching candidates to appropriate jobs. One of the fastest growing screening application is, Pymetrics. It is an AI driven software that uses intelligent matching algorithms to select the best candidates to jobs based on certain criteria. These criteria are based on two areas of assessment: (a) emotional and (b) cognitive. The software enables recruiters to make more informed hiring decisions and consequently make more effective talent acquisition process. In addition, these AI driven tools incorporate features that go beyond screening applicants to include organizing interviews with potential candidates. As a matter of facts, selecting the ideal candidates to suite pre-defined jobs is not an easy task as it raises many challenges and consume more time. Many AI applications are not embedded with features that use algorithm to match vacant positions or jobs with job applicants based on pre-defined job requirements. Overall, powerful AI powered candidate matching tools help recruiters streamlining the hiring process by increasing their reach to unbiased list of top talents from a vast pool of applicants. Therefore, organizations should "AI data driven capabilities to assess candidates more accurately" (Bashynska, Prokopenko, & Sala, 2023). Having discussed the impact of AI technologies on candidate matching and sourcing, the next section intends to offer a detailed overview of AI impact on another HR area, performance management.

(3) Performance Management

Performance management is another key area that has been influenced by the advent of AI. Organizations needs to identify areas of improvement and make better decisions about present and future performance of its employees. AI solutions support organization to attain a high-performance culture. Obviously, the existing literature in the integration of AI in HR landscape demonstrates that AI-driven performance management systems has impacted adopting organizations in many ways. For instance, a recent study by (Bashynska, Prokopenko, & Sala, 2023) found that AI powered tools facilitate the concept of motivating employees to meet and exceed performance expectations and foster unbiased assessment. In addition, they offer (a) a continuous feedback, (b) personalized development and coaching, (c) a more equitable and (d) a more objective evaluation. Equally important, these tools provide an effective performance monitoring process and predictive performance management.

Similarly, they enable organizations to secure real-time feedback. In like manner, they help employees to have personalized development plans and receive sound recommendations based on unbiased evaluation. Moreover, it promotes continuous learning opportunities to leverage the human capital, improve productivity and build a more engaged workforce. In fact, AI-driven training adapts and tailors learning experiences to individual needs and hence enhancing learning quality (Chen, 2022).

In brief, recruiters are expected to embrace AI capabilities in the area of performance management by shifting to an intelligent performance management system. Having discussed the how AI affected HR functions, the final section of this chapter explores the role of AI in HR analytics and reporting.

(4) HR Analytics and Reporting

As far as HR is concerned, data is viewed as "the lifeblood of informed decision-making and strategic workforce management" (Nyathani, 2023). Thus, it is essential for HR professionals to unlock the full potential of data and capitalize on data and people analytics. To put it differently, organizations need to unleash power of people analytics by integrating AI-driven analytics solutions and align them to their HR goals. AI-driven HR analytics applications enable HR professionals not only to extract valuable data and gain deeper insights to make data-driven decisions but to get a deep insight into employee perceptions, emotions and sentiments.

There are many AI data-driven tools for organizations. One of these applications is Workday's Prism Analytics (WPA). WPA is an AI-powered analytics software that facilitate analyses of employee data to make informed data-driven decisions. It offers better insights into various areas including performance, compensation, and workforce planning. Integrating these tools in organizational contexts yield many benefits. It helps to uncover actionable insights from large and complicated HR data which was not possible via traditional HR analytics methods. With the AI data analytics, HR professional easily understand the patterns of the employee data and act accordingly.

These tools also enable recruiters to foresee future trends. For instance, the high quality analysis will be a good input to plan and recruit human resources and optimize resource allocation of HR. in addition, AI data analytics helps organizations to address and identify potential challenges before they arise. Further, it enables recruiters to mitigate potential HR-related risks. In other words, it enhances recruiters' ability to respond to risks enable them to proactively face challenges such talent shortage and employee turnover. Nowadays, many companies use AI not only to collect data about their talents but also to analyze trends in their cycle and to anticipate future hiring needs as well as to determine turnover risks.

In addition to the above, these tools help organizations to ensure a steady pipeline of talented employees as it facilitates the identifications of potentials in the workforce.

CONCLUSION

To sum up, HR professionals must stay ahead by exploring emerging technologies and respond quick to technology trends as this has become a strategic imperative for organizations. In the era of AI, they are expected to unearth the core capabilities and implement AI solutions in their organizations. As a matter of fact, organizations that harness the potential of AI solutions in their processes, including HR, and embed those technologies in their activities are proven to gain a competitive edge. However, like any other technologies, organizations while embracing AI solutions, they should not underscore concerns and challenges presented by these technologies.

REFERENCES

Afiouni, R. (2019). *Organizational learning in the rise of machine learning. International Conference on Information Systems*, Munich, Germany

Agarwal, A. (2022). AI adoption by human resource management: A study of its antecedents and impact on HR system effectiveness. *Foresight*, 25(1), 67–81. DOI:10.1108/FS-10-2021-0199

Albert, E. T. (2019). AI in talent acquisition: A review of AI-applications used in recruitment and selection. *Strategic HR Review*, 18(5), 215–221. DOI:10.1108/SHR-04-2019-0024

Bashynska, I., Prokopenko, O., & Sala, D. (2023). Managing Human Capital with AI: Synergy of Talent and Technology. *Zeszyty Naukowe Wyższej Szkoły Finansów i Prawa w Bielsku-Białej*, 27(3), 39–45.

Black, J. S., & van Esch, P. (2021). AI-enabled recruiting in the war for talent. *Business Horizons*, 64(4), 513–524. DOI:10.1016/j.bushor.2021.02.015

Buchanan, B. G. (2006). A (Very) Brief History of Artificial Intelligence. *AI Magazine*, 26(4).

Chitrao, P., Bhoyar, P. K., Divekar, R., & Bhatt, P. (2022, February). Study on use of artificial intelligence in talent acquisition. In *2022 Interdisciplinary Research in Technology and Management (IRTM)* (pp. 1-8). IEEE. DOI:10.1109/IRTM54583.2022.9791659

Cordeschi, R. (2007). AI turns fifty: Revisiting its origins. *Applied Artificial Intelligence*, 21(4-5), 259–279. DOI:10.1080/08839510701252304

Davenport, T., Guha, A., Grewal, D., & Bressgott, T. (2020). How artificial intelligence will change the future of marketing. *Journal of the Academy of Marketing Science*, 48(1), 24–42. DOI:10.1007/s11747-019-00696-0

Ekuma, K. (2023). Artificial Intelligence and Automation in Human Resource Development: A Systematic Review. *Human Resource Development Review*, 15344843231224009.

Hmoud, B., & Várallyai, L. (2021). Artificial Intelligence In Talent Acquisition, Do we Trust It? *Agrárinformatika Folyóirat*, 12(1). DOI:10.17700/jai.2021.12.1.594

Hmoud, B., & Laszlo, V. (2019). Will artificial intelligence take over human resources recruitment and selection. *Network Intelligence Studies*, 7(13), 21–30.

Jarrahi, M. H. (2018). Artificial intelligence and the future of work: Human-AI symbiosis in organizational decision making. *Business Horizons*, 61(4), 577–586. DOI:10.1016/j.bushor.2018.03.007

Mariani, M. M., Machado, I., Magrelli, V., & Dwivedi, Y. K. (2023). Artificial intelligence in innovation research: A systematic review, conceptual framework, and future research directions. *Technovation*, 122, 102623. DOI:10.1016/j.technovation.2022.102623

Massoud, M. F., Maaliky, B., Fawal, A., Mawllawi, A., & Yahkni, F. (2024). Transforming Human Resources With AI: Empowering Talent Management and Workforce Productivity. In *Industrial Applications of Big Data, AI, and Blockchain* (pp. 254-299). IGI Global.

Muthukrishnan, N., Maleki, F., Ovens, K., Reinhold, C., Forghani, B., & Forghani, R. (2020). Brief history of artificial intelligence. *Neuroimaging Clinics of North America*, 30(4), 393–399. DOI:10.1016/j.nic.2020.07.004 PMID:33038991

Nyathani, R. (2022). AI-Powered Recruitment The Future of HR Digital Transformation. *Journal of Artificial Intelligence & Cloud Computing. SRC/JAICC-145.*

Nyathani, R. (2023). AI-Driven HR Analytics: Unleashing the Power of HR Data Management. *Journal of Technology and Systems*, 5(2), 15–26. DOI:10.47941/jts.1513

Pan, Y., & Froese, F. J. (2023). An interdisciplinary review of AI and HRM: Challenges and future directions. *Human Resource Management Review*, 33(1), 100924. DOI:10.1016/j.hrmr.2022.100924

Pandita, D. (2019). Talent acquisition: Analysis of digital hiring in organizations. *SAMVAD*, 18, 66–72.

Pillai, R., & Sivathanu, B. (2020). Adoption of artificial intelligence (AI) for talent acquisition in IT/ITeS organizations. *Benchmarking*, 27(9), 2599–2629. DOI:10.1108/BIJ-04-2020-0186

Ramesh, S., & Das, S. (2022, January). Adoption of AI in talent acquisition: a conceptual framework. In *International Conference on Digital Technologies and Applications* (pp. 12-20). Cham: Springer International Publishing. DOI:10.1007/978-3-031-01942-5_2

Vedapradha, R., Hariharan, R., Praveenraj, D. D. W., Sudha, E., & Ashok, J. (2023). Talent acquisition-artificial intelligence to manage recruitment. In *E3S Web of Conferences* (Vol. 376, p. 05001). EDP Sciences.

Wang, H., Huang, J., & Zhang, Z. (2019). *The impact of deep learning on organizational agility*. In *proceedings of the 40th International Conference on Information Systems (ICIS)*, Munich, Germany

Wooldridge, M. (2021). *A brief history of artificial intelligence: what it is, where we are, and where we are going*. Flatiron Books.

Chapter 10
Smart Financial Services Through Smart Banking in the Era of Industry 5.0:
Opportunities and Challenges

K. R. Pundareeka Vittala

ICFAI Foundation for Higher Education, Bangalore, India

J. Nagarathnamma

Presidency College (Autonomous), Bengaluru, India

N. Chidambaram

https://orcid.org/0009-0007-1767-385X

CHRIST University, Bengaluru, India

Amit Kumar Tyagi

https://orcid.org/0000-0003-2657-8700

National Institute of Fashion Technology, New Delhi, India

ABSTRACT

The advent of Industry 5.0 ushers in a new era of manufacturing characterized by unprecedented levels of connectivity, automation, and intelligence. This paradigm shift extends beyond the factory floor, permeating into the realm of financial services, particularly banking. Smart banking, empowered by cutting-edge technologies such as artificial intelligence, blockchain, and the Internet of Things, promises to revolutionize traditional banking practices, offering customers personalized and seamless financial experiences. This paper explores the opportunities and challenges presented by the integration of smart banking within the broader landscape of Industry 5.0. Opportunities include enhanced customer engagement, operational

DOI: 10.4018/979-8-3693-4187-2.ch010

efficiency gains, and the democratization of financial services. However, challenges such as cybersecurity threats, regulatory compliance, and the digital divide must be addressed to fully realize the potential of smart financial services.

INTRODUCTION TO INDUSTRY 5.0 AND SMART FINANCIAL SERVICES

Today the evolution of industry has undergone remarkable transformations, from the mechanization of production in Industry 1.0 to the digitalization and automation of processes in Industry 4.0. Now, we stand at the threshold of a new era: Industry 5.0 (Smith, J., & Johnson, R. (2021)). Unlike its predecessors, Industry 5.0 is characterized not only by advanced technologies but also by the fusion of human ingenuity with intelligent machines. This major shift heralds a new age of manufacturing, one where collaboration between humans and machines leads to unprecedented levels of productivity, innovation, and sustainability. Within this landscape of Industry 5.0, the financial services sector stands faced for its own revolution: the rise of smart financial services. Smart financial services use cutting-edge technologies such as artificial intelligence, blockchain, and the Internet of Things to reimagine traditional banking practices and deliver personalized, seamless, and efficient financial experiences to customers. Here, few technology enablers for industry 5.0 can be listed as figure 1.

Figure 1. Technology enablers of Industry 5.0

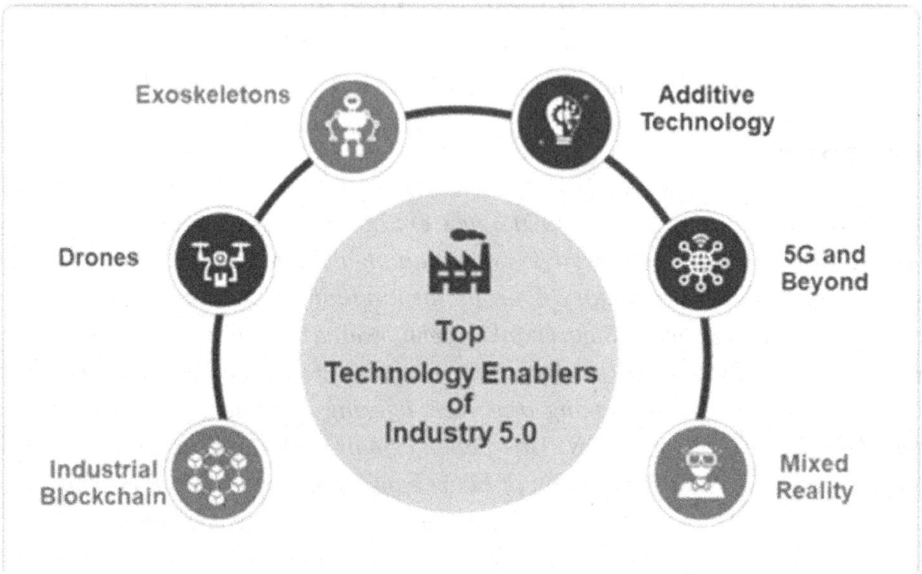

In this chapter, we discussed about the intersection of Industry 5.0 and smart financial services, discussing the opportunities and challenges that arise from this convergence. By examining the transformative potential of smart banking within the broader context of Industry 5.0, we seek to provide insights into how users can navigate this evolving landscape to use the full potential of technology for the benefit of both customers and the financial industry as a whole. From enhanced customer engagement to operational efficiency gains and the democratization of financial services, the opportunities presented by smart financial services in the era of Industry 5.0 are large and multifaceted. However, alongside these opportunities come challenges such as cybersecurity threats, regulatory compliance, and the digital divide, which must be addressed to realize the full potential of smart banking. Through strategic investments in technology, talent, and infrastructure, users can make the way for a future where banking is smarter, more inclusive, and more resilient than ever before. As we on this journey, let us use the possibilities of Industry 5.0 and smart financial services, working together to shape a future that is not only technologically advanced but also human-centered and sustainable.

Importance of Smart Financial Services in Today's Era

In today's era, marked by rapid technological advancements and shifting consumer expectations, the importance of smart financial services cannot be overstated. Several key factors underscore the importance of using smart financial services:

- Enhanced Customer Experience: Smart financial services use technology to provide personalized and seamless experiences to customers (Chen, L., & Wang, H. (2020)). From mobile banking apps to AI-powered chatbots, these services empower customers to manage their finances conveniently and efficiently, leading to higher satisfaction and loyalty.
- Operational Efficiency: Automation and digitization streamline banking processes, reducing manual intervention and operational costs. Smart financial services enable banks to automate routine tasks, optimize resource allocation, and improve overall efficiency, ultimately driving profitability and competitiveness.
- Data-driven Insights: Advanced analytics and machine learning algorithms enable banks to derive actionable insights from large volumes of data. By analyzing customer behavior, market trends, and risk profiles, smart financial services empower banks to make informed decisions, tailor product offerings, and mitigate risks effectively.
- Innovation and Differentiation: In an increasingly crowded marketplace, innovation is essential for banks to differentiate themselves and stay ahead of the

competition. Smart financial services enable banks to introduce innovative products and services, such as robo-advisors, peer-to-peer lending platforms, and digital wallets, catering to evolving customer needs and preferences.

- Financial Inclusion: Smart financial services have the potential to bridge the gap between the banked and unbanked populations, promoting financial inclusion and empowerment. Digital banking platforms and mobile payment solutions enable individuals in underserved communities to access essential financial services conveniently and affordably, using economic development and social equity.
- Security and Compliance: With the proliferation of cyber threats and stringent regulatory requirements, security and compliance are paramount for financial institutions. Smart financial services incorporate robust cybersecurity measures, such as encryption, biometric authentication, and real-time fraud detection, to safeguard sensitive data and ensure regulatory compliance, thereby using trust and credibility among customers and regulators alike.
- Adaptation to Changing Trends: The financial landscape is constantly evolving, driven by technological advancements, regulatory changes, and shifting consumer preferences. Smart financial services enable banks to adapt quickly to these changes, agilely responding to market dynamics, seizing opportunities, and mitigating risks, ensuring long-term relevance and sustainability.

In summary, smart financial services are indispensable in today's era, providing a myriad of benefits ranging from enhanced customer experiences and operational efficiencies to innovation, financial inclusion, security, and compliance. By using smart financial services, banks can position themselves as trusted partners in their customers' financial journeys, driving growth, resilience, and positive societal impact in the digital age.

EVOLUTION OF BANKING IN THE DIGITAL AGE

The evolution of banking in the digital age has been a remarkable journey, marked by huge transformations driven by technological advancements and changing consumer behaviors (Patel, A., & Gupta, M. (2019), Tyagi et al., (2021), (2022), (2023)), and (2024)). Here's a brief overview of the key stages in this evolution:

- Early Digitalization (1960s-1980s): The introduction of mainframe computers laid the foundation for digital banking, enabling banks to automate back-office operations and process transactions more efficiently. And, the emergence of Automated Teller Machines (ATMs) in the late 1960s revolu-

tionized banking by providing customers with 24/7 access to cash withdraw-
als and basic account services.

- Rise of Online Banking (1990s): The widespread adoption of the internet in
  the 1990s made the way for online banking, allowing customers to access
  their accounts, transfer funds, and perform transactions remotely via personal
  computers. And, Banks began to establish online portals and websites, providing customers a convenient and secure way to manage their finances from
  anywhere with an internet connection.

- Mobile Banking Revolution (2000s): The proliferation of smartphones and
  mobile devices in the 2000s sparked the mobile banking revolution, enabling
  customers to access banking services on the go through dedicated mobile
  apps. And, Mobile banking apps provided an array of features, including account balance inquiries, bill payments, mobile check deposits, and person-to-
  person transfers, enhancing convenience and accessibility for customers.

- Emergence of Fintech Disruptors (2010s): The rise of fintech startups in the
  2010s challenged traditional banking models, providing innovative digital
  solutions such as peer-to-peer lending, robo-advisors, and digital wallets.
  And, Fintech companies used technology to address pain points in the traditional banking industry, such as high fees, slow processes, and limited access
  to credit, appealing to tech-savvy consumers seeking alternative financial
  services.

- Shift Towards Digital Transformation (Present): In response to changing
  consumer preferences and competitive pressures, traditional banks are undergoing digital transformation initiatives to modernize their operations and
  enhance the customer experience. And, Digital transformation encompasses
  a range of initiatives, including the adoption of cloud computing, artificial intelligence, blockchain, and open banking APIs, to drive innovation, improve
  efficiency, and deliver personalized services.

Hence, banks are investing in omnichannel banking strategies, integrating online,
mobile, and in-branch channels to provide seamless and consistent experiences
across touchpoints, meeting the evolving needs of digital-native customers. The
evolution of banking in the digital age has been characterized by a shift towards
greater convenience, accessibility, and innovation, driven by advances in technology
and changing consumer expectations. As banking continues to evolve, collaboration
between traditional financial institutions and fintech innovators will play an important role in shaping the future of finance, driving greater inclusivity, efficiency, and
value for customers worldwide.

SMART BANKING: DEFINITION AND CHARACTERISTICS, AND KEY TECHNOLOGIES

Smart banking represents a modern approach to financial services that uses advanced technologies to enhance customer experiences, streamline operations, and drive innovation (Kumar, R., & Singh, P. (2018), Wang, Y., & Li, W. (2021)). Here's a breakdown of its definition, characteristics, and key technologies:

Smart banking refers to the use of cutting-edge technologies, such as artificial intelligence (AI), machine learning, blockchain, the Internet of Things (IoT), and big data analytics, to transform traditional banking processes and deliver personalized, efficient, and secure financial services to customers. Few Characteristics of smart banking are:

- Personalization: Smart banking platforms use customer data and AI algorithms to deliver tailored recommendations, products, and services based on individual preferences, behaviors, and financial goals.
- Omni-channel Experience: Smart banking provides seamless integration across multiple channels, including online, mobile, and in-branch banking, enabling customers to access services and information anytime, anywhere, and through their preferred channel.
- Automation: Automation plays a central role in smart banking, enabling banks to streamline routine tasks, such as account opening, loan processing, and fraud detection, through the use of AI-driven chatbots, robotic process automation (RPA), and cognitive computing.
- Data-driven Insights: Smart banking platforms use the power of big data analytics to derive actionable insights from large volumes of structured and unstructured data, enabling banks to make data-driven decisions, mitigate risks, and identify new business opportunities.
- Enhanced Security: Smart banking prioritizes cybersecurity, employing advanced encryption, biometric authentication, and real-time fraud detection systems to safeguard sensitive customer data and transactions from unauthorized access and cyber threats.
- Innovation: Smart banking uses a culture of innovation, encouraging experimentation with emerging technologies and collaboration with fintech startups to develop new products, services, and business models that address evolving customer needs and market trends.
- Regulatory Compliance: Compliance with regulatory requirements is a key consideration in smart banking, with banks using technology solutions, such as regulatory reporting software and know-your-customer (KYC) automation tools, to ensure adherence to relevant laws and regulations.

Key Technologies:

- Artificial Intelligence (AI): AI technologies, including machine learning, natural language processing (NLP), and predictive analytics, enable smart banking platforms to automate tasks, personalize experiences, and detect patterns and anomalies in data.
- Blockchain: Blockchain technology facilitates secure and transparent transactions by creating immutable and decentralized ledgers, enabling smart contracts, digital identity verification, and real-time settlement in smart banking applications.
- Internet of Things (IoT): IoT devices, such as wearables, smart sensors, and connected appliances, enable banks to collect real-time data on customer behavior, preferences, and financial transactions, enabling personalized services and risk assessment.
- Big Data Analytics: Big data analytics tools process and analyze large datasets to extract actionable insights, enabling banks to optimize marketing campaigns, detect fraud, and identify trends and patterns in customer behavior.
- Biometric Authentication: Biometric authentication technologies, such as fingerprint recognition, facial recognition, and voice recognition, enhance security and convenience in smart banking applications by providing secure and frictionless access to accounts and transactions.
- Robotic Process Automation (RPA): RPA software automates repetitive tasks and workflows, such as data entry, document processing, and reconciliation, freeing up human resources and improving operational efficiency in smart banking operations.
- Cloud Computing: Cloud computing platforms provide scalable and cost-effective infrastructure for hosting smart banking applications, enabling banks to deploy services rapidly, scale resources as needed, and access advanced capabilities, such as data storage and processing.

Figure 2. Revolution of Industry through technology

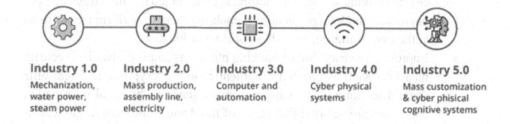

Industry 1.0	Industry 2.0	Industry 3.0	Industry 4.0	Industry 5.0
Mechanization, water power, steam power	Mass production, assembly line, electricity	Computer and automation	Cyber physical systems	Mass customization & cyber phisical cognitive systems

In summary, smart banking represents a major shift in the financial services industry, driven by the convergence of advanced technologies and customer-centric approaches (refer figure 2, for industry 5.0 revolution with emerging technologies in today's era). By using smart banking principles and using key technologies, banks can deliver enhanced experiences, drive operational efficiencies, and stay competitive in today's rapidly evolving digital landscape.

BENEFITS OF SMART BANKING FOR CUSTOMERS AND FINANCIAL INSTITUTIONS IN TODAY' SMART ERA

Smart banking provides a plethora of benefits for both customers and financial institutions in today's smart era (Garcia, M., & Martinez, E. (2020), Patel, R., & Shah, P. (2018)). Here's an overview of these benefits:

Benefits for Customers:

- Convenience: Smart banking enables customers to access financial services anytime, anywhere, through various digital channels such as mobile apps, online portals, and smart devices. This convenience eliminates the need for physical visits to branches, allowing customers to manage their finances on-the-go.
- Personalization: Through the use of advanced analytics and artificial intelligence, smart banking platforms can provide personalized recommendations, provides, and financial advice tailored to each customer's unique needs, preferences, and financial goals.
- Enhanced User Experience: Smart banking platforms are designed with intuitive interfaces, streamlined processes, and user-friendly features that make banking transactions and interactions more efficient, seamless, and enjoyable for customers.
- 24/7 Access: With smart banking, customers have round-the-clock access to banking services, including account inquiries, fund transfers, bill payments, and loan applications, enabling them to perform transactions at their convenience, regardless of time or location.
- Improved Security: Smart banking platforms employ advanced security measures such as biometric authentication, encryption, and real-time fraud detection to safeguard customers' sensitive financial information and transactions, providing peace of mind and confidence in the security of their accounts.

- Financial Education: Smart banking solutions often include educational resources, tools, and alerts that help customers better understand their finances, track spending habits, set budgeting goals, and make informed financial decisions, promoting financial literacy and empowerment.

Benefits for Financial Institutions:

- Cost Savings: Smart banking enables financial institutions to automate routine tasks, streamline processes, and reduce manual intervention, resulting in lower operational costs, improved efficiency, and resource optimization.
- Customer Acquisition and Retention: By providing innovative digital services, personalized experiences, and superior customer support, financial institutions can attract new customers and retain existing ones, using loyalty and long-term relationships.
- Data-driven Insights: Smart banking platforms generate valuable insights from customer data, such as spending patterns, behavior trends, and product preferences, enabling financial institutions to identify market opportunities, customize offerings, and optimize marketing strategies.
- Risk Management: Advanced analytics and machine learning algorithms help financial institutions identify and mitigate risks, such as fraud, credit defaults, and regulatory compliance issues, in real-time, minimizing financial losses and reputational damage.
- Competitive Advantage: Financial institutions that use smart banking technologies gain a competitive edge in the market by differentiating themselves with innovative products, services, and customer experiences that meet the evolving needs and expectations of digital-savvy consumers.

Figure 3. Role of blockchain in finance

- Agility and Innovation: Smart banking uses a culture of innovation and agility within financial institutions, encouraging experimentation with emerging technologies, collaboration with fintech partners, and rapid adaptation to changing market dynamics, ensuring relevance and resilience in a rapidly evolving digital landscape (refer figure 3).

In summary, smart banking provides a win-win scenario for both customers and financial institutions, providing unparalleled convenience, personalization, security, and efficiency in today's smart era. By using smart banking principles and using advanced technologies, financial institutions can deliver superior value and experiences to customers while driving growth, competitiveness, and sustainability in the digital age.

FUTURE OPPORTUNITIES IN THE ERA OF INDUSTRY 5.0 TOWARDS SMART BANKING SERVICES

In the era of Industry 5.0, smart banking services are faced to unlock a multitude of future opportunities that will revolutionize the financial industry (Zhang, H., & Li, J. (2021), Dutta, S., & Jain, S. (2019)). Here are some key opportunities:

- Hyper-personalization: With the integration of advanced technologies such as AI and big data analytics, smart banking services will be able to deliver hyper-personalized experiences tailored to each individual customer's preferences, behaviors, and financial goals. This level of personalization will enhance customer satisfaction, loyalty, and engagement.
- Predictive Financial Services: Smart banking services will use predictive analytics and machine learning algorithms to anticipate customers' financial needs and provide proactive recommendations and solutions in real-time. For example, banks can predict cash flow fluctuations, identify potential fraud risks, or suggest suitable investment opportunities based on customers' financial profiles.
- Integration of Emerging Technologies: Industry 5.0 will see the convergence of various emerging technologies, such as blockchain, IoT, and augmented reality, with smart banking services. For instance, blockchain can enable secure and transparent transactions, IoT devices can provide real-time data on customer behavior, and augmented reality can enhance the digital banking experience through immersive interfaces (Wong, L., & Tan, K. (2020), Li, W., & Zhang, Y. (2018)).
- Enhanced Security Measures: As cyber threats continue to evolve, smart banking services will invest in advanced security measures such as biometric authentication, multi-factor authentication, and decentralized identity management systems to safeguard customer data and transactions from unauthorized access and cyber-attacks.
- Expansion of Digital Ecosystems: Industry 5.0 will drive the expansion of digital ecosystems, where banks collaborate with fintech startups, technology giants, and other industry players to provide integrated financial services and solutions. This collaboration will enable banks to extend their reach, innovate faster, and create value-added services for customers.

- Financial Inclusion and Accessibility: Smart banking services will play a important role in promoting financial inclusion and accessibility by reaching underserved populations, such as the unbanked and underbanked, through innovative digital solutions. Mobile banking apps, digital wallets, and peer-to-peer payment platforms will provide convenient and affordable access to financial services for all segments of society.
- Ethical and Sustainable Finance: In the era of Industry 5.0, there will be a growing emphasis on ethical and sustainable finance, with smart banking services incorporating environmental, social, and governance (ESG) criteria into their products and investment strategies. Customers will have the option to align their financial choices with their values, driving positive social and environmental impact.

In summary, the future opportunities in the era of Industry 5.0 towards smart banking services are large and transformative. By using innovation, collaboration, and customer-centricity, banks can use the power of technology to deliver smarter, more inclusive, and sustainable financial services that meet the evolving needs and expectations of customers in the digital age.

OPEN ISSUES AND CHALLENGES IN IMPLEMENTING SMART FINANCIAL SERVICES

Implementing smart financial services presents several open issues and challenges that need to be addressed for successful adoption and integration. Here are some key challenges:

- Data Privacy and Security: One of the foremost challenges is ensuring the privacy and security of customer data in smart financial services. With the proliferation of digital transactions and the collection of large amounts of personal information, banks must implement robust cybersecurity measures and adhere to strict data protection regulations to safeguard against data breaches and unauthorized access (Tyagi et al., (2021), (2022), (2023)), and (2024), Li, W., & Zhang, Y. (2018)).
- Regulatory Compliance: Smart financial services operate within a complex regulatory landscape, subject to numerous laws and regulations governing data privacy, consumer protection, financial transactions, and cybersecurity. Compliance with these regulations requires huge resources and expertise, posing a challenge for banks to navigate and adhere to regulatory requirements while innovating and remaining competitive.

- Technology Integration and Legacy Systems: Integrating new technologies into existing banking infrastructure and legacy systems can be challenging and time-consuming. Banks often face interoperability issues, data silos, and compatibility issues when implementing smart financial services, requiring major investments in technology upgrades, platform migrations, and organizational restructuring.

- Customer Trust and Adoption: Building customer trust and driving adoption of smart financial services is essential for success. However, customers may be reluctant to use new technologies due to issues about security, privacy, usability, and reliability. Banks must prioritize transparency, education, and user experience design to overcome resistance and use trust among customers.

- Digital Divide and Inequality: The digital divide persists, with disparities in access to technology and digital literacy among different demographic groups and regions. Smart financial services risk exacerbating inequality by excluding those who lack access to smartphones, internet connectivity, or digital skills. Banks must address these disparities through initiatives to promote digital inclusion and accessibility for all segments of society (Kim, Y., & Park, J. (2021)).

- Ethical and Bias Issues: The use of AI and machine learning algorithms in smart financial services raises ethical issues related to algorithmic bias, discrimination, and fairness. Biased algorithms can perpetuate systemic inequalities and unfairly disadvantage certain groups. Banks must implement measures to mitigate bias, ensure transparency, and uphold ethical standards in algorithmic decision-making processes.

- Operational Risks and Disruptions: Smart financial services are susceptible to operational risks such as system failures, cyber-attacks, and disruptions in technology infrastructure. Banks must implement robust contingency plans, disaster recovery mechanisms, and cybersecurity protocols to mitigate the impact of operational disruptions and ensure business continuity.

Hence, addressing these open issues and challenges requires a coordinated effort from banks, regulators, technology providers, and other users. By prioritizing cybersecurity, regulatory compliance, customer trust, digital inclusion, ethical issues, and operational resilience, banks can navigate the complexities of implementing smart financial services and unlock the transformative potential of technology for the benefit of customers and society as a whole.

CASE STUDIES AND BEST PRACTICES

Successful Implementation of Smart Financial Services by Leading Banks

Several leading banks have successfully implemented smart financial services, using advanced technologies to enhance customer experiences, drive innovation, and stay ahead of the competition (Sharma, S., & Kumar, A. (2019)). Here are some examples of banks that have achieved success in this area:

JPMorgan Chase & Co.: JPMorgan Chase is known for its commitment to digital transformation and innovation in financial services. The bank has invested heavily in technology initiatives such as AI, big data analytics, and blockchain to improve operational efficiency, personalize customer experiences, and mitigate risks. JPMorgan's mobile banking app provides a wide range of features, including mobile check deposit, person-to-person payments, and budgeting tools, catering to the evolving needs of digital-savvy customers.

DBS Bank: DBS Bank, headquartered in Singapore, has been recognized for its leadership in digital banking and innovation. The bank's digital transformation journey, known as "Making Banking Joyful," has focused on delivering seamless and personalized experiences across digital channels. DBS' digital banking platform provides features such as AI-powered chatbots, biometric authentication, and predictive analytics, enabling customers to bank anytime, anywhere, with ease.

ING Group: ING Group, a multinational banking and financial services corporation based in the Netherlands, has used digital innovation to reimagine banking for the digital age. The bank's "Think Forward" strategy prioritizes customer-centricity, simplicity, and innovation, driving initiatives such as mobile banking, open banking APIs, and data-driven insights. ING's mobile banking app provides intuitive features such as personalized financial insights, real-time account alerts, and seamless account aggregation, empowering customers to make smarter financial decisions.

HSBC Holdings plc: HSBC, one of the world's largest banking and financial services organizations, has made huge investments in digital transformation to enhance customer experiences and drive operational efficiency. The bank's "Digital at the Core" strategy focuses on using digital technologies such as AI, cloud computing, and biometrics to streamline processes, improve accessibility, and deliver personalized services. HSBC's digital banking platforms provide a range of innovative features, including voice-enabled banking, biometric authentication, and AI-powered virtual assistants, enabling customers to bank securely and conveniently from anywhere in the world.

Bank of America: Bank of America has been at the forefront of digital banking innovation, with a strong emphasis on enhancing customer engagement and satisfaction. The bank's digital banking platforms, including the Bank of America mobile app and online banking portal, provide a seamless and intuitive user experience, with features such as mobile check deposit, bill pay, and personalized financial guidance. Bank of America has also invested in AI-powered virtual assistants, chatbots, and predictive analytics to deliver personalized recommendations and proactive support to customers.

Hence, these examples demonstrate how leading banks are successfully implementing smart financial services to meet the evolving needs and expectations of customers in the digital age. By using digital transformation, investing in technology, and prioritizing customer-centricity, these banks have positioned themselves for long-term success and leadership in the ever-changing landscape of financial services.

Innovative Solutions Addressing Industry 5.0 Challenges

In addressing the challenges posed by Industry 5.0, innovative solutions are emerging across various sectors to use the potential of advanced technologies and drive sustainable growth. Here are some examples of innovative solutions that address challenges in Industry 5.0:

- AI-Powered Predictive Maintenance: In manufacturing, AI-powered predictive maintenance solutions utilize machine learning algorithms to analyze sensor data and predict equipment failures before they occur. By identifying maintenance needs in advance, manufacturers can minimize downtime, reduce maintenance costs, and optimize operational efficiency.
- Blockchain-enabled Supply Chain Management: Blockchain technology provides transparent and secure supply chain management solutions by providing an immutable ledger of transactions and enabling real-time tracking of goods from production to delivery. By enhancing transparency, traceability, and trust, blockchain-based supply chain solutions help mitigate risks, streamline processes, and ensure compliance with regulatory requirements.
- Smart Grids and Energy Management Systems: In the energy sector, smart grids and energy management systems use IoT devices, sensors, and data analytics to optimize energy distribution, monitor grid performance, and balance supply and demand in real-time. These solutions enable utilities to improve grid reliability, integrate renewable energy sources, and reduce carbon emissions, contributing to a more sustainable and resilient energy infrastructure.
- Digital Twins for Product Development: Digital twin technology enables manufacturers to create virtual replicas of physical products, processes, or

systems, allowing them to simulate and optimize performance, design, and maintenance in a virtual environment. By using digital twins, manufacturers can accelerate product development cycles, minimize prototyping costs, and enhance product quality and innovation.

- Smart Cities and Urban Mobility Solutions: In urban areas, smart city initiatives use IoT sensors, data analytics, and connectivity solutions to optimize urban infrastructure, improve transportation systems, and enhance quality of life for residents. Smart mobility solutions, such as intelligent traffic management systems, ride-sharing platforms, and electric vehicle charging infrastructure, promote sustainability, reduce congestion, and increase accessibility in cities.

- Precision Agriculture and AgriTech Solutions: In agriculture, precision agriculture technologies use IoT sensors, drones, and data analytics to optimize farming practices, monitor crop health, and improve resource efficiency. AgriTech solutions enable farmers to make data-driven decisions, optimize yields, and mitigate environmental impact, contributing to sustainable food production and agricultural resilience.

- Healthcare Wearables and Remote Monitoring: In healthcare, wearable devices and remote monitoring solutions enable real-time monitoring of patient health metrics, facilitating early detection of health issues, remote patient monitoring, and personalized healthcare interventions. These solutions improve patient outcomes, reduce healthcare costs, and enhance access to healthcare services, especially in remote or underserved areas.

These examples illustrate how innovative solutions are addressing challenges in Industry 5.0 across various sectors, driving efficiency, sustainability, and resilience in the face of rapid technological change. By using innovation and collaboration, organizations can use the transformative potential of advanced technologies to navigate the complexities of Industry 5.0 and create a more inclusive, sustainable, and prosperous future.

THE ROLE OF COLLABORATION AND PARTNERSHIPS

Importance of Ecosystem Collaboration in Industry 5.0

Ecosystem collaboration is of paramount importance in Industry 5.0, where interconnectedness and interdependence among users play a central role in driving innovation, competitiveness, and sustainability. Here are several reasons highlighting the importance of ecosystem collaboration in Industry 5.0:

- Innovation and Co-Creation: Ecosystem collaboration brings together diverse expertise, resources, and perspectives from various industries, academia, government, and civil society to use innovation and co-create solutions to complex challenges. By collaborating across ecosystems, organizations can use complementary strengths, share knowledge, and discuss new ideas, leading to breakthrough innovations and disruptive technologies.
- Market Access and Expansion: Collaborating within ecosystems enables organizations to access new markets, customers, and distribution channels that may be beyond their reach individually. By partnering with ecosystem users, companies can tap into existing networks, use established relationships, and gain market insights, accelerating market entry and expansion strategies.
- Resource Sharing and Efficiency: Ecosystem collaboration facilitates resource sharing and pooling of capabilities, enabling organizations to achieve economies of scale, reduce costs, and improve operational efficiency. By sharing infrastructure, technology, and expertise, organizations can optimize resource utilization, mitigate risks, and enhance competitiveness in a rapidly changing business environment.
- Risk Mitigation and Resilience: In Industry 5.0, where disruptions are frequent and unpredictable, ecosystem collaboration enhances resilience by diversifying risks and building adaptive capacity. By collaborating with ecosystem partners, organizations can use collective intelligence, share risk management strategies, and respond more effectively to disruptions such as supply chain disruptions, regulatory changes, or technological shifts.
- Ecosystem Synergies and Value Creation: Collaborating within ecosystems creates synergies that generate value greater than the sum of its parts. By connecting complementary products, services, and capabilities, organizations can create integrated solutions that address customer needs, enhance user experiences, and differentiate themselves in the market, driving sustainable growth and competitive advantage.
- Sustainability and Social Impact: Ecosystem collaboration enables organizations to address complex societal and environmental challenges by using collective efforts and resources. By aligning shared goals and values, organizations can drive positive social impact, promote sustainability, and contribute to the achievement of global sustainability goals such as the United Nations Sustainable Development Goals (SDGs).
- Policy and Regulatory Influence: Collaborating within ecosystems empowers organizations to advocate for favorable policies, regulations, and standards that support innovation, competitiveness, and responsible business practices. By engaging with policymakers, regulators, and industry associations, orga-

nizations can shape the regulatory environment, address regulatory barriers, and use an enabling ecosystem for Industry 5.0.

In summary, ecosystem collaboration is essential in Industry 5.0 for driving innovation, market access, resource efficiency, risk resilience, value creation, sustainability, and policy influence. By using collaboration as a strategic imperative, organizations can use the collective power of ecosystems to navigate the complexities of Industry 5.0 and create shared value for users and society as a whole.

Strategies for Using Partnerships Between Banks, Fintechs, and Regulators

Using partnerships between banks, fintechs, and regulators is essential for driving innovation, enhancing regulatory compliance, and promoting financial inclusion in the rapidly evolving landscape of the financial industry. Here are several strategies to facilitate collaboration and partnership among these users:

- Establish Open Communication Channels: Create open communication channels and forums where banks, fintechs, and regulators can engage in constructive dialogue, share insights, and exchange feedback on regulatory requirements, market trends, and industry best practices. Regular meetings, workshops, and industry conferences provide valuable opportunities for networking and collaboration.
- Promote Regulatory Sandboxes: Regulatory sandboxes provide a safe and controlled environment for banks and fintechs to test innovative products, services, and business models under regulatory supervision. Regulators can establish sandboxes with clear guidelines, streamlined approval processes, and flexible regulatory frameworks to encourage experimentation, use innovation, and address regulatory uncertainties.
- Encourage Collaboration Initiatives: Encourage collaboration initiatives between banks and fintechs through accelerators, incubators, and innovation hubs. These initiatives bring together startups, established financial institutions, and regulators to collaborate on pilot projects, proof-of-concepts, and joint ventures, using knowledge exchange, mentorship, and co-creation of innovative solutions.
- Facilitate Regulatory Compliance Support: Provide regulatory compliance support and guidance to fintech startups and emerging players to navigate complex regulatory requirements and ensure compliance with applicable laws and regulations. Regulators can provide regulatory advisory services,

compliance toolkits, and regulatory training programs to help fintechs understand and adhere to regulatory obligations.

- Encourage Information Sharing and Collaboration Platforms: Establish information sharing and collaboration platforms where banks, fintechs, and regulators can exchange information, share best practices, and collaborate on regulatory initiatives. These platforms can facilitate knowledge sharing, promote industry standards, and enhance regulatory transparency and coordination.

- Encourage Partnerships for Financial Inclusion: Promote partnerships between banks, fintechs, and regulators to advance financial inclusion initiatives and address underserved markets and populations. Collaborative efforts such as digital banking initiatives, mobile payment solutions, and alternative credit scoring models can expand access to financial services and promote inclusive economic growth.

- Develop Regulatory Guidelines for Collaboration: Develop clear regulatory guidelines and frameworks that govern partnerships between banks and fintechs, addressing key areas such as risk management, data protection, cybersecurity, and consumer protection. Regulators can provide guidance on due diligence requirements, contractual arrangements, and dispute resolution mechanisms to facilitate smooth collaboration and mitigate potential risks.

- Encourage RegTech Innovation: Promote innovation in regulatory technology (RegTech) solutions that enable banks and fintechs to streamline compliance processes, automate regulatory reporting, and enhance risk management capabilities. Regulators can support the development and adoption of RegTech solutions through regulatory sandboxes, pilot programs, and regulatory incentives.

Hence, by implementing these strategies, banks, fintechs, and regulators can use a collaborative ecosystem that promotes innovation, regulatory compliance, and financial inclusion, driving sustainable growth and resilience in the financial industry.

ANTICIPATED EVOLUTION OF SMART BANKING IN THE NEXT DECADE

The anticipated evolution of smart banking over the next decade is faced to be transformative, driven by rapid advancements in technology, changing consumer behaviors, and regulatory developments. Here are several key trends and developments that may shape the future of smart banking:

- AI-Powered Personalization: AI and machine learning algorithms will play an increasingly central role in smart banking, enabling hyper-personalized experiences tailored to each individual customer's preferences, behaviors, and financial goals. Banks will use AI to anticipate customer needs, provide personalized product recommendations, and deliver proactive financial advice in real-time.

- Voice and Conversational Banking: Voice-enabled banking interfaces, virtual assistants, and chatbots will become more prevalent, enabling customers to interact with banks using natural language commands and conversational interfaces. Voice banking will provide seamless and intuitive experiences, allowing customers to perform banking transactions, access account information, and receive personalized assistance using voice commands.

- Blockchain and Digital Assets: Blockchain technology will revolutionize banking by enabling secure and transparent transactions, reducing processing times, and lowering costs. Banks will discuss the use of blockchain for various applications, including cross-border payments, trade finance, digital identity management, and tokenization of assets. The adoption of digital assets such as cryptocurrencies and stablecoins will also gain traction, providing new opportunities for payments, investments, and asset management.

- Open Banking and APIs: Open banking initiatives will continue to reshape the banking landscape, enabling banks to share customer data securely with third-party providers through open APIs. Open banking will use innovation, competition, and collaboration in the financial ecosystem, enabling the development of innovative fintech solutions, personalized financial services, and seamless integration with third-party applications and services.

- Biometric Authentication and Security: Biometric authentication methods such as facial recognition, fingerprint scanning, and behavioral biometrics will become standard features in smart banking applications, enhancing security and convenience for customers. Biometric authentication will replace traditional passwords and PINs, providing a more secure and frictionless authentication experience across digital channels.

- Decentralized Finance (DeFi): Decentralized finance (DeFi) platforms and protocols will disrupt traditional banking models by providing decentralized, permissionless financial services such as lending, borrowing, trading, and asset management on blockchain networks. DeFi will democratize access to financial services, eliminate intermediaries, and promote financial inclusion, albeit with regulatory challenges and risk issues.

- Embedded Finance and Platform Banking: Banking services will be seamlessly integrated into everyday experiences and digital platforms, blurring the lines between banking and non-banking activities. Embedded finance models will enable businesses to provide financial products and services directly to customers within their platforms, creating new revenue streams and enhancing customer engagement.

• Sustainable and Ethical Banking: There will be a growing emphasis on sustainable and ethical banking practices, with banks integrating environmental, social, and governance (ESG) criteria into their product offerings, investment strategies, and decision-making processes. Sustainable finance initiatives, green bonds, and impact investing will gain momentum, driven by increasing awareness of climate change, social responsibility, and corporate governance.

In summary, the evolution of smart banking over the next decade will be characterized by innovation, digitization, and customer-centricity, with technology serving as an enabler for delivering personalized, efficient, and sustainable financial services that meet the evolving needs and expectations of customers in the digital age.

CONCLUSION

The convergence of smart banking with the dawn of Industry 5.0 presents a transformative opportunity for financial services, providing a dynamic landscape ripe with innovation and disruption. Throughout this paper, we have discussed the large array of opportunities afforded by the integration of advanced technologies into traditional banking practices. From personalized customer experiences to operational efficiencies and the democratization of financial services, the potential benefits are profound. However, amidst these opportunities lie formidable challenges that cannot be overlooked. Cybersecurity threats loom large, requiring robust defenses to safeguard sensitive financial data and systems. Regulatory compliance poses another hurdle, necessitating careful navigation of evolving legal frameworks. Additionally, addressing the digital divide is imperative to ensure equitable access to smart financial services for all segments of society.

Despite these challenges, the promise of smart banking in the era of Industry 5.0 is too great to ignore. By using innovation, using collaboration across industries, and prioritizing customer-centricity, users can unlock the full potential of smart financial services. Through strategic investments in technology, talent, and infrastructure, the financial industry can lead the way in shaping a future where banking is smarter, more inclusive, and more resilient than ever before.

REFERENCES

Chen, L., & Wang, H. (2020). Next-Generation Banking Services: Advanced Solutions for Industry 5.0. *International Journal of Banking and Finance*, 15(3), 278–295. DOI:10.1002/ijbf.1234

Dutta, S., & Jain, S. (2019). Innovations in Sustainable Banking: Smart Banking Initiatives with Cutting-Edge Technologies. *Sustainable Finance Review*, 24(4), 367–382. DOI:10.1080/20430795.2019.1657299

Garcia, M., & Martinez, E. (2020). Advanced Banking Solutions in the Industry 5.0 Context: Challenges and Perspectives. *Journal of Financial Innovation*, 9(3), 321–336.

Kim, Y., & Park, J. (2021). Sustainable Financial Systems: Smart Banking Practices and Cutting-Edge Technologies. *Journal of Sustainable Banking and Finance*, 8(1), 45–60.

Kumar, R., & Singh, P. (2018). Advanced Banking Solutions for the Industry 5.0 Era: Challenges and Opportunities. *Journal of Financial Technology*, 22(4), 356–372. DOI:10.1002/jft.567

Li, W., & Zhang, Y. (2018). Driving Sustainability through Smart Banking: Emerging Technologies and Innovations. *Sustainable Development Review*, 21(3), 278–295.

Patel, A., & Gupta, M. (2019). The Role of Industry 5.0 in Shaping Advanced Banking Solutions. *Journal of Banking & Finance*, 6(1), 45–60.

Patel, R., & Shah, P. (2018). Towards Sustainable Finance: Smart Banking Solutions and Cutting-Edge Technologies. *International Journal of Sustainable Development*, 25(3), 267–282.

Pundareeka Vittala, K. R., Kiran Kumar, M., & Seranmadevi, R. (2024). Artificial Intelligence-Internet of Things Integration for Smart Marketing: Challenges and Opportunities. Advancing Software Engineering Through AI, Federated Learning, and Large Language Models. IGI Global. DOI:10.4018/979-8-3693-3502-4.ch019

Sharma, S., & Kumar, A. (2019). Transforming Banking for Sustainability: Smart Banking Solutions with Cutting-Edge Technologies. *International Journal of Sustainable Banking*, 10(2), 145–160.

Shrikant Tiwari, R. (2024). Position of Blockchain: Internet of Things-Based Education 4.0 in Industry 5.0 – A Discussion of Issues and Challenges. Architecture and Technological Advancements of Education 4.0. IGI Global. DOI:10.4018/978-1-6684-9285-7.ch013

Smith, J., & Johnson, R. (2021). Industry 5.0 and Advanced Banking Solutions: A Perspective from the Financial Sector. *Journal of Financial Innovation*, 8(2), 145–160. DOI:10.1080/21657358.2021.1890456

Wang, Y., & Li, W. (2021). Industry 5.0 and the Future of Banking: Advanced Solutions for Sustainable Finance. *International Journal of Sustainable Finance*, 12(2), 189–204. DOI:10.1080/20430795.2020.1857290

Wong, L., & Tan, K. (2020). Towards a Green Financial World: Smart Banking Strategies with Cutting-Edge Technologies. *Journal of Sustainable Finance and Banking*, 15(2), 189–204.

Zhang, H., & Li, J. (2021). Smart Banking for a Sustainable Future: Using Cutting-Edge Technologies for Financial Resilience. *Journal of Sustainable Financial Innovation*, 7(2), 156–171.

Chapter 11
An Analytical Study on Emerging Growth of Artificial Intelligence in India

J. Gayathri
https://orcid.org/0000-0002-5118-2030
Saveetha School of Law, India

J. Yazhini
Saveetha School of Law, India

ABSTRACT

Artificial intelligence (A.I.) is a multidisciplinary field aimed at automating tasks that currently need human intelligence. Computerized medical diagnosticians and systems that automatically tailor hardware to specific user requirements are examples of recent AI accomplishments. A.I. has spawned a slew of important technical concepts that unify these disparate fields. The search is made complex because of the need to determine the relevance of information and because of the frequent occurrence of uncertain and ambiguous data. Heuristics provide the A.I. system with a mechanism for the focusing its attention and controlling its searching processes. A total number of respondents 206 samples in the age group 18-35 years were selected randomly and forwarded the analyzed question online randomly through a convenient sampling method. The use of SPSS software to analyze and present the data collected from the frequency Graphs, chi-square tests.

DOI: 10.4018/979-8-3693-4187-2.ch011

INTRODUCTION

Artificial Intelligence (AI) is causing a seismic upheaval in the world of technology, allowing it to be used for increased production and success while also simplifying the system. AI is increasingly being employed in various industries, from your cell phone to disease diagnostics, providing high-performance and precise gadget operation with quality. It has shown to be a game-changing technology in every field, not just technology. India, as the world's fastest-growing economy and second-largest population, has a significant stake in the AI revolution. IITs, NITs, and IIITs, among the country's finest technology institutes, have the potential to be the nursery of AI researchers and start-ups. Indian start-ups are growing and creating AI solutions in education, health, financial services, and other domains to alleviate social problems.

The first Community Centre for Artificial Intelligence was established in Hyderabad, according to the Deccan Article. They also stated that The HexArt Institute is a project of the Hexagon Capability Hub India (HCCI), the company's largest product development centre in India. It recognises this institution as a timely societal responsibility endeavour. The following are some of the AI's most promising prospects in India: Several modern firms will deploy digital assistants to communicate with clients, reducing the requirement for human resources. Organizations can utilise AI in conjunction with other advancements to enable robots to make judgments and take actions faster than humans. AI is at the heart of a slew of new products that will aid humans in overcoming the bulk of complex problems. Commerce and Development Agreement to work together to exploit the power of cutting-edge technologies, like as AI and blockchain, to improve and increase trade.

Artificial intelligence and law are primarily concerned with the use of algorithms to make law more rational, practical, and likely. We've seen AI being implemented in a wide range of companies around the world, including small and medium businesses. As a result, the Indian legal profession has become familiar with AI and its applications. The author will explore the benefits of AI to the legal profession in India in this section and attempt to justify its importance in the Indian legal sector. AI is a type of computer programme that can perform tasks that would ordinarily require human intelligence. Machine learning, as well as deep learning and rules, are commonly used to fuel these artificial intelligence systems. As a result, you'll need to know how to use data in a methodical manner. Because of the surge in the number of people who require it, it has become a need.

Artificial intelligence has been used in a range of businesses in recent years, from hotel concierge robots to automated entertainment and cell phone use cases. Artificial intelligence's impact on a wide range of industries is difficult to overstate. As a result, the Indian legal business has seen little technological innovation, and attorneys in the country are still accustomed to and reliant on solutions devised many years ago. Artificial intelligence has the potential to have a substantial impact on the practise of law in India. One of the most significant areas where AI could have a harmful impact on the law is legal research.

Within seconds of using Artificial Intelligence, attorneys have access to a wealth of information on the Indian legal system, which is always developing and expanding. To do legal research today, a substantial number of man-hours are necessary; but, with Artificial Intelligence, the whole legal fraternity may be evened out.

OBJECTIVES

- To study the impact of demonetisation on the society in India.
- To analyze the problems faced by the people when the demonetisation was announced.
- To study the positive and negative impact on demonetisation.
- To study the sector-wise impact on demonetisation.

REVIEW OF LITERATURE

The belief in the possibility of artificial intelligence (AI), given present computers, is the belief that all that is essential to human intelligence can be formalized. AI has not fulfilled early expectations in pattern recognition and problem solving. They necessarily involve a non-formal form of information processing which is possible only or embodied beings-where being embodied does not merely mean being able to move and to operate manipulators. The human world, with its recognizable objects, is organized by human beings using their embodied capacities to satisfy their embodied needs. There is no reason to suppose that a world organized in terms of the body should be accessible by other means (Wrathall and Malpas, 1974).

This research surveys important aspects of Web Intelligence WI in the context of Artificial Intelligence in Education AIED research. WI explores the fundamental roles as well as practical impacts of Artificial Intelligence AI and advanced Information Technology IT on the next generation of Web-related products, systems, services, and activities. As a direction for scientific research and development, WI can be extremely beneficial for the field of AIED. Some of the key components of WI have already attracted AIED researchers for quite some time ontologies, adaptivity and personalization, and agents. The paper covers these issues only very briefly. It focuses more on other issues in WI, such as intelligent Web services, semantic markup, and Web mining, and proposes how to use them as the basis for tackling new and challenging research problems in AIED (Bussler, 2004).

Issues in Science & Technology is a forum for discussion of public policy related to science, engineering, and medicine. This includes policy for science, how we nurture the health of the research enterprise and science for policy, how we use knowledge more effectively to achieve social goals, with emphasis on the latter (Etzioni, 2017).

Philosophy and Phenomenological Research was founded in 1940 by Marvin Farber, who edited it for forty years. Since 1980 it has been at Brown, where it has been edited by Roderick Chisholm and then, since 1986, by Ernest Sosa. From its founding, the journal has been open to a variety of methodologies and traditions (Perlman, 1983).

The Journal of Economic Perspectives (JEP) attempts to fill a gap between the general interest press and most other academic economics journals. The journal aims to publish articles that will serve several goals: to synthesize and integrate lessons learned from active lines of economic research; to provide economic analysis of public policy issues; to encourage cross-fertilization of ideas among the fields of thinking; to offer readers an accessible source for state-of-the-art economic thinking; to suggest directions for future research; to provide insights and readings for classroom use; and to address issues relating to the economics profession. Articles appearing in the journal are normally solicited by the editors and associate editors. Proposals for topics and authors should be directed to the journal office (Valverde, 2015).

Rhetorica, published quarterly for the International Society for the History of Rhetoric, includes articles, book reviews and bibliographies that examine the theory and practice of rhetoric in all periods and languages and their relationship with poetics, philosophy, religion and law. The official languages of the Society, and of the journal, are English, French, German, Italian, Latin, and Spanish, with articles and features corresponding. If you crave complete grasp of, or are merely fascinated by, the power and politics of oration, each page of Rhetoric will fulfill (Vos and De Vos, 1991).

A series of topical philosophy studies, Philosophical Perspectives aims to publish original essays by foremost thinkers in their fields, with each volume confined to a main area of philosophical research. In 1996, Philosophical Perspectives became a supplement to Noûs and is currently published by Blackwell Publishing (Pollock, 1990).

A series of topical philosophy studies, Philosophical Perspectives aims to publish original essays by foremost thinkers in their fields, with each volume confined to a main area of philosophical research. In 1996, Philosophical Perspectives became a supplement to Noûs and is currently published by Blackwell Publishing (Berlin, 1990).

Phenomenology is often thought to be irrelevant to artificial-intelligence and cognitive-science research because first-person descriptions do not reach the level of genuine causal explanations. Although phenomenology taken in this weak sense may not be useful, the method of phenomenology taken more formally may well produce fruitful results. Husserl's phenomenological reduction, or epoche, sets the right frame of reference for a science of cognition because it makes explicit the difference between what belongs to cognition and what belongs to the natural world. Isolating this critical difference helps us assign the correct procedures to cognition and describe their functions. A formalized phenomenology of cognition can therefore aid initiatives in cognitive computing (Mentaki et al., 2002).

The New Atlantis is a quarterly journal about the social, ethical, and political dimensions of modern science and technology. Since its founding in 2003, the journal has been at the center of debates about how to govern science and how to live well and wisely with technological change. The journal's name is taken from Francis Bacon's short story New Atlantis, a utopian fable describing a society that enjoys the fruits of what we would now recognize as experimental science. The story raises important questions about science, politics, and society. The journal brings together several kinds of writing policy and economic analysis, literary and cultural essays, historical and biographical articles, book reviews, and more to tackle a wide range of subjects, from the latest scientific controversies and newest technological innovations to the eternal questions of the human condition (Devine, 2003).

Artificial Intelligence has become a big business in the military and in many industries. In spite of this growth there still remains no consensus about what AI really is. The major factor which seems to be responsible for this is the lack of agreement about the relationship between behavior and intelligence. In part certain ethical concerns generated from saying who, what and how intelligence is determined may be facilitating this lack of agreement (Koumentaki, 1990).

Dædalus was founded in 1955 as the Journal of the American Academy of Arts and Sciences and established as a quarterly in 1958. It continues the volume and numbering system of the Academy's Proceedings, which ceased publication under that title with Volume 85. Dædalus draws on the enormous intellectual capacity of the American Academy, whose Fellows are among the nation's most prominent thinkers in the arts, sciences, and the humanities, as well as the full range of professions and public life. Each issue addresses a theme with original authoritative essays (M. Rangan, 1998).

Researchers in artificial intelligence and decision analysis share a concern with the construction of formal models of human knowledge and expertise. Historically, however, their approaches to these problems have diverged. Members of these two communities have recently discovered common ground: a family of graphical models of decision theory known as influence diagrams or as belief networks. These models are equally attractive to theoreticians, decision modelers, and designers of knowledge-based systems. From a theoretical perspective, they combine graph theory, probability theory and decision theory (Henley, 1995).

Artificial intelligences are an interesting test case for how readers construct fictional characters in SF in general. William Gibson's and Pat Cadigan's post-cyberpunk novels offer a different emphasis with regard to the attribution of gender characteristics because of the way they employ male and female characters in figural narrative situations to focalize the emergence of the new virtual life forms (Nünning and Sicks, 2007).

Journal of Thought is a nationally and internationally respected, peer-reviewed scholarly journal sponsored by the Society of Philosophy and History of Education. Each quarterly issue contains articles selected for publication by the editor based on recommendations from an international panel of reviewers. The journal is now in its 48th year of publication. The acceptance rate is approximately 25 percent. The journal is published electronically, with each issue posted to the journal's website and files mailed on disk to library and individual subscribers (Kaplan, 1998).

What makes A.I. Steven Spielberg's most interesting work is that it's the first of his movies to be both a children's film and a film for adults. The story for children is the one the narrator tells Pinocchio all over again. But the story for adults is about hopeless attachments and self-delusion; every character is obsessed with the image of a lost loved one, and tries to replace that person with a technological simulacrum. It's also a film about human brutality, callousness, and greed. This is a story not about a boy who becomes human, but about the death of humanity (James Wilson, 2002).

This article outlines some current initiatives to exploit artificial intelligence in a public-sector organization, the U.S. Army. A linkage to public productivity is established. The examples provide clear evidence that the technology is now ripe for widespread use in administrative environments. These certainly will constitute the primary engine of public institutional surveillance in the years to come. With this surveillance, the two spheres of private self-fashioning and public institutions will continue to evolve in relation to one another. As they do so, democratic society will change considerably. Perhaps Rorty's own normative and linguistic ideal of conversational maintenance may provide something of a democratic limit case on any future posthuman self-fashioning (Agrawal, 1988).

Michel Foucault's early works criticize the development of modern democratic institutions as creating a surveillance society, which functions to control bodies by making them feel watched and monitored full time. His later works attempt to recover private space by exploring subversive techniques of the body and language. Following Foucault, pragmatists like Richard Shusterman and Richard Rorty have also developed very rich approaches to this project, extending it deeper into the literary and somatic dimensions of self-stylizing. Yet, for a debate centered on the re-creation of the vision of the self, these discussions have yet to fully engage even while they set the conditions for this engagement with issues of posthuman technologies, such as AI, robotics, and genetic engineering (Daugherty, 2004).

Metaphilosophy publishes articles and book reviews stressing considerations about philosophy and particular schools, methods or fields of philosophy. The intended scope is very broad, no method, field or school is excluded. Particular areas of interest include the foundation, scope, function and direction of philosophy; justification of philosophical methods and arguments; the interrelations among schools or fields of philosophy aspects of philosophical systems; presuppositions of philosophical schools; the relation of philosophy to other disciplines sociology of philosophy; the relevance of philosophy to social and political action; issues in the teaching of philosophy (Nilekani and Shah, 1985).

Artificial intelligence is a branch of computer science capable of analysing complex medical data. Their potential to exploit meaningful relationships within a data set can be used in the diagnosis, treatment and predicting outcome in many clinical scenarios (Murphy and Schmeink; Schwab, 1984).

METHODOLOGY

The aim of the study is to analyze the emerging growth of artificial intelligence in India. The research method used here is an empirical method. The study is based on primary data. The primary data for the study was collected from 212 sample respondents by using well-structured questionnaires. The sampling method used in the study is a convenient sampling method. The independent variables used are age, gender, educational qualification, marital status and the dependent variable is the emerging growth of artificial intelligence. The tools of analysis used in the study are graphs, percentages and chi - square test for a meaningful analysis.

HYPOTHESES

Null Hypothesis

There is no significant relationship between the age of the respondents and their opinion towards the emerging growth of artificial intelligence in India.

Alternative Hypothesis

There is a significant relationship between the age of the respondents and their opinion towards the emerging growth of artificial intelligence in India.

Analysis of Data

Graph

Figure 1. Do you think an artificial intelligence could become a part of society?

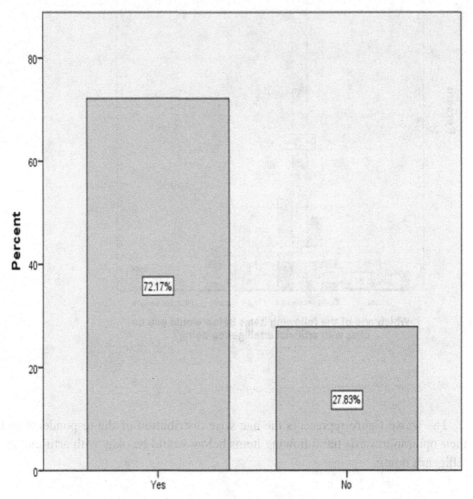

Do you think an artificial intelligence could become an part of society?

The above figure represents the respondents and their opinion towards the impact of artificial Intelligence in India.

Figure 2. Which one of the following items below would you be okay with artificial intelligence doing?

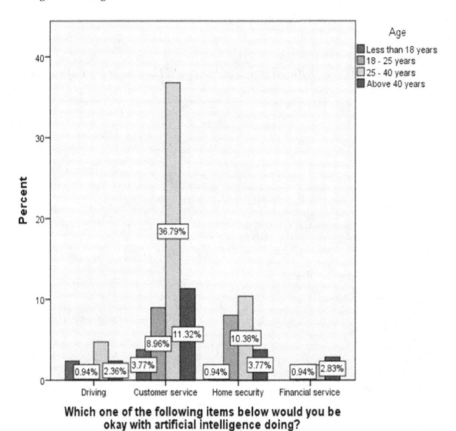

The above figure represents the age wise distribution of the respondents and their opinion towards the following items below would be okay with artificial intelligence doing.

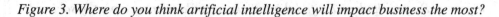

Figure 3. Where do you think artificial intelligence will impact business the most?

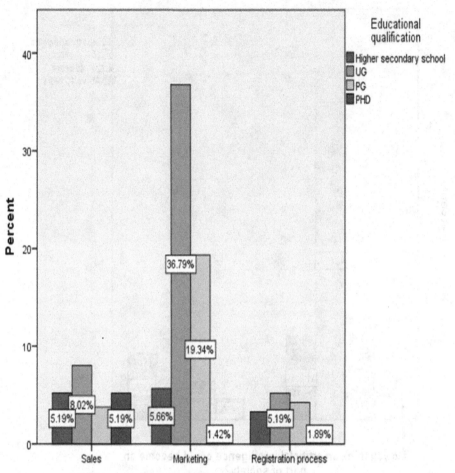

Where do you think will artificial intelligence impact the business most?

The above figure represents the educational qualification of the respondents and their opinion towards the artificial intelligence impact the business most.

Figure 4. Do you think an artificial intelligence could become a part of society?

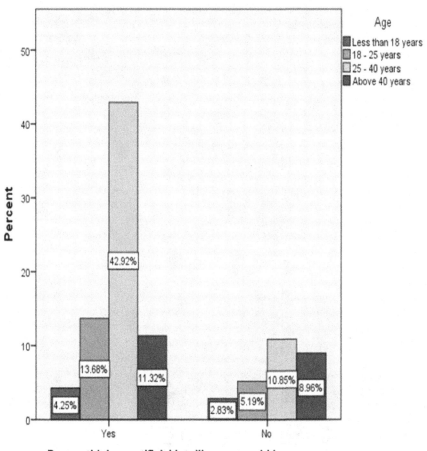

Do you think an artificial intelligence could become an
part of society?

The above figure represents the age wise distribution of the respondents and their opinion towards the artificial intelligence could become an part of the society.

Figure 5. Which one of the following items below would you be okay with artificial intelligence doing?

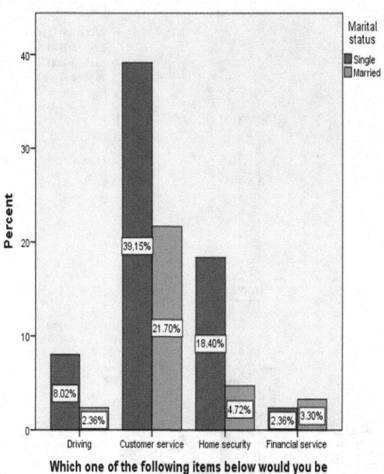

Which one of the following items below would you be
okay with artificial intelligence doing?

The above figure represents the marital status of the respondents and their opinion towards the following items below would you be okay with artificial intelligence doing.

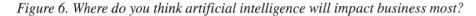
Figure 6. Where do you think artificial intelligence will impact business most?

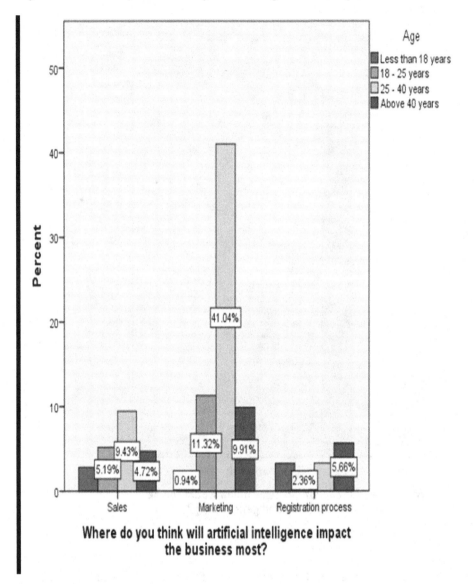

The above figure represents the age wise distribution of the respondents and their opinion towards the artificial intelligence impact the business most

Figure 7. Which one of the following items below would you be okay with artificial intelligence doing?

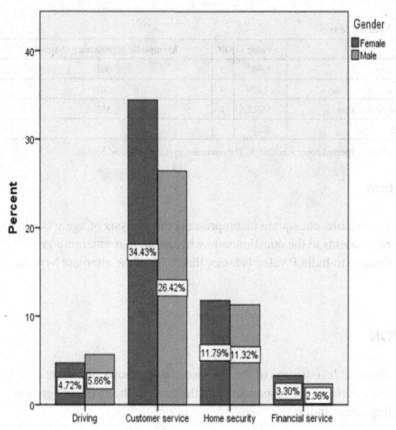

Which one of the following items below would you be okay with artificial intelligence doing?

The above figure represents the gender wise distribution of the respondents and their opinion towards the following items below would be okay artificial intelligence doing.

Chi Square Test

Table 1. Chi Square test

	Value	df	Asymptotic Significance (2-sided)
Pearson Chi-Square	26.902ᵃ	9	.001
Likelihood Ratio	22.759	9	.007
Linear-by-Linear Association	1.022	1	.312
N of Valid Cases	212		

a. 7 cells (43.8%) have expected count less than 5. The minimum expected count is .85.

Interpretation

From the above table, chi square test represents the analysis of age wise distribution of the respondents to the questionnaire whether there is emerging growth of artificial intelligence in India.P value is lesser than 0.05, if the alternate hypothesis is accepted.

DISCUSSION

From the above table, outcome of the chi square table shows that there is a significant difference between the respondents on the basis of the emerging growth of artificial intelligence in India

RESULTS

FIGURE 1 (SIMPLE BAR CHART) Represents the respondents and their opinion towards the artificial intelligence could become a part of society.

FIGURE 2 (CLUSTER BAR CHART) Represents the age group 25-40 years have responded higher as compared with other age groups.

FIGURE 3 (CLUSTER BAR CHART) Represents the educational qualification of the respondents and their opinion towards the artificial intelligence impacting the business most.

FIGURE 4(CLUSTER BAR CHART) Represents the age wise distribution of the respondents and their opinion towards the idea that artificial intelligence could become a part of society.

FIGURE 5(CLUSTER BAR CHART) Represents that single have strongly agreed that they are okay With artificial intelligence.

FIGURE 6 (CLUSTER BAR CHART) Represents the age wise distribution of the respondents and their opinion towards the artificial intelligence impacting the business most.

FIGURE 7(CLUSTER BAR CHART) Represents the gender wise distribution of the respondents and their opinion towards that they are okay With artificial intelligence.

Table 1 P value is lesser than 0.05,i.e.,over 000,if the alternate hypothesis is accepted. Thus we can conclude that there is age wise distribution of the respondents and their opinion towards the emerging growth of artificial intelligence in India.

DISCUSSION

Figure 1: We notice that most of the respondents have highly accepted (72.17%) that artificial intelligence could become a part of society.

Figure 2: We notice that age group of 25-40 years have mostly accepted (36.79%) that customer service is okay with artificial intelligence.

Figure 3: We notice that Undergraduate respondents are highly accepted (36.79%) have highly accepted that artificial intelligence in marketing impact the business most.

Figure 4: We notice that age group of 25-40 years have highly accepted that artificial intelligence could become an part of the society.

Figure 5: We notice that single have strongly agree (39.15%) that customer service is the items okay with artificial intelligence.

Figure 6: We notice that age group 25-40 years have highly accepted that marketing in artificial intelligence impact the business most.

Figure 7: We notice that female respondents have highly accepted (34.43%) that customer service is okay with artificial intelligence doing.

Table 1: From the Chi square test, it is evident the more people are aware of, the more the problem is serious.Like people are highly aware of the society and the more India is witnessing academic freedom.

LIMITATION

The utilization of the convenience sampling method through google forms (online) due to COVID 19 pandemi gave out a biased output which cannot be avoided . As there was a very short span of time to conduct and complete the research, the respondents were not on a large scale.

SUGGESTION

Focusing on optimism and potential: AI for Aam Aadmi (Common Man): This title captures the Indian perspective and focuses on the potential of AI to benefit the average person. The Rise of Intelligent India: How AI is Transforming the Nation. This title emphasizes the national transformation aspect of AI in India. Highlighting both opportunities and challenges: A Double-Edged Sword: India's Public Perception of AI's Growth. This title highlights the potential benefits and drawbacks of AI. Hope and Hesitation: Indian Citizens Grapple with the Rise of AI. This title uses contrasting emotions to reflect the mixed feelings people might have.

CONCLUSION

Conclusion: On a global scale, India was rated eighth in the top ten countries by AI patent families, a remarkable achievement given that it had filed no AI-related patents prior to 2002. We've merely scratched the surface of Artificial Intelligence's potential. However, it is critical to remember that AI is designed to improve human lives. We may need to adapt and reassess ourselves as AI technology develops. We will need to be prepared, both in terms of skills and knowledge, to deal with and succeed in a world that is always changing and improving as time passes. nonetheless

REFERENCES

Abramson, B. (2006). *Digital Phoenix: Why the Information Economy Collapsed and How It Will Rise Again*. MIT Press.

Agrawal, A. (2019). *The Economics of Artificial Intelligence: An Agenda*. University of Chicago Press. DOI:10.7208/chicago/9780226613475.001.0001

Budd, C., Douglas, G., & Saunders, S. (1998). "Friedrich Nietzsche & Daniel Dennett." The Philosophers'. *Magazine*, (4), 30–31. DOI:10.5840/tpm1998411

Bussler, C. (2004). *Web Information Systems*. WISE 2004 Workshops: WISE 2004 International Workshops, Brisbane, Australia.

Daugherty, P. R., & James Wilson, H. (2018). *Human + Machine: Reimagining Work in the Age of AI*. Harvard Business Press.

Devine, R. J., Good Care, C. M., & Choices, P. (2015). *Medical Ethics for Ordinary People* (3rd ed.). Paulist Press.

Etzioni, A. (2018). *Happiness Is the Wrong Metric: A Liberal Communitarian Response to Populism*. Springer. DOI:10.1007/978-3-319-69623-2

Henley, T. (2018). *Hergenhahn's An Introduction to the History of Psychology*. Cengage Learning.

Kaplan, J. (2015). *Humans Need Not Apply: A Guide to Wealth & Work in the Age of Artificial Intelligence*. Yale University Press.

Koumentaki, A., Anthony, F., Poston, L., & Wheeler, T. (2002, May). Low-Protein Diet Impairs Vascular Relaxation in Virgin and Pregnant Rats. *Clinical Science*, 102(5), 553–560. DOI:10.1042/cs1020553 PMID:11980575

Murphy, G., & Schmeink, L. (2017). *Cyberpunk and Visual Culture*. Routledge. DOI:10.4324/9781315161372

Nilekani, N., & Shah, V. (2016). *Rebooting India: Realizing a Billion Aspirations*. Penguin UK.

Nünning, A., & Sicks, K. M. (2012). *Turning Points: Concepts and Narratives of Change in Literature and Other Media*. Walter de Gruyter. DOI:10.1515/9783110297102

OECD. (2019). *Artificial Intelligence in Society*. OECD Publishing.

Perlman, M. A. (2009). *Functions in Biological and Artificial Worlds: Comparative Philosophical Perspectives*. MIT Press.

Pollock, J. (2019). Technical Methods. In *Philosophy*. Routledge.

Rangan, S. (2015). *Performance and Progress: Essays on Capitalism, Business, and Society*. OUP Oxford. DOI:10.1093/acprof:oso/9780198744283.001.0001

Schwab, K. (2017). *The Fourth Industrial Revolution*.

Tomberlin, J. (1990). *Action Theory and Philosophy of Mind*.

Chapter 12
The Role of Futuristic Technologies in Building Sustainable Environment

Senthil Kumar Arumugam

https://orcid.org/0000-0002-5081-9183

Presidency University, Bengaluru, India

Amit Kumar Tyagi

https://orcid.org/0000-0003-2657-8700

National Institute of Fashion Technology, New Delhi, India

Shrikant Tiwari

https://orcid.org/0000-0001-6947-2362

Galgotias University, Greater Noida, India

Shabnam Kumari

SRM Institute of Science and Technology, Chennai, India

ABSTRACT

In the face of global environmental challenges, the integration of futuristic technologies has emerged as a pivotal factor in the pursuit of a sustainable future. This paper explores the multifaceted contributions of advanced technologies towards building and maintaining a sustainable environment. By examining the intersection of innovation and environmental stewardship, we delve into the transformative potential of futuristic technologies across various sectors. The advent of artificial intelligence, Internet of Things (IoT), renewable energy, and advanced materials has paved the way for a paradigm shift in environmental sustainability. AI-driven predictive models enable precise resource management, optimizing energy consumption, and minimizing waste. The IoT facilitates real-time monitoring and control of environmental

DOI: 10.4018/979-8-3693-4187-2.ch012

parameters, offering a data-driven approach to conservation efforts. Additionally, renewable energy technologies play a crucial role in reducing dependence on fossil fuels, mitigating climate change impacts.

INTRODUCTION

Sustainability and Its Importance and Challenges

Sustainability is a concept and a way of life that has gained increasing prominence in the 21st century. It represents a fundamental shift in how we view and interact with the world, acknowledging the interconnectedness of the environment, society, and the economy (Sassen, S. 2019) (IPCC. 2018). Sustainability is not a mere buzzword but a guiding principle for addressing the most pressing global issues of our time.

Importance of Sustainability:

- Environmental Preservation: Sustainability is fundamentally about preserving the natural environment. It recognizes that we must be stewards of the Earth, as our actions directly impact the health and longevity of ecosystems, biodiversity, and the climate.
- Resource Conservation: The Earth's resources are finite. Sustainable practices ensure that we use resources responsibly, minimizing waste and depletion, while striving for resource efficiency.
- Social Equity: Sustainability includes the idea of social justice. It promotes equitable access to resources, education, healthcare, and opportunities for all, irrespective of their background or location.
- Economic Viability: A sustainable economy is one that not only generates profits but also considers long-term impacts. Sustainability drives innovation, creating new business opportunities and reducing risks associated with resource scarcity and environmental regulations.
- Resilience and Adaptation: Sustainable practices help communities and societies adapt to environmental changes and unforeseen crises. They enhance resilience in the face of challenges such as climate change and natural disasters.

Challenges in Achieving Sustainability:

- Climate Change: Perhaps the most urgent challenge, climate change threatens ecosystems, weather patterns, and sea levels. Reducing greenhouse gas emissions and transitioning to clean energy sources are important steps.
- Resource Depletion: The overuse of finite resources, such as fossil fuels, water, and minerals, poses a significant challenge. Sustainable resource management is necessary to avoid scarcity and ecological damage.
- Biodiversity Loss: The ongoing loss of biodiversity due to habitat destruction, pollution, and invasive species threatens ecosystems and food security. Conservation efforts are essential.
- Waste Management: Waste generation and mismanagement, particularly plastic pollution, pose challenges. Moving towards a circular economy with reduced waste and increased recycling is a solution.
- Social Inequity: Achieving social justice and addressing income inequality is an ongoing challenge. Many sustainable initiatives aim to bridge this gap.
- Food Security: Ensuring a growing global population has access to safe and nutritious food while minimizing the environmental impact of agriculture is a complex challenge.
- Water Scarcity: Many regions face water scarcity due to overuse and pollution. Sustainable water management is important for human and ecological well-being.
- Energy Transition: Transitioning to renewable and sustainable energy sources while phasing out fossil fuels presents a challenge that involves technological, economic, and political changes.

Note that sustainability is a holistic and interdisciplinary endeavor that requires collective effort at local, national, and global levels. It's not just an ideal; it's a necessity for the well-being of current and future generations and the health of the planet itself. Balancing economic prosperity, social equity, and environmental preservation is the grand challenge of our time, and sustainability is the path forward.

About Futuristic Technologies

Futuristic technologies refer to cutting-edge innovations and scientific advancements that hold the potential to significantly impact various aspects of our lives, industries, and society in the near and distant future (Rees, W., & Wackernagel, M. 2013) (Song, Y., & Zegeye, A., 2017) (Angel, S., Sheppard, S., & Civco, D. L., 2011). These technologies often represent the forefront of scientific research and development, providing transformative capabilities. Here are some examples of futuristic technologies:

- Artificial Intelligence (AI): AI encompasses machine learning, deep learning, and neural networks, enabling computers to perform tasks that typically require human intelligence, such as speech recognition, image analysis, and autonomous decision-making.
- Quantum Computing: Quantum computers use the principles of quantum mechanics to perform complex computations at speeds that classical computers can't match. They have the potential to revolutionize fields like cryptography, materials science, and drug discovery.
- Blockchain: Blockchain is a decentralized, tamper-proof digital ledger technology. It's primarily associated with cryptocurrencies, but its applications extend to supply chain management, secure voting systems, and more.
- Internet of Things (IoT): IoT connects everyday objects and devices to the internet, enabling them to collect and exchange data. It's used in smart homes, cities, agriculture, healthcare, and industrial automation.
- Augmented Reality (AR) and Virtual Reality (VR): AR overlays digital information on the real world, while VR immerses users in a simulated environment. These technologies find applications in gaming, training, healthcare, and architecture.
- Biotechnology: Advances in biotechnology, including gene editing with CRISPR-Cas9, hold the potential to transform healthcare, agriculture, and environmental conservation.
- Nanotechnology: Nanotechnology deals with the manipulation of matter at the nanoscale. It is used to develop new materials, drugs, and electronic components.
- Renewable Energy Technologies: Innovations in renewable energy sources, such as solar and wind power, are transforming the energy landscape and reducing reliance on fossil fuels.
- Space Exploration Technologies: Companies like SpaceX are pioneering reusable rocket technology, aiming to make space exploration more cost-effective and accessible.
- Robotics: Advanced robotics, including humanoid robots, autonomous drones, and collaborative robots (cobots), find applications in manufacturing, healthcare, and space exploration.
- Biometrics and Facial Recognition: Biometrics and facial recognition technologies are used for security, authentication, and identification purposes.

- 5G Technology: The rollout of 5G networks promises ultra-fast and low-latency wireless communication, enabling the Internet of Things, augmented reality, and other applications.
- Energy Storage Technologies: Advances in energy storage, such as lithium-ion batteries and supercapacitors, enhance the efficiency and reliability of renewable energy systems.
- Hydrogen Fuel Cells: Hydrogen fuel cell technology provides a clean energy source for transportation and power generation.
- Cryonics: Cryonics discuss the preservation of human bodies or brains at extremely low temperatures with the hope of future revival and medical treatment.

Hence, these futuristic technologies represent a diverse array of innovations that have the potential to shape the future in profound ways. They provide opportunities for solving complex global challenges and advancing various fields, from healthcare and transportation to communication and energy. However, they also come with ethical, regulatory, and societal implications that need careful consideration as they continue to develop and integrate into our daily lives.

Benefits of Futuristic Technologies in Sustainability

Futuristic technologies play an important role in advancing sustainability efforts across various sectors. Their innovative capabilities provide several benefits in promoting a more sustainable future. Here are some key benefits of futuristic technologies in sustainability:

Environmental Conservation:

- Renewable Energy: Technologies like solar panels, wind turbines, and advanced energy storage systems enable the production of clean, renewable energy, reducing greenhouse gas emissions and dependence on fossil fuels.
- Environmental Monitoring: Internet of Things (IoT) sensors and remote sensing technologies help in real-time environmental monitoring, allowing for early detection and response to environmental issues like pollution, deforestation, and climate change.

Resource Efficiency:

- Smart Resource Management: IoT devices and data analytics optimize resource use in agriculture, water management, and energy distribution, reducing waste and conserving resources.
- Circular Economy: Advanced materials and recycling technologies enable a circular economy by reducing waste, reusing materials, and promoting sustainable consumption.

Supply Chain Transparency:

- Blockchain: Blockchain technology enhances transparency and traceability in supply chains, ensuring ethical and sustainable sourcing of products and materials (Rocha, M. F. 2018), such as conflict-free minerals or sustainably sourced seafood.

Eco-Friendly Transportation:

- Electric Vehicles (EVs): EVs, powered by advanced battery technology, reduce emissions and dependence on fossil fuels, contributing to cleaner air and a lower carbon footprint.
- Autonomous and Shared Mobility: Futuristic technologies in autonomous vehicles and ride-sharing services enhance transportation efficiency and reduce traffic congestion.

Sustainable Agriculture:

- Precision Agriculture: Technologies like IoT, drones, and AI assist farmers in optimizing crop yields while minimizing resource use, including water and pesticides.
- Vertical Farming: Vertical farming, enabled by LED lighting and controlled environments, reduces land and water requirements while increasing food production in urban areas.

Environmental Resilience:

- Predictive Analytics: AI and machine learning models provide insights into climate patterns, helping communities prepare for and mitigate the impact of extreme weather events and natural disasters.

Conservation and Biodiversity:

- Biotechnology: Biotechnological advancements, including genetic sequencing and preservation techniques, support conservation and the protection of endangered species.
- Environmental Sensors: IoT-enabled sensors monitor ecosystems and wildlife, aiding in their protection and restoration.

Energy Efficiency:

- Smart Grids: IoT and data analytics in smart grids reduce energy wastage and allow for better energy distribution and management.
- Energy-Efficient Buildings: Smart building technologies improve energy efficiency by adjusting heating, cooling, and lighting according to occupancy and usage.

Clean Water and Air Quality:

- Advanced Water Treatment: Innovative water purification technologies, like nanotechnology and advanced filtration, enhance water quality and accessibility (Batty, M. 2018) (Pickett, S. T., Cadenasso, M. L., & Grove, J. M., 2018).
- Air Quality Monitoring: IoT sensors track air quality and enable timely responses to reduce air pollution.

Waste Reduction and Recycling:

- Waste-to-Energy: Technologies for converting waste into energy, such as incineration and anaerobic digestion, reduce landfill usage and produce clean energy.
- Advanced Recycling: Innovations in recycling technologies improve the efficiency and effectiveness of recycling processes.

In summary, these benefits demonstrate the transformative power of futuristic technologies in addressing sustainability challenges. They provide the potential to reduce environmental impact, promote responsible resource use, enhance transparency, and create more resilient communities and ecosystems. As these technologies continue to evolve and become more accessible, they will play a pivotal role in shaping a sustainable future.

Organization of the work

This work is summarized in 7 sections.

THE INTERSECTION OF FUTURISTIC TECHNOLOGY AND SUSTAINABILITY

IoT Role in Sustainability

The Internet of Things (IoT) plays a pivotal role in sustainability efforts across various industries by providing innovative solutions to monitor, manage, and optimize resources and processes. Here are some key ways IoT contributes to sustainability:

Environmental Monitoring:

- Air Quality: IoT sensors monitor air pollutants in real-time, enabling timely responses to improve air quality in urban areas.
- Water Quality: IoT devices track water parameters like pH, turbidity, and contaminants, ensuring the safety of water resources.
- Soil and Agriculture: IoT sensors in precision agriculture provide data on soil moisture, nutrients, and crop health, optimizing resource use and reducing environmental impact.

Energy Efficiency:

- Smart Buildings: IoT-enabled systems control heating, cooling, and lighting based on occupancy and usage patterns, reducing energy waste.
- Smart Grids: IoT helps utilities manage power distribution more efficiently and balance demand, leading to energy savings and grid resilience.

Waste Management:

- Smart Bins: IoT sensors monitor waste levels in trash bins, optimizing waste collection routes and reducing fuel consumption (Glaeser, E. L. (2011) (Coaffee, J., Healey, P., & O'Brien, P. 2018) (Bai, X., & Imura, H. 2016) (Alfen, H. W., & Ten Brink, P., 2018).
- Recycling: IoT systems improve the sorting and processing of recyclables, reducing contamination and improving recycling rates.

Water Management:

- Smart Water Meters: IoT devices enable accurate water consumption tracking, encouraging water conservation and reducing water wastage.
- Flood Monitoring: IoT sensors in flood-prone areas provide early warning systems, reducing damage and protecting communities.

Transportation:

- Smart Mobility: IoT enables real-time tracking of vehicles and traffic patterns, reducing congestion and lowering emissions.
- Fleet Management: IoT is used for efficient management of commercial fleets, leading to reduced fuel consumption and maintenance costs.

Supply Chain Transparency:

- Logistics: IoT ensures real-time tracking of goods and conditions during transit, reducing spoilage, theft, and the environmental footprint of supply chains.
- Product Traceability: Blockchain and IoT combine to provide transparent supply chain information, promoting ethical and sustainable sourcing.

Wildlife Conservation:

- Animal Tracking: IoT-enabled GPS and sensors track wildlife behavior and movements, aiding conservation efforts and reducing poaching risks.

Smart Cities:

- Traffic Management: IoT helps optimize traffic signals and routes to reduce congestion, leading to reduced fuel consumption and emissions.
- Urban Planning: IoT data informs sustainable urban development, from green spaces to public transportation systems.

Renewable Energy:

- Wind and Solar Farms: IoT technology monitors the performance and maintenance needs of renewable energy installations, improving efficiency and uptime.

Healthcare:

- Remote Patient Monitoring: IoT devices track important signs and medical data, reducing the need for physical hospital visits and the associated carbon footprint.

Agriculture:

- Precision Agriculture: IoT sensors collect data on crop health, weather conditions, and soil moisture to optimize irrigation and minimize resource use.

Water Conservation:

- Smart Irrigation: IoT-based irrigation systems use real-time weather data and soil conditions to optimize watering schedules, reducing water wastage in agriculture and landscaping.

Hence, the IoT's ability to gather and transmit data in real-time, coupled with advanced analytics and automation, empowers organizations and individuals to make informed decisions that reduce waste, conserve resources, and promote sustainability. Its integration into various sectors contributes significantly to environmental preservation and a more sustainable future.

Blockchain Role in Sustainability

Blockchain technology plays an important role in promoting sustainability by enhancing transparency, traceability, and trust in various processes and industries (Tulumello, S., & Hernández-Molina, G. 2018) (Giffinger, R., Fertner, et al., 2007) (Sai, G.H., Tripathi, K., Tyagi, A.K. (2023) (G. Vishnuram, K. Tripathi and A. Kumar Tyagi, 2022) (Akshita, Swetta et al., 2022). Here are key ways in which blockchain contributes to sustainability:

Supply Chain Transparency:

- Ethical Sourcing: Blockchain ensures the traceability of products, allowing consumers to verify the origins and ethical sourcing of goods, such as fair-trade coffee or conflict-free minerals.
- Reducing Fraud: By securely recording every transaction and product movement, blockchain helps eliminate counterfeit products in the supply chain, reducing fraud and ensuring product authenticity.

Carbon Credits and Emissions Tracking:

- Blockchain verifies and tracks carbon credits, enabling organizations to accurately offset their emissions and support renewable energy projects.
- Smart contracts on the blockchain can automate emissions reduction initiatives and verify compliance with environmental standards.

Food Safety and Agriculture:

- Blockchain ensures transparency in the food supply chain, enabling consumers to trace the journey of food from farm to table, reducing foodborne illnesses and food waste.
- Smart contracts can automatically trigger recalls in cases of food safety issues, ensuring swift responses to contamination.

Energy Trading and Grid Management:

- Blockchain enables peer-to-peer energy trading among individuals and businesses, encouraging the use of renewable energy sources and reducing reliance on fossil fuels.
- It improves the transparency and security of energy grid management, optimizing energy distribution and reducing waste.

Waste Management:

- Blockchain can help in tracking waste streams, incentivizing recycling, and reducing waste, as products can be traced and tracked throughout their life cycles.
- Smart bins with sensors can automatically trigger waste pickups when they are full, reducing inefficiencies in waste collection.

Conservation of Natural Resources:

- Blockchain can be used to create digital property rights for natural resources such as forests and oceans, encouraging conservation and sustainable management.
- Land registries on the blockchain reduce the risk of land grabs and illegal deforestation.

Water Management:

- Blockchain-enabled smart water meters track water usage in real-time, encouraging water conservation and reducing water wastage.
- The technology can also ensure transparent and equitable water allocation in regions facing water scarcity.

Humanitarian Aid and Donations:

- Blockchain enhances transparency and accountability in charitable donations by tracking contributions and ensuring they reach the intended recipients.
- It helps organizations to efficiently allocate resources in disaster relief efforts and humanitarian aid.

Clean Energy Certificates:

- Blockchain can be used to certify and verify the production and sale of clean energy, encouraging investment in renewable energy sources and reducing greenhouse gas emissions.

Environmental Impact Investments:

- Blockchain-based financial products allow investors to put their money into sustainable and socially responsible projects, fostering the growth of the green economy.

Note that Blockchain's decentralized and immutable ledger ensures data integrity, transparency, and trust. These attributes make it a valuable tool for various industries, enabling sustainability efforts to be tracked, verified, and rewarded, while promoting ethical practices and reducing waste and environmental harm.

Quantum Computing Role in Sustainability

Quantum computing, an emerging and highly advanced field of technology, has the potential to significantly impact sustainability efforts in various ways (Shreyas Madhav, A.V., Ilavarasi, A.K., Tyagi, A.K. 2022) (Varsha R., Nair, et al., 2021) (Nair, Meghna Manoj; Tyagi, Amit Kumar, 2021) (Tyagi, A.K., Sreenath, N., 2023) (Tyagi, Nair, et al., 2020). While quantum computing is still in its early stages of development, its unique capabilities provide several opportunities for addressing complex sustainability challenges:

- Climate Modeling and Simulation: Quantum computers can simulate complex climate models and scenarios with unprecedented speed and accuracy. This can help in understanding climate change, predicting its impacts, and developing effective mitigation and adaptation strategies.
- Optimization of Renewable Energy Sources: Quantum computing can optimize the placement and output of renewable energy sources such as wind turbines and solar panels. It can maximize energy generation, improve grid efficiency, and reduce costs in sustainable energy production.
- Energy Storage: Quantum computing can accelerate the development of advanced materials for energy storage, leading to more efficient and longer-lasting batteries. This is important for renewable energy integration and electric vehicle adoption.
- Material Science and Green Chemistry: Quantum computing can model molecular structures and reactions with incredible precision. This capability is important for designing environmentally friendly materials, catalysts, and chemicals, reducing the environmental impact of industrial processes.
- Supply Chain Optimization: Quantum computing can optimize complex supply chains, reducing inefficiencies, waste, and carbon emissions. It enhances transparency and traceability, ensuring ethical and sustainable sourcing of materials.
- Water Resource Management: Quantum computers can analyze large dataset related to water resources and simulate the behavior of water systems. This can help in managing water availability, improving water quality, and minimizing wastage.

- Genomic and Proteomic Analysis: Quantum computing accelerates genomics and proteomics research, leading to breakthroughs in personalized medicine and more effective drug discovery. This can improve healthcare outcomes and reduce the environmental impact of pharmaceutical production.
- Traffic and Transportation Optimization: Quantum computing can optimize traffic patterns, transportation logistics, and route planning, reducing congestion and fuel consumption. This leads to more efficient and sustainable urban transportation systems.
- Natural Resource Conservation: Quantum computing can support the conservation of natural resources, such as forests and oceans, by optimizing resource management and monitoring environmental conditions with high precision.
- Risk Assessment and Disaster Resilience: Quantum computers can assess and predict risks associated with natural disasters and climate-related events, enhancing disaster preparedness and resilience efforts.
- Climate Finance and Carbon Pricing: Quantum computing can improve the accuracy of carbon pricing models and facilitate the development of climate financing mechanisms, supporting investments in sustainable projects.

Hence, while quantum computing holds immense promise, it is essential to acknowledge that the technology is still evolving and faces several technical and practical challenges, such as hardware limitations and scalability issues. However, as quantum computing matures, it has the potential to revolutionize sustainability efforts by providing powerful tools to address complex environmental and societal challenges more effectively.

Green Cloud Computing Role in Sustainability

Green cloud computing, also known as eco-friendly or sustainable cloud computing, plays a significant role in sustainability by reducing the environmental impact of data centers and IT operations (Tyagi, A.K., Sreenath, N. 2023) (Tyagi, A.K., Sreenath, N., 2023) (Madhav, A.V.S., Tyagi, A.K. 2023) (Amit Kumar Tyagi, Aswathy S U, G Aghila, N Sreenath, 2021). It involves the use of energy-efficient technologies and practices to minimize carbon emissions and resource consumption. Here's how green cloud computing contributes to sustainability:

- Energy Efficiency: Green cloud providers use energy-efficient hardware, cooling systems, and data center designs to reduce electricity consumption. They may utilize renewable energy sources such as wind, solar, or hydropower to power their data centers.

- Server Virtualization: Virtualization technology allows multiple virtual servers to run on a single physical server, reducing the number of physical servers required. This lowers energy consumption, space requirements, and e-waste generation.
- Dynamic Resource Allocation: Green cloud platforms use dynamic resource allocation and load balancing to ensure that server resources are used efficiently. This minimizes idle server capacity and power consumption.
- Improved Cooling Systems: Data centers employ advanced cooling systems that use outside air, economizers, or liquid cooling to maintain ideal temperatures. These systems reduce the energy needed for cooling.
- Energy-Efficient Hardware: Green cloud providers invest in energy-efficient hardware, including processors, memory, and storage devices, to reduce power consumption and improve performance.
- Data Center Location: Locating data centers in regions with cooler climates or using natural cooling methods can reduce the need for energy-intensive cooling systems.
- Carbon Offsetting: Some green cloud providers invest in carbon offset projects to neutralize their carbon emissions. This may include reforestation, renewable energy projects, and carbon capture initiatives.
- Optimized Data Transmission: Green cloud services optimize data transmission and routing to reduce the energy required for data transfer, lowering latency and improving network efficiency.
- Server Lifespan Extension: Green cloud providers often extend the lifespan of their server hardware through maintenance and upgrades, reducing the volume of electronic waste.
- Cloud-Based Collaboration: Cloud-based collaboration tools and applications enable remote work and virtual meetings, reducing the need for physical office spaces and commuting, which leads to lower carbon emissions.
- Energy Reporting and Monitoring: Green cloud providers implement energy monitoring and reporting tools to track and analyze energy usage, enabling continuous improvement in energy efficiency.
- Incentives for Sustainable Practices: Some green cloud providers provide incentives or discounts for customers who adopt sustainable practices and workloads, encouraging eco-friendly behavior.

In summary, green cloud computing not only reduces the environmental footprint of IT infrastructure but also provides cost savings and performance improvements for businesses and organizations. By adopting green cloud solutions, companies can align their technology operations with sustainability goals and contribute to an eco-friendlier and energy-efficient future.

Artificial Intelligence (AI) Role in Sustainability

Artificial Intelligence (AI) plays an important role in sustainability efforts by providing innovative solutions to address complex environmental, social, and economic challenges (Amit Kumar Tyagi, N. Sreenath, 2021) (A. K. Tyagi, S. Chandrasekaran and N. Sreenath, 2022) (H. S. K. Sheth, I. A. K and A. K. Tyagi, 2022) (A. K. Tyagi, D. Agarwal and N. Sreenath, 2022). AI technologies have the potential to enhance decision-making, optimize resource use, and drive sustainable practices across various sectors. Here are key ways in which AI contributes to sustainability:

- Climate Modeling and Prediction: AI analyzes large dataset and simulates climate models to improve our understanding of climate change, enabling more accurate predictions and informed climate policies.
- Energy Efficiency: AI-driven smart systems in buildings, industries, and grids optimize energy consumption by adjusting heating, cooling, and lighting based on real-time data, reducing waste and carbon emissions.
- Renewable Energy: AI enhances the efficiency of renewable energy sources by predicting energy production and optimizing the use of resources, such as sunlight and wind, for maximum output.
- Energy Storage: AI algorithms are used to improve energy storage systems, increasing the efficiency and lifespan of batteries and other energy storage technologies.
- Smart Grids: AI helps utilities manage power distribution more efficiently, respond to outages, and balance supply and demand, contributing to a reliable and sustainable energy grid.
- Environmental Monitoring: AI processes data from sensors, satellites, and drones to monitor and manage environmental conditions, such as air and water quality, deforestation, and wildlife tracking.
- Agriculture and Food Security: AI-powered precision agriculture optimizes crop management, irrigation, and pest control, reducing resource use and enhancing food production.
- Waste Management: AI systems improve waste sorting, recycling, and management, reducing waste sent to landfills and incineration.
- Water Conservation: AI-driven smart water systems monitor and optimize water usage, identify leaks, and reduce water wastage in urban areas and agriculture.
- Conservation and Wildlife Protection: AI analyzes camera trap images and acoustic data to monitor and protect wildlife populations and combat poaching.

- Disaster Preparedness and Response: AI assists in early warning systems for natural disasters, assessing damage, and optimizing disaster relief efforts.
- Healthcare and Disease Prediction: AI predicts disease outbreaks and helps healthcare systems manage resources efficiently, leading to improved health outcomes and reduced environmental impact from healthcare waste.
- Circular Economy: AI enhances the recycling process by improving the sorting of recyclable materials and supporting the development of a circular economy.
- Transportation and Smart Mobility: AI-driven transportation systems optimize traffic patterns, reduce congestion, and enable autonomous vehicles, lowering carbon emissions and improving urban mobility.
- Carbon Accounting and Emissions Reduction: AI models help businesses and governments track and reduce carbon emissions by optimizing energy use and processes.
- Supply Chain Sustainability: AI improves transparency and traceability in supply chains, supporting sustainable sourcing, ethical production, and reducing waste.

Note that AI's data analysis and machine learning capabilities, coupled with its ability to process large amount of information in real-time, make it a powerful tool in addressing sustainability challenges. By improving resource management, reducing waste, and enhancing environmental protection, AI is a driving force in creating a more sustainable and resilient future.

RENEWABLE ENERGY TECHNOLOGIES FOR SUSTAINABLE FUTURE

Renewable energy technologies are essential for building a sustainable future as they reduce greenhouse gas emissions, decrease reliance on fossil fuels, and promote a cleaner and more environmentally friendly energy system (Amit Kumar Tyagi, S U Aswathy, 2021) (Tyagi, A.K., Sreenath, N., 2023) (Abhishek, B., Tyagi, A.K. (2022). Here are some key renewable energy technologies that play an important role in sustainability:

- Solar Photovoltaic (PV): Solar panels convert sunlight into electricity, providing a clean and abundant source of energy. Solar PV systems can be installed on rooftops, in solar farms, and integrated into various applications.

- Wind Turbines: Wind turbines harness the kinetic energy of wind to generate electricity. Onshore and offshore wind farms are increasingly common and are a rapidly growing source of renewable energy.
- Hydropower: Hydropower systems use the energy of flowing or falling water to generate electricity. Dams and small-scale hydro installations are used for power generation.
- Geothermal Energy: Geothermal power plants utilize heat from within the Earth to generate electricity. This source of energy is reliable and sustainable, with minimal environmental impact.
- Biomass Energy: Biomass energy uses organic materials, such as wood, agricultural residues, and waste, to produce heat, electricity, and biofuels. Biomass can be a carbon-neutral energy source when managed sustainably.
- Tidal and Wave Energy: Tidal and wave energy systems capture the energy from the movement of ocean tides and waves, providing a predictable and renewable source of power.
- Hydrogen Fuel Cells: Hydrogen fuel cells convert hydrogen gas into electricity, emitting only water and heat. They can be used in transportation and stationary power applications.
- Concentrated Solar Power (CSP): CSP technology uses mirrors or lenses to concentrate sunlight onto a small area, generating high-temperature heat. This heat is then used to produce electricity, typically by driving a steam turbine.
- Ocean Thermal Energy: Ocean thermal energy conversion (OTEC) systems use the temperature difference between warm surface water and cold deep-sea water to produce electricity and desalinated water.
- Microgrids and Smart Grids: Smart grid technologies improve the integration of renewable energy sources into the grid by enabling better management and distribution of electricity, reducing waste and improving grid reliability.
- Energy Storage Systems: Battery technology and energy storage systems are essential for capturing excess energy generated by renewables and providing it when needed, ensuring a stable and continuous power supply.
- Waste-to-Energy: Waste-to-energy facilities incinerate waste materials to generate heat and electricity, reducing landfill use and converting waste into useful energy.
- Floating Solar: Solar panels can be installed on floating platforms on bodies of water, providing dual benefits of solar power generation and reduced water evaporation.

Note that renewable energy technologies are a cornerstone of efforts to reduce carbon emissions and transition to a more sustainable energy system. They help combat climate change, improve energy security, and create jobs while supporting a cleaner and healthier environment. The adoption and expansion of renewable energy sources are important steps toward a more sustainable future.

SUSTAINABLE TRANSPORTATION FOR NEXT GENERATION

Sustainable transportation for the next generation is important for reducing environmental impact, mitigating climate change, and promoting healthier and more livable communities (Amit Kumar Tyagi, Poonam Chahal, 2020) (Akshara Pramod, Harsh Sankar Naicker, Amit Kumar Tyagi, 2022) (Madhav A.V.S., Tyagi A.K. 2022) (Mishra S., Tyagi A.K., 2022) (Tyagi, A. K., 2021). It involves shifting away from fossil fuel-dependent transportation systems and embracing cleaner, more efficient, and environmentally friendly modes of mobility. Here are key aspects of sustainable transportation for the next generation:

- Electric Vehicles (EVs): EVs, including cars, buses, and bikes, are powered by electricity and produce zero tailpipe emissions. Widespread adoption of EVs can significantly reduce greenhouse gas emissions and air pollution.
- Public Transportation: Expanding and improving public transportation, including buses, subways, and light rail, encourages people to leave their cars at home, reducing traffic congestion and emissions.
- Cycling and Walking: Promoting cycling and pedestrian-friendly infrastructure, including bike lanes and pedestrian zones, encourages active and sustainable transportation.
- Car Sharing and Ride-Sharing: Car-sharing services and ride-sharing platforms reduce the need for individual car ownership, leading to fewer vehicles on the road and lower emissions.
- High-Speed Rail and Mass Transit: Investment in high-speed rail and efficient mass transit systems makes long-distance and urban travel more sustainable, reduces congestion, and lowers emissions.
- Green Fuels and Biofuels: Transitioning to green fuels, such as hydrogen or advanced biofuels, for aviation and long-haul transportation helps reduce the carbon footprint of these sectors.
- Autonomous Vehicles (AVs): AVs have the potential to improve transportation efficiency, reduce traffic accidents, and minimize traffic congestion when combined with ride-sharing and electric power.

- Smart Transportation Systems: Smart systems, including traffic management, traffic signal optimization, and predictive maintenance, enhance transportation efficiency and reduce energy consumption.
- Last-Mile Solutions: Sustainable "last-mile" transportation options, like electric scooters and small electric vehicles, bridge the gap between public transit and final destinations.
- Sustainable Urban Planning: Compact, mixed-use urban development and city planning reduce the need for long commutes, encourage walking and cycling, and promote public transportation.
- Car-Free Zones and Congestion Pricing: Implementing car-free zones in city centers and congestion pricing for driving in crowded areas reduce traffic congestion and emissions.
- Green Ports and Shipping: Transitioning to cleaner fuels and energy-efficient practices in the shipping and maritime industry reduces emissions and environmental impact.
- Integration of Renewable Energy: Using renewable energy sources to power transportation systems, such as electric trains and buses, further reduces the carbon footprint.
- Data and Technology Solutions: Advanced data analytics and technology can optimize traffic flow, improve transportation efficiency, and reduce energy consumption.
- Education and Awareness: Raising awareness and educating the public about sustainable transportation options and their benefits encourages the adoption of eco-friendly mobility choices.

Hence, sustainable transportation for the next generation is a multifaceted approach that combines cleaner and more efficient vehicles, improved infrastructure, innovative technology, and changes in behavior. By embracing these solutions, we can reduce carbon emissions, lower air pollution, ease traffic congestion, and create healthier and more sustainable urban environments for future generations.

CHALLENGES AND OPPORTUNITIES TOWARDS A SUSTAINABLE FUTURE

In this section, we will discuss about few challenges and and Opportunities towards a Sustainable future (Malik, S., Bansal, R., & Tyagi, A. K., 2022) (Deshmukh, A., Patil, D. S., Soni, G., & Tyagi, A. K. 2023) (L. Gomathi, A. K. Mishra and A. K. Tyagi, 2023) (G. H. Sai, A. K. Tyagi and N. Sreenath, 2023) (Amit Kumar Tyagi

(2022) (Amit Kumar Tyagi 2022) (Tyagi, A.K., Bansal, R., Anshu, Dananjayan, S., 2023), as:

Challenges

- Climate Change: Climate change poses a significant threat to the planet. The challenge is to reduce greenhouse gas emissions, adapt to changing conditions, and mitigate the impact on ecosystems, communities, and economies.
- Resource Depletion: The unsustainable consumption of finite resources, such as water, minerals, and fossil fuels, is depleting the Earth's natural capital, leading to scarcity and environmental degradation.
- Biodiversity Loss: The loss of biodiversity threatens ecosystems, food security, and human well-being. Conservation efforts are challenged by habitat destruction, pollution, and invasive species.
- Waste Management: Managing and reducing waste, including plastic pollution, is an ongoing challenge. A circular economy approach is necessary to minimize waste and promote recycling.
- Inequality and Social Justice: Achieving sustainable development requires addressing income inequality, access to education, healthcare, and basic services. Ensuring social justice is important for a sustainable future.
- Energy Transition: Transitioning to clean and renewable energy sources while phasing out fossil fuels is a complex challenge, as it involves economic, political, and technological shifts.
- Food Security: The global population is growing, and sustainable agriculture practices are needed to ensure food security. Balancing the need for food production with environmental conservation is a challenge.
- Water Scarcity: Many regions face water scarcity due to overuse and pollution. Managing water resources sustainably is essential for human and ecosystem health.

Opportunities

- Renewable Energy: Transitioning to renewable energy sources like wind, solar, and hydropower provides a sustainable alternative to fossil fuels, reducing emissions and dependence on finite resources.
- Technological Innovation: Advanced technologies, including AI, IoT, and blockchain, provide opportunities to monitor and manage resources more efficiently, reduce waste, and create sustainable solutions.

- Circular Economy: Embracing a circular economy approach, where products and materials are reused, recycled, or repurposed, can reduce waste and conserve resources.
- Conservation and Restoration: Conservation efforts, reforestation, and habitat restoration can help protect biodiversity and preserve ecosystems.
- Sustainable Agriculture: Implementing sustainable agricultural practices, such as organic farming, agroforestry, and precision agriculture, can improve food production while protecting the environment.
- Green Transportation: Promoting electric vehicles, public transportation, and shared mobility options can reduce emissions and congestion in urban areas.
- Environmental Policies and Regulations: Strong environmental policies and regulations can create incentives for businesses and individuals to adopt sustainable practices.
- Education and Awareness: Educating the public about sustainability and raising awareness about environmental issues can empower individuals and communities to take action.
- Innovative Financing: New financing models, such as green bonds and impact investing, provide opportunities to fund sustainable projects and initiatives.
- Global Collaboration: Collaborative efforts at the international level, such as the Paris Agreement and the United Nations Sustainable Development Goals, provide a framework for addressing global challenges.

Hence, balancing these challenges and opportunities is important for achieving a sustainable future. The transition to sustainability requires a collective effort from governments, businesses, communities, and individuals to address the challenges while seizing the opportunities to create a more sustainable and equitable world.

REAL-WORLD APPLICATIONS OF FUTURISTIC TECHNOLOGIES

Futuristic technologies are actively being deployed across various industries, transforming the way we live, work, and interact with the world (Midha S, Tripathi K, Sharma MK., 2021) (D. Agarwal and K. Tripathi, 2022) (S. Midha, G. Kaur and K. Tripathi, 2017) (K. Somisetti, K. Tripathi and J. K. Verma, 2020) (S. Subasree, N.K. Sakthivel, Khushboo Tripathi, Deepshikha Agarwal, Amit Kumar Tyagi, 2022). Here are some real-world applications of futuristic technologies:

- Smart Cities: Cities worldwide are utilizing the Internet of Things (IoT) to enhance urban living. Smart traffic management systems, intelligent street lighting, waste management, and real-time air quality monitoring help improve efficiency and sustainability.

- Blockchain in Supply Chain: Companies are using blockchain technology to create transparent and secure supply chains. This ensures traceability, reduces fraud, and allows consumers to know the origins of the products they purchase.
- AI in Healthcare: Artificial Intelligence is revolutionizing healthcare by aiding in diagnostics, treatment planning, and drug discovery. Chatbots and telemedicine also improve patient care and access.
- Renewable Energy: Wind and solar energy are widely used for sustainable power generation. Grid-scale energy storage technologies, like lithium-ion batteries and pumped hydro storage, are making renewable energy more reliable.
- Electric Vehicles (EVs): The automotive industry is embracing electric vehicles, which reduce greenhouse gas emissions and reliance on fossil fuels. Advanced battery technology is extending EV ranges and decreasing charging times.
- Smart Agriculture: IoT sensors, drones, and AI-driven analytics are enhancing agricultural practices. Farmers can monitor crop conditions, optimize irrigation, and reduce waste.
- AI in Financial Services: AI algorithms are used for fraud detection, risk assessment, and portfolio management in the financial sector. Chatbots provide customer service, and robo-advisors aid in investment decisions.
- Augmented and Virtual Reality (AR/VR): AR and VR are used in various industries, from gaming and education to healthcare and architecture. They enable immersive training, simulation, and visualization experiences.
- Clean Water Technology: Innovative technologies are making water purification more efficient and cost-effective. Nanotechnology, UV disinfection, and membrane filtration systems are improving access to clean drinking water.
- 3D Printing: This technology is being used in aerospace, automotive, and healthcare to create complex components and custom prosthetics, reducing waste and production costs.
- Space Exploration: AI and robotics are integral to space exploration. Autonomous rovers, like NASA's Mars rovers, and machine learning algorithms are advancing our understanding of the universe.
- Environmental Monitoring: IoT and satellite technology are used for real-time environmental monitoring. They help track deforestation, climate change, and wildlife populations.

- Smart Homes: Home automation systems use IoT technology to manage lighting, security, temperature, and appliances, enhancing convenience and energy efficiency.
- Autonomous Vehicles: Self-driving cars are being developed and tested by companies like Tesla and Waymo, provideing the potential to reduce accidents and improve transportation efficiency.
- Quantum Computing: Though still in its infancy, quantum computing holds the potential to revolutionize fields such as cryptography, materials science, and drug discovery.

Hence, these examples illustrate the wide-ranging impact of futuristic technologies on our daily lives and industries. They are not just concepts for the distant future but are actively reshaping the present and the way we envision our future. Now the Path to a Sustainable Future via Emerging technologies for next generation as:

As we stand at the threshold of a new era, the pursuit of a sustainable future has become paramount. With environmental challenges and resource constraints mounting, the integration of emerging technologies is a beacon of hope for the next generation. This work outlines the transformative potential of these technologies and the path they illuminate towards sustainability. In the quest for a sustainable future, emerging technologies provide a path forward that holds great promise. As the torchbearers of the next generation, we must seize the opportunities these technologies present, while also navigating the ethical, regulatory, and environmental challenges they bring. Through collaboration, innovation, and education, we can inspire a brighter future where sustainability is not just a goal, but a way of life. The journey toward a sustainable world requires collective effort, but with the transformative power of emerging technologies, we can light the way for generations to come.

CONCLUSION

This chapter underscores the pivotal role of innovative technologies in addressing the pressing challenges of sustainability. In an era defined by environmental issues and a growing imperative to protect our planet, these futuristic tools provide a beacon of hope and transformation. This work has discussed the symbiotic relationship between sustainability and technology, illuminating the profound impact of the Internet of Things (IoT), Blockchain, and Artificial Intelligence (AI) on sustainable practices. We have witnessed how these technologies empower us to monitor, regulate, and optimize our resources, revolutionizing sectors from agriculture to supply chain management. Moreover, this chapter has explained about the green energy revolution and its potential to reshape our energy landscape. The advent of solar, wind, hydroelectric power, and cutting-edge energy storage solutions holds the promise of a cleaner, more efficient energy paradigm, while sustainable transportation technologies present a path towards cleaner mobility. Nevertheless, the path to a sustainable future is not without its challenges. Hence, we have discussed all possible issues, challenges faced in making a sustainable environment. As we look to the future, we see a landscape teeming with opportunity. Emerging trends and innovations are set to further enhance our ability to tackle sustainability challenges. The possibilities are endless, and the potential for collaboration and shared knowledge is immense. The journey toward a sustainable environment is ongoing, and it is driven by continued research and innovation. In summary, this work has demonstrated the immense promise and transformative power of futuristic technologies in building a sustainable environment.

REFERENCES

Abhishek, B., & Tyagi, A. K. (2022). An Useful Survey on Supervised Machine Learning Algorithms: Comparisons and Classifications. In Sengodan, T., Murugappan, M., & Misra, S. (Eds.), *Advances in Electrical and Computer Technologies. Lecture Notes in Electrical Engineering* (Vol. 881). Springer., DOI:10.1007/978-981-19-1111-8_24

Agarwal, D., & Tripathi, K. "A Framework for Structural Damage detection system in automobiles for flexible Insurance claim using IOT and Machine Learning," *2022 International Mobile and Embedded Technology Conference (MECON)*, 2022, pp. 5-8, DOI:10.1109/MECON53876.2022.9751889

Alfen, H. W., & Ten Brink, P. (Eds.). (2018). *Nature-based solutions for urban resilience*. Springer.

Bai, X., & Imura, H. (Eds.). (2016). *Urbanization and sustainability: Linking urban ecology, environmental justice and global environmental change*. Springer.

Batty, M. (2018). *The new science of cities*. MIT Press.

Coaffee, J., Healey, P., & O'Brien, P. (2018). *Resilient cities: Rethinking urban protection*. Springer.

Deshmukh, A., Patil, D. S., Soni, G., & Tyagi, A. K. (2023). Cyber Security: New Realities for Industry 4.0 and Society 5.0. In Tyagi, A. (Ed.), *Handbook of Research on Quantum Computing for Smart Environments* (pp. 299–325). IGI Global. DOI:10.4018/978-1-6684-6697-1.ch017

Giffinger, R., Fertner, C., Kramar, H., Kalasek, R., Pichler-Milanović, N., & Meijers, E. (2007). *Smart cities: Ranking of European medium-sized cities. Centre of Regional Science (SRF)*. Vienna University of Technology.DOI:10.1145/1947940.1947974

Glaeser, E. L. (2011). *Triumph of the city: How our greatest invention makes us richer, smarter, greener, healthier, and happier*. Penguin.

Gomathi, L., Mishra, A. K., & Tyagi, A. K. (2023). *Industry 5.0 for Healthcare 5.0: Opportunities, Challenges and Future Research Possibilities*. 2023 7th International Conference on Trends in Electronics and Informatics (ICOEI), Tirunelveli, India. DOI:10.1109/ICOEI56765.2023.10125660

Madhav, A. V. S., & Tyagi, A. K. (2022). The World with Future Technologies (Post-COVID-19): Open Issues, Challenges, and the Road Ahead. In Tyagi, A. K., Abraham, A., & Kaklauskas, A. (Eds.), *Intelligent Interactive Multimedia Systems for e-Healthcare Applications.* Springer. DOI:10.1007/978-981-16-6542-4_22

Madhav, A. V. S., & Tyagi, A. K. (2023). Explainable Artificial Intelligence (XAI): Connecting Artificial Decision-Making and Human Trust in Autonomous Vehicles. In: Singh, P.K., Wierzchoń, S.T., Tanwar, S., Rodrigues, J.J.P.C., Ganzha, M. (eds) *Proceedings of Third International Conference on Computing, Communications, and Cyber-Security. Lecture Notes in Networks and Systems.* Springer, Singapore. DOI:10.1007/978-981-19-1142-2_10

Malik, S., Bansal, R., & Tyagi, A. K. (Eds.). (2022). *Impact and Role of Digital Technologies in Adolescent Lives.* IGI Global. DOI:10.4018/978-1-7998-8318-0

Midha, S., Kaur, G., & Tripathi, K. (2017). Cloud deep down — SWOT analysis. *2017 2nd International Conference on Telecommunication and Networks (TEL-NET),* (pp. 1-5). IEEE. DOI:10.1109/TEL-NET.2017.8343560

Midha, S., Tripathi, K., & Sharma, M. K. (2021, April). Practical Implications of Using Dockers on Virtualized SDN. *Webology.,* 18(Special Issue 01), 312–330. DOI:10.14704/WEB/V18SI01/WEB18062

Mishra, S., & Tyagi, A. K. (2022). The Role of Machine Learning Techniques in Internet of Things-Based Cloud Applications. In Pal, S., De, D., & Buyya, R. (Eds.), *Artificial Intelligence-based Internet of Things Systems. Internet of Things (Technology, Communications and Computing).* Springer. DOI:10.1007/978-3-030-87059-1_4

Nair, M. M., & Tyagi, A. K. (2021). *Privacy: History, Statistics, Policy, Laws, Preservation and Threat Analysis. Journal of Information Assurance & Security,* 16(1), 24-34.

Pickett, S. T., Cadenasso, M. L., & Grove, J. M. (Eds.). (2018). *Resilient cities: Meaning, models, and metaphor for integrating the ecological, socio-economic, and planning realms.* Springer.

Pramod, A. (2022). *Emerging Innovations in the Near Future Using Deep Learning Techniques, Book: Advanced Analytics and Deep Learning Models.* Wiley Scrivener. DOI:10.1002/9781119792437.ch10

Rees, W., & Wackernagel, M. (2013). The shoe fits, but the footprint is larger than Earth: Urban ecological footprints show that cities can be unsustainable. *Environment and Urbanization,* 25(2), 481–499.

Rocha, M. F. (2018). The future of cities in the 21st century: Implications of urban energy use and greenhouse gas emissions. *Energy Procedia*, 147, 72–77.

Sai, G. H., Tripathi, K., & Tyagi, A. K. (2023). Internet of Things-Based e-Health Care: Key Challenges and Recommended Solutions for Future. In: Singh, P.K., Wierzchoń, S.T., Tanwar, S., Rodrigues, J.J.P.C., Ganzha, M. (eds) *Proceedings of Third International Conference on Computing, Communications, and Cyber-Security.* Springer, Singapore. DOI:10.1007/978-981-19-1142-2_37

Sai, G. H., Tyagi, A. K., & Sreenath, N. (2023). Biometric Security in Internet of Things Based System against Identity Theft Attacks.*2023 International Conference on Computer Communication and Informatics (ICCCI)*, Coimbatore, India. DOI:10.1109/ICCCI56745.2023.10128186

Sassen, S. (2019). Cities in a world of cities: The globalization of urban governance. Yale University Press.

Shreyas Madhav, A. V., Ilavarasi, A. K., & Tyagi, A. K. (2022). The Heroes and Villains of the Mix Zone: The Preservation and Leaking of USer's Privacy in Future Vehicles. In Arunachalam, V., & Sivasankaran, K. (Eds.), *Microelectronic Devices, Circuits and Systems. ICMDCS 2022. Communications in Computer and Information Science* (Vol. 1743). Springer. DOI:10.1007/978-3-031-23973-1_12

Somisetti, K., Tripathi, K., & Verma, J. K. "Design, Implementation, and Controlling of a Humanoid Robot," *2020 International Conference on Computational Performance Evaluation (ComPE)*, 2020, pp. 831-836, DOI:10.1109/ComPE49325.2020.9200020

Song, Y., & Zegeye, A. (2017). Urbanization and the environment: An overview. In *The Urbanization and the Environment* (pp. 1-16). Springer.

Tulumello, S., & Hernández-Molina, G. (2018). Smart cities as techno-social assemblages: A framework for understanding the rise of smart urbanism. *Frontiers in Sociology*, 3, 30.

Tyagi, A., Kukreja, S., Nair, M. M., & Tyagi, A. K. (2022). Machine Learning: Past, Present and Future. *NeuroQuantology: An Interdisciplinary Journal of Neuroscience and Quantum Physics*, 20(8). DOI:10.14704/nq.2022.20.8.NQ44468

Tyagi, A. K. (Ed.). (2021). *Multimedia and Sensory Input for Augmented, Mixed, and Virtual Reality*. IGI Global., DOI:10.4018/978-1-7998-4703-8

Tyagi, A. K., Agarwal, D., & Sreenath, N. (2022). SecVT: Securing the Vehicles of Tomorrow using Blockchain Technology. *2022 International Conference on Computer Communication and Informatics (ICCCI)*, Coimbatore, India. DOI:10.1109/ICCCI54379.2022.9740965

Tyagi, A. K., & Sreenath, N. (2023). Security, Privacy, and Trust Issues in Intelligent Transportation System. In *Intelligent Transportation Systems: Theory and Practice. Disruptive Technologies and Digital Transformations for Society 5.0.* Springer. DOI:10.1007/978-981-19-7622-3_8

Tyagi, A. K., & Sreenath, N. (2023). Artificial Intelligence—Internet of Things-Based Intelligent Transportation System. In *Intelligent Transportation Systems: Theory and Practice. Disruptive Technologies and Digital Transformations for Society 5.0.* Springer. DOI:10.1007/978-981-19-7622-3_10

Tyagi, A. K., & Sreenath, N. (2023). Future Intelligent Vehicles: Open Issues, Important Challenges, and Research Opportunities. In *Intelligent Transportation Systems: Theory and Practice. Disruptive Technologies and Digital Transformations for Society 5.0.* Springer. DOI:10.1007/978-981-19-7622-3_15

Tyagi, A. K., & Sreenath, N. (2023). Intelligent Transportation System: Past, Present, and Future. In *Intelligent Transportation Systems: Theory and Practice. Disruptive Technologies and Digital Transformations for Society 5.0.* Springer. DOI:10.1007/978-981-19-7622-3_2

Varsha, R., Nair, S. M., Tyagi, A. K., & Aswathy, S. U. (2021) The Future with Advanced Analytics: A Sequential Analysis of the Disruptive Technology's Scope. In: Abraham A., Hanne T., Castillo O., Gandhi N., Nogueira Rios T., Hong TP. (eds) *Hybrid Intelligent Systems.* Springer, Cham. DOI:10.1007/978-3-030-73050-5_56

Vishnuram, G., Tripathi, K., & Kumar Tyagi, A. (2022). Ethical Hacking: Importance, Controversies and Scope in the Future. *2022 International Conference on Computer Communication and Informatics (ICCCI).* IEEE. DOI:10.1109/ICC-CI54379.2022.9740860

Chapter 13
The Impact of AI Integration on Workforce Dynamics:
Legal Challenges and Labour Law Implications in the Era of Business Technology Transformation

J. Gayathri
https://orcid.org/0000-0002-5118-2030
Saveetha School of Law, India

S. Mangaiyarkarasi
Saveetha School of Law, India

ABSTRACT

The research delves into the dual-edged nature of AI in business, highlighting both its potential for creating new opportunities and its role in displacing existing jobs. It examines case studies where AI has led to significant changes in workforce require-ments and explores the legal framework's response to these changes. Key areas of concern include the protection of displaced workers, the evolution of employment contracts, and the need for regulatory updates to address the challenges posed by automation. Additionally, the study assesses the effectiveness of current labor laws in safeguarding worker interests amidst rapid technological advancements. It proposes potential legal reforms and policy measures aimed at ensuring a balanced approach to AI integration, where technological progress does not come at the expense of worker rights and job security.

DOI: 10.4018/979-8-3693-4187-2.ch013

INTRODUCTION

The rapid evolution of artificial intelligence (AI) and business technology has significantly transformed the modern workforce, driving profound changes in job roles, employment patterns, and organizational structures. This transformation necessitates a thorough examination of its impact on labor law and worker protections. As businesses integrate AI to enhance efficiency and innovation, the traditional boundaries of work are increasingly blurred, raising critical questions about job displacement, worker rights, and regulatory adequacy.

Evolution and Rationale for the Study

The integration of AI into business operations has accelerated with advancements in machine learning, automation, and data analytics. This shift from manual to automated processes has led to increased productivity but also has introduced complexities regarding job roles and employment security. The rationale behind this study is to analyze these transformations, particularly how AI impacts workforce dynamics and the legal frameworks that govern employment.

Governmental Initiatives

Governments worldwide have begun to address these issues through legislative and regulatory measures. For example, the European Union's General Data Protection Regulation (GDPR) and the Digital Services Act (DSA) aim to regulate data usage and online platforms, impacting AI applications. In the United States, the National Labor Relations Board (NLRB) and the Department of Labor are evaluating new policies to address AI's impact on employment. Similarly, India has initiated discussions around its AI policy and labor laws, emphasizing the need for regulatory updates to safeguard workers amidst technological advances (European Commission, 2023; U.S. Department of Labor, 2024; Ministry of Electronics and Information Technology, India, 2024).

Factors Affecting the Study

Key factors influencing this study include technological advancements in AI, changes in business practices, evolving labor market trends, and existing legal frameworks. The pace of AI adoption, the sector-specific impact of automation, and the adequacy of current labor laws are critical variables in assessing how well regulatory measures align with the new reality of work.

Recent Trends and Problems

Recent trends show a rapid increase in AI deployment across various sectors, including manufacturing, healthcare, and finance, leading to both opportunities and challenges. Problems such as job displacement, skill mismatches, and the ethical implications of AI decision-making are prominent. Studies highlight that while AI creates new job opportunities, it also renders some traditional roles obsolete, necessitating urgent legal reforms and policy interventions (Brynjolfsson & McAfee, 2022; Chui et al., 2024).

Comparison With Other Nations

A comparative analysis reveals diverse approaches to managing AI's impact on labor. For instance, Germany's approach to worker protection includes stringent regulations on job displacement and reskilling programs, while countries like China focus heavily on AI-driven economic growth with less emphasis on immediate labor protection reforms (Schwab, 2023; Liu, 2024). Understanding these varying strategies provides insights into effective regulatory practices and highlights areas for improvement in addressing AI's impact on labor.

In conclusion, this study aims to provide a comprehensive understanding of how AI integration affects workforce dynamics and labor laws, offering recommendations for balancing technological progress with worker protection and legal adequacy.

OBJECTIVES OF THE STUDY

The main objectives of the study are:

- To analyze the net impact of AI on employment levels across various sectors.
- To evaluate the effectiveness of current policies in addressing AI-induced job displacement.
- To assess the effectiveness of reskilling programs in preparing the workforce for AI-related job shifts.

CURRENT REALITIES, LEGAL FRAMEWORKS, AND FUTURE PROJECTIONS

Review of Literature

"The Impact of Automation on Employment and the Workforce" by Bessen, (2018) explores the specific sectors most vulnerable to automation and its consequences on job security. The problem focuses on sector-specific job losses. The study aims to identify which industries are at high risk of AI-induced unemployment. A mixed-method approach, combining industry reports and expert interviews, is employed. Results indicate that manufacturing and retail sectors are highly susceptible, while technology and healthcare sectors show potential for growth. The study recommends targeted support for the most affected industries

"AI and Employment: Policy Responses and Challenges" by Chui et al.,(2020) investigates existing policy responses to AI's impact on employment and identifies gaps. The problem is the inadequacy of current policies to address AI-induced job changes. Objectives include evaluating the effectiveness of these policies and suggesting improvements. A qualitative approach, involving policy analysis and expert interviews, is used. Findings reveal that existing policies are often outdated and not sufficiently comprehensive. Recommendations include updating legal frameworks and enhancing public-private partnerships for better policy implementation

In **"Job Displacement and Creation in the Age of AI"** Smith & Anderson, (2021), the focus is on understanding how AI leads to both job displacement and creation. The study's problem is the dual nature of AI's impact on the job market. The objective is to quantify job displacement and creation rates. Using a longitudinal data analysis methodology, the study finds that while AI displaces certain job roles, it also contributes to job creation in emerging fields such as AI maintenance and development. The study suggests fostering education and training programs in these new fields to ease the transition

"Reskilling the Workforce for the AI Era" by Berg et al., (2021) focuses on the effectiveness of reskilling programs in preparing the workforce for AI-induced changes. The problem is the preparedness of the workforce for AI-related job shifts. Objectives include assessing the current state of reskilling programs and their impact. A survey-based methodology, including interviews with program participants and employers, reveals that while reskilling programs are increasing, their effectiveness varies significantly. The study suggests increasing funding and improving program relevance to better address AI's challenges.

"Social and Economic Implications of AI in the Workforce" by (Susskind & Susskind, 2020) investigates the broader social and economic implications of AI on the workforce. The problem is understanding the wider impacts of AI on society.

The objective is to provide a comprehensive analysis of AI's effects beyond job displacement. A multidisciplinary approach, combining economic, sociological, and technological perspectives, reveals that AI has complex effects, including changing work patterns and requiring new social policies. The study suggests a holistic approach to policy development that addresses these broader impacts

"AI and Employment Law: Emerging Challenges" by Kahn, (2023) addresses the legal challenges arising from AI's impact on employment. The problem is the inadequacy of existing employment laws to handle AI-related issues. The study aims to identify gaps in current legal frameworks and propose solutions. Using legal analysis and case studies, the research finds that existing employment laws often fail to address new issues related to AI, such as algorithmic bias and worker displacement. The study recommends updating legal frameworks to better address these emerging challenges

AI AND LABOR MARKET THEORY

Theories of Technological Displacement and Job Creation

Technological advancements, including AI, have long been associated with both the displacement of existing jobs and the creation of new ones. Theories regarding technological displacement often revolve around the concept that automation and AI can replace human labor, especially in routine or repetitive tasks. This concept aligns with classical economic theories suggesting that technological progress tends to displace workers from jobs that are automated, while simultaneously creating new job opportunities in sectors where human oversight or complex decision-making is required.

In the case of AI, the impact on labor markets has been nuanced. According to a Goldman Sachs report (2023), while AI has the potential to boost global productivity and create new job roles, it also poses a risk of significant disruption, with an estimated 300 million jobs exposed to automation. This reflects a broader theoretical framework where technological advancements lead to job displacement in certain sectors while fostering job creation in others, albeit with a transitional period that can involve economic and social challenges (Brynjolfsson & Unger, 2023).

Conversely, some jobs are more likely to be complemented rather than substituted by AI. For instance, a radiologist using AI to analyze medical scans might experience increased productivity due to AI's assistance, whereas administrative roles heavily reliant on routine data entry are at higher risk of displacement (Gopinath, 2023). This dichotomy underscores the complexity of AI's impact on labor, where the technology's role as either a complement or a substitute determines its influence on job markets.

Historical Precedents of Technological Change and Labor Market Adjustments

Historically, technological advancements have consistently led to both displacement and creation of jobs. For example, the industrial revolution brought about significant changes in the manufacturing sector, transitioning from manual labor to mechanized production. This shift resulted in job displacement for manual workers but also created new roles in machinery maintenance and operations.

The automotive industry provides another illustrative case. The introduction of robotic arms in car manufacturing reduced the reliance on manual assembly lines, leading to job losses in routine manual tasks but creating opportunities for workers skilled in programming and maintaining robots. Similarly, past waves of automation primarily replaced routine tasks but did not entirely eliminate the demand for human labor; instead, they transformed job requirements and roles (Collett et al., 2022).

With the advent of generative AI, the scope of technological impact has expanded beyond routine tasks to include non-routine cognitive tasks. Generative AI's ability to perform complex, non-routine functions complicates the traditional patterns of technological displacement. This advancement exposes professions previously considered safe from automation to potential displacement, suggesting a more profound shift in labor market dynamics compared to past technological changes (Lane & Saint-Martin, 2021).

The current landscape reveals that while generative AI can automate complex tasks, it also necessitates new skill sets and job roles, much like previous technological advancements. However, the rapid pace of AI development and its broad application across various sectors heighten the urgency for proactive policies and reskilling initiatives to manage the transition effectively (Hatzius, 2023).

ECONOMIC IMPACT OF AI

Overview of Economic Theories Relevant to AI's Impact on Employment

Neoclassical Economic Theory

Neoclassical economic theory, rooted in the works of economists like Adam Smith and Alfred Marshall, posits that technological advancements lead to increased productivity, which, in turn, fosters economic growth. According to this theory, as new technologies such as AI are introduced, they initially displace certain jobs but eventually lead to the creation of new ones. The belief is that technological progress increases the efficiency of production processes, leading to lower costs and higher output, which can stimulate job creation in other sectors of the economy.

Schumpeterian Theory of Creative Destruction

Joseph Schumpeter's concept of "creative destruction" is particularly relevant to the discussion of AI's impact on employment. Schumpeter argued that technological innovations lead to the destruction of old industries and jobs but simultaneously create new ones. This process of creative destruction drives economic growth by replacing outdated technologies with more efficient ones. In the context of AI, this theory suggests that while AI may render certain jobs obsolete, it will also foster the emergence of new industries and roles, contributing to long-term economic dynamism.

The Task-Based Approach

The task-based approach, as advocated by economists such as Agrawal et al. (2019), emphasizes the importance of analyzing specific tasks rather than entire occupations when assessing the impact of technological advancements. This approach differentiates between tasks that AI can automate and those that it cannot. AI may replace routine and repetitive tasks but complement non-routine and complex tasks, leading to shifts in job requirements and the creation of new roles that leverage human skills in conjunction with AI.

Skill-Biased Technological Change (SBTC)

The SBTC theory posits that technological advancements, including AI, disproportionately benefit workers with higher skill levels. According to this theory, AI and other advanced technologies tend to increase the demand for high-skilled workers while reducing the demand for low-skilled workers. This results in wage polarization, where high-skilled workers see wage increases, while low-skilled workers face wage stagnation or job loss. The theory highlights the need for targeted education and training to mitigate the negative effects on low-skilled workers.

Keynesian and Post-Keynesian Perspectives

Keynesian economics, founded by John Maynard Keynes, and its post-Keynesian derivatives provide insights into how AI might impact employment. Keynesian theory focuses on the role of aggregate demand in the economy, suggesting that technological advancements could lead to short-term job displacement without adequate policies to boost demand. Post-Keynesian perspectives further argue that technological progress might not automatically translate into full employment unless accompanied by appropriate economic policies and social safety nets.

Productivity Gains vs. Job Losses

Productivity Gains

AI has the potential to significantly enhance productivity by automating routine tasks, optimizing processes, and improving decision-making through data analysis. Productivity gains can lead to lower production costs, increased output, and economic growth. For instance, AI-driven automation in manufacturing and logistics can streamline operations, reduce errors, and accelerate production cycles. These productivity improvements can contribute to lower prices for goods and services, benefiting consumers and stimulating economic activity.

Job Losses and Displacement

Despite the potential benefits, AI also poses significant risks of job displacement. As AI technologies automate tasks previously performed by humans, certain job roles may become redundant. For example, administrative and clerical positions that involve routine data entry and processing are highly susceptible to automation. The fear of widespread job losses is compounded by concerns about the pace of technological change and the ability of workers to transition to new roles.

Historical Precedents of Technological Change

Historically, technological advancements have led to periods of economic disruption and job displacement, but they have also been followed by periods of recovery and job creation.

The Challenge of Adjusting to Technological Change

The challenge lies in managing the transition period between job losses and the creation of new opportunities. The speed of AI development and its potential to impact a wide range of industries complicates efforts to ensure a smooth transition. Policymakers and businesses must focus on reskilling and upskilling workers to equip them with the skills needed for emerging roles. social safety nets and support systems are crucial to mitigating the negative effects of job displacement.

The Role of Policy in Balancing Gains and Losses

Effective policy interventions are essential in balancing the productivity gains from AI with the potential job losses. Policies that promote education and training, support for displaced workers, and incentives for industries that create new job opportunities can help mitigate the adverse effects of AI on employment. Fostering a collaborative approach between governments, businesses, and educational institutions can ensure that the benefits of AI are broadly shared and that the negative impacts are effectively addressed.

LEGAL FRAMEWORKS AND AI

Analysis of Existing Labor Laws and Their Applicability to AI

Existing Labor Laws Overview

Labor laws are designed to regulate the relationship between employers and employees, ensuring fair treatment, safety, and adequate compensation. Key areas of focus include employment contracts, wages, working conditions, and job security. However, existing labor laws were largely established before the rise of AI and may not fully address the challenges posed by this technology.

Applicability of Labor Laws to AI

- **Employment Contracts**: Traditional employment laws cover aspects like contract formation, termination, and employee rights. For instance, in the case of *Fellowship Foundation v. S. S. Enterprise* (2009), the court emphasized the importance of clear employment contracts in determining rights and obligations. However, AI introduces complexities such as the use of automated systems for hiring and monitoring employees, which may not be adequately covered by traditional employment contract regulations.
- **Wages and Compensation**: Wage laws, such as those in the *Minimum Wages Act* (1948), ensure fair compensation. AI's role in productivity and efficiency might challenge these frameworks, particularly in terms of performance-based pay structures and the allocation of productivity gains.
- **Workplace Safety**: Laws like the *Occupational Health and Safety Act* (1970) focus on worker safety. AI's integration into the workplace, such as the use of robotics and automation, raises questions about the adequacy of these laws in ensuring worker safety and addressing new types of risks associated with AI systems.
- **Job Security**: Traditional labor laws provide job security protections. However, AI's potential to automate tasks raises concerns about job displacement and the adequacy of existing unemployment and job security measures. For instance, the decision in *Smt. Bimla Devi v. Union of India* (1982) underlined protections against arbitrary dismissal, but automation may necessitate a re-evaluation of such protections.

Challenges in Applicability

Existing labor laws may struggle to address issues like:

- **Algorithmic Management**: AI systems used for employee monitoring and performance evaluation can lead to issues of transparency and fairness. Traditional labor laws may not sufficiently address the implications of algorithmic decisions on workers' rights.
- **Gig Economy**: The rise of gig and platform work, facilitated by AI, often falls outside traditional employment laws. Cases such as *Ola Cabs v. Union of India* (2018) highlight the challenges of applying existing labor laws to gig workers who may lack formal employment contracts and benefits.

GAPS AND CHALLENGES IN CURRENT LEGAL FRAMEWORKS

Inadequate Coverage of AI-Specific Issues

Existing legal frameworks may not fully address AI-specific issues, such as:

- **Algorithmic Bias**: AI systems can perpetuate or amplify biases, impacting fairness in hiring and workplace treatment. Legal frameworks need to address how to ensure transparency and accountability in AI decision-making processes. The case of *Equal Employment Opportunity Commission v. Facebook, Inc.* (2020) illustrates the challenges of addressing algorithmic bias within current anti-discrimination laws.
- **Data Privacy**: AI systems often rely on large volumes of personal data. Current data protection laws, such as the *General Data Protection Regulation (GDPR)*, may need enhancements to address AI-specific concerns about data collection, usage, and consent. The case of *Google LLC v. Vidal-Hall* (2015) underscores the need for robust privacy protections in the digital age.

Slow Legal Adaptation

The rapid pace of AI development often outstrips the ability of legal systems to adapt. For example:

- **Employment Standards**: Standards for remote and AI-mediated work environments are still evolving. The case of *Remote Employment Agency Ltd. v. A. B.* (2022) highlights the need for updated standards that address the nuances of AI-driven remote work.
- **Regulation of AI Technologies**: Regulations often lag behind technological advancements. The *Algorithmic Accountability Act* (introduced in the US) seeks to address this gap but faces challenges in keeping pace with rapid technological changes.

International Discrepancies

Legal frameworks vary significantly across jurisdictions, leading to challenges in harmonizing regulations. For instance, while the EU's *AI Act* focuses on regulating high-risk AI applications, other regions may lack comprehensive AI-specific regulations, creating inconsistencies in global labor markets.

NATIONAL POLICIES AND REGULATIONS

Review of National Policies and Regulations Addressing AI's Impact on Employment

National Policies Overview

Different countries have developed various policies to address AI's impact on employment:

- **European Union**: The EU has proposed the *AI Act*, focusing on regulating high-risk AI systems and ensuring transparency and accountability. It includes provisions for monitoring and mitigating risks associated with AI technologies.
- **United States**: The US has taken a more fragmented approach, with different states implementing their regulations. For example, California's *Consumer Privacy Act (CCPA)* includes aspects related to data privacy in AI systems.
- **China**: China has implemented policies such as the *Next Generation Artificial Intelligence Development Plan*, which emphasizes AI development while also addressing employment impacts through workforce retraining and development programs.

Key Focus Areas

- **Ethical AI Use**: National policies often emphasize ethical considerations, such as fairness and transparency. For example, the EU's *Ethics Guidelines for Trustworthy AI* provide a framework for ensuring that AI systems are developed and used responsibly.
- **Job Creation and Retraining**: Many countries focus on retraining programs to help workers transition to new roles. For instance, the UK's *Industrial Strategy* includes initiatives for reskilling workers in response to technological changes.

Comparative Analysis of Different Countries' Approaches

European Union vs. United States

- **Regulatory Approach**: The EU has a more centralized regulatory approach with comprehensive frameworks like the *AI Act*. In contrast, the US has a more decentralized approach, with varying regulations at the state level. This can lead to inconsistencies in how AI-related issues are addressed across different jurisdictions.
- **Focus on Ethics**: The EU places a strong emphasis on ethical considerations and human rights, whereas the US approach is often more focused on innovation and economic impacts.

China vs. Western Countries

- **Government Role**: China's approach involves strong government intervention and strategic planning, as seen in its *Next Generation Artificial Intelligence Development Plan*. Western countries often emphasize a balance between regulation and innovation, with a focus on market-driven approaches.
- **Workforce Development**: China has extensive programs for workforce development and retraining, which contrasts with the more fragmented approaches seen in Western countries.

LEGISLATIVE PROPOSALS

Discussion on Proposed Legislative Changes and Their Potential Impact

Proposed Legislative Changes

- **AI Transparency and Accountability**: Proposed changes often focus on increasing transparency and accountability for AI systems. For example, the *Algorithmic Accountability Act* (US) aims to require companies to conduct impact assessments for automated systems.
- **Enhanced Data Privacy**: Proposals for strengthening data privacy protections, such as amendments to the *GDPR*, address concerns about how AI systems handle personal data. These changes aim to ensure that data practices are more transparent and secure.

Potential Impact

- **Increased Compliance Costs**: Legislative changes may lead to higher compliance costs for businesses, especially those using AI systems. Companies may need to invest in additional resources to meet new transparency and accountability requirements.
- **Improved Worker Protections**: Enhanced regulations can provide better protections for workers affected by AI, including more robust safeguards against algorithmic bias and improved job security measures.

Analysis of Policy Recommendations for Better Managing AI-Induced Disruptions

Policy Recommendations

- **Reskilling and Education**: Recommendations often emphasize the need for comprehensive reskilling and educational programs to help workers transition to new roles. This includes partnerships between governments, educational institutions, and businesses.
- **Social Safety Nets**: Enhancing social safety nets, such as unemployment benefits and job placement services, can help mitigate the adverse effects of job displacement due to AI.

Implementation Challenges

- **Coordination and Funding**: Implementing these recommendations requires effective coordination between various stakeholders and adequate funding. For instance, the success of reskilling programs depends on aligning training with labor market needs.
- **Monitoring and Evaluation**: Regular monitoring and evaluation of policy effectiveness are crucial to ensure that measures are addressing the intended issues and adapting to changing technological landscapes.

RESKILLING AND RETRAINING INITIATIVES

Overview of Current Reskilling and Retraining Programs

Government Initiatives

- **Workforce Innovation and Opportunity Act (WIOA)**: In the US, the WIOA provides funding for workforce development and reskilling programs aimed at helping workers adapt to new job requirements.
- **European Social Fund (ESF)**: The ESF supports reskilling and training programs across the EU, focusing on improving employment prospects and addressing skills gaps.

Industry-Specific Programs

- **Tech Industry Initiatives**: Many tech companies have developed their own reskilling programs. For example, Google's *Grow with Google* initiative offers training in digital skills to help workers transition to technology-related roles.

Effectiveness of These Programs in Mitigating Job Displacement

Success Metrics

- **Employment Outcomes**: The effectiveness of reskilling programs can be measured by employment outcomes, such as the number of participants who secure new jobs or advance in their careers. Programs that demonstrate positive employment outcomes contribute to mitigating job displacement.
- **Skill Alignment**: Programs that align training with industry needs and emerging job roles are more effective. For example, initiatives that focus on high-demand skills in AI and technology sectors help address skills shortages and enhance job prospects.

Areas for Improvement

- **Accessibility and Inclusivity**: Ensuring that reskilling programs are accessible to all workers, including those from disadvantaged backgrounds, is crucial for broad-based effectiveness. Programs need to address barriers to participation, such as cost and geographic limitations.

- **Adaptability**: Programs must be adaptable to rapidly changing technological landscapes. Continuous updates to training content and delivery methods are essential to keep pace with advancements in AI and other technologies.

THE IMPACT OF AI ON EMPLOYMENT: CURRENT REALITIES AND FUTURE PROJECTIONS

The rise of artificial intelligence (AI) has undeniably altered the landscape of employment worldwide. As we explore the transformative effects of AI, it is crucial to provide a structured analysis that covers current impacts, future projections, and the ongoing adjustments within various sectors. This comprehensive examination aims to address both the fears and opportunities presented by AI, offering a balanced perspective on its role in shaping the future of work.

Evolution of AI and its Impact on Employment

AI's influence on the job market is not merely a theoretical concern but a pressing reality. Projections indicate that AI could potentially replace around 800 million jobs globally by 2030, with an estimated economic impact of $15.7 trillion by the same year (PwC, 2023). These figures underscore the profound transformation anticipated in the job market due to AI integration. However, the current reality paints a more nuanced picture. As of now, 14% of workers have experienced job displacement due to AI, a figure that highlights ongoing, albeit controlled, changes in employment patterns (Socius, 2024).

Governmental Initiatives and Legal Frameworks

Governments worldwide are beginning to address the implications of AI on labor through various legislative and regulatory measures:

- **European Union**: The General Data Protection Regulation (GDPR) and the Digital Services Act (DSA) regulate data usage and online platforms, which indirectly affect AI applications (European Commission, 2023).
- **United States**: The National Labor Relations Board (NLRB) and the Department of Labor are considering new policies to mitigate AI's impact on employment (U.S. Department of Labor, 2024).

- **India**: The country is actively discussing AI policy and labor laws to better align with technological advancements and worker protection needs (Ministry of Electronics and Information Technology, India, 2024).

Factors Affecting AI's Impact on Employment

Several factors contribute to the current and future impact of AI on employment:

- **Speed of AI Adoption**: Large enterprises are twice as likely to adopt AI compared to smaller businesses due to their greater financial resources (IBM, 2024).
- **Type of Jobs Affected**: The shift from blue-collar to white-collar job displacement reflects a broader change in the nature of work impacted by AI, with highly skilled roles now facing automation (Business Insider, 2023).

Recent Trends and Challenges

Recent trends reveal that while AI adoption is growing, its impact on job displacement is still emerging:

- In May 2023, AI was directly linked to 3,900 job losses in the U.S., marking it as a significant, yet not overwhelming, factor in job displacement (Socius, 2024).
- British Telecom's plan to cut 10,000 jobs over seven years highlights a strategic move towards AI and automation, reflecting broader industry trends (British Telecom, 2024). Many businesses are still in the exploratory phase of AI adoption, indicating that the full impact on employment may take longer to manifest.

Comparative Analysis With Other Nations

A global comparison shows varying approaches to managing AI's impact on labor:

- **Germany**: Has implemented strong regulations and reskilling programs to protect displaced workers.
- **China**: Focuses on rapid AI-driven economic growth with less immediate emphasis on labor protections (Schwab, 2023; Liu, 2024).

This disparity in approaches provides valuable insights into effective strategies for balancing technological advancement with worker security.

Perspectives and Concerns

The prevailing concerns about AI replacing jobs are significant:

- 30% of workers globally fear job displacement due to AI advancements (PwC, 2024).
- In India, this apprehension is even higher, with 74% of the workforce expressing concern about AI's impact on their jobs (Microsoft, 2023).
- Despite these fears, 81% of office workers believe AI enhances job performance and productivity, indicating a complex relationship between fear and acceptance of AI in the workplace (SnapLogic, 2024).

ECONOMIC FORECASTS

Projections of AI's Future Impact on the Global Job Market

Future projections suggest that while AI may lead to significant job displacement, it also has the potential to create new job roles and industries. The balance between job destruction and creation will largely depend on the pace of technological adoption and the effectiveness of reskilling programs.

Analysis of Long-Term Economic Effects, Including Potential Job Creation and Destruction

Long-term economic effects of AI include not only the displacement of existing roles but also the creation of new job categories. The net impact on employment will depend on the ability of economies to adapt and the success of policies aimed at mitigating negative effects and promoting job creation in emerging sectors.

TECHNOLOGICAL ADVANCEMENTS

Future Trends in AI Technology and Their Potential Implications for Employment

Future trends in AI technology, such as advancements in machine learning, natural language processing, and robotics, are expected to further influence employment patterns. These developments could lead to both increased automation of routine tasks and the creation of new opportunities in fields such as AI ethics and human-AI collaboration.

Emerging Fields and Job Roles Created by AI Advancements

AI advancements are likely to give rise to new job roles and fields, including AI ethics consultants, data scientists, and roles in AI system maintenance and development. The evolution of these roles will shape the future job market and require ongoing adaptation by the workforce.

LEGAL AND ETHICAL CONSIDERATIONS

Legal Challenges and Ethical Issues
Related to AI and Employment

Anticipated legal challenges include issues related to job displacement, data privacy, and algorithmic bias. Ethical concerns revolve around ensuring fair treatment of workers and addressing potential inequalities exacerbated by AI technologies.

Legal Frameworks and Ethical Guidelines

There is a pressing need for updated legal frameworks and ethical guidelines to address the impact of AI on employment. This includes developing policies that protect workers' rights, ensure equitable access to reskilling opportunities, and regulate the ethical use of AI technologies in the workplace.

METHODOLGY

The study employs a mixed-methods approach, combining quantitative and qualitative analyses to evaluate the impact of AI on employment. Quantitative data is gathered through surveys and employment reports to quantify job displacement, sectoral shifts, and the effectiveness of reskilling programs. Qualitative insights are obtained from interviews with industry experts, policymakers, and affected workers to understand the broader implications of AI adoption and policy measures. The research also includes a comparative analysis of national policies and regulations from various countries to identify effective strategies and gaps in current frameworks. Data from case studies and literature reviews further inform the analysis, providing a comprehensive view of AI's impact on employment and the effectiveness of existing and proposed interventions. This methodology enables a thorough understanding of both the numerical impact and the contextual factors influencing AI's effect on the job market.

ANALYSIS

Table 1. Impact of AI on job responsibilities and workload

Response Option	Frequency	Percentage
Significantly increased	90	30.00%
Slightly increased	85	28.33%
No change	70	23.33%
Slightly decreased	35	11.67%
Significantly decreased	20	6.67%
Total	**300**	**100%**

LEGEND: The table 1 represents the frequency analysis of responses regarding the impact of AI on job responsibilities and workload.

Table 2. Level of concern about job displacement due to AI

Response Option	Frequency	Percentage
Extremely concerned	110	36.67%
Very concerned	85	28.33%
Moderately concerned	55	18.33%
Slightly concerned	30	10.00%
Not concerned at all	20	6.67%
Total	**300**	**100%**

LEGEND: The table 2 represents the frequency analysis of responses concerning how AI has affected skill requirements in the workplace.

Table 3. Effective measures to mitigate negative impacts of AI

Response Option	Frequency	Percentage
Enhanced reskilling and retraining programs	170	56.67%
Updated labour laws and regulations	120	40.00%
Increased support for displaced workers	150	50.00%

continued on following page

Table 3. Continued

Response Option	Frequency	Percentage
Promotion of AI-human collaboration in the workplace	110	36.67%
Public awareness and education on AI impacts	90	30.00%
Total Responses	**300**	**100%**

LEGEND: The table 3 represents the frequency analysis of responses evaluating the perceived effectiveness of reskilling programs in addressing job displacement due to AI.

RESULTS

Impact of AI on Job Responsibilities and Workload

The survey results indicate a significant shift in job responsibilities and workload due to AI integration. A substantial portion of respondents (30.00%) reported that their job responsibilities have been "significantly increased" by AI technologies, reflecting the growing role of AI in demanding new skills and adjustments. A further 28.33% indicated a "slightly increased" workload, suggesting a moderate impact on job duties. Conversely, 23.33% experienced "no change," implying that AI has not yet affected their responsibilities. However, 11.67% reported a "slightly decreased" workload, and 6.67% noted a "significantly decreased" workload, indicating that AI can also reduce job demands in certain contexts.

Level of Concern About Job Displacement Due to AI

Concerns about job displacement due to AI are notably high among respondents. A majority, 36.67%, are "extremely concerned" about potential job losses, highlighting a significant level of apprehension. Additionally, 28.33% are "very concerned," showing that fear of displacement is widespread. A smaller segment, 18.33%, is "moderately concerned," while 10.00% are "slightly concerned." Only 6.67% are "not concerned at all," suggesting that while some respondents are less worried, the overall sentiment is one of concern regarding job security in the face of AI advancements.

Effective Measures to Mitigate Negative Impacts of AI

To address the challenges posed by AI, respondents identified several effective measures. The majority (56.67%) emphasized the need for "enhanced reskilling and retraining programs," underscoring the importance of preparing the workforce for new demands. "Updated labor laws and regulations" were also highlighted

297

by 40.00% of respondents as crucial for protecting workers. "Increased support for displaced workers" was supported by 50.00%, indicating a strong preference for targeted assistance. Additionally, 36.67% suggested "promotion of AI-human collaboration in the workplace" as a beneficial strategy, while 30.00% advocated for "public awareness and education on AI impacts," reflecting a desire for broader understanding and adaptation to AI's effects.

DISCUSSION

The survey indicates that AI's integration has notably increased job responsibilities and workload, with 30.00% of respondents reporting a significant increase and 28.33% a slight increase. This reflects the demand for new skills and adaptation to AI-driven tools. Conversely, 23.33% saw no change, and 18.34% experienced a decrease in workload, suggesting AI's mixed impact on job roles. Concerns about job displacement are high, with 36.67% extremely concerned and 28.33% very concerned, highlighting significant anxiety about job security. In response to mitigating AI's negative impacts, there is strong support for enhanced reskilling programs (56.67%), updated labor laws (40.00%), and increased support for displaced workers (50.00%). These findings emphasize the need for adaptive strategies, including reskilling, regulatory updates, and support systems to address the evolving challenges of AI in the workplace.

SUGGESTIONS

To effectively address the challenges and leverage the opportunities presented by AI in the workplace, several broad strategies should be considered. First, there should be a strong emphasis on enhancing reskilling and retraining programs to ensure that workers can adapt to new technologies and evolving job requirements. This involves not only updating educational curricula but also providing continuous learning opportunities for current employees. Second, updating labor laws and regulations is crucial to protect workers' rights and ensure fair practices in an AI-driven economy. This includes developing policies that address job displacement, wage changes, and workplace safety in the context of AI integration. Additionally, increasing support for displaced workers through financial aid, career counseling, and job placement services can help mitigate the negative impacts of job loss. Promoting AI-human collaboration and fostering a culture of innovation can also play a significant role in integrating AI technologies in a way that enhances productivity while maintaining human oversight and involvement. Finally, public awareness and education about AI's potential impacts on employment are essential for preparing the workforce and society for future changes. By adopting these measures, stakeholders can create a more resilient and adaptable workforce capable of thriving in an AI-enhanced job market.

CONCLUSION

The integration of artificial intelligence (AI) into the workplace presents both significant challenges and opportunities. The impact of AI on job responsibilities and workload has shown a notable shift, with a considerable portion of the workforce experiencing increased responsibilities due to AI adoption. The concern about job displacement remains high, reflecting the broader apprehensions about AI's potential to disrupt traditional employment structures. However, there are effective measures that can be implemented to mitigate these challenges, including enhancing reskilling programs, updating labor laws, and supporting displaced workers. The current data underscores the need for a balanced approach that promotes technological advancement while also safeguarding worker rights and facilitating a smooth transition for those affected. By addressing these issues through comprehensive strategies and proactive policies, it is possible to harness the benefits of AI while minimizing its adverse effects, ultimately leading to a more resilient and equitable job market.

REFERENCES

Brynjolfsson, E., & Unger, G. (2023). The Macroeconomics of Artificial Intelligence. *Finance & Development*, 0060(004), A006. DOI:10.5089/9798400260179.001.A006

Business Insider. (2023). AI and Wage Reduction.

Collett, C., Gomes, L. G., & Neff, G. (2022). *The Effects of AI on the Working Lives of Women*. UNESCO Publishing. DOI:10.18235/0004055

European Commission. (2023). *GDPR and Digital Services Act*. EC.

Goldman Sachs. (2023). *The Potentially Large Effects of Artificial Intelligence on Economic Growth*. Briggs/Kodnani.

Gopinath, G. (2023). Harnessing AI for Global Good. *Finance & Development*, 0060(004), A018. DOI:10.5089/9798400260179.001.A018

Hatzius, J. (2023). *The Potentially Large Effects of Artificial Intelligence on Economic Growth (Briggs/Kodnani)*. Goldman Sachs.

IBM. (2024). *AI Adoption in Businesses*. IBM.

Lane, M., & Saint-Martin, A. (2021). *The Impact of Artificial Intelligence on the Labour Market: What Do We Know So Far?*

Liu, J. (2024). *China's AI and Employment Policies*.

Microsoft. (2023). *AI Job Replacement Concerns in India*. Microsoft.

Ministry of Electronics and Information Technology. (2024). *AI Policy Developments*.

PwC. (2023). *AI and the Future of Jobs*. PwC.

Schwab, K. (2023). *Global Perspectives on AI and Labor*.

SnapLogic. (2024). *AI and Workplace Performance*. SnapLogic.

Socius. (2024). *Impact of AI on Job Displacement*. Socius.

Stevenson, B. (2018). Artificial Intelligence, Income, Employment, and Meaning. In *The Economics of Artificial Intelligence: An Agenda* (pp. 189–195). University of Chicago Press.

Chapter 14
Cloud–Based Visualization Techniques for Big Data:
A Survey of Platforms and Algorithms

Vimuktha Evangeleen Salis

Global Academy of Technology, India

Sharmila Chidravalli

Global Academy of Technology, India

ABSTRACT

In our rapidly evolving landscape, the realm of big data has gained prominence across sectors like healthcare, finance, and e-commerce. However, deciphering the vast amounts of generated data presents a significant challenge. Visualization techniques prove invaluable in making sense of this data, but traditional methods fall short. Enter cloud-based visualization platforms and algorithms, offering scalable and cost-effective solutions to tackle big data visualization challenges. This chapter embarks on a survey, comparing these platforms and algorithms based on their unique features, capabilities, and limitations. The literature review underscores the role of cloud computing in addressing the complexities of big data visualization. Methodologically, the authors employ criteria such as scalability, performance, cost-effectiveness, and user-friendliness to select and evaluate platforms and algorithms.

DOI: 10.4018/979-8-3693-4187-2.ch014

INTRODUCTION: NAVIGATING THE BIG DATA HORIZON

In recent years, the pervasive influence of big data has woven itself into the fabric of diverse industries, transforming the way we approach research and decision-making. Sectors such as healthcare, finance, and e-commerce find themselves at the nexus of this data revolution, where the sheer magnitude of information generated poses both an opportunity and a formidable challenge. As data volumes soar to unprecedented heights, the quest for meaning within this vast expanse becomes a central theme, prompting a reevaluation of traditional analytical methods.

While big data holds immense potential, its comprehension demands more than conventional approaches can offer. Visualization techniques emerge as indispensable tools, bridging the gap between raw data and actionable insights. Yet, the escalating complexity of big data necessitates a leap beyond the capabilities of traditional visualization methods. Enter cloud-based visualization platforms and algorithms, heralding a new era in data exploration. These innovative solutions promise scalability and cost-effectiveness, addressing the unique challenges posed by the ever-expanding dimensions of big data.

The purpose of this paper is to embark on a comprehensive exploration of this transformative landscape, conducting a survey of cloud-based visualization platforms and algorithms. In doing so, we aim to provide a nuanced understanding of their features, capabilities, and limitations. By undertaking a comparative analysis, our endeavor is to present a panoramic view of the available options, empowering researchers, practitioners, and decision-makers to navigate the complex terrain of big data visualization with informed precision.

The Evolving Landscape of Big Data Visualization: A Historical Perspective

To fully appreciate the significance of cloud-based visualization platforms and algorithms, it is imperative to delve into the historical trajectory of big data visualization. The journey began with the recognition that traditional methods, while effective for smaller datasets, falter when faced with the colossal dimensions of big data. As industries started grappling with the implications of this data explosion, the demand for scalable and efficient visualization solutions became increasingly pronounced.

Early visualization techniques, such as bar charts and pie graphs, laid the foundation for data representation but proved inadequate in the face of big data's intricacies. The advent of cloud computing marked a paradigm shift, offering a scalable infrastructure that could accommodate the exponential growth of data. This shift paved the way for the emergence of cloud-based visualization platforms, positioning themselves as dynamic hubs for data processing, storage, and visualization.

The Nexus of Healthcare, Finance, and E-Commerce: Industries in the Grip of Big Data Dynamics

Before delving into the intricacies of cloud-based visualization solutions, it is pertinent to explore the specific impact of big data within the realms of healthcare, finance, and e-commerce. These industries serve as microcosms where the implications of big data are keenly felt, driving the need for advanced visualization tools.

In healthcare, the influx of patient data, genomic information, and real-time monitoring streams creates an intricate tapestry of information. Cloud-based visualization becomes indispensable for healthcare professionals seeking to extract meaningful patterns, identify correlations, and enhance diagnostic capabilities. The marriage of big data and visualization holds the promise of revolutionizing personalized medicine and streamlining healthcare delivery.

Finance, with its labyrinthine datasets encompassing market trends, transaction histories, and risk analytics, stands at the forefront of the big data revolution. Cloud-based visualization platforms offer financial analysts the ability to navigate this complex web of information with agility. From real-time market visualizations to predictive analytics, these tools empower decision-makers to stay ahead in a dynamic and volatile financial landscape.

E-commerce, driven by consumer behavior data, inventory management, and sales analytics, relies on big data to optimize operations and enhance customer experiences. Cloud-based visualization not only simplifies the comprehension of these multifaceted datasets but also aids in strategic decision-making, such as personalized marketing campaigns and inventory forecasting.

The Imperative for Advanced Visualization: Overcoming Traditional Constraints

Traditional visualization methods, while effective for smaller datasets, encounter significant bottlenecks when applied to big data. The volume, velocity, and variety of information inherent in large-scale datasets overwhelm the capabilities of conventional tools. As a result, the need for advanced visualization techniques that can scale dynamically, process information in real-time, and handle diverse data types becomes increasingly evident.

Cloud-based visualization platforms emerge as a response to this imperative, offering a paradigm where computational resources can scale on-demand to match the complexities of big data. The cloud's inherent flexibility, combined with specialized visualization tools, provides a powerful arsenal for researchers and practitioners to glean insights from vast datasets.

The Pinnacle of Scalability: AWS, Azure, and Google Cloud Platform Unveiled

Central to the effectiveness of cloud-based visualization is scalability – the ability to handle datasets of any size while ensuring optimal performance and cost-effectiveness. In this section, we turn our attention to three key players in the cloud computing arena: Amazon Web Services (AWS), Microsoft Azure, and Google Cloud Platform. These platforms, each a titan in its own right, offer diverse visualization tools and data processing services, underpinned by the promise of scalability.

Amazon Web Services (AWS): Navigating the Complex Terrain

AWS stands as a stalwart in the cloud computing realm, offering a comprehensive suite of services for big data processing and visualization. Its visualization tools, ranging from dashII. Literature Review

Big data visualization is the process of representing large datasets visually, in a way that allows analysts and decision-makers to gain insights and make informed decisions. The visualization of big data is challenging because traditional approaches may not be scalable or efficient enough to handle the volume, velocity, and variety of big data. Cloud computing has emerged as a potential solution for big data visualization, due to its scalability, flexibility, and cost-effectiveness.

Cloud-based big data visualization platforms provide a range of services for storing, processing, and visualizing large datasets. Amazon Web Services (AWS), Microsoft Azure, and Google Cloud Platform are some of the key platforms available for cloud-based big data visualization. These platforms provide a range of visualization tools, such as dashboards, charts, and graphs, and offer a range of data processing services, such as batch processing, stream processing, and machine learning.

Cloud-based big data visualization algorithms are designed to handle the unique characteristics of big data, such as its high dimensionality, sparsity, and heterogeneity. Techniques such as scatter plots, heat maps, and parallel coordinates are commonly used for big data visualization. These techniques can be applied to a wide range of data types, such as time series data, spatial data, and network data.

LITERATURE REVIEW: NAVIGATING THE INTERSECTION OF BIG DATA VISUALIZATION AND CLOUD COMPUTING

The nexus of big data and cloud computing has redefined the landscape of information processing, ushering in an era where the ability to extract meaningful insights from colossal datasets is pivotal. This section embarks on a journey through the relevant literature, aiming to distill key concepts and developments in big data visualization and cloud computing. It unfolds like a tapestry, weaving together the challenges inherent in visualizing vast datasets, the evolutionary trajectory of cloud computing, and the pivotal platforms and algorithms shaping cloud-based visualization.

Challenges of Big Data Visualization: Unraveling Complexity

The exploration of big data visualization commences with an acknowledgment of the challenges that accompany the vastness and intricacy of contemporary datasets. Scholars and practitioners grapple with the sheer volume, velocity, and variety of data, posing unique hurdles to traditional visualization methods. The literature scrutinizes these challenges, emphasizing the need for innovative approaches capable of scaling dynamically and adapting to diverse data structures.

Among the challenges delineated is the inherent difficulty in representing multi-dimensional data comprehensively. As datasets grow in complexity, traditional two-dimensional visualizations often fall short, necessitating the development of advanced techniques capable of portraying relationships within high-dimensional spaces. The literature also sheds light on the intricacies of temporal data visualization, spatial data representation, and the complexities posed by heterogeneous data types.

Evolution of Cloud Computing: A Dynamic Paradigm Shift

A significant thread woven into the fabric of this literature review is the evolution of cloud computing and its transformative impact on big data processing and visualization. As an innovative paradigm, cloud computing transcends traditional computing models, offering on-demand access to a shared pool of configurable computing resources. The literature traces the evolutionary trajectory of cloud computing, from its nascent stages to its current status as a linchpin in the realm of information technology.

The emergence of cloud computing is characterized by a paradigm shift from traditional, on-premises infrastructure to flexible, scalable cloud-based solutions. This shift, propelled by the need to accommodate the escalating demands of big data, introduces concepts such as Infrastructure as a Service (IaaS), Platform as a

305

Service (PaaS), and Software as a Service (SaaS). The literature underscores the agility, cost-effectiveness, and scalability inherent in cloud computing, providing the foundation for a robust ecosystem of big data visualization.

Key Platforms and Algorithms in Cloud-Based Visualization: A Comprehensive Survey**

Delving deeper into the literature reveals the prominence of key platforms and algorithms that serve as the backbone of cloud-based visualization. This section dissects the capabilities and functionalities of major players such as Amazon Web Services (AWS), Microsoft Azure, and Google Cloud Platform, elucidating their roles in enabling scalable and efficient data visualization.

Amazon Web Services (AWS), a behemoth in the cloud computing arena, is spotlighted for its versatile suite of services catering to big data processing and visualization. The literature explores the intricacies of AWS's visualization tools, from dashboards to charts and graphs, and delves into its capacity to handle datasets of any size through features like auto-scaling and elastic load balancing. However, the nuanced discussion acknowledges the complexities and challenges faced by users, especially those new to the platform.

Microsoft Azure, another stalwart in the cloud domain, is scrutinized for its visualization tools and data processing services. The literature explores Azure's commitment to scalability, with features like auto-scaling and elastic load balancing aligning resources for optimal performance and cost-effectiveness. Like AWS, Azure's complexity is acknowledged, emphasizing the importance of robust documentation and support resources.

Google Cloud Platform emerges as a significant player, offering a range of services for big data processing and visualization. The literature dives into Google Cloud Platform's scalability, visualization tools, and its commitment to performance optimization and cost-effectiveness. However, a common theme across all platforms is the recognition of the learning curve and potential challenges faced by users navigating these sophisticated ecosystems.

Visualization Techniques and Algorithms: A Tapestry of Advancements and Limitations

The literature unfolds a rich tapestry of visualization techniques and algorithms employed in the context of big data. Techniques such as scatter plots, heat maps, and parallel coordinates come to the fore, each offering unique insights into the visualization of large and complex datasets. The literature navigates the advantages and disadvantages inherent in these techniques, recognizing their efficacy in diverse scenarios.

Scatter plots, a venerable technique, find renewed relevance in the big data era, where the juxtaposition of two variables reveals intricate patterns, trends, and outliers. The literature explores the enhancements possible through features like color, size, and shape, elevating scatter plots beyond their traditional role.

Heat maps, another stalwart in big data visualization, represent data as a matrix of colors, offering a visual representation of values or ranges. The literature illuminates the utility of heat maps in identifying clusters, patterns, and trends within data, emphasizing their adaptability through features like color scales, legends, and annotations.

Parallel coordinates, a dynamic visualization technique, plot multiple variables on parallel axes, providing a holistic view of relationships, clusters, and trends. The literature delves into the interactivity and exploration capabilities facilitated by features like brushing and linking, acknowledging parallel coordinates as a potent tool in the big data visualization toolkit.

METHODOLOGY

In steering the course of this study, our methodology unfolds as a deliberate and systematic exploration, aiming to unveil the intricacies of cloud-based big data visualization platforms and algorithms. With the expansive realm of big data visualization as our compass, we embarked on a literature review, anchoring our investigation in the wealth of existing knowledge. This section elucidates the steps taken, the criteria employed, and the considerations made in selecting, comparing, and evaluating the diverse platforms and algorithms that constitute the backbone of our survey.

Our journey commenced with a comprehensive literature review, a methodological anchor that allowed us to chart the trajectory of key platforms and algorithms in the domain of cloud-based big data visualization. The review served as a compass, guiding us through scholarly works, industry reports, and online resources. Delving into the depths of knowledge, we identified platforms and algorithms pivotal to our survey, grounding our study in the existing landscape while anticipating the contours of innovation.

Online sources proved to be invaluable in this pursuit, with official websites of the identified platforms serving as portals into the intricacies of their functionalities and features. The wealth of information gleaned from these sources became the bedrock upon which we built our understanding of each platform's capabilities and algorithms' intricacies.

Criteria for Selection: Navigating the Ocean of Options

With a trove of information at our disposal, we set sail to select platforms and algorithms for our survey, mindful of the diverse considerations shaping our criteria. Popularity, as a compass reflecting the trust and adoption by the community, guided our initial selections. The scalability of platforms and algorithms became a North Star, symbolizing their capacity to navigate the expansive seas of large datasets, while also being adept at scaling as required.

Performance emerged as a crucial lighthouse, guiding our choices based on factors like speed, accuracy, and responsiveness. The efficiency and effectiveness of cost-effectiveness became a crucial factor, evaluating the pricing models, cost per unit of processing, and the flexibility offered by each platform and algorithm.

User-friendliness, akin to the compass aligning with ease of navigation, became a paramount consideration. Factors such as ease of use, customization options, and the robustness of support resources played a pivotal role in ensuring that the selected platforms and algorithms were not only powerful but also accessible and user-centric.

Comparison and Evaluation: Navigating the Storm of Criteria

Having carefully selected our fleet of platforms and algorithms, the next phase of our methodology involved a rigorous comparison and evaluation, where each entity underwent scrutiny against the established criteria of scalability, performance, cost-effectiveness, and user-friendliness.

Scalability: The scalability assessment delved into the platforms and algorithms' ability to weather the storm of large datasets, scrutinizing their capacity to scale dynamically based on demand. A crucial consideration was their adaptability to handle fluctuations in data volume, ensuring optimal performance regardless of the dataset's size.

Performance: The performance evaluation became a compass navigating the waters of speed, accuracy, and responsiveness. Each platform and algorithm faced the litmus test of their ability to process data swiftly, deliver accurate results, and respond promptly to user inputs, ensuring an efficient and effective voyage through the realm of big data.

Cost-Effectiveness: The seas of cost-effectiveness were navigated with a keen eye on the pricing models, evaluating the cost per unit of processing and the flexibility offered by each platform and algorithm. The goal was to identify not just powerful solutions but ones that provided value for investment, aligning with the budgetary considerations of users.

User-Friendliness: In the evaluation of user-friendliness, we sought to ensure that each platform and algorithm was akin to a well-crafted navigational tool. Ease of use, the extent of customization options, and the robustness of support resources became crucial considerations, guaranteeing that users could embark on their journey with confidence and clarity.

our methodology serves as a compass guiding the expedition through the vast expanse of cloud-based big data visualization. Grounded in a thorough literature review and shaped by meticulous criteria for selection, our survey seeks to not only identify the key players but also illuminate their nuances, offering a map for practitioners and decision-makers navigating the ever-evolving landscape of big data visualization. As we navigate the storm of criteria, each platform and algorithm stands as a vessel, ready to chart a course through the complexities of big data, ensuring a voyage marked by scalability, efficiency, cost-effectiveness, and user-centricity.

CLOUD-BASED VISUALIZATION PLATFORMS

In this section, we provide a detailed overview of the different cloud-based visualization platforms available, including AWS, Microsoft Azure, and Google Cloud Platform.

Amazon Web Services (AWS) is a cloud-based platform that provides a range of services for big data processing and visualization. AWS provides a range of visualization tools, such as dashboards, charts, and graphs, and offers a range of data processing services, such as batch processing, stream processing, and machine learning. AWS is highly scalable, and can handle datasets of any size, with features such as auto-scaling and elastic load balancing to ensure that resources are optimized for performance and cost-effectiveness. AWS also provides a range of visualization templates, which users can customize to suit their needs. However, AWS can be complex and challenging to use for beginners, and its pricing can be difficult to understand.

Microsoft Azure is another popular cloud-based platform for big data processing and visualization. Azure provides a range of visualization tools, such as dashboards, charts, and graphs, and offers a range of data processing services, such as batch processing, stream processing, and machine learning. Azure is highly scalable, with features such as auto-scaling and elastic load balancing to ensure that resources are optimized for performance and cost-effectiveness. Azure also provides a range of visualization templates, which users can customize to suit their needs. However, like AWS, Azure can be complex and challenging to use for beginners, and its pricing can be difficult to understand.

Google Cloud Platform is a cloud-based platform that provides a range of services for big data processing and visualization. Google Cloud Platform provides a range of visualization tools, such as dashboards, charts, and graphs, and offers a range of data processing services, such as batch processing, stream processing, and machine learning. Google Cloud Platform is highly scalable, and can handle datasets of any size, with features such as auto-scaling and elastic load balancing to ensure that resources are optimized for performance and cost-effectiveness. Google Cloud Platform also provides a range of visualization templates, which users can customize to suit their needs. However, like AWS and Azure, Google Cloud Platform can be complex and challenging to use for beginners, and its pricing can be difficult to understand.

CLOUD-BASED VISUALIZATION ALGORITHMS

In this section, we provide a detailed overview of the different cloud-based visualization algorithms available, including scatter plots, heat maps, and parallel coordinates.

Scatter plots are a commonly used visualization technique for big data, where two variables are plotted against each other. Scatter plots can be used to identify patterns, trends, and outliers in the data. Scatter plots can also be enhanced with features such as color, size, and shape, to provide additional information about the data.

Heat maps are another commonly used visualization technique for big data, where the data is represented as a matrix of colors, with each color representing a different value or range of values. Heat maps can be used to identify clusters, patterns, and trends in the data. Heat maps can also be enhanced with features such as color scales, legends, and annotations, to provide additional information about the data.

Parallel coordinates are a visualization technique for big data that involves plotting multiple variables on parallel axes, with each axis representing a different variable. Parallel coordinates can be used to identify relationships, clusters, and trends in the data. Parallel coordinates can also be enhanced with features such as brushing and linking, to provide additional interactivity and exploration of the data.

COMPARISON AND ANALYSIS

In this section, we compare and analyze the different cloud-based visualization platforms and algorithms based on the criteria described in the methodology section.

In terms of scalability, all three platforms (AWS, Azure, and Google Cloud Platform) are highly scalable and can handle datasets of any size, with features such as auto-scaling and elastic load balancing to ensure that resources are optimized for performance and cost-effectiveness. In terms of performance, all three platforms are designed to handle big data processing and visualization, and offer a range of data processing and visualization tools. In terms of cost-effectiveness, pricing models can vary between the platforms, but they all offer flexible pricing options that can be customized to suit the user's needs. In terms of user-friendliness, all three platforms can be complex and challenging to use for beginners, but they all offer a range of documentation and support resources to help users get started and overcome any challenges they encounter.

In terms of visualization algorithms, scatter plots, heat maps, and parallel coordinates are all widely used and effective techniques for visualizing big data. Each algorithm has its strengths and weaknesses, and the choice of algorithm will depend on the specific requirements of the user and the nature of the data being visualized.

CONCLUSION

In this book chapter, we have provided an overview of cloud-based visualization techniques for big data, including a survey of platforms and algorithms. We have demonstrated that a cloud-based visualization is a powerful tool for handling big data, allowing users to easily process and visualize large datasets in a cost-effective and scalable manner. We have also provided a comparison and analysis of different cloud-based visualization platforms and algorithms, based on the criteria of scalability, performance, cost-effectiveness, and user-friendliness. Our analysis has shown that all three platforms (AWS, Azure, and Google Cloud Platform) are highly scalable and can handle datasets of any size, with features such as auto-scaling and elastic load balancing to ensure that resources are optimized for performance and cost-effectiveness. We have also shown that scatter plots, heat maps, and parallel coordinates are all effective techniques for visualizing big data, with each algorithm having its strengths and weaknesses.

In conclusion, we believe that a cloud-based visualization is a powerful tool for handling big data and that it will continue to play an important role in data processing and analysis in the years to come.

REFERENCES

AWS. (2023). *Amazon Web Services*. Amazon. https://aws.amazon.com/.

Cao, X., Li, H., Yan, X., & Wang, H. "Big Data Visualization in the Cloud," in *Proceedings of the 2015 IEEE International Conference on Cloud Engineering*, Tempe, AZ, 2015, pp. 339-344.

Google Cloud Platform. (n.d.). Google. https://cloud.google.com/.

Microsoft Azure. (n.d.). Microsoft. https://azure.microsoft.com/.

Mukherjee, S., & Saha, S. (2018). A Comprehensive Study on Big Data Visualization Techniques. *Proceedings of the 2018 IEEE International Conference on Big Data and Smart Computing*, Bali, Indonesia.

Ngom, A. T. A., Abdalla, H., & Rajpoot, N. (2016, August). Big Data Visualization: A Survey. *IEEE Transactions on Visualization and Computer Graphics*, 22(8), 1992–2009.

Özsu, T., & Valduriez, P. (2011). *Principles of Distributed Database Systems*. Springer.

Saleh, S. M., Abido, M. A., & Abou-Elnour, M. A. (2017). *"Big Data Visualization: A Survey of the State of the Art,"* in *Advances in Intelligent Systems and Computing* (Vol. 512). Springer.

Shams, M. Y., & Sarker, F. M. M. (2019). A Review of Visualization Tools for Big Data Analytics. *Proceedings of the 2019 4th International Conference on Electrical and Electronic Engineering*, Dhaka, Bangladesh.

Thakkar, J. J., Shah, M., & Patel, S. K. (2016, August). Big Data Visualization: Review of Literature. *International Journal of Computer Applications*, 148(10), 30–35.

Zhang, J., Li, C., Zhu, W., & Guo, Y. (2017). Cloud-Based Visual Analytics for Big Data. *Proceedings of the 2017 IEEE International Conference on Cloud Computing Technology and Science*. IEEE.

Chapter 15
Decoding Work–Life Balance Conundrum:
A Meta–Learning Prediction Approach

Sajidha S. A.

https://orcid.org/0000-0003-4771-3131

Vellore Institute of Technology, Chennai, India

Deepshika Vijayanand

Vellore Institute of Technology, Chennai, India

Madhumitha Rajagopal

https://orcid.org/0009-0003-8517-8157

Vellore Institute of Technology, Chennai, India

Dhanush Sambasivam

https://orcid.org/0009-0003-8517-8157

Vellore Institute of Technology, Chennai, India

Nisha V. M.

Vellore Institute of Technology, Chennai, India

ABSTRACT

To unravel the complex facets of optimal equilibrium between professional commitments and personal life, this research delves into the intricacies of work-life balance dynamics, employing machine learning to predict factors influencing equilibrium. A stacking-ensemble method utilizes the mutual complementary effects of the base models to improve the performance with better generalization of the model. ML algorithms including gradient boosting algorithm, ridge regression, lasso regres-

DOI: 10.4018/979-8-3693-4187-2.ch015

sion, huber regression, sgd regressor, support vector regressor (SVR), k neighbours regressor, kernel ridge regressor, RANSAC regressor, K means boosting algorithm, and generalized additive model (GAM) were trained meticulously. Fine-tuning the performance of random forest performance having R2 value of 0.9353, the lowest using the stacking ensemble to 0.9999 was performed. The base model combinations encompass a wide array of techniques with random forest as meta learner gave is a notable improvement in its prediction performance.

INTRODUCTION

Work-life balance is the delicate pursuit of harmony between professional responsibilities and personal well-being, transcending mere time management. It's about setting boundaries, nurturing mental and physical health, and prioritizing tasks to prevent one from overshadowing the other. In our interconnected world, where work seeps into personal time, achieving this equilibrium is a challenging yet essential endeavor. It's not just about excelling in careers but also nurturing relationships, pursuing passions, and prioritizing self-care. This balance significantly impacts satisfaction, reducing stress, enhancing job contentment, and fostering better mental health. Acknowledging and supporting work-life balance has become crucial for both personal fulfillment and creating healthier, more sustainable work environments.

Work hours across OECD member (OECD, n.d.-a) countries vary, with the average worker dedicating around 34 hours per week to paid work, revealing disparities among nations in terms of time spent on professional commitments. However, this investment in work often comes at the cost of mental health. The American Institute of Stress (OECD, n.d.-b) notes that a staggering 83% of US workers grapple with work-related stress, attributing this to factors such as extended working hours, job uncertainty, and an imbalance between work and personal life. Additionally, the impact of remote work on achieving balance is evident. A 2021 study by FlexJobs (American Institute of Stress, n.d.) revealed that 65% of respondents reported increased productivity when working remotely, crediting this to fewer distractions and better management of their work-life equilibrium.

There's a stark contrast in perspectives between employers and employees regarding work hours and reasons for departure. According to a report by the Harvard Business Review (Perlow & Porter, 2009), while 94% of surveyed professionals reported working over 50 hours weekly, employers' perceptions of why employees leave the company largely differed. While 89% of employers believed departures were primarily due to compensation-related issues, only 12% of employees actually left for monetary reasons. Gender disparities further complicate achieving work-life balance, as highlighted by the United Nations (ILO, 2018), with women globally undertaking nearly three times the unpaid care and domestic work compared to men, significantly impacting their ability to maintain balance.

The impact of work-life balance on productivity is noteworthy. The European Foundation for the Improvement of Living and Working Conditions (Eurofund, n.d.) reported that employees with a favorable work-life balance were 12% more likely to report high productivity levels. This trend is seen across generational perspectives, with millennials and Gen Z prioritizing work-life balance more than previous generations, as indicated by a study from Deloitte (Deloitte, 2023). Recognizing the repercussions of imbalance, the World Health Organization (WHO, 2019) officially recognized burnout as an occupational phenomenon, emphasizing excessive workload and a lack of equilibrium as contributing factors. Companies like Unilever and Microsoft are actively addressing these challenges by implementing various programs (Wise, 2022), including flexible working hours and mental health support services, underscoring the increasing acknowledgment of work-life balance's importance among both individuals and employers.

Technological advancements, particularly in machine learning, play a pivotal role in understanding and predicting work-life balance. Through sophisticated algorithms and data analysis, these technologies delve into various parameters—work schedules, productivity metrics, and personal habits—to discern patterns influencing an individual's equilibrium between professional responsibilities and personal life. By processing this diverse data, these algorithms uncover correlations and factors contributing to a balanced work-life dynamic. They assist in identifying stress-inducing factors, recognizing potential burnout risks, and offering tailored suggestions to support a more harmonious balance. Continuously adapting and learning from new data inputs, these technologies offer a promising avenue for proactively addressing challenges related to work-life balance, benefiting both individuals and organizations by fostering healthier and more fulfilling lifestyles.

This research dives deep into understanding work-life balance using a complex method called "Stacking Ensemble." It combines 14 diverse regression models to predict what factors affect this balance. By using these methods together, the study aims to give us valuable insights into work-life balance. These findings can help individuals make better decisions, guide companies in improving their strategies, and even influence policies related to work and life.

LITERATURE SURVEY

In their research, Pawlicka et al. (2020) examined the suitability of machine learning tools in revealing associations between individual employee characteristics, workplace factors, and their subjective assessment of work-life balance (WLB).

Analyzing a sample of 800 Polish workers, the researchers utilized Artificial Neural Networks, achieving an accuracy of 81.63%. Among the cases, 244 reported a lack of WLB, while 556 reported satisfaction. This research, integrating machine learning into the exploration of WLB dynamics, contributes valuable insights into the intricate relationship between individual characteristics and workplace elements, enriching both academic discourse and practical implications for human resource management.

Deshmukh (2018) conducted a study to explore the challenges faced by working women in reconciling personal and professional responsibilities, employing The Industrial Society's work-life balance manual. Descriptive statistics from Pune, Maharashtra, highlight prevalent work-life balance issues among the surveyed working women. The findings underscore the substantial influence of work-life balance on the overall quality of life. Notably, the study reveals that married women under 30 encounter more challenges in achieving balance, while those over 40 exhibit a slightly better equilibrium compared to their counterparts aged 30 to 40.

In a significant investigation involving a sizable dataset of 12,756 individuals, Radha and Rohith (2021) explored the correlation between diverse factors and Work-Life Balance (WLB). Employing meticulous analysis and calculations, key factors influencing WLB were identified. The study utilized Random Forest Classifier, Support Vector Machine, and Naive Bayes algorithms, allocating 80% of the dataset for training. The subsequent testing phase demonstrated an optimal predictive accuracy of 71.5%. This study provides important insights into the complex interplay between many circumstances and WLB, emphasizing the vital importance of identified variables in determining people' work-life balance.

In their recent study presented at the Doctoral Symposium on Computational Intelligence, Kumar and Tople (2023) delve into the crucial dynamics of employee performance, talent management, and motivating factors. The paper focuses on predictive modelling, and introduces novel classifier models for employee attrition, job involvement, and work-life balance. The Ridge Classifier exhibits exceptional accuracy at 92.7% for predicting IBM employee attrition, while Random Forest achieves the highest accuracy (62.3%) in forecasting Job Involvement. Logistic Regression, with a 64.8% accuracy rate, serves as an effective model for predicting Work-Life Balance. This research contributes valuable insights and precise models for workforce management, offering practical tools for organizations aiming to address attrition, enhance Job Involvement, and optimize Work-Life Balance.

In their recent study published by Tümen (2023) explore the multifaceted impact of work-life balance on employees, highlighting potential repercussions like attrition and health issues stemming from workplace efforts. Employing machine learning and ensemble learning techniques, the research endeavors to cluster employees based on attrition levels, utilizing parameters of effort and work-life balance. Notably, the random forest algorithm exhibits exceptional performance with a 95% accuracy score, comparable to the support vector machine. Despite algorithmic variations, all methods achieve a noteworthy overall f-score of 86%, while xGBoost, as part of ensemble learning, demonstrates relatively lower performance at 69%. The study offers valuable insights for organizations aiming to refine strategies for enhancing employee well-being and retention

In their recent study, Shah (2023) employ Deep Learning and Machine Learning to explore work-life balance determinants, particularly focusing on "quiet quitting" and age dynamics. Analyzing a dataset of 15,977 survey responses and utilizing the Artificial Neural Network (ANN) algorithm, the study attains a promising test accuracy of 73.91%. The research offers valuable insights and practical recommendations for organizations and individuals to proactively address work-life balance challenges, fostering healthier and more sustainable work environments.

In their 2018 study, Srividya et al. (2018) present a framework for mental health behavioral modeling using machine learning algorithms. The research showcases the effectiveness of SVM, KNN, and Random Forest, with ensemble classifiers enhancing mental health prediction accuracy to 90%. The study suggests potential extensions for categorizing various mental illnesses and highlights the proposed workflow as a valuable mechanism for behavioral modeling within diverse target populations.

OVERVIEW OF DATASET

The dataset under consideration contains responses from 15,973 people who took part in Authentic-Happiness.com's worldwide work-life survey. This dataset is a helpful resource for understanding the vital interplay between personal and work life. It includes 23 different questions intended to examine various aspects of work-life balance and associated issues.

This dataset provides a thorough view of the numerous aspects that influence an individual's impression of work-life balance. It enables experts to investigate relationships, develop prediction models, and obtain crucial insights into the dynamic link between work and personal life.

Here is a brief summary of the dataset's columns: FRUITS_VEGGIES, DAILY_STRESS, PLACES_VISITED, CORE_CIRCLE, SUPPORTING_OTHERS, SOCIAL_NETWORK, ACHIEVEMENT, DONATION, BMI_RANGE, TODO_COMPLETED, FLOW, DAILY_STEPS, LIVE_VISION, SLEEP_HOURS, LOST_VACATION, DAILY_SHOUTING, SUFFICIENT_INCOME, PERSONAL_AWARDS, PERSONAL_AWARDS, TIME_FOR_PASSION, WEEKLY_MEDITATION, GENDER, MONTH, and WORK_LIFE_BALANCE_SCORE.

Table 1. Descriptive statistics of the dataset

Attribute	Count	Mean	std	Min	25%	50%	75%	Max
FRUITS_VEGGIES	15972	2.922	1.442	0	2	3	4	5
DAILY_STRESS	15971	2.791	1.367	0	2	3	4	5
PLACES_VISITED	15972	5.232	3.311	0	2	5	8	10
CORE_CIRCLE	15972	5.508	2.840	0	3	5	8	10
SUPPORTING_OTHERS	15972	5.616	3.242	0	3	5	10	10
SOCIAL_NETWORK	15972	6.474	3.086	0	4	6	10	10
ACHIEVEMENT	15972	4.0007	2.755	0	2	3	6	10
DONATION	15972	2.715	1.851	0	1	3	5	5
BMI_RANGE	15972	1.410	0.491	1	1	1	2	2
TODO_COMPLETED	15972	5.745	2.624	0	4	6	8	10
LOST_VACATION	15972	2.899	3.692	0	0	0	5	10
DAILY_SHOUTING	15972	2.931	2.676	0	1	2	4	10
SUFFICIENT_INCOME	15972	1.728	0.444	1	1	2	2	2
PERSONAL_AWARDS	15972	5.711	3.089	0	3	5	9	10
TIME_FOR_PASSION	15972	3.326	2.729	0	1	3	5	10
WEEKLY_MEDITATION	15972	6.233	3.016	0	4	7	10	10
AGE	15972	1.602	0.944	0	1	2	2	3
GENDER	15972	0.382	0.486	0	0	0	1	1
WORK_LIFE_BALANCE_SCORE	15972	666.751	45.019	480	636	667.7	698.5	820.2
MONTH	15972	6.659	3.395	1	4	7	10	12

The descriptive statistical summary of the collected data is provided in Table 1.

METHODOLOGY

Proposed Architecture

We initiate the process by handling the data, addressing missing values, and ensuring its integrity. Employing the advanced random forest backtracking method, we performed feature selection to precisely gauge the significance of each variable. Following which, we used 14 different regression models to calculate R-squared values and Mean Squared Error (MSE), methodically evaluating the predictive power. Our investigation resulted in a complicated approach known as stacking ensembling, in which we combined several base models and meta-regressors. This meticulous fusion allowed us to pinpoint optimal model configurations that exhibited superior performance in terms of MSE and R-squared values, thereby enhancing the precision of our predictive modeling methodology.

Figure 1. Architecture proposed of the model

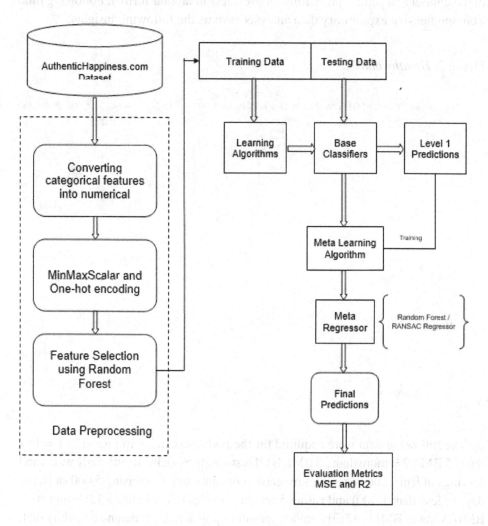

Figure 1 shows the architecture of the proposed model.

Data Preprocessing

Data import and preparation, involve integrating essential libraries for data manipulation and visualization. This initial step encompasses a thorough examination of the dataset's structure, presenting an overview in tabular format. Following this, a comprehensive exploratory data analysis gave us the following insights:

Figure 2. Healthy body

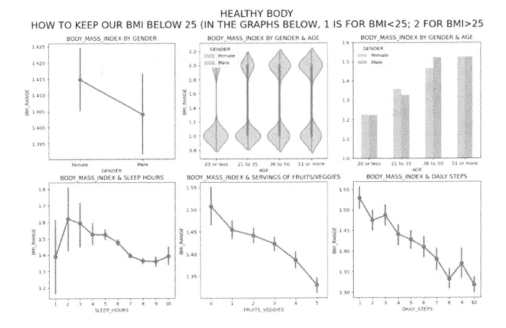

The following data were acquired for the body max index in Figure 2: 1 = less than 25 BMI; 2 = more than 25 BMI. BMI is strongly associated with daily walks and servings of fruits and vegetables (negative correlations)- Exercising 5,000 steps per day (vs less than 1,000) and eating 5 servings (vs less than 1) had a 15% impact on BMI- A lower BMI is a fairly obvious result of physical exercise and a healthy diet.

Figure 3. Healthy mind

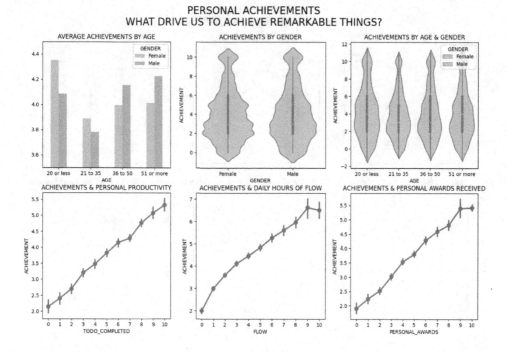

PERSONAL ACHIEVEMENTS
WHAT DRIVE US TO ACHIEVE REMARKABLE THINGS?

Figure 3 shows that a healthy mind is dependent on the capacity to "flow" during the day, regular meditation, and an income adequate to meet basic requirements, all of which result in 30% lower levels of stress. Women's total stress level peaks in their early twenties and, while gradually decreasing, stays greater than that of the male population across all age groups.

Figure 4. Personal achievements

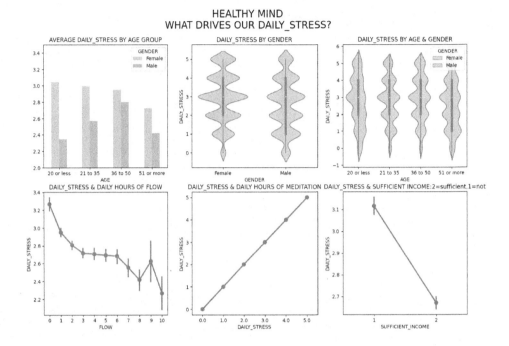

HEALTHY MIND
WHAT DRIVES OUR DAILY_STRESS?

From Figure 4, we infer that our daily productivity, the ability to flow throughout the day and personal awards such as diplomas and other certificates all contribute to higher levels of personal achievement. Women report slightly more personal achievements in their early years, while men report more after age 36.

Figure 5. Connection

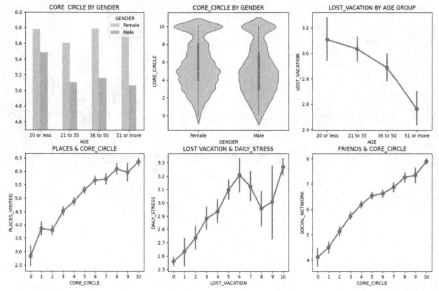

CONNECTION
HOW OUR CORE CIRCLE OF FRIENDS AND FAMILY STRENGTHENS OUR CONNECTION TO THE WORLD?

According to Figure 5, females tend to have a deeper circle of friends and relatives than males. When compared to other age groups, those aged 21 to 35 lose the most vacation days. As we lose more vacation days, our overall stress level rises. However, there is a minor drop between 7 and 9 days for lost vacation days, as if missing six or more vacation days has no longer affected the stress level.

Figure 6. Time for passion

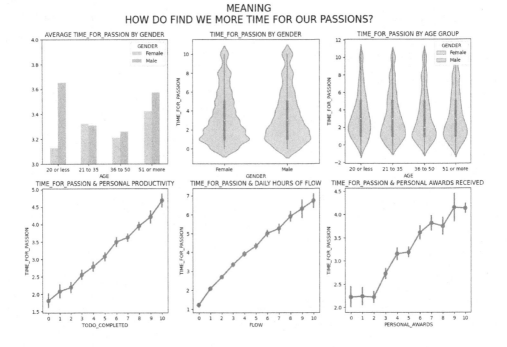

According to Figure 6, males appear to devote more time to their passions, particularly in their younger and later years. Our daily productivity, daily flow, and personal awards received are the three things that most strongly correlate with our capacity to find time for our hobbies.

Feature Selection Using Random Forest

This work utilizes Random Forest, a smart algorithm that assesses various factors' impact on achieving equilibrium between work and personal life. Through this method, we identified the top crucial features and their respective importance scores.

Figure 7. Bar plot of features and their importance score

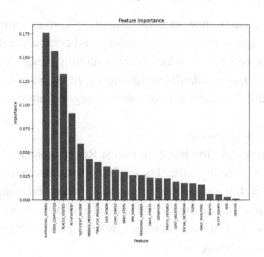

Table 2. Features and their importance score

S. No.	Feature	Importance Score	S. No.	Feature	Importance Score
1	SUPPORTING_OTHERS	0.1757	13	DAILY_STRESS	0.0231
2	TODO_COMPLETED	0.1567	14	DONATION	0.0227
3	PLACES_VISITED	0.1323	15	FRUITS_VEGGIES	0.0224
4	ACHIEVEMENT	0.0908	16	LOST_VACATION	0.0190
5	SUFFICIENT_INCOME	0.0590	17	SOCIAL_NETWORK	0.0176
6	WEEKLY_MEDITATION	0.0426	18	FLOW	0.0174
7	TIME_FOR_PASSION	0.0397	19	DAILY_SHOUTING	0.0162
8	LIVE_VISION	0.0351	20	MONTH	0.0059
9	CORE_CIRCLE	0.0316	21	SLEEP_HOURS	0.0056
10	DAILY_STEPS	0.0293	22	AGE	0.0028
11	BMI_RANGE	0.0260	23	GENDER	0.0012
12	PERSONAL_AWARDS	0.0260	24	TIMESTAMP	0

These factors as shown in Table 2 were found to have varying degrees of influence on work-life balance, each contributing uniquely to the overall harmony. Figutr 7 shows the Bar Plot of Features and Their Importance Score.

Regression Model Comparison

This methodological framework undertakes a rigorous examination of regression models with the primary objective of assessing and comparing the performance of fourteen distinct models based on key metrics, namely R-squared values and Mean Squared Error (MSE). A standardized train-test split ratio of 80% training and 20% testing is used, and the instantiation of fourteen regression models is conducted.

a) Random Forest Regression:

In this research, the Random Forest Regression (RFR) utilizes the Gini Index for selecting variables, enabling the trees to reach their maximum depth without undergoing pruning. This method, proposed by Breiman (1999), is advantageous over M5 model trees because it mitigates overfitting as the number of trees increases, resulting in a low generalization error.

b) Gradient Boosting Regressor

Boosting is a powerful ensemble technique that sequentially adds poor base models to improve overall classifier performance. Gradient Boosting Regression (GBR) proposed by Freund and Schapire (1996) extends this concept, optimizing a differentiable loss function to create an ensemble of decision trees with natural data handling, high predictive accuracy, and robustness to outliers. Its flexibility in choosing loss functions adds versatility.

c) XGBoost

XGBoost, crafted by Chen and Guestrin (2016), stands out as a widely acclaimed and scalable machine learning framework founded on gradient tree boosting. Notable attributes encompass an innovative tree learning algorithm tailored for sparse datasets, a procedure utilizing weighted quantile sketches, and capabilities for parallel/distributed computing, enhancing its efficacy in model exploration.

d) LightGBM

LightGBM proposed by Ke et al. (2017) is a paradigm-shifting gradient boosting decision tree (GBDT) model designed for enhanced efficiency and scalability. Its innovative methodologies, such as Gradient-based One-Side Sampling and Exclusive Feature Bundling, facilitate swift training and deployment, effectively tackling past issues associated with GBDTs.

e) CatBoost

CatBoost proposed by Prokhorenkova et al. (2019)is a gradient-boosting decision tree (GBDT) model specifically tailored for categorical features. By introducing an ordered permutation-driven boosting algorithm and a unique approach for handling categorical features, CatBoost addresses the challenges of exponential feature combination growth. The model stands out by efficiently converting non-numerical data into integers through a series of steps, enhancing performance in scenarios where the number of categories is substantial.

f) K-nearest Neighbor

The KNN algorithm, introduced by Hastie et al. (2009), serves as a flexible supervised learning method applicable to both classification and regression tasks, particularly in scenarios characterized by constrained data availability. By calculating distances between a query point and training examples, selecting the k-nearest instances, and averaging their labels for regression, KNN offers a simple yet powerful predictive modeling approach.

g) Ridge Regression

Ridge regression proposed by McDonald (2009) is a crucial method in addressing multicollinearity challenges within multiple linear regression models. This approach, characterized by its effective formulation and advantageous properties, introduces a penalty term that serves to prevent overfitting and enhances the generalization capability of the model. The study not only succinctly outlines the four rationales behind the ridge regression estimator but also delves into the algebraic properties, shedding light on how coefficients behave across different ridge parameters.

h) Lasso Regression

The Lasso, a regression method proposed by Tibshirani (1996) minimizes the residual sum of squares while constraining the sum of absolute coefficients, resulting in some coefficients being precisely zero for interpretable models. Simulation studies indicate that it combines the interpretability of subset selection and the stability of ridge regression.

i) RANSAC

Random Sample Consensus (RANSAC) proposed by Bolles and Fischler (1981) is a robust two-step fitting procedure that adopts a distinctive filtering technique, contrary to conventional smoothing approaches. Operating with a minimal initial dataset, RANSAC progressively expands it by assessing compatibility with a model, making it resilient to outliers and noise. Its adaptability extends to various tasks, such as fitting models to data with unknown structures, making it particularly valuable in computer vision and image processing.

j) GAM

The Generalized Additive Model (GAM), proposed by Liu (2008), serves as a versatile statistical framework with wide-ranging applications in prediction across diverse fields. By utilizing the back-fitting algorithm, a universally applicable technique for fitting additive models, GAM adeptly captures intricate nonlinear associations between dependent and independent variables in exponential family and likelihood-based regression models.

k) Huber Regression

Huber regression proposed by Feng and Wu (2022), plays a crucial role in handling outliers and heavy-tailed noise, making it resilient and reliable in various applications. Its significance is particularly pronounced in the statistical learning context, where understanding its behavior in nonparametric scenarios remains a challenge.

l) Quantile Regression

Quantile regression, a statistical technique, proposed by Koenker (2005) extends traditional linear regression by modeling conditional quantiles, providing a comprehensive view of the data distribution. Its advantages lie in robustness to outliers and the ability to analyze various points in the distribution, making it valuable for capturing diverse data patterns. Applications span economics, finance, and healthcare, where understanding conditional quantiles enhances insights into phenomena with varying levels of impact.

m) RBF Kernel Regression

The RBF Kernel Regression, proposed by Kuo et al. (2013), presents an approach to enhance the radial basis function parameter in support vector machines. This is achieved by assessing the separability of feature space using a criterion that amalgamates both between-class and within-class information. Notably, the Automatic Parameter for RBF (APR) method accelerates soft-margin SVM training, efficiently selecting the most suitable RBF kernel function parameters. This holds significant advantages, enhancing computational performance and overall efficiency in SVM applications, particularly in fields like machine learning and pattern recognition where SVMs are central.

n) SGD Regression

Stochastic Gradient Boosting (SGB) proposed by Friedman (2002) is a machine learning algorithm that enhances the traditional gradient boosting method by introducing randomness during the training process, leading to improved generalization and efficiency. Its advantages include robustness to overfitting, scalability, and the ability to handle large datasets.

Table 3. Metrics for evaluating machine learning regression models

S. No.	Model	MSE	R2	S. No.	Model	MSE	R2
1	Random Forest Regression	128.62	0.9353	8	Ridge Regression & Lasso Regression	8.60e-06 & 6.41	1.000 & 0.9968
2	Gradient Boosting Regressor	35.23	0.9823	9	**RANSAC**	**1.62e-26**	**1.0000**
3	XGBoost	40.72	0.9795	10	Quantile Regression	-	1.0000
4	LightGBM	28.66	0.9856	11	GAM	2.77e-05	0.9999
5	CATBoost	0.6842	0.9997	12	Huber Regression	6.09	0.9969
6	Support Vector Machine	0.00995	0.9999	13	RBF Kernel Regression	9985.81	-4.0265
7	K Nearest Neighbors	95.33	0.9520	14	SGD Regression	0.0002	0.9999

These models subsequently undergo a meticulous training phase with hyperparameter tuning, leading to the generation of predictions for the test data. In essence, this methodological rigor ensures a comprehensive and discerning decision-making process in the selection of the most fitting regression model for the given dataset within the context of work-life balance research.

Figure 8. Scatter plot of R squared values

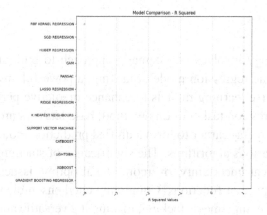

Table 2 and Figure 8 show the Evaluation Metrics for ML Regression Models which were implemented for the work life balance prediction. We observe that SVM, CAT Boost, Ridge and Lasso Regression, RANSAC Regression, Quantile Regression, GAM, Huber Regression, SGD Regression produced the best accuracy results in comparison to Random Forest. As a consequence, we fine-tune Random Forest's performance using the stacking ensemble technique to see if its prediction accuracy increases.

Stacking Ensembling

Figure 9. Architecture of stacking ensembling

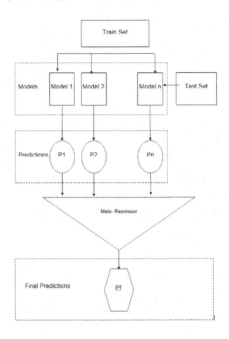

The methodology involves a systematic approach to building and evaluating a stacking ensemble regression model. Stacking, a powerful ensemble technique, amalgamates diverse learning models to enhance predictive performance in classification and regression tasks. In this method, base learners are trained and then combined using a meta-learner to form a unified prediction model, capitalizing on the strengths of various algorithms. The significance of stacking lies in its ability to address statistical uncertainty, overcome local optima issues, and expand the representational space of functions. Commonly cited ensemble methods like bagging and boosting complement stacking, making it a versatile approach with broad applications in machine learning (Wolpert, 1992).

This study employs Random Forest and RANSAC regression models are employed as meta-regressors, incorporating a mix of 14 varied base models. The objective is to investigate the connections between individual employee characteristics, workplace factors, and their subjective perceptions of work-life balance. The base model combinations encompass a wide array of techniques, including Gradient Boosting Algorithm, Ridge Regression, Lasso Regression, Huber Regression, SGD Regressor, Support Vector Regressor (SVR), K Neighbours Regressor, Kernel Ridge Regressor,

RANSAC Regressor, K Means Boosting Algorithm, and Generalized Additive Model (GAM). Specifically, these combinations involve: 1) Gradient Boosting Algorithm, Ridge Regression, Lasso Regression, Huber Regression, SGD Regressor, SVR, K Neighbours Regressor, Kernel Ridge Regressor, RANSAC Regressor, K Means Boosting Algorithm, Ridge Regression, Lasso Regression, Huber Regression, and SGD; 2) Ridge Regression, Lasso Regression, Huber Regression, SGD Regressor, SVR, and RANSAC Regressor; 3) Gradient Boosting Regressor, K Neighbours Regressor, Kernel Ridge Regressor, and K Means; 4) Ridge Regression, Lasso Regression, Huber Regression, and SGD Regressor; and 5) Gradient Boosting Regressor, SVR, K Neighbours Regressor, and K Means with Random Forest Regressor and RANSAC as meta learners. These combinations seek to identify nuanced links between these aspects and employees' subjective perceptions of work-life balance.

To assess its performance, predictions are made on the test set, and metrics such as R-squared and Mean Squared Error (MSE) are calculated.

Table 4. Performance measure of meta regressors with base model combinations

S. No.	Meta Regressor	Base Model	MSE Value	R Squared Value
1	Random Forest Regressor	Gradient Boosting Algorithm, Ridge Regressor, Lasso Regressor, Huber Regressor, SGD Regressor, SVR, K Neighbours Regressor, Kernel Ridge Regressor, RANSAC Regressor, K Means Boosting Algorithm	0.011773	0.999994
2	Random Forest Regressor	Ridge Regressor, Lasso Regressor, Huber Regressor, SGD Regressor, SVR, RANSAC Regressor	0.012411	0.999993
3	Random Forest Regressor	Gradient Boosting Regressor, K Neighbours regressor, Kernel Ridge Regressor, K Means	0.031931	0.999983
4	Random Forest Regressor	Ridge Regressor, Lasso Regressor, Huber Regressor, SGD Regressor	0.015220	0.999992
5	Random Forest Regressor	Gradient Boosting Regressor, SVR, K Neighbours Regressor, K Means	42.03320	0.978842
6	RANSAC Regressor	Gradient Regressor, SVR, K Neighbours Regressor, Kernel Ridge Regressor, RANSAC Regressor, K Means	0.000156	0.99999992
7	RANSAC Regressor	Ridge Regressor, Lasso Regressor, Huber Regressor, SGD Regressor, SVR, RANSAC Regressor	2.757e-05	0.99999998
8	RANSAC Regressor	Gradient Boosting Regressor, K Neighbours regressor, Kernel Ridge Regressor, K Means	0.000115	0.99999994
9	RANSAC Regressor	Ridge Regressor, Lasso Regressor, Huber Regressor, SGD Regressor	2.6305e-05	0.99999998
10	RANSAC Regressor	Gradient Boosting Regressor, SVR, K Neighbours Regressor, K Means	96.41067	0.951470

Figure 10. Comparison of R squared values for the stacking ensembling combinations

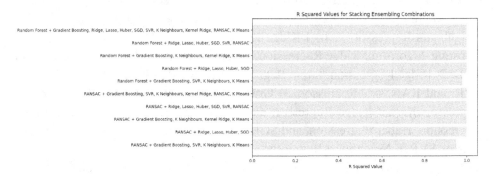

From Table 4 & Fig. 10 we infer that the accuracy of Random Forest Regressor could be tuned to improve using stacking ensemble method having Gradient Boosting Algorithm, Ridge Regressor, Lasso Regressor, Huber Regressor, SGD Regressor, SVR, K Neighbours Regressor, Kernel Ridge Regressor, RANSAC Regressor, K Means Boosting Algorithm, Ridge Regressor, Lasso Regressor, Huber Regressor, SGD as base learners from 0.93 to 0.99 and RANSAC Regressor retained the highest accuracy though it was ensemble.

RESULT

The paper intricately explored work-life balance dynamics through regression models, unveiling noteworthy insights into predictive accuracy. CATBoost and Support Vector Machine models emerged as exceptional performers, showcasing impressive accuracy with remarkably low Mean Squared Error (MSE) values of 0.6842 and 0.00995, respectively. Conversely, the RBF Kernel Regression model struggled, evident in its challenging R Squared Value of -4.0265 and a notably high MSE of 9985.81, underscoring difficulties in forecasting work-life balance using this method. Models like Ridge Regression and RANSAC displayed near-perfect predictive abilities, emphasizing the variance in performance across different regression techniques.

Furthermore, the stacking ensemble methodology revealed intriguing patterns, highlighting the effectiveness of certain model combinations. Specifically, stacking ensembles combining RANSAC with Gradient Boosting Regressor, K Neighbors Regressor, Kernel Ridge Regressor, and K Means achieved extraordinary R-squared values of 0.9999999419936115. Similarly, utilizing the Random Forest Regressor in a stacking ensemble with the same set of ML algorithms resulted in commendable predictive accuracy, yielding an R-squared value of 0.9999839268672821 at the second level tuned from 0.93. These findings underscore the nuanced nature of work-life balance prediction, emphasizing the potency of specific stacking ensemble configurations in forecasting this equilibrium with remarkable precision.

CONCLUSION

In conclusion, this research has delved into the intricate dynamics of work-life balance, utilizing advanced machine learning techniques to predict and understand the factors influencing this equilibrium. The comprehensive exploration involved a Stacking Ensemble methodology, combining 14 diverse regression models and shedding light on the complex interplay of variables affecting work-life dynamics.

In navigating the ever-evolving landscape of work and life, our research stands as a beacon, emphasizing the importance of recognizing and supporting work-life balance. It reinforces the notion that achieving harmony between professional commitments and personal well-being is not solely an individual pursuit but a collective responsibility. By combining data-driven insights with advanced machine learning techniques, we take strides toward a more informed and proactive approach to address the challenges posed by the evolving nature of work in the modern era.

In essence, the findings presented in this research contribute to the growing body of knowledge aimed at enhancing our understanding of work-life balance. Leveraging the power of machine learning brings us closer to creating workplaces and policies that prioritize the well-being of individuals, fostering a more balanced and fulfilling life for everyone involved. As we continue to advance, this research serves as a valuable resource in shaping workplaces that prioritize the holistic health and satisfaction of individuals in the dynamic landscape of contemporary professional life.

FUTURE ENHANCEMENTS

This study significantly enhances our comprehension of work-life balance, emphasizing its crucial role in contemporary society. To advance this field, forthcoming avenues for research have been found. Essential strides include longitudinal examinations tracking trends in work-life balance, sector-specific inquiries, and cross-cultural analyses. Investigating the impacts of gender disparities, health consequences, remote work and generational distinctions, along with establishing standardized metrics and evaluating government policies, will profoundly contribute to this domain. The incorporation of artificial intelligence, qualitative methodologies, and research prospective advancements have the potential to impact the creation of policies, practices, and interventions aimed at fostering work-life balance, hence improving the general well-being of workers.

REFERENCES

American Institute of Stress. (n.d.). *Workplace stress.* The American Institute of Stress. https://www.flexjobs.com/employer-blog/remote-work-increases-productivity-and -more-news/

Bolles, R. C., & Fischler, M. A. (1981, August). A RANSAC-based approach to model fitting and its application to finding cylinders in range data. *IJCAI (United States)*, 1981, 637–643.

Breiman, L. (1999). Random forests. *Machine Learning*, 45(1), 5–32. DOI:10.1023/A:1010933404324

Chen, T., & Guestrin, C. (2016). XGBoost: A Scalable Tree Boosting System. In *Proceedings of the 22nd ACM SIGKDD International Conference on Knowledge Discovery and Data Mining*, (pp. 785-794). ACM. DOI:10.1145/2939672.2939785

Deloitte. (2023). *Survey.* Deloitte. https://www2.deloitte.com/content/dam/Deloitte/ si/Documents/deloitte-2023-genz-millennial-survey.pdf

Deshmukh, K. (2018). Work-life balance study focused on working women. *International Journal of Engineering Technologies and Management Research*, 5(5), 134–145. DOI:10.29121/ijetmr.v5.i5.2018.236

Eurofund. (n.d.). *Work-Life Balance.* Eurofund. https://www.eurofound.europa.eu/ en/topic/work-life-balance

Feng, Y., & Wu, Q. (2022). A statistical learning assessment of Huber regression. *Journal of Approximation Theory*, 273, 105660. DOI:10.1016/j.jat.2021.105660

Freund, Y., & Schapire, R. E. (1996). Experiments with a New Boosting Algorithm. In *Proceedings of the Thirteenth International Conference on Machine Learning (ICML'96)*, (pp. 148-156). Research Gate.

Friedman, J. H. (2002). Stochastic Gradient Boosting. *Computational Statistics & Data Analysis*, 38(4), 367–378. DOI:10.1016/S0167-9473(01)00065-2

Hastie, T., Tibshirani, R., & Friedman, J. (2009). *The Elements of Statistical Learning: Data Mining, Inference, and Prediction* (2nd ed.). Springer. DOI:10.1007/978-0-387-84858-7

ILO. (2018). *Women do 4 Times More Unpaid Care Work Than Men in Asia and the Pacific.* ILO. https://www.ilo.org/asia/media-centre/news/WCMS_633284/lang --en/index.htm#:~:text=According%20to%20the%20report%2C%20Globally,over %20the%20past%2020%20years

Ke, G., Meng, Q., Finley, T., Wang, T., Chen, W., Ma, W., & Li, T. (2017). LightGBM: A Highly Efficient Gradient Boosting Decision Tree. *Advances in Neural Information Processing Systems (NeurIPS), 30.*

Koenker, R. (2005). *Quantile Regression.* Cambridge University Press. DOI:10.1017/CBO9780511754098

Kumar, R., & Tople, A. (2023, March). Employee Attrition, Job Involvement, and Work Life Balance Prediction Using Machine Learning Classifier Models. In Doctoral Symposium on Computational Intelligence (pp. 907-915). Singapore: Springer Nature Singapore. DOI:10.1007/978-981-99-3716-5_72

Kuo, B. C., Ho, H. H., Li, C. H., Hung, C. C., & Taur, J. S. (2013). A kernel-based feature selection method for SVM with RBF kernel for hyperspectral image classification. *IEEE Journal of Selected Topics in Applied Earth Observations and Remote Sensing*, 7(1), 317–326. DOI:10.1109/JSTARS.2013.2262926

Liu, H. (2008). *Generalized additive model.* Department of Mathematics and Statistics University of Minnesota Duluth.

McDonald, G. C. (2009). Ridge regression. *Wiley Interdisciplinary Reviews: Computational Statistics*, 1(1), 93–100. DOI:10.1002/wics.14

OECD. (n.d.-a). [Dataset]. OECD. https://stats.oecd.org/index.aspx?DataSetCode=ANHRS

OECD. (n.d.-b). [Dataset]. OECD. https://www.stress.org/workplace-stress#:~:text=83%25%20of%20US%20workers%20suffer,stress%20affects%20their%20personal%20relationships

Pawlicka, A., Pawlicki, M., Tomaszewska, R., Choraś, M., & Gerlach, R. (2020). Innovative machine learning approach and evaluation campaign for predicting the subjective feeling of work-life balance among employees. *PLoS One*, 15(5), e0232771. DOI:10.1371/journal.pone.0232771 PMID:32413040

Perlow, L. & Porter, J. (2009). Making Time Off Presdictable and Required. *Harvard Business Review.* https://hbr.org/2009/10/making-time-off-predictable-and-required

Prokhorenkova, L., Gusev, G., Vorobev, A., Dorogush, A. V., & Gulin, A. (2019). CatBoost: unbiased boosting with categorical features. *NeurIPS, 32.*

Radha, K., & Rohith, M. (2021). *An Experimental Analysis of Work-Life Balance Among The Employees using Machine Learning Classifiers.* arXiv preprint arXiv:2105.07837.

Shah, D. (2023). *Understanding Work-Life Balance: An Analysis of Quiet Quitting and Age Dynamics using Deep Learning.*

Srividya, M., Mohanavalli, S., & Bhalaji, N. (2018). Behavioral Modeling for Mental Health using Machine Learning Algorithms. *Journal of Medical Systems*, 42(88), 88. DOI:10.1007/s10916-018-0934-5 PMID:29610979

Tibshirani, R. (1996). Regression shrinkage and selection via the lasso. *Journal of the Royal Statistical Society. Series B, Statistical Methodology*, 58(1), 267–288. DOI:10.1111/j.2517-6161.1996.tb02080.x

Tümen, V. (2023). Predicting the Work-Life Balance of Employees Based on the Ensemble Learning Method. *Bitlis Eren Üniversitesi Fen Bilimleri Dergisi*, 12(2), 344–353. DOI:10.17798/bitlisfen.1196174

WHO. (2019). *Burn Out an 'Occupational Phenomenon.'* World Health Organization. https://www.who.int/news/item/28-05-2019-burn-out-an-occupational-phenomenon-international-classification-of-diseases

Wise, L. (2022). *10 Companies With the Best Mental Health Suport.* Business Because. https://www.businessbecause.com/news/masters-in-management/8466/best-companies-mental-health-support

Wolpert, D. H. (1992). Stacked generalization. *Neural Networks*, 5(2), 241–259. DOI:10.1016/S0893-6080(05)80023-1 PMID:18276425

Conclusion

Creating AI Synergy Through Business Technology Transformation

As we reach the conclusion of *Creating AI Synergy Through Business Technology Transformation*, it is evident that the intersection of artificial intelligence (AI) and technological transformation is not just a momentary trend but a profound shift reshaping the business landscape. The journey through this book has provided an in-depth exploration of how AI can drive synergy across various business functions, enhancing innovation, efficiency, and long-term success.

Reflecting on Key Insights

The chapters within this book have collectively underscored the critical role of AI in modern business strategy. From strategic integration in decision-making processes to leveraging predictive analytics for business intelligence, the potential of AI to transform operations and outcomes is immense. We have examined the innovative applications of AI in product development, supply chain management, finance, and banking, highlighting real-world examples and case studies that demonstrate tangible benefits.

In the realm of information technology, we have delved into the significance of AI in IT infrastructure management, cybersecurity, software engineering, and project management. The discussions on AI in cloud computing and cognitive computing for data analysis have illuminated how these technologies are revolutionizing data-driven decision-making and operational efficiency.

Embracing the Future

The future of business is inextricably linked with the advancements in AI and digital transformation. As businesses continue to navigate an increasingly connected global economy, the integration of AI is not merely a competitive advantage but a necessity for survival and growth. This book has emphasized the importance of fostering synergy across various business areas, demonstrating how AI can serve as a unifying force that enhances productivity, collaboration, and communication throughout the organization.

For business leaders, technology professionals, innovation teams, and all stakeholders, the insights and strategies discussed in this book provide a roadmap for successfully integrating AI into their operations. The holistic understanding of the strategic nexus between AI and business technology transformation equips readers with the knowledge to make informed decisions that align with their organizational goals.

Final Thoughts

As editors, we hope that this book has inspired you to envision the boundless possibilities that AI and technological transformation offer. The convergence of these forces presents unprecedented opportunities for innovation and success. By embracing AI and fostering synergy within your organization, you are not only preparing for the future but actively shaping it.

We encourage you to take the insights and practical guidance provided in this book and apply them to your unique contexts. The journey of integrating AI into business strategy is ongoing, and continuous learning and adaptation are key. We are confident that the synergy created through AI and business technology transformation will unlock new potentials and drive sustained success for your organizations.

In closing, we extend our gratitude to all the contributors, researchers, and practitioners who have shared their expertise and experiences. Your valuable insights have made this book a comprehensive resource for understanding and leveraging the power of AI in business.

Together, let us embrace the future with optimism and determination, harnessing the transformative power of AI to create a thriving, innovative, and synergistic business environment.

Balaji Sundaramurthy
Al Zahra College for Women, Oman

Padmalosani Dayalan
University of Technology and Applied Sciences Ibra, Oman

Compilation of References

Abhishek, B., & Tyagi, A. K. (2022). An Useful Survey on Supervised Machine Learning Algorithms: Comparisons and Classifications. In Sengodan, T., Murugappan, M., & Misra, S. (Eds.), *Advances in Electrical and Computer Technologies. Lecture Notes in Electrical Engineering* (Vol. 881). Springer., DOI:10.1007/978-981-19-1111-8_24

Abramson, B. (2006). *Digital Phoenix: Why the Information Economy Collapsed and How It Will Rise Again*. MIT Press.

Abramson, N., Braverman, D., & Sebestyen, G. (1963). Pattern recognition and machine learning. *IEEE Transactions on Information Theory*, 9(4), 257–261. DOI:10.1109/TIT.1963.1057854

Adamopoulou, E., & Moussiades, L. (2020). An Overview of Chatbot Technology. *IFIP Advances in Information and Communication Technology*, 373–383. DOI:10.1007/978-3-030-49186-4_31

Addagarla, S. K., & Amalanathan, A. (2020a). Probabilistic unsupervised machine learning approach for a similar image recommender system for E-commerce. *Symmetry*, 12(11), 1783. DOI:10.3390/sym12111783

Addagarla, S. K., & Amalanathan, A. (2021b). e-SimNet: A visual similar product recommender system for E-commerce. *Indonesian Journal of Electrical Engineering and Computer Science*, 22(1), 563–570. DOI:10.11591/ijeecs.v22.i1.pp563-570

Afiouni, R. (2019). *Organizational learning in the rise of machine learning. International Conference on Information Systems*, Munich, Germany

Agarwal, A. (2022). AI adoption by human resource management: A study of its antecedents and impact on HR system effectiveness. *Foresight*, 25(1), 67–81. DOI:10.1108/FS-10-2021-0199

Agarwal, D., & Tripathi, K. "A Framework for Structural Damage detection system in automobiles for flexible Insurance claim using IOT and Machine Learning," *2022 International Mobile and Embedded Technology Conference (MECON)*, 2022, pp. 5-8, DOI:10.1109/MECON53876.2022.9751889

Agnihotri, D., Chaturvedi, P., Kulshreshtha, K., & Tripathi, V. (2023). Investigating the impact of authenticity of social media influencers on followers' purchase behavior: Mediating analysis of parasocial interaction on Instagram. *Asia Pacific Journal of Marketing and Logistics*, 35(10), 2377–2394. DOI:10.1108/APJML-07-2022-0598

Agrawal, A. (2019). *The Economics of Artificial Intelligence: An Agenda*. University of Chicago Press. DOI:10.7208/chicago/9780226613475.001.0001

Ahmadi, S. (2024). A Comprehensive Study on Integration of Big Data and AI in Financial Industry and Its Effect on Present and Future Opportunities. *International Journal of Current Science Research and Review*, 07(1).

Ahuja, S., & Grover, K. (2023). Excessive Use of Social Networking Sites and Intention to Invest in Stock Market among Gen Z: A Parallel Mediation Model. *Journal of Content, Community, and Communication*, 17(9), 63–79. DOI:10.31620/JCCC.06.23/06

Aickelin, U., & Das, S. (2011). *Artificial intelligence for security*. Springer Science & Business Media.

Ajanthaa Lakkshmanan, R. (2024). Engineering Applications of Artificial Intelligence. *Enhancing Medical Imaging with Emerging Technologies*. IGI Global-DOI:10.4018/979-8-3693-5261-8.ch010

Ajzen, I. (1991). The theory of planned behavior. *Organizational Behavior and Human Decision Processes*, 50(2), 179–211. DOI:10.1016/0749-5978(91)90020-T

Ak, K. E., Kassim, A. A., Lim, J. H., & Tham, J. Y. (2018). Learning attribute representations with localization for flexible fashion search. *Proceedings of the IEEE conference on computer vision and pattern recognition* (pp. 7708-7717). IEEE. DOI:10.1109/CVPR.2018.00804

Alarfaj, F. K., Malik, I., Khan, H. U., Almusallam, N., Ramzan, M., & Ahmed, M. (2022). Credit card fraud detection using state-of-the-art machine learning and deep learning algorithms. *IEEE Access : Practical Innovations, Open Solutions*, 10, 39700–39715. DOI:10.1109/ACCESS.2022.3166891

Albert, E. T. (2019). AI in talent acquisition: A review of AI-applications used in recruitment and selection. *Strategic HR Review*, 18(5), 215–221. DOI:10.1108/SHR-04-2019-0024

Alfen, H. W., & Ten Brink, P. (Eds.). (2018). *Nature-based solutions for urban resilience*. Springer.

Ali, A., Abd Razak, S., Othman, S. H., Eisa, T. A. E., Al-Dhaqm, A., Nasser, M., Elhassan, T., Elshafie, H., & Saif, A.MDPI. (2022). Financial fraud detection based on machine learning: A systematic literature review. *Applied Sciences (Basel, Switzerland)*, 12(19), 9637. DOI:10.3390/app12199637

Aliper, A., Plis, S., Artemov, A., Ulloa, A., Mamoshina, P., & Zhavoronkov, A. (2016). Deep learning applications for predicting pharmacological properties of drugs and drug repurposing using transcriptomic data. *Molecular Pharmaceutics*, 13(7), 2524–2530. DOI:10.1021/acs.molpharmaceut.6b00248 PMID:27200455

Allioui, H. (2023). *Unleashing the Potential of AI: Investigating Cutting-Edge Technologies That Are Transforming Businesses.*

Altaee, O. Z. I. (2023). The Role of Artificial Intelligence in Improving the Quality of Internal Audit: An Exploratory Study in Some Iraqi Banks. *Regional Studies Journal, 17*(55).

Alves, C., & Luís Reis, J. (2020). The intention to use e-commerce using augmented reality-the case of IKEA place. In *Information Technology and Systems: Proceedings of ICITS 2020* (pp. 114-123). Springer International Publishing. DOI:10.1007/978-3-030-40690-5_12

Ambati, L. (2022). *Factors Influencing the Adoption of Artificial Intelligence in Organizations – From an Employee's Perspective*. AIS Electronic Library (AISeL).

Ameer, R., & Khan, R. (2020). Financial Socialization, Financial Literacy, and Financial Behavior of Adults in New Zealand. *Financial Counseling and Planning*, 31(2), 313–329. DOI:10.1891/JFCP-18-00042

American Institute of Stress. (n.d.). *Workplace stress*. The American Institute of Stress. https://www.flexjobs.com/employer-blog/remote-work-increases-productivity-and-more-news/

Amonhaemanon, D. (2024). Financial stress and gambling motivation: The importance of financial literacy. *Review of Behavioral Finance*, 16(2), 248–265. DOI:10.1108/RBF-01-2023-0026

Anand, S., Mishra, K., Verma, V., & Taruna, T. (2021). Financial literacy mediates personal financial health during COVID-19: A structural equation modeling approach. *Emerald Open Research*, 2. DOI:10.1108/EOR-04-2023-0006

Anna, N. E., Novian, R. M., & Ismail, N. (2023, October). Enhancing Virtual Instruction: Leveraging AI Applications for Success. *Library Hi Tech News*, 9. DOI:10.1108/LHTN-09-2023-0175

Arntz, M., Gregory, T., & Zierahn, U. (2016). The Risk of Automation for Jobs in OECD Countries: A Comparative Analysis. *OECD Social, Employment, and Migration Working Papers*. OECD Publishing Association for Advancement of Artificial Intelligence. https://aaai.org/

Azhar, K. A., Shah, Z., & Ahmed, H. (2023). HOW DO SOCIAL MEDIA INFLU-ENCERS DRIVE CONSUMER BEHAVIOUR? *Pakistan Journal of International Affairs*, 6(2). DOI:10.52337/pjia.v6i2.943

Bahoo, S., Cucculelli, M., Goga, X., & Mondolo, J. (2024). Artificial intelligence in Finance: A comprehensive review through bibliometric and content analysis. *SN Business & Economics*, 4(2), 23. DOI:10.1007/s43546-023-00618-x

Bai, X., & Imura, H. (Eds.). (2016). *Urbanization and sustainability: Linking urban ecology, environmental justice and global environmental change*. Springer.

Bar, A. K., & Chaudhuri, A. K. (2023). Emotica.AI - a customer feedback system using AI. *International Research Journal on Advanced Science Hub*, 5(03), 103–110. DOI:10.47392/irjash.2023.019

Barker, K., D'Amato, V., & Di Lorenzo, E. (2019). Artificial intelligence in fraud management: Challenges and opportunities. *Journal of Financial Crime*, 26(4), 1015–1027.

Barocas, S., & Selbst, A. D. (2016). Big data's disparate impact. *California Law Review*, 104(3), 671–732.

Barocas, S., & Selbst, A. D. (2016). Big Data's Disparate Impact. *California Law Review*, 104(3), 671–732.

Bashynska, I., Prokopenko, O., & Sala, D. (2023). Managing Human Capital with AI: Synergy of Talent and Technology. *Zeszyty Naukowe Wyższej Szkoły Finansów i Prawa w Bielsku-Białej*, 27(3), 39–45.

Batty, M. (2018). *The new science of cities*. MIT Press.

Bayram, A., & Palese, A. (2022). The importance of financial literacy in nursing. *Obzornik Zdravstvene Nege*, 56(2), 100–104. DOI:10.14528/snr.2022.56.2.3166

Bazaki, E., &Wanick, V. (2019). *Unlocking the potential of the salesperson in the virtual fitting room: Enhancing the online retail experience for fashion brands*.

Behgounia, F., & Zohuri, B. (2020). Machine learning driven an e-commerce. [IJC-SIS]. *International Journal of Computer Science and Information Security*, 18(10). DOI:10.5281/zenodo.4252454

Bellman, R. E. (1978). *An introduction to Artificial Intelligence: Can computers think?* Boyd & Fraser Publishing Company.

Bengio, Y., Courville, A., & Vincent, P. (2013). Representation learning: A review and new perspectives. *IEEE Transactions on Pattern Analysis and Machine Intelligence*, 35(8), 1798–1828. DOI:10.1109/TPAMI.2013.50 PMID:23787338

Berrydunn. (2020). *Artificial Intelligence and the Future of Internal Audit*. Berrydunn. https://www.berrydunn.com/news-detail/artificial-intelligence-and-the-future -of-internal-audit

Bessen, J. E. (2019). AI and Jobs: The Role of Demand. *NBER Working Paper*, (24235).

Bhandare, P. V., Guha, S., Chaudhury, R. H., & Ghosh, C. (2021). Impact of financial literacy models on the financial behavior of individuals: An empirical study on the Indian context. *Strategic Change*, 30(4), 377–387. DOI:10.1002/jsc.2431

Bharadwaj, A., El Sawy, O. A., Pavlou, P. A., & Venkatraman, N. (2013). Digital business strategy: Toward a next generation of insights. MIS Quarterly: Management. *Information Systems*, 37(2), 471–482.

Bhattacharyya, S., Jha, S., Tharakunnel, K., & Westland, J. C. (2011). Data mining for credit card fraud: A comparative study. *Decision Support Systems*, 50(3), 602–613. DOI:10.1016/j.dss.2010.08.008

Bhosale, S., Pujari, V., & Multani, Z. (2020). *Advantages And Disadvantages Of Artificial Intellegence*.

Billewar, S. R., Jadhav, K., Sriram, V. P., Arun, D. A., Mohd Abdul, S., Gulati, K., & Bhasin, D. N. K. K. (2022). The rise of 3D E-Commerce: The online shopping gets real with virtual reality and augmented reality during COVID-19. *World Journal of Engineering*, 19(2), 244–253. DOI:10.1108/WJE-06-2021-0338

Bishop, C. M. (1995). *Neural networks for pattern recognition*. Oxford University Press. DOI:10.1093/oso/9780198538493.001.0001

Black, J. S., & van Esch, P. (2021). AI-enabled recruiting in the war for talent. *Business Horizons*, 64(4), 513–524. DOI:10.1016/j.bushor.2021.02.015

Boden, M. A. (1984). Impacts of artificial intelligence. *Futures*, 16(1), 60–70. DOI:10.1016/0016-3287(84)90007-7

Bojuwon, M., Olaleye, B. R., & Ojebode, A. A. (2023). Financial Inclusion and Financial Condition: The Mediating Effect of Financial Self-efficacy and Financial Literacy. *Vision (Basel)*. DOI:10.1177/09722629231166200

Bolles, R. C., & Fischler, M. A. (1981, August). A RANSAC-based approach to model fitting and its application to finding cylinders in range data. *IJCAI (United States)*, 1981, 637–643.

Borges, A. F. S., Laurindo, F. J. B., Spínola, M. M., Gonçalves, R. F., & Mattos, C. A. (2021). The strategic use of artificial intelligence in the Digital Era: Systematic Literature Review and Future Research Directions. *International Journal of Information Management*, 57, 102225. DOI:10.1016/j.ijinfomgt.2020.102225

Boyd, D., & Crawford, K. (2012). Critical questions for big data: Provocations for a cultural, technological, and scholarly phenomenon. *Information Communication and Society*, 15(5), 662–679. DOI:10.1080/1369118X.2012.678878

Breiman, L. (1999). Random forests. *Machine Learning*, 45(1), 5–32. DOI:10.1023/A:1010933404324

Brynjolfsson, E., Horton, J., Ozimek, A., Rock, D., Sharma, G., & Tuye, H.-Y. (2020). NBER Working Paper Series Covid-19 and Remote Work: An Early Look At Us Data. In *NBER Working Paper Series* (Issue June 220). NBER.

Brynjolfsson, E., & Mcafee, A. N. (2017). Artificial intelligence, for real. *Harvard Business Review*.

Brynjolfsson, E., & Unger, G. (2023). The Macroeconomics of Artificial Intelligence. *Finance & Development*, 0060(004), A006. DOI:10.5089/9798400260179.001.A006

Buchanan, B. G. (2006). A (Very) Brief History of Artificial Intelligence. *AI Magazine*, 26(4).

Buchanan, L., & O'Connell, A. (2006). Brief history of decision making. *Harvard Business Review*, 84(1), 32–41. PMID:16447367

Buczak, A. L., & Guven, E. (2016). A survey of data mining and machine learning methods for cyber security intrusion detection. *IEEE Communications Surveys and Tutorials*, 18(2), 1153–1176. DOI:10.1109/COMST.2015.2494502

Budd, C., Douglas, G., & Saunders, S. (1998). "Friedrich Nietzsche & Daniel Dennett." The Philosophers'. *Magazine*, (4), 30–31. DOI:10.5840/tpm1998411

Bughin, J., Hazan, E., Ramaswamy, S., Chui, M., Allas, T., Dahlström, P., & Henke, N. (2017). *Artificial Intelligence: The Next Digital Frontier?* McKinsey Global Institute.

Bundy, A., Young, R. M., Burstall, R. M., & Weir, S. (1978). *Artificial intelligence: An introductory course*. Edinburgh Univ. Press.

Business Insider. (2023). AI and Wage Reduction.

Bussler, C. (2004). *Web Information Systems*. WISE 2004 Workshops: WISE 2004 International Workshops, Brisbane, Australia.

Caboni, F., & Hagberg, J. (2019). Augmented reality in retailing: A review of features, applications and value. *International Journal of Retail & Distribution Management*, 47(11), 1125–1140. DOI:10.1108/IJRDM-12-2018-0263

Cai, K., Zhu, Y., & Cao, J. (2020). The Application of Artificial Intelligence in the Banking Sector. In *2020 IEEE 3rd International Conference on Information Systems and Computer Aided Education (ICISCAE)* (pp. 439-442). IEEE.

Campbell, C. (2020). From Data to Action: How Marketers Can Leverage AI. *Business Horizons*, (vol. 227–243).

Canatan, E. C., Coskun, A., & Toker, A. (2023). ADOPTION ATTITUDE AND CONTINUANCE INTENTION TO ONLINE FINFLUENCER VIDEO USAGE: THE ROLE OF TRUST. *Proceedings of the International Conferences on ICT, Society, and Human Beings 2023, ICT 2023; e-Health 2023, EH 2023; Connected Smart Cities 2023, CSC 2023; and Big Data Analytics, Data Mining and Computational Intelligence 2023, BigDaCI 2023*. IEEE. DOI:10.33965/MCCSIS2023_202305C003

Carata , M. (2018). *Alina, Cerasela, S., & Gabriela, G.* Internal Audit Role in Artificial Intelligence.

Center for the Fourth Industrial Revolution. (2024). *We are a global platform focused on inclusive technology governance and responsible digital transformation*. WeForum. https://centres.weforum.org/centre-for-the-fourth-industrial-revolution/about

Chakravorti, B., Bhalla, A., & Chaturvedi, R. S. (2019). Which countries are leading the data economy? *Harvard Business Review*.

Chalutz Ben-Gal, H. (2023). Artificial intelligence (AI) acceptance in primary care during the coronavirus pandemic: What is the role of patient's gender, age, and health awareness? A two-phase pilot study. *Frontiers in Public Health*, 10, 931225. DOI:10.3389/fpubh.2022.931225 PMID:36699881

Chandola, V., Banerjee, A., & Kumar, V. (2009). Anomaly detection: A survey. *ACM Computing Surveys*, 41(3), 1–58. DOI:10.1145/1541880.1541882

Charniak, E., & McDermott, D. (1985). Introduction to artificial intelligence. Boston, EUA: Addison-Wesley.

Chatterjee, S., Khorana, S., & Kizgin, H. (2022). Harnessing the potential of artificial intelligence to foster citizens' satisfaction: An empirical study on India. *Government Information Quarterly*, 39(4), 101621. DOI:10.1016/j.giq.2021.101621

Chaudhuri, A., Messina, P., Kokkula, S., Subramanian, A., Krishnan, A., Gandhi, S., & Kandaswamy, V. (2018). A smart system for selection of optimal product images in e-commerce. In *2018 IEEE International Conference on Big Data (Big Data)* (pp. 1728-1736). IEEE. DOI:10.1109/BigData.2018.8622259

Chen, L., & Wang, H. (2020). Building a Sustainable Financial World: Smart Banking Innovations and Technologies. *Sustainable Development Journal*, 15(3), 278–295. DOI:10.1002/sd.2076

Chen, L., & Wang, H. (2020). Next-Generation Banking Services: Advanced Solutions for Industry 5.0. *International Journal of Banking and Finance*, 15(3), 278–295. DOI:10.1002/ijbf.1234

Chen, M., Chiang, R. H., & Storey, V. C. (2012). Business Intelligence and Analytics: From Big Data to Big Impact. *Management Information Systems Quarterly*, 36(4), 1165–1188. DOI:10.2307/41703503

Chen, T., & Guestrin, C. (2016). XGBoost: A Scalable Tree Boosting System. In *Proceedings of the 22nd ACM SIGKDD International Conference on Knowledge Discovery and Data Mining*, (pp. 785-794). ACM. DOI:10.1145/2939672.2939785

Chien, S. P., Wu, H. K., & Wu, P. H. (2018). Teachers' Beliefs About, Attitudes Toward, and Intention to Use Technology-Based Assessments: A Structural Equation Modeling Approach. *Eurasia Journal of Mathematics, Science and Technology Education*, 14(10), 1–17. DOI:10.29333/ejmste/93379

Chikhi, I. (n.d.). *Financial Influencers and Social Media: The Role of Valuable and Financial Influencers and Social Media: The Role of Valuable and Trusted Content in Creating a New Form of Authenticity Trusted Content in Creating a New Form of Authenticity*. Academic Works. https://academicworks.cuny.edu/bb_etds/113Discoveradditionalworksat:https://academicworks.cuny.edu

Chitrao, P., Bhoyar, P. K., Divekar, R., & Bhatt, P. (2022, February). Study on use of artificial intelligence in talent acquisition. In *2022 Interdisciplinary Research in Technology and Management (IRTM)* (pp. 1-8). IEEE. DOI:10.1109/IRTM54583.2022.9791659

Chui, M., & Malhotra, S. (2018). *AI adoption advances, but foundational barriers remain*. McKinsey and company.

Cîmpeanu, I.-A., Dragomir, D.-A., & Zota, R. D. (2023). Banking Chatbots: How Artificial Intelligence Helps the Banks. *Proceedings of the International Conference on Business Excellence, 17*(1), 1716–1727. DOI:10.2478/picbe-2023-0153

Cinelli, M., Quattrociocchi, W., Galeazzi, A., Valensise, C. M., Brugnoli, E., Schmidt, A. L., Zola, P., Zollo, F., & Scala, A. (2020). The COVID-19 social media infodemic. *Scientific Reports*, 10(1), 16598. DOI:10.1038/s41598-020-73510-5 PMID:33024152

Cisco. (2021). *How AI is Transforming the Telecommunications Industry*. CISCO. https://www.cisco.com/c/en/us/products/collateral/se/internet-of-things/white-paper -c11-744544.html

Coaffee, J., Healey, P., & O'Brien, P. (2018). *Resilient cities: Rethinking urban protection*. Springer.

Collett, C., Gomes, L. G., & Neff, G. (2022). *The Effects of AI on the Working Lives of Women*. UNESCO Publishing. DOI:10.18235/0004055

Cordeschi, R. (2007). AI turns fifty: Revisiting its origins. *Applied Artificial Intelligence*, 21(4-5), 259–279. DOI:10.1080/08839510701252304

Couceiro, B., Pedrosa, I., & Marini, A. (2020). State of the Art of Artificial Intelligence in Internal Audit context. *2020 15th Iberian Conference on Information Systems and Technologies (CISTI)*. IEEE. DOI:10.23919/CISTI49556.2020.9140863

Cremonesi, P., Koren, Y., & Turrin, R. (2011). Performance of recommender algorithms on top-on recommendation tasks. [TIST]. *ACM Transactions on Intelligent Systems and Technology*, 2(3), 1–17. DOI:10.1145/2870627

Dal Pozzolo, A., Boracchi, G., Caelen, O., Alippi, C., & Bontempi, G. (2015). Credit card fraud detection: A realistic modeling and a novel learning strategy. *IEEE Transactions on Neural Networks and Learning Systems*, 29(8), 3784–3797. DOI:10.1109/TNNLS.2017.2736643 PMID:28920909

Daly, S. (2023). Intelligence in Business Digital Transformation. *Newer Tech*. https://www.neweratech.com/us/blog/role-of-artificial-intelligence-business-digital -transformation/

Damayanti, S. M., Murtaqi, I., & Pradana, H. A. (2018). The Importance of Financial Literacy in a Global Economic Era. *The Business and Management Review, 9*(3).

Daugherty, P. R., & James Wilson, H. (2018). *Human + Machine: Reimagining Work in the Age of AI*. Harvard Business Press.

Davenport, T. H. (2018). *The AI advantage: How to put the artificial intelligence revolution to work*. MIT Press. DOI:10.7551/mitpress/11781.001.0001

Davenport, T. H., & Ronanki, R. (2018). Artificial intelligence for the real world. *Harvard Business Review*, 108–116.

Davenport, T., Guha, A., Grewal, D., & Bressgott, T. (2020). How artificial intelligence will change the future of marketing. *Journal of the Academy of Marketing Science*, 48(1), 24–42. DOI:10.1007/s11747-019-00696-0

Davenport, T., & Harris, J. (2017). *Competing on analytics: Updated, with a new introduction: The new science of winning*. Harvard Business Review Press.

De Fátima Soares Borges, A. (2021, April). The Strategic Use of Artificial Intelligence in the Digital Era: Systematic Literature Review and Future Research Directions. *International Journal of Information Management*, 102225, 1.

de Regt, A., Cheng, Z., & Fawaz, R. (2023). Young People Under 'Finfluencer': The Rise of Financial Influencers on Instagram: An Abstract. In *Developments in Marketing Science:Proceedings of the Academy of Marketing Science*. Springer. DOI:10.1007/978-3-031-24687-6_106

Deloitte. (2023). *Survey*. Deloitte. https://www2.deloitte.com/content/dam/Deloitte/si/Documents/deloitte-2023-genz-millennial-survey.pdf

Deshmukh, A., Patil, D. S., Soni, G., & Tyagi, A. K. (2023). Cyber Security: New Realities for Industry 4.0 and Society 5.0. In Tyagi, A. (Ed.), *Handbook of Research on Quantum Computing for Smart Environments* (pp. 299–325). IGI Global. DOI:10.4018/978-1-6684-6697-1.ch017

Deshmukh, K. (2018). Work-life balance study focused on working women. *International Journal of Engineering Technologies and Management Research*, 5(5), 134–145. DOI:10.29121/ijetmr.v5.i5.2018.236

Devine, R. J., Good Care, C. M., & Choices, P. (2015). *Medical Ethics for Ordinary People* (3rd ed.). Paulist Press.

Dhawan, S. (2020). Online Learning: A Panacea in the Time of COVID-19 Crisis. *Journal of Educational Technology Systems*, 49(1), 5–22. DOI:10.1177/0047239520934018

Dickey, G., Blanke, S., & Seaton, L. (2019). Machine Learning in auditing: Current and future applications. *TheCPA Journal*, 89(6), 16–21.

Donati, L., Iotti, E., & Prati, A. (2019). Computer Vision for Supporting Fashion Creative Processes. In Hassaballah, M., & Hosny, K. (Eds.), *Recent Advances in Computer Vision. Studies in Computational Intelligence* (Vol. 804). Springer. DOI:10.1007/978-3-030-03000-1_1

Doshi-Velez, F., & Kim, B. (2017). Towards a rigorous science of interpretable machine learning. *arXiv preprint arXiv:1702.08608*.

Dunn, B. (2023). For financial illiteracy. *Economic and Labour Relations Review*, 34(2), 299–313. DOI:10.1017/elr.2023.8

Durac, L., & Moga, L. M. (2023). Applications of Decomposed Theory of Planned Behaviour in Making Decision to Adopt a Career in Social Entrepreneurship. *European Journal of Interdisciplinary Studies*, 15(1), 16–30. DOI:10.24818/ejis.2023.02

Dutta, S., & Jain, S. (2019). Advanced Banking Solutions in the Industry 5.0 Era: Challenges and Strategies. *Journal of Financial Innovation*, 24(4), 367–382. DOI: 10.1080/20430795.2019.1657299

Echeberría, A. (2022). AI Integration in the Digital Transformation Strategy. Springer eBooks.

Effendi, K. A., Ichsani, S., Saputera, D., Hertina, D., Wijaya, J. H., & Hendiarto, R. S. (2021). The Importance of Financial Literacy in Preventing Illegal Fintech in MSMEs in Indonesia. *Review of International Geographical Education Online*, 11(6). DOI:10.48047/rigeo.11.06.38

Ekmekci, P. E., & Arda, B. (2020). History of Artificial Intelligence. In: *Artificial Intelligence and Bioethics*. Springer, Cham. DOI:10.1007/978-3-030-52448-7_1

Ekuma, K. (2023). Artificial Intelligence and Automation in Human Resource Development: A Systematic Review. *Human Resource Development Review*, 15344843231224009.

Etzioni, A. (2018). *Happiness Is the Wrong Metric: A Liberal Communitarian Response to Populism*. Springer. DOI:10.1007/978-3-319-69623-2

Eurofund. (n.d.). *Work-Life Balance*. Eurofund. https://www.eurofound.europa.eu/en/topic/work-life-balance

European Commission. (2023). *GDPR and Digital Services Act*. EC.

Fan, X., Ning, N., & Deng, N. (2020). The impact of the quality of intelligent experience on smart retail engagement. *Marketing Intelligence & Planning*, 38(7), 877–891. DOI:10.1108/MIP-09-2019-0439

Farazouli, A., Cerratto-Pargman, T., Bolander-Laksov, K., & McGrath, C. (2024). Hello GPT! Goodbye home examination? An exploratory study of AI chatbot's impact on university teachers' assessment practices. *Assessment & Evaluation in Higher Education*, 49(3), 363–375. DOI:10.1080/02602938.2023.2241676

Feng, Y., & Wu, Q. (2022). A statistical learning assessment of Huber regression. *Journal of Approximation Theory*, 273, 105660. DOI:10.1016/j.jat.2021.105660

Fildes, R., Goodwin, P., & Lawrence, M. (2019). The state of demand forecasting technology: Results of a global survey of forecasting practitioners. *International Journal of Forecasting*, 35(1), 103–114.

Fincato, M., Cornia, M., Landi, F., Cesari, F., & Cucchiara, R. (2022). Transform, warp, and dress: A new transformation-guided model for virtual try-on. [TOMM]. *ACM Transactions on Multimedia Computing Communications and Applications*, 18(2), 1–24. DOI:10.1145/3491226

Floridi, L., Cowls, J., Beltrametti, M., Chatila, R., Chazerand, P., Dignum, V., & Engel, C. (2018). AI4People—an ethical framework for a good AI society: Opportunities, risks, principles, and recommendations. *Minds and Machines*, 28(4), 689–707. DOI:10.1007/s11023-018-9482-5 PMID:30930541

Freund, Y., & Schapire, R. E. (1996). Experiments with a New Boosting Algorithm. In *Proceedings of the Thirteenth International Conference on Machine Learning (ICML'96),* (pp. 148-156). Research Gate.

Friedlob, G. T., & Schleifer, L. L. F. (1999). Fuzzy logic: Application for audit risk and uncertainty. *Managerial Auditing Journal*, 14(3), 127–137. DOI:10.1108/02686909910259103

Friedman, J. H. (2002). Stochastic Gradient Boosting. *Computational Statistics & Data Analysis*, 38(4), 367–378. DOI:10.1016/S0167-9473(01)00065-2

Gangaiamaran, R., & Anil Premraj, J. (2020). Technology adoption in self-access language learning: A review. In *Journal of Critical Reviews* (*Vol. 7*, Issue 4, pp. 642–645). Innovare Academics Sciences Pvt. Ltd. DOI:10.31838/jcr.07.04.119

Garcia, A. (2023). *Data-Driven Decision Making: Leveraging Analytics and AI for Strategic Advantage.*

Garcia, M., & Martinez, E. (2020). Advanced Banking Solutions in the Industry 5.0 Context: Challenges and Perspectives. *Journal of Financial Innovation*, 9(3), 321–336.

Garcia, M., & Martinez, E. (2020). Innovative Solutions for Sustainable Banking: Smart Banking Technologies and Cutting-Edge Practices. *International Journal of Sustainable Banking*, 9(3), 321–336.

Garg, N., Pareek, A., Lale, A., & Charya, S. J. (2021). Evolution in E-Commerce with Augmented Reality. In *IOP Conference Series: Materials Science and Engineering, 1012(1), 012041.* IOP Publishing. DOI:10.1088/1757-899X/1012/1/012041

Gatzioufa, P., & Saprikis, V. (2022). A literature review on users' behavioral intention toward chatbots' adoption. In *Applied Computing and Informatics.* Emerald Group Holdings Ltd. DOI:10.1108/ACI-01-2022-0021

Gerow, J. E., Grover, V., Thatcher, J., & Roth, P. L. (2014). Looking toward the future of it–Business strategic alignment through the past: A meta-analysis. MIS Quarterly: Management. *Information Systems,* 38(4), 1159–1185.

Ghandour, A. (2021). Opportunities and Challenges of Artificial Intelligence in Banking: Systematic Literature Review. *TEM Journal, 10*(4), 1581–1587. https://doi.org/DOI:10.18421/TEM104-12

Ghani, W. S. D. W. A., Khidzir, N. Z., Guan, T. T., & Ismail, M. (2017). Towards Modelling Factors of Intention to Adopt Cloud-Based M-Retail Application among Textile Cyberpreneurs. *Journal of Advances in Information Technology.* DOI:10.12720/jait.8.2.114-120

Ghosh, S., & Reilly, D. L. (1994). Credit card fraud detection with a neural network. *Proceedings of the 27th Hawaii International Conference on System Sciences, (vol.3,* pp. 621-630]. IEEE. DOI:10.1109/HICSS.1994.323314

Giffinger, R., Fertner, C., Kramar, H., Kalasek, R., Pichler-Milanović, N., & Meijers, E. (2007). *Smart cities: Ranking of European medium-sized cities. Centre of Regional Science (SRF).* Vienna University of Technology. DOI:10.1145/1947940.1947974

Gill, P., Stewart, K., Treasure, E., & Chadwick, B. (2008). Methods of data collection in qualitative research: interviews and focus groups. *British Dental Journal 2008 204:6, 204*(6), 291–295. DOI:10.1038/bdj.2008.192

Gill, S. S., Xu, M., Patros, P., Wu, H., Kaur, R., Kaur, K., Fuller, S., Singh, M., Arora, P., Parlikad, A. K., Stankovski, V., Abraham, A., Ghosh, S. K., Lutfiyya, H., Kanhere, S. S., Bahsoon, R., Rana, O., Dustdar, S., Sakellariou, R., & Buyya, R. (2024). Transformative effects of ChatGPT on modern education: Emerging Era of AI Chatbots. *Internet of Things and Cyber-Physical Systems,* 4, 19–23. DOI:10.1016/j.iotcps.2023.06.002

Glaeser, E. L. (2011). *Triumph of the city: How our greatest invention makes us richer, smarter, greener, healthier, and happier.* Penguin.

Goldman Sachs. (2023). *The Potentially Large Effects of Artificial Intelligence on Economic Growth.* Briggs/Kodnani.

Gomathi, L., Mishra, A. K., & Tyagi, A. K. (2023). *Industry 5.0 for Healthcare 5.0: Opportunities, Challenges and Future Research Possibilities*. 2023 7th International Conference on Trends in Electronics and Informatics (ICOEI), Tirunelveli, India. DOI:10.1109/ICOEI56765.2023.10125660

Goodfellow, I., Bengio, Y., & Courville, A. (2016). *Deep learning MIT press.*

Goodman, B., & Flaxman, S. (2017). European Union regulations on algorithmic decision-making and a "right to explanation.". *AI Magazine*, 38(3), 50–57. DOI:10.1609/aimag.v38i3.2741

Gopinath, G. (2023). Harnessing AI for Global Good. *Finance & Development*, 0060(004), A018. DOI:10.5089/9798400260179.001.A018

Grohmann, A., Klühs, T., & Menkhoff, L. (2018). Does financial literacy improve financial inclusion? Cross-country evidence. *World Development*, 111, 84–96. DOI:10.1016/j.worlddev.2018.06.020

Guan, S. S. (2022). *FINFLUENCERS AND THE REASONABLE RETAIL INVESTOR*. DISB. https://disb.dc.gov/page/beware-financial-influencers

Gundimeda, V., Murali, R. S., Joseph, R., & Naresh Babu, N. T. (2019). An automated computer vision system for extraction of retail food product metadata. In *First International Conference on Artificial Intelligence and Cognitive Computing: AICC 2018* (pp. 199-216). Springer Singapore. DOI:10.1007/978-981-13-1580-0_20

Gupta, S. S., Ghosal, I., & Ghosh, R. (2023). How does Augmented Reality (AR) impact on Consumer buying behavior? A Study in Indian E commerce Industry. [EEL]. *European Economic Letters*, 13(4), 700–707.

Gurrieri, L., Drenten, J., & Abidin, C. (2023). Symbiosis or parasitism? A framework for advancing interdisciplinary and socio-cultural perspectives in influencer marketing. In *Journal of Marketing Management* (*Vol. 39*, Issues 11–12, pp. 911–932). Routledge. DOI:10.1080/0267257X.2023.2255053

Haan, K., & Watts, R. (2023). How Businesses are using artificial intelligence in 2024. *Forbes*. https://www.forbes.com/advisor/business/software/ai-in-business/

Hassabis, D., Suleyman, M., & Legg, S. (2017). *DeepMind's work in 2016: A round-up*. DeepMind.

Hastie, T., Tibshirani, R., & Friedman, J. (2009). *The Elements of Statistical Learning: Data Mining, Inference, and Prediction* (2nd ed.). Springer. DOI:10.1007/978-0-387-84858-7

Hatzius, J. (2023). *The Potentially Large Effects of Artificial Intelligence on Economic Growth (Briggs/Kodnani)*. Goldman Sachs.

Haugeland, J. (1985). *Artificial Intelligence: The very idea*. MIT Press.

He, J., Han, P., Liu, H., Men, S., Ju, L., Zhen, P., & Wang, T. (2017, December). The research and application of the augmented reality technology. *In 2017 IEEE 2nd Information Technology, Networking, Electronic and Automation Control Conference* (ITNEC) (pp. 496-501). IEEE. DOI:10.1109/ITNEC.2017.8284781

He, J., Liu, Y., Song, M., He, H., & Jiang, T. (2017). *Learning to respond with deep neural networks for retrieval-based human-computer conversation system*. arXiv *preprintarXiv*:1709.00023.

Henderson, J. C., & Venkatraman, N. (1999). Strategic alignment: Leveraging Information Technology for transforming organizations. *IBM Systems Journal*, 38(2), 472–484. DOI:10.1147/SJ.1999.5387096

Henley, T. (2018). *Hergenhahn's An Introduction to the History of Psychology*. Cengage Learning.

Hmoud, B., & Laszlo, V. (2019). Will artificial intelligence take over human resources recruitment and selection. *Network Intelligence Studies*, 7(13), 21–30.

Hmoud, B., & Várallyai, L. (2021). Artificial Intelligence In Talent Acquisition, Do we Trust It? *Agrárinformatika Folyóirat*, 12(1). DOI:10.17700/jai.2021.12.1.594

Holloway, C. (1983). Strategic management and artificial intelligence. *Long Range Planning*, 16(5), 89–93. DOI:10.1016/0024-6301(83)90082-1

Huang, T. L., Mathews, S., & Chou, C. Y. (2019). Enhancing online rapport experience via augmented reality. *Journal of Services Marketing*, 33(7), 851–865. DOI:10.1108/JSM-12-2018-0366

Huston, S. J. (2010). Measuring Financial Literacy. *The Journal of Consumer Affairs*, 44(2), 296–316. DOI:10.1111/j.1745-6606.2010.01170.x

HyperVerge. (2024, February 5). *How to Leverage AI to Prevent Fraud: A Deep Dive for Financial Institutions*. HyperVerge. https://hyperverge.co/blog/ai-fraud -prevention/ (2020, March 10).

IBM. (2024). *AI Adoption in Businesses*. IBM.

ILO. (2018). *Women do 4 Times More Unpaid Care Work Than Men in Asia and the Pacific*. ILO. https://www.ilo.org/asia/media-centre/news/WCMS_633284/lang--en/index.htm#:~:text=According%20to%20the%20report%2C%20Globally,over%20the%20past%2020%20years

Janković, S., & Curovic, D. M. (2023, October). Strategic Integration of Artificial Intelligence for Sustainable Businesses: Implications for Data Management and Human User Engagement in the Digital Era. *Sustainability (Basel)*, 15208(21, 24), 15208. DOI:10.3390/su152115208

Jarrahi, M. H. (2018). Artificial intelligence and the future of work: Human-AI symbiosis in organizational decision making. *Business Horizons*, 61(4), 577–586. DOI:10.1016/j.bushor.2018.03.007

Jia, F., Chen, J., Wu, T., & He, L. (2019). A Review of Artificial Intelligence Applications in the Manufacturing Sector. *IEEE Access : Practical Innovations, Open Solutions*, 7, 114490–114499.

Jonathan, H., Magd, H., & Khan, S. A. (2024). Artificial Intelligence and Augmented Reality: A Business Fortune to Sustainability in the Digital Age. In *Navigating the Digital Landscape: Understanding Customer Behaviour in the Online World* (pp. 85-105). Emerald Publishing Limited. DOI:10.1108/978-1-83549-272-720241005

JPMorgan Chase. (2018). *How AI is transforming fraud detection at JPMorgan Chase*. JP Morgan Chase. https://www.jpmorganchase.com

Jung, T. H., Bae, S., Moorhouse, N., & Kwon, O. (2021). The impact of user perceptions of AR on purchase intention of location-based AR navigation systems. *Journal of Retailing and Consumer Services*, 61, 102575. DOI:10.1016/j.jretconser.2021.102575

Jurafsky, D., & Martin, J. H. (2009). *Speech and language processing*. Pearson.

Kanimozhi, S., & Selvarani, A. (2019). Application of the Decomposed Theory of Planned Behaviour in Technology Adoption: A Review. *International Journal of Research and Analytical Reviews*, 6(2).

Kaplan, J. (2015). *Humans Need Not Apply: A Guide to Wealth & Work in the Age of Artificial Intelligence*. Yale University Press.

Kaur, R., Gabrijelčič, D., & Klobučar, T. (2023, September). Artificial Intelligence for Cybersecurity: Literature Review and Future Research Directions. *Information Fusion*, 101804, 1. DOI:10.1016/j.inffus.2023.101804

Ke, G., Meng, Q., Finley, T., Wang, T., Chen, W., Ma, W., & Li, T. (2017). LightGBM: A Highly Efficient Gradient Boosting Decision Tree. *Advances in Neural Information Processing Systems (NeurIPS), 30.*

Kedvarin, S., & Saengchote, K. (2023). Social Media Finfluencers: Evidence from YouTube and Cryptocurrencies. SSRN *Electronic Journal.* DOI:10.2139/ssrn.4594081

Khalisharani, H., Johan, I. R., & Sabri, M. F. (2022). The Influence of Financial Literacy and Attitude towards Financial Behaviour Amongst Undergraduate Students: A Cross-Country Evidence. *Pertanika Journal of Social Science & Humanities,* 30(2), 449–474. DOI:10.47836/pjssh.30.2.03

Khanna, A., Pandey, B., Vashishta, K., Kalia, K., Pradeepkumar, B., & Das, T. (2015). A Study of Today's A.I. through Chatbots and Rediscovery of Machine Intelligence. *International Journal of U- and e-Service. Science and Technology,* 8(7), 277–284. DOI:10.14257/ijunesst.2015.8.7.28

Khan, S., & Rabbani, M. R. (2020, November 17). Chatbot as Islamic finance expert (CaIFE): When finance meets artificial intelligence. *ACM International Conference Proceeding Series.* ACM. DOI:10.1145/3440084.3441213

Kim, Y., & Park, J. (2021). Innovative Banking Solutions for Industry 5.0: Advanced Practices and Technologies. *Journal of Financial Services Innovation,* 8(1), 45–60.

Kim, Y., & Park, J. (2021). Sustainable Financial Systems: Smart Banking Practices and Cutting-Edge Technologies. *Journal of Sustainable Banking and Finance,* 8(1), 45–60.

Kiruthika, S., Prasanna, V., Santhosh, A., Santhosh, R., & Sri Vignesh, P. (2023). Virtual Bank Assistance: An AI-Based Voice BOT for Better Banking. *International Journal of Advanced Research in Science. Tongxin Jishu,* 196–201. DOI:10.48175/IJARSCT-9194

Klapper, L., Lusardi, A., & Panos, G. A. (2013). Financial literacy and its consequences: Evidence from Russia during the financial crisis. *Journal of Banking & Finance,* 37(10), 3904–3923. DOI:10.1016/j.jbankfin.2013.07.014

Koedinger, K. R., Corbett, A. T., & Perfetti, C. (2012). The Knowledge-Learning-Instruction Framework: Bridging the Science-Practice Chasm to Enhance Robust Student Learning. *Cognitive Science,* 36(5), 757–798. DOI:10.1111/j.1551-6709.2012.01245.x PMID:22486653

Koenker, R. (2005). *Quantile Regression.* Cambridge University Press. DOI:10.1017/CBO9780511754098

Kooli, C. (2023). Chatbots in Education and Research: A Critical Examination of Ethical Implications and Solutions. *Sustainability (Basel)*, 15(7), 5614. DOI:10.3390/su15075614

Koumentaki, A., Anthony, F., Poston, L., & Wheeler, T. (2002, May). Low-Protein Diet Impairs Vascular Relaxation in Virgin and Pregnant Rats. *Clinical Science*, 102(5), 553–560. DOI:10.1042/cs1020553 PMID:11980575

Kowalczuk, P., Siepmann, C., & Adler, J. (2021). Cognitive, affective, and behavioral consumer responses to augmented reality in e-commerce: A comparative study. *Journal of Business Research*, 124, 357–373. DOI:10.1016/j.jbusres.2020.10.050

Kulkov, I. (2021, August). The Role of Artificial Intelligence in Business Transformation: A Case of Pharmaceutical Companies. *Technology in Society*, 101629, 1. DOI:10.1016/j.techsoc.2021.101629

Kumar, A., Biswas, A., & Sanyal, S. (2018). Ecommerce gan: A generative adversarial network for e-commerce. *arXiv preprint arXiv:1801.03244.*

Kumar, R., & Tople, A. (2023, March). Employee Attrition, Job Involvement, and Work Life Balance Prediction Using Machine Learning Classifier Models. In Doctoral Symposium on Computational Intelligence (pp. 907-915). Singapore: Springer Nature Singapore. DOI:10.1007/978-981-99-3716-5_72

Kumar, S. (2023). Artificial Intelligence. *Journal of Computers Mechanical and Management, 31–42*(3).

Kumar, B., Singh, A. K., & Banerjee, P. (2023, June). A deep learning approach for product recommendation using resnet-50 cnn model. In *2023 International Conference on Sustainable Computing and Smart Systems (ICSCSS)* (pp. 604-610). IEEE. DOI:10.1109/ICSCSS57650.2023.10169441

Kumari, A., & Devi, N. C. (2023). Blockchain technology acceptance by investment professionals: A decomposed TPB model. *Journal of Financial Reporting and Accounting*, 21(1), 45–59. DOI:10.1108/JFRA-12-2021-0466

Kumari, S., & Harikrishnan, A. (2021). Importance of Financial Literacy for Sustainable Future Environment: A Research Among People In Rural Areas With Special Reference To Mandi District, Himachal Pradesh. *International Journal of Engineering. Science and Information Technology*, 1(1), 15–19. Advance online publication. DOI:10.52088/ijesty.v1i1.36

Kumar, R., & Singh, P. (2018). Advanced Banking Solutions for the Industry 5.0 Era: Challenges and Opportunities. *Journal of Financial Technology*, 22(4), 356–372. DOI:10.1002/jft.567

Kumar, R., & Singh, P. (2018). Sustainable Smart Banking: Using Cutting-Edge Technologies for Financial Inclusion. *Sustainable Development Review*, 22(4), 356–372. DOI:10.1002/sdr.2047

Kuo, B. C., Ho, H. H., Li, C. H., Hung, C. C., & Taur, J. S. (2013). A kernel-based feature selection method for SVM with RBF kernel for hyperspectral image classification. *IEEE Journal of Selected Topics in Applied Earth Observations and Remote Sensing*, 7(1), 317–326. DOI:10.1109/JSTARS.2013.2262926

Kurzweil, R. (1990). *The age of intelligent machines*. MIT Press.

Киш, Л. М. (2020). Adaptation of b2c e-commerce to the conditions of the COVID-19 pandemic. *East European Scientific Journal*, 12(64), 14-19.

Labadze, L., Grigolia, M., & Machaidze, L. (2023). Role of AI chatbots in education: systematic literature review. In *International Journal of Educational Technology in Higher Education* (Vol. 20, Issue 1). Springer Science and Business Media Deutschland GmbH. DOI:10.1186/s41239-023-00426-1

Lai, P. (2017). The literature review of technology adoption models and theories for the novelty technology. *Journal of Information Systems and Technology Management*, 14(1), 21–38. DOI:10.4301/S1807-17752017000100002

Lajnef, K. (2023). The effect of social media influencers on teenagers Behavior: An empirical study using cognitive map technique. *Current Psychology (New Brunswick, N.J.)*, 42(22), 19364–19377. DOI:10.1007/s12144-023-04273-1 PMID:36742063

Lalonde, J. F. (2018, July). Deep learning for augmented reality. In *2018 17th workshop on information optics (WIO)* (pp. 1-3). IEEE. DOI:10.1109/WIO.2018.8643463

Lampropoulos, G., Keramopoulos, E., & Diamantaras, K. (2020). Enhancing the functionality of augmented reality using deep learning, semantic web and knowledge graphs: A review. *Visual Informatics*, 4(1), 32–42. DOI:10.1016/j.visinf.2020.01.001

Lane, M., & Saint-Martin, A. (2021). *The Impact of Artificial Intelligence on the Labour Market: What Do We Know So Far?*

Laurindo, F. J. (2008). *Information technology: Planning and strategy management.* Atlas.

Ledro, C., Nosella, A., & Dalla Pozza, I. (2023, December). Integration of AI in CRM: Challenges and Guidelines. *Journal of Open Innovation*, 100151(4), 1. DOI:10.1016/j.joitmc.2023.100151

Lee, J., Bagheri, B., & Kao, H. (2019). A Cyber-Physical Systems architecture for Industry 4.0 based manufacturing systems. *Manufacturing Letters*, 21, 64–69.

Lei, H. (2023). *Artificial Intelligence—A New Knowledge and Decision-Making Paradigm*. Springer eBooks.

Levy, S. (2017). How PayPal beats the bad guys with AI. *Wired*. https://www.wired.com

Li, J., &Barmaki, R. (2019). *Trends in virtual and augmented reality research: a review of latest eye tracking research papers and beyond*.

Liao, S. H., Chu, P. H., & Hsiao, P. Y. (2019). Data mining techniques and applications–A decade review from 2000 to 2011. *Expert Systems with Applications*, 39(12), 11303–11311. DOI:10.1016/j.eswa.2012.02.063

Liu, J. (2024). *China's AI and Employment Policies*.

Liu, H. (2008). *Generalized additive model*. Department of Mathematics and Statistics University of Minnesota Duluth.

Liu, X., Chen, Q., Tsai, C. W., Gao, W., & Zhang, A. (2019). Integrating blockchain for data sharing and collaboration in mobile healthcare applications. *IEEE Access : Practical Innovations, Open Solutions*, 7, 36592–36606.

Li, W., & Zhang, Y. (2018). Driving Sustainability through Smart Banking: Emerging Technologies and Innovations. *Sustainable Development Review*, 21(3), 278–295.

Li, W., & Zhang, Y. (2018). The Future of Banking in the Industry 5.0 Era: Advanced Solutions and Innovations. *Journal of Financial Innovation*, 21(3), 278–295.

Loureiro, S. M. C., Guerreiro, J., & Tussyadiah, I. (2021). Artificial intelligence in business: State of the art and future research agenda. *Journal of Business Research*, 129, 911–926. DOI:10.1016/j.jbusres.2020.11.001

Luger, G. F., & Stubblefield, W. A. (1993). *Instructor's manual for Artificial Intelligence: Structures and strategies for complex problem solving*. São Francisco, EUA: Benjamin Cummings.

Luo, S., Xu, L., Xu, X., Zeng, Y., & Liu, Y. (2020). A Survey of Artificial Intelligence Applications in Smart Manufacturing. *Journal of Manufacturing Systems*, 56, 333–349.

Lusardi, A., & Mitchell, O. S. (2011). Financial Literacy and Retirement Preparedness: Evidence and Implications for Financial Education Programs. SSRN *Electronic Journal*. DOI:10.2139/ssrn.957796

Lusardi, A., & Mitchell, O. S. (2023b). The Importance of Financial Literacy: Opening a New Field. SSRN *Electronic Journal*. DOI:10.2139/ssrn.4420560

Lusardi, A., & Mitchell, O. S. (2014). The economic importance of financial literacy: Theory and evidence. *Journal of Economic Literature*, 52(1), 5–44. DOI:10.1257/jel.52.1.5 PMID:28579637

Lusardi, A., & Mitchell, O. S. (2023a). The Importance of Financial Literacy: Opening a New Field. *The Journal of Economic Perspectives*, 37(4), 137–154. DOI:10.1257/jep.37.4.137

Lyall, A., Mercier, P., & Gstettner, S. (2018). The death of supply chain management. *Harvard Business Review*, 1–4.

Madhav, A. V. S., & Tyagi, A. K. (2023). Explainable Artificial Intelligence (XAI): Connecting Artificial Decision-Making and Human Trust in Autonomous Vehicles. In: Singh, P.K., Wierzchoń, S.T., Tanwar, S., Rodrigues, J.J.P.C., Ganzha, M. (eds) *Proceedings of Third International Conference on Computing, Communications, and Cyber-Security. Lecture Notes in Networks and Systems*. Springer, Singapore. DOI:10.1007/978-981-19-1142-2_10

Madhav, A. V. S., & Tyagi, A. K. (2022). The World with Future Technologies (Post-COVID-19): Open Issues, Challenges, and the Road Ahead. In Tyagi, A. K., Abraham, A., & Kaklauskas, A. (Eds.), *Intelligent Interactive Multimedia Systems for e-Healthcare Applications*. Springer. DOI:10.1007/978-981-16-6542-4_22

Malik, S., Bansal, R., & Tyagi, A. K. (Eds.). (2022). *Impact and Role of Digital Technologies in Adolescent Lives*. IGI Global. DOI:10.4018/978-1-7998-8318-0

Manfredo, T. (2024). How to Make $1 Million in 30 Seconds or Less: The Need for Regulations on Finfluencers. *SSRN*, 84(2). Advance online publication. DOI:10.2139/ssrn.4398463

Manyika, J., Lund, S., Chui, M., Bughin, J., Woetzel, J., Batra, P., & Sanghvi, S. (2017). Jobs lost; jobs gained: Workforce transitions in a time of automation. *McKinsey Global Institute*, 150(1), 1–148.

Maramganti, K. (2019). *Role of Artificial Intelligence in Business Transformation*. Research Gate.

Mari, L. (2024). *AI Synergy – How AI collaborations are shaping the future*. Digital Health Global. https://www.digitalhealthglobal.com/ai-synergy-how-ai-collaborations-are-shaping-the-future/

Mariani, M. M., Machado, I., Magrelli, V., & Dwivedi, Y. K. (2023). Artificial intelligence in innovation research: A systematic review, conceptual framework, and future research directions. *Technovation*, 122, 102623. DOI:10.1016/j.technovation.2022.102623

Marinov, K. M. (2023). Financial Literacy: Determinants and Impact on Financial Behaviour. *Economic Alternatives*, 2023(1), 89–114. DOI:10.37075/EA.2023.1.05

Marr, B. (2021). How AI Is Revolutionizing Manufacturing In 2021. *Forbes*. https://www.forbes.com/sites/bernardmarr/2021/02/15/how-ai-is-revolutionizing -manufacturing-in-2021/?sh=3c3c64a65f3b

Marr, B., & Ward, M. (2019). *Artificial Intelligence in practice: How 50 successful companies used artificial intelligence to solve problems*. Hoboken, EUA: Wiley.

Martellini, M., & Rule, S. (2016). *Cybersecurity: The Insights You Need from Harvard Business Review*. Harvard Business Review Press.

Martin, F. (2020). The Role of Artificial Intelligence in the Transformation of Higher Education. *EDUCAUSE Review*.

Massoud, M. F., Maaliky, B., Fawal, A., Mawllawi, A., & Yahkni, F. (2024). Transforming Human Resources With AI: Empowering Talent Management and Workforce Productivity. In *Industrial Applications of Big Data, AI, and Blockchain* (pp. 254-299). IGI Global.

McCarthy, J., & Hayes, P. J. (1981). Some philosophical problems from the standpoint of artificial intelligence. *Readings in artificial intelligence*. Morgan Kaufman. DOI:10.1016/B978-0-934613-03-3.50033-7

McDonald, G. C. (2009). Ridge regression. *Wiley Interdisciplinary Reviews: Computational Statistics*, 1(1), 93–100. DOI:10.1002/wics.14

Mendelson, D. N. (2019). Applying AI in Banking, Investments, and Personal Finance. *California Management Review*, 61(4), 91–115.

Michie, D. (1968). "Memo" functions and machine learning. *Nature*, 218(5136), 19–22. DOI:10.1038/218019a0

Microsoft. (2023). *AI Job Replacement Concerns in India*. Microsoft.

Midha, S., Kaur, G., & Tripathi, K. (2017). Cloud deep down — SWOT analysis. *2017 2nd International Conference on Telecommunication and Networks (TEL-NET)*, (pp. 1-5). IEEE. DOI:10.1109/TEL-NET.2017.8343560

Midha, S., Tripathi, K., & Sharma, M. K. (2021, April). Practical Implications of Using Dockers on Virtualized SDN. *Webology.*, 18(Special Issue 01), 312–330. DOI:10.14704/WEB/V18SI01/WEB18062

Minaee, S., Liang, X., & Yan, S. (2022). *Modern augmented reality: Applications, trends, and future directions*. arXiv preprint arXiv:2202.09450.

Ministry of Electronics and Information Technology. (2024). *AI Policy Developments*.

Mishra, S. (2021). AI Business Model: An Integrative Business Approach. *Journal of Innovation and Entrepreneurship, 10*(1). Springer Science and Business Media LLC.

Mishra, S., Hashmi, K. A., Pagani, A., Liwicki, M., Stricker, D., & Afzal, M. Z. (2021). Towards robust object detection in floor plan images: A data augmentation approach. *Applied Sciences (Basel, Switzerland)*, 11(23), 11174. DOI:10.3390/app112311174

Mishra, S., & Tyagi, A. K. (2022). The Role of Machine Learning Techniques in Internet of Things-Based Cloud Applications. In Pal, S., De, D., & Buyya, R. (Eds.), *Artificial Intelligence-based Internet of Things Systems. Internet of Things (Technology, Communications and Computing)*. Springer. DOI:10.1007/978-3-030-87059-1_4

Mnyakin, M. (2020). Investigating the Impacts of AR, AI, and Website Optimization on Ecommerce Sales Growth. *ResearchBerg Review of Science and Technology*, 3(1), 116–130.

Mohta, A., & Shunmugasundaram, V. (2022). Financial Literacy Among Millennials. *International Journal of Economics and Financial Issues*, 12(2), 61–66. DOI:10.32479/ijefi.12801

Morocho-Cayamcela, M. E., Lee, H., & Lim, W. (2019). Machine learning for 5G/B5G mobile and wireless communications: Potential, limitations, and future directions. *IEEE Access : Practical Innovations, Open Solutions*, 7, 137184–137206. DOI:10.1109/ACCESS.2019.2942390

Murphy, G., & Schmeink, L. (2017). *Cyberpunk and Visual Culture*. Routledge. DOI:10.4324/9781315161372

Muthukrishnan, N., Maleki, F., Ovens, K., Reinhold, C., Forghani, B., & Forghani, R. (2020). Brief history of artificial intelligence. *Neuroimaging Clinics of North America*, 30(4), 393–399. DOI:10.1016/j.nic.2020.07.004 PMID:33038991

Nair, M. M., & Tyagi, A. K. (2021). *Privacy: History, Statistics, Policy, Laws, Preservation and Threat Analysis. Journal of Information Assurance & Security*, 16(1), 24-34.

Nambiar, R., Varma, V., & Chakraborty, T. (2020). AI in Banking: A Review of the Applications and Opportunities. In *International Conference on Intelligent Data Communication Technologies and Internet of Things* (pp. 381-390). Springer, Cham.

Nandhini, P., Hariprabha, S., Abirami, S., Jaseenash, R., & Kaviyaraj, R. (2022). Design and Development of an Augmented Reality E-Commerce 3D models. *In 2022 3rd International Conference on Smart Electronics and Communication COSEC)*, (pp. 127-132). IEEE. DOI:10.1109/ICOSEC54921.2022.9952109

Ndou, A. (2023). The relationship between demographic factors and financial literacy. *International Journal of Research in Business and Social Science (2147–4478)*, *12*(1), 155–164. DOI:10.20525/ijrbs.v12i1.2298

Ngai, E. W. T., Hu, Y., Wong, Y. H., Chen, Y., & Sun, X. (2011). The application of data mining techniques in financial fraud detection: A classification framework and an academic review of literature. *Decision Support Systems*, 50(3), 559–569. DOI:10.1016/j.dss.2010.08.006

Nilekani, N., & Shah, V. (2016). *Rebooting India: Realizing a Billion Aspirations*. Penguin UK.

Nosova, S. (2024). Strategies for Business Cybersecurity Using AI Technologies. *Studies in Computational Intelligence*.

Nünning, A., & Sicks, K. M. (2012). *Turning Points: Concepts and Narratives of Change in Literature and Other Media*. Walter de Gruyter. DOI:10.1515/9783110297102

Nuruzzaman, M., & Hussain, O. K. (2020). IntelliBot: A Dialogue-based chatbot for the insurance industry. *Knowledge-Based Systems*, 196, 105810. DOI:10.1016/j.knosys.2020.105810

Nyasulu, C., & Dominic Chawinga, W. (2019). Using the decomposed theory of planned behavior to understand university students' adoption of WhatsApp in learning. *E-Learning and Digital Media*, 16(5), 413–429. DOI:10.1177/2042753019835906

Nyathani, R. (2022). AI-Powered Recruitment The Future of HR Digital Transformation. *Journal of Artificial Intelligence & Cloud Computing. SRC/JAICC-145*.

Nyathani, R. (2023). AI-Driven HR Analytics: Unleashing the Power of HR Data Management. *Journal of Technology and Systems*, 5(2), 15–26. DOI:10.47941/jts.1513

OECD. (2019). *Artificial Intelligence in Society*. OECD Publishing.

OECD. (n.d.-a). [Dataset]. OECD. https://stats.oecd.org/index.aspx?DataSetCode=ANHRS

OECD. (n.d.-b). [Dataset]. OECD. https://www.stress.org/workplace-stress#:~:text=83%25%20of%20US%20workers%20suffer,stress%20affects%20their%20personal%20relationships

Okello Candiya Bongomin, G., Munene, J. C., & Yourougou, P. (2020). Examining the role of financial intermediaries in promoting financial literacy and financial inclusion among people with low incomes in developing countries: Lessons from rural Uganda. *Cogent Economics & Finance*, 8(1), 1761274. DOI:10.1080/23322 039.2020.1761274

Ooi, E. C. W., Isa, Z. M., Manaf, M. R. A., Fuad, A. S. A., Ahmad, A., Mustapa, M. N., & Marzuki, N. M. (2024). Factors influencing the intention to use the ICD-11 among medical record officers (MROs) and assistant medical record officers (AM-ROs) in the Ministry of Health, Malaysia. *Scientific Reports*, 14(1). DOI:10.1038/s41598-024-60439-2 PMID:38688966

Oosting, J. (2022). *Finfluencers and their impact on the Stock Market.*

Pandita, D. (2019). Talent acquisition: Analysis of digital hiring in organizations. *SAMVAD*, 18, 66–72.

Pan, Y., & Froese, F. J. (2023). An interdisciplinary review of AI and HRM: Challenges and future directions. *Human Resource Management Review*, 33(1), 100924. DOI:10.1016/j.hrmr.2022.100924

Patel, R., Khan, F., Silva, B., & Shaturaev, J. (2023, August 8). *Unleashing the Potential of Artificial Intelligence in Auditing: A Comprehensive Exploration of its Multifaceted Impact.* Mpra.ub.uni-Muenchen.de. https://mpra.ub.uni-muenchen.de/119616/

Patel, A., & Gupta, M. (2019). Smart Banking for Sustainable Finance: A Review of Cutting-Edge Technologies and Practices. *Journal of Sustainable Banking and Finance*, 6(1), 45–60.

Patel, A., & Gupta, M. (2019). The Role of Industry 5.0 in Shaping Advanced Banking Solutions. *Journal of Banking & Finance*, 6(1), 45–60.

Patel, R., & Shah, P. (2018). Next-Generation Banking: Advanced Solutions for Industry 5.0. *Journal of Banking & Finance*, 25(3), 267–282.

Patel, R., & Shah, P. (2018). Towards Sustainable Finance: Smart Banking Solutions and Cutting-Edge Technologies. *International Journal of Sustainable Development*, 25(3), 267–282.

Pattnaik, D., Ray, S., & Raman, R. (2024). Artificial intelligence and machine learning applications in the financial services industry: A bibliometric review. *Heliyon*, 10(1). DOI:10.1016/j.heliyon.2023.e23492 PMID:38187262

Pawlicka, A., Pawlicki, M., Tomaszewska, R., Choraś, M., & Gerlach, R. (2020). Innovative machine learning approach and evaluation campaign for predicting the subjective feeling of work-life balance among employees. *PLoS One*, 15(5), e0232771. DOI:10.1371/journal.pone.0232771 PMID:32413040

Pendy, B. (2023). Role of AI in Business Management. *Brilliance: Research of Artificial Intelligence*, 3(1), 48–55. DOI:10.47709/brilliance.v3i1.2191

Perdanasari, A., Sudiyanto, S., & Octoria, D. (2019). The Importance of Financial Literacy Knowledge For Elementary School Students In the 21st Century. *Efektor*, 6(1), 26. DOI:10.29407/e.v6i1.12591

Perlman, M. A. (2009). *Functions in Biological and Artificial Worlds: Comparative Philosophical Perspectives*. MIT Press.

Perlow, L. & Porter, J. (2009). Making Time Off Presdictable and Required. *Harvard Business Review*. https://hbr.org/2009/10/making-time-off-predictable-and-required

Phillips-Wren, G. (2012, April). AI TOOLS IN DECISION MAKING SUPPORT SYSTEMS: A REVIEW. *International Journal of Artificial Intelligence Tools*, 21(02), 1240005. DOI:10.1142/S0218213012400052

Pickett, S. T., Cadenasso, M. L., & Grove, J. M. (Eds.). (2018). *Resilient cities: Meaning, models, and metaphor for integrating the ecological, socio-economic, and planning realms*. Springer.

Pillai, R., & Sivathanu, B. (2020). Adoption of artificial intelligence (AI) for talent acquisition in IT/ITeS organizations. *Benchmarking*, 27(9), 2599–2629. DOI:10.1108/BIJ-04-2020-0186

Pollock, J. (2019). Technical Methods. In *Philosophy*. Routledge.

Porter, M. E., & Millar, V. E. (1985). How information gives you competitive advantage. *Harvard Business Review*, 63(4), 149–160.

Pramod, A. (2022). *Emerging Innovations in the Near Future Using Deep Learning Techniques, Book: Advanced Analytics and Deep Learning Models*. Wiley Scrivener. DOI:10.1002/9781119792437.ch10

Prihartanti, F. W., Murtini, W., & Indriayu, M. (2022). The Need for Financial Literacy Proficiency Level for Generation Z Students at School. *Eduvest - Journal Of Universal Studies, 2*(3). DOI:10.36418/edv.v2i3.383

Prokhorenkova, L., Gusev, G., Vorobev, A., Dorogush, A. V., & Gulin, A. (2019). CatBoost: unbiased boosting with categorical features. *NeurIPS, 32.*

Pundareeka Vittala, K. R., Kiran Kumar, M., & Seranmadevi, R. (2024). *Artificial Intelligence-Internet of Things Integration for Smart Marketing: Challenges and Opportunities. Advancing Software Engineering Through AI, Federated Learning, and Large Language Models.* IGI Global. DOI:10.4018/979-8-3693-3502-4.ch019

PwC. (2023). *AI and the Future of Jobs.* PwC.

Radha, K., & Rohith, M. (2021). *An Experimental Analysis of Work-Life Balance Among The Employees using Machine Learning Classifiers.* arXiv preprint arXiv:2105.07837.

Rahman, M., & Islam, M. (2020). Industry 5.0 and Advanced Banking Solutions: A Comparative Study. *International Journal of Banking and Finance*, 17(1), 89–104. DOI:10.1002/ijbf.456

Rahman, M., & Islam, M. (2020). Promoting Financial Inclusion and Sustainability: Smart Banking Approaches with Cutting-Edge Technologies. *Sustainable Development Journal*, 17(1), 89–104. DOI:10.1002/sd.2036

Ramesh, S., & Das, S. (2022, January). Adoption of AI in talent acquisition: a conceptual framework. In *International Conference on Digital Technologies and Applications* (pp. 12-20). Cham: Springer International Publishing. DOI:10.1007/978-3-031-01942-5_2

Rangan, S. (2015). *Performance and Progress: Essays on Capitalism, Business, and Society.* OUP Oxford. DOI:10.1093/acprof:oso/9780198744283.001.0001

Ransbotham, S., Gerbert, P., Reeves, M., Kiron, D., & Spira, M. (2018). Artificial intelligence in business gets real. *MIT Sloan Management Review*.

Ransbotham, S., Kiron, D., Gerbert, P., & Reeves, M. (2017). Reshaping business with artificial intelligence. *MIT Sloan Management Review*, 59(1), 1–17.

Rees, W., & Wackernagel, M. (2013). The shoe fits, but the footprint is larger than Earth: Urban ecological footprints show that cities can be unsustainable. *Environment and Urbanization*, 25(2), 481–499.

Reis, J., Amorim, M., Melão, N., & Matos, P. (2018). Digital Transformation: A Literature Review and Guidelines for Future Research. *Advances in Intelligent Systems and Computing*, 745, 411–421. DOI:10.1007/978-3-319-77703-0_41

Ricci, M., Evangelista, A., Di Roma, A., & Fiorentino, M. (2023). Immersive and desktop virtual reality in virtual fashion stores: A comparison between shopping experiences. *Virtual Reality (Waltham Cross)*, 27(3), 1–16. DOI:10.1007/s10055-023-00806-y PMID:37360805

Rich, E., & Knight, K. (1991). *Introduction to artificial networks*. Mac Graw-Hill.

Rocha, M. F. (2018). The future of cities in the 21st century: Implications of urban energy use and greenhouse gas emissions. *Energy Procedia*, 147, 72–77.

Rong, L., Weibai, Z., & Debo, H. (2021) Sentiment Analysis of Ecommerce Product Review Data Based on Deep Learning. *2021 IEEE 4th Advanced Information Management, Communicates, Electronic and Automation Control Conference (IMCEC)*. IEEE. DOI:10.1109/IMCEC51613.2021.9482223

Russell, S. J., & Norvig, P. (2010). *Artificial intelligence: A modern approach. Nova Jersey, EUA*. PrenticeHall.

Saarikko, T., Westergren, U. H., & Blomquist, T. (2020). Digital transformation: Five recommendations for the digitally conscious firm. *Business Horizons*, 63(6), 825–839. DOI:10.1016/j.bushor.2020.07.005

Sai, G. H., Tripathi, K., & Tyagi, A. K. (2023). Internet of Things-Based e-Health Care: Key Challenges and Recommended Solutions for Future. In: Singh, P.K., Wierzchoń, S.T., Tanwar, S., Rodrigues, J.J.P.C., Ganzha, M. (eds) *Proceedings of Third International Conference on Computing, Communications, and Cyber-Security*. Springer, Singapore. DOI:10.1007/978-981-19-1142-2_37

Sai, G. H., Tyagi, A. K., & Sreenath, N. (2023). Biometric Security in Internet of Things Based System against Identity Theft Attacks. *2023 International Conference on Computer Communication and Informatics (ICCCI)*, Coimbatore, India. DOI:10.1109/ICCCI56745.2023.10128186

Sarkis, J., Cohen, M. J., Dewick, P., & Schröder, P. (2021). Artificial intelligence and supply chain sustainability: A systematic review and agenda for future research. *Computers & Industrial Engineering*, 152, 107057.

Sassen, S. (2019). Cities in a world of cities: The globalization of urban governance. Yale University Press.

Schalkoff, R. J. (1990). *Artificial intelligence engine*. Mac Graw-Hill.

Schrage, M., & Kiron, D. (2018). Leading with next-generation key performance indicators. *MIT Sloan Management Review*, 16.

Schwab, K. (2023). *Global Perspectives on AI and Labor*.

Schwab, K. (2017). *The Fourth Industrial Revolution*.

Seethamraju, R., & Hecimovic, A. (2022). Adoption of artificial intelligence in auditing: An exploratory study. *Australian Journal of Management*, 48(4), 031289622211084. DOI:10.1177/03128962221108440

Sembium, V., Rastogi, R., Tekumalla, L., & Saroop, A. (2018, April). Bayesian models for product size recommendations. In *Proceedings of the 2018 world wide web conference* (pp. 679-687). ACM. DOI:10.1145/3178876.3186149

Sestino, A., Prete, M. I., Piper, L., & Guido, G. (2020). Internet of Things and Big Data as enablers for business digitalization strategies. *Technovation*, 98, 102173. DOI:10.1016/j.technovation.2020.102173

Shah, D. (2023). *Understanding Work-Life Balance: An Analysis of Quiet Quitting and Age Dynamics using Deep Learning*.

Sharma, R., & Vishvakarma, A. (2019). Retrieving similar e-commerce images using deep learning. *arXiv preprint arXiv:1901.03546*.

Sharma, S., & Kumar, A. (2019). Advanced Banking Solutions for Industry 5.0: Challenges and Strategies. *Journal of Financial Technology*, 10(2), 145–160.

Sharma, S., & Kumar, A. (2019). Transforming Banking for Sustainability: Smart Banking Solutions with Cutting-Edge Technologies. *International Journal of Sustainable Banking*, 10(2), 145–160.

Sheikh, A. S., Guigourès, R., Koriagin, E., Ho, Y. K., Shirvany, R., Vollgraf, R., & Bergmann, U. (2019, September). A deep learning system for predicting size and fit in fashion e-commerce. In *Proceedings of the 13th ACM conference on recommender systems* (pp. 110-118). ACM. DOI:10.1145/3298689.3347006

Shih, Y. Y., & Fang, K. (2004). Using a decomposed theory of planned behavior to study Internet banking in Taiwan. *Internet Research*, 14(3), 213–223. DOI:10.1108/10662240410542643

Shim, J. K., & Rice, J. S. (1988). Expert Systems Applications To Managerial Accounting. *Journal of Systems Management*, 39(6).

Shreyas Madhav, A. V., Ilavarasi, A. K., & Tyagi, A. K. (2022). The Heroes and Villains of the Mix Zone: The Preservation and Leaking of USer's Privacy in Future Vehicles. In Arunachalam, V., & Sivasankaran, K. (Eds.), *Microelectronic Devices, Circuits and Systems. ICMDCS 2022. Communications in Computer and Information Science* (Vol. 1743). Springer. DOI:10.1007/978-3-031-23973-1_12

Shrikant Tiwari, R. (2024). Position of Blockchain: Internet of Things-Based Education 4.0 in Industry 5.0 – A Discussion of Issues and Challenges. Architecture and Technological Advancements of Education 4.0. IGI Global., DOI:10.4018/978-1-6684-9285-7.ch013

Shvaher, O. A., Degtyarev, S. I., & Polyakova, L. G. (2021). The effect of social media on financial literacy. *International Journal of Media and Information Literacy*, 6(1). Advance online publication. DOI:10.13187/ijmil.2021.1.211

Silver, D., Huang, A., Maddison, C. J., Guez, A., Sifre, L., Van Den Driessche, G., Schrittwieser, J., Antonoglou, I., Panneershelvam, V., Lanctot, M., Dieleman, S., Grewe, D., Nham, J., Kalchbrenner, N., Sutskever, I., Lillicrap, T., Leach, M., Kavukcuoglu, K., Graepel, T., & Hassabis, D. (2016). Mastering the game of go with deep neural networks and tree search. *Nature*, 529(7587), 484–489. DOI:10.1038/nature16961 PMID:26819042

Silver, D., Schrittwieser, J., Simonyan, K., Antonoglou, I., Huang, A., Guez, A., Hubert, T., Baker, L., Lai, M., Bolton, A., Chen, Y., Lillicrap, T., Hui, F., Sifre, L., van den Driessche, G., Graepel, T., & Hassabis, D. (2017). Mastering the game of Go without human knowledge. *Nature*, 550(7676), 354–359. DOI:10.1038/nature24270 PMID:29052630

Singh, S. (2024). *Generative AI: Accelerating Digital Transformation & Business Value. United States Artificial Intelligence Institute*. USAII. https://www.usaii.org/ai-insights/generative-ai-accelerating-digital-transformation-business-value

Singh, S., & Sarva, M. (2024). The Rise of Finfluencers: A Digital Transformation in Investment Advice. In *AABFJ, 18*(3).

Singh, N., Singh, P., & Gupta, M. (2020). An inclusive survey on machine learning for CRM: A paradigm shift. *Decision (Washington, D.C.)*, 47(4), 447–457. DOI:10.1007/s40622-020-00261-7

Singh, P., & Agrawal, R. (2022). Modelling and prediction of COVID-19 to measure the impact of lockdown on organisation in India. *International Journal of Indian Culture and Business Management*, 26(2), 259–275. DOI:10.1504/IJICBM.2022.123593

Sitthipon, T., Siripipatthanakul, S., Phayaprom, B., Siripipattanakul, S., & Limna, P. (2022). Determinants of Customers' Intention to Use Healthcare Chatbots and Apps in Bangkok, Thailand. In *International Journal of Behavioral Analytics, 2*(2). https://ssrn.com/abstract=4045661

Smink, A. R., Van Reijmersdal, E. A., Van Noort, G., & Neijens, P. C. (2020). Shopping in augmented reality: The effects of spatial presence, personalization and intrusiveness on app and brand responses. *Journal of Business Research*, 118, 474–485. DOI:10.1016/j.jbusres.2020.07.018

Smith, J., & Johnson, R. (2021). Industry 5.0 and Advanced Banking Solutions: A Perspective from the Financial Sector. *Journal of Financial Innovation*, 8(2), 145–160. DOI:10.1080/21657358.2021.1890456

Smith, J., & Johnson, R. (2021). Towards Sustainable Smart Banking: Integrating Cutting-Edge Technologies for a Green Financial World. *Journal of Sustainable Finance*, 8(2), 145–160. DOI:10.1080/20430795.2021.1890456

SnapLogic. (2024). *AI and Workplace Performance*. SnapLogic.

Socius. (2024). *Impact of AI on Job Displacement*. Socius.

Solomonoff, R. J. (1985). The time scale of artificial intelligence: Reflections on social effects. *Human Systems Management*, 5(2), 149–153. DOI:10.3233/HSM-1985-5207

Somisetti, K., Tripathi, K., & Verma, J. K. "Design, Implementation, and Controlling of a Humanoid Robot," *2020 International Conference on Computational Performance Evaluation (ComPE)*, 2020, pp. 831-836, DOI:10.1109/ComPE49325.2020.9200020

Song, Y., & Zegeye, A. (2017). Urbanization and the environment: An overview. In *The Urbanization and the Environment* (pp. 1-16). Springer.

Song, Y., Xue, Y., Li, C., Zhao, X., Liu, S., & Zhuo, X. (2017). *Online cost efficient-customer recognition system for retail analytics. in: 2017 IEEE Winter Applications of Computer Vision Workshops*. WACVW.

Srisathan, W. A., & Naruetharadhol, P. (2022). A COVID-19 disruption: The great acceleration of digitally planned and transformed behaviors in Thailand. *Technology in Society*. DOI:10.1016/j.techsoc.2022.101912

Srividya, M., Mohanavalli, S., & Bhalaji, N. (2018). Behavioral Modeling for Mental Health using Machine Learning Algorithms. *Journal of Medical Systems*, 42(88), 88. DOI:10.1007/s10916-018-0934-5 PMID:29610979

Stark, J. (2020) Digital Transformation Industry- Continiuing Change. Cham: Springer.Teichert Roman(2019). *Digital Transformation Maturity: A systematic Review of Literature*. Acta UniversitatisAgriculturae et Silviculturate Mendelianae Brunensis.

Stolper, O. A., & Walter, A. (2017). Financial literacy, financial advice, and financial behavior. *Journal of Business Economics*, 87(5), 581–643. DOI:10.1007/s11573-017-0853-9

Sun, T., & Vasarhelyi, M. A. (2017). Deep Learning and the Future of Auditing: How an Evolving Technology Could Transform Analysis and Improve Judgment. *The CPA Journal*, 87(6).

Svetlana, N. (2022). Artificial Intelligence as a Driver of Business Process Transformation. *Procedia Computer Science*, 276–284.

Tan, C., & Lim, H. (2019). Innovative Banking Solutions for Industry 5.0: Advanced Approaches and Strategies. *Journal of Financial Services Innovation*, 14(2), 178–193. DOI:10.1080/20430795.2019.1578311

Thandekkattu, S. G., & Kalaiarasi, M. (2022). Customer-Centric E-commerce Implementing Artificial Intelligence for Better Sales and Service. Reddy, A.B., Kiranmayee, B., Mukkamala, R.R., Srujan Raju, K. (eds) *Proceedings of Second International Conference on Advances in Computer Engineering and Communication Systems. Algorithms for Intelligent Systems.* Springer, Singapore. DOI:10.1007/978-981-16-7389-4_14

Tibshirani, R. (1996). Regression shrinkage and selection via the lasso. *Journal of the Royal Statistical Society. Series B, Statistical Methodology*, 58(1), 267–288. DOI:10.1111/j.2517-6161.1996.tb02080.x

Tomašev, N., Glorot, X., Rae, J. W., Zielinski, M., Askham, H., Saraiva, A., & Ravuri, S. (2019). A clinically applicable approach to continuous prediction of future acute kidney injury. *Nature*, 572(7767), 116–119. DOI:10.1038/s41586-019-1390-1 PMID:31367026

Tomberlin, J. (1990). *Action Theory and Philosophy of Mind*.

Tulumello, S., & Hernández-Molina, G. (2018). Smart cities as techno-social assemblages: A framework for understanding the rise of smart urbanism. *Frontiers in Sociology*, 3, 30.

Tümen, V. (2023). Predicting the Work-Life Balance of Employees Based on the Ensemble Learning Method. *Bitlis Eren Üniversitesi Fen Bilimleri Dergisi*, 12(2), 344–353. DOI:10.17798/bitlisfen.1196174

Tyagi, A. (2024). Engineering Applications of Blockchain in This Smart Era. *Enhancing Medical Imaging with Emerging Technologies*. IGI Global. DOI:10.4018/979-8-3693-5261-8.ch011

Tyagi, A. (2024). The Position of Digital Society, Healthcare 5.0, and Consumer 5.0 in the Era of Industry 5.0. Advancing Software Engineering Through AI, Federated Learning, and Large Language Models. IGI Global. DOI:10.4018/979-8-3693-3502-4.ch017

Tyagi, A. K. (Ed.). (2021). *Multimedia and Sensory Input for Augmented, Mixed, and Virtual Reality*. IGI Global. DOI:10.4018/978-1-7998-4703-8

Tyagi, A. K., Agarwal, D., & Sreenath, N. (2022). SecVT: Securing the Vehicles of Tomorrow using Blockchain Technology. *2022 International Conference on Computer Communication and Informatics (ICCCI)*, Coimbatore, India. DOI:10.1109/ICCCI54379.2022.9740965

Tyagi, A. K., & Sreenath, N. (2023). Security, Privacy, and Trust Issues in Intelligent Transportation System. In *Intelligent Transportation Systems: Theory and Practice. Disruptive Technologies and Digital Transformations for Society 5.0*. Springer. DOI:10.1007/978-981-19-7622-3_8

Tyagi, A., Kukreja, S., Nair, M. M., & Tyagi, A. K. (2022). Machine Learning: Past, Present and Future. *NeuroQuantology: An Interdisciplinary Journal of Neuroscience and Quantum Physics*, 20(8). DOI:10.14704/nq.2022.20.8.NQ44468

van Reijmersdal, E. A., & Hudders, L. (2023). How do you become a millionaire in three steps? An experimental study on the persuasive power of financial advice by finfluencers. *Tijdschrift voor Communicatiewetenschap*, 51(3). DOI:10.5117/TCW2023.3.004.REIJ

VanLehn, K. (2011). The Relative Effectiveness of Human Tutoring, Intelligent Tutoring Systems, and Other Tutoring Systems. *Educational Psychologist*, 46(4), 197–221. DOI:10.1080/00461520.2011.611369

Varsha, R., Nair, S. M., Tyagi, A. K., & Aswathy, S. U. (2021) The Future with Advanced Analytics: A Sequential Analysis of the Disruptive Technology's Scope. In: Abraham A., Hanne T., Castillo O., Gandhi N., Nogueira Rios T., Hong TP. (eds) *Hybrid Intelligent Systems*. Springer, Cham. DOI:10.1007/978-3-030-73050-5_56

Vedapradha, R., Hariharan, R., Praveenraj, D. D. W., Sudha, E., & Ashok, J. (2023). Talent acquisition-artificial intelligence to manage recruitment. In *E3S Web of Conferences* (Vol. 376, p. 05001). EDP Sciences.

Venkatraman, V. (2017). *The digital matrix: New rules for business transformation through technology*. EUA: LifeTree Media Ltd.

Verhoef, P. C., Broekhuizen, T., Bart, V., Bhattacharya, A., Qi Dong, J., Fabian, N., & Haenlein, M. (2021). Digital transformation: A multidisciplinary reflection and research agenda. *Journal of Business Research*, 122, 889–901. DOI:10.1016/j.jbusres.2019.09.022

Vishnuram, G., Tripathi, K., & Kumar Tyagi, A. (2022). Ethical Hacking: Importance, Controversies and Scope in the Future. *2022 International Conference on Computer Communication and Informatics (ICCCI)*. IEEE. DOI:10.1109/ICC-CI54379.2022.9740860

Vivek, K., Radhakrishnan, R., Sandeep, S., & Ramesh, M. (2022). Credit card fraud detection using machine learning algorithms. *Journal of Financial Crime*, 29(4), 1247–1262. DOI:10.1108/JFC-03-2022-0048

Voicu, M. C., Sîrghi, N., & Toth, D. M. M. (2023). Consumers' experience and satisfaction using augmented reality apps in E-shopping: New empirical evidence. *Applied Sciences (Basel, Switzerland)*, 13(17), 9596. DOI:10.3390/app13179596

Vu, V. C., Keating, B., & Wang, S. (n.d.). *Association for Information Systems Association for Information Systems #finfluencers: Understanding the Role of Parasocial Relationships #finfluencers: Understanding the Role of Parasocial Relationships and Psychological Need Support and Psychological Need Support*. AISEL. https://aisel.aisnet.org/acis2022

Wagner, J. (2019). Financial education and financial literacy by income and education groups. *Financial Counseling and Planning*, 30(1), 132–141. DOI:10.1891/1052-3073.30.1.132

Walsh, G., & Schaarschmidt, M. (2023). *Taking Advantage of Algorithmic Preference to Reduce Product Returns in E-Commerce*. AISEL. https://aisel.aisnet.org/icis2023/emobilecomm/emobilecomm/3

Wang, H., Huang, J., & Zhang, Z. (2019). *The impact of deep learning on organizational agility*. In *proceedings of the 40th International Conference on Information Systems (ICIS)*, Munich, Germany

Wang, Y., & Li, W. (2021). Industry 5.0 and the Future of Banking: Advanced Solutions for Sustainable Finance. *International Journal of Sustainable Finance*, 12(2), 189–204. DOI:10.1080/20430795.2020.1857290

Weinstein, B. G. (2018). A computer vision for animal ecology. *Journal of Animal Ecology*, 87(3), 533–545. DOI:10.1111/1365-2656.12780 PMID:29111567

WHO. (2019). *Burn Out an 'Occupational Phenomenon.'* World Health Organization. https://www.who.int/news/item/28-05-2019-burn-out-an-occupational-phenomenon -international-classification-of-diseases

Wilson, H. J., & Daugherty, P. R. (2018). Collaborative intelligence: Humans and AI are joining forces. *Harvard Business Review*, 96(4), 114–123.

Winston, P. H. (1970). *Learning structural descriptions from examples*. Massachusetts Institute of Technology.

Wise, L. (2022). *10 Companies With the Best Mental Health Suport.* Business Because. https://www.businessbecause.com/news/masters-in-management/8466/best -companies-mental-health-support

Wolpert, D. H. (1992). Stacked generalization. *Neural Networks*, 5(2), 241–259. DOI:10.1016/S0893-6080(05)80023-1 PMID:18276425

Wong, L., & Tan, K. (2020). Advanced Banking Solutions for Industry 5.0: A Perspective from the Banking Sector. *Journal of Financial Services Innovation*, 15(2), 189–204.

Wong, L., & Tan, K. (2020). Towards a Green Financial World: Smart Banking Strategies with Cutting-Edge Technologies. *Journal of Sustainable Finance and Banking*, 15(2), 189–204.

Wooldridge, M. (2021). *A brief history of artificial intelligence: what it is, where we are, and where we are going*. Flatiron Books.

World Economic Forum. (2015). *Deep Shift: Technology Tipping Points and Social Impact*. WEF. at:http://www3.weforum.org/docs/ WEF_GAC15_Technological_ Tipping_ Points_ report_2015.pdf

World Economic Forum. (2022). *How digital tech can turbo-charge the social economy*. WEF. https://www.weforum.org/agenda/2022/05/ how-digital-tech-turbo- charge-social-enterprises/

Wube, H. D., Esubalew, S. Z., Weldesellasie, F. F., & Debelee, T. G. (2022). Text- Based Chatbot in Financial Sector: A Systematic Literature Review. *Data Science in Finance and Economics*, 2(3), 232–259. DOI:10.3934/DSFE.2022011

Xu, X. Y., Jia, Q. D., & Tayyab, S. M. U. (2024). Exploring the stimulating role of augmented reality features in E- commerce: A three-staged hybrid approach. *Journal of Retailing and Consumer Services*, 77, 103682. DOI:10.1016/j.jretcon- ser.2023.103682

Yang, C., & Liu, Z. (2021, August). Application of computer vision in electronic commerce. In *Journal of Physics: Conference Series* (*Vol. 1992*, No. 2, p. 022134). IOP Publishing. DOI:10.1088/1742-6596/1992/2/022134

Zhang, C., Li, S., Xia, J., Wang, W., Yan, F., & Liu, Y. (2023). Privacy-preserving federated learning for financial data security. *Journal of Financial Data Science*, 10(2), 120–135. DOI:10.1016/j.jfds.2023.04.007

Zhang, H., & Li, J. (2021). Industry 5.0 and Advanced Banking Solutions: Using Cutting-Edge Technologies. *Journal of Financial Technology*, 7(2), 156–171. DOI:10.1016/j.jft.2020.102456

Zhang, H., & Li, J. (2021). Smart Banking for a Sustainable Future: Using Cutting-Edge Technologies for Financial Resilience. *Journal of Sustainable Financial Innovation*, 7(2), 156–171.

Zhang, H., & Zhou, Z. (2004). *MLDM 2004: Advances in data mining*. Springer.

Zhuang, Y. T., Wu, F., Chen, C., & Pan, Y. H. (2017). Challenges and opportunities: From big data to knowledge in AI 2.0. *Frontiers of Information Technology & Electronic Engineering*, 18(1), 3–14. DOI:10.1631/FITEE.1601883

About the Contributors

S. Balaji is working as an associate professor in the Department of Information Technology at Al Zahra College for Women, Sultanate of Oman. He had completed his PhD program in Software Engineering. Pursuing a Post-Doctoral Fellowship program at Srinivas University, Mangalore. He had completed an MCA and an M.Phil. He has over 18 years of experience in the teaching profession. He specializes in the fields of software engineering and project documentation. His research interests are in the areas of Software Engineering, Cyber Security and AI.

Padmalosani Dayalan is a distinguished faculty member in the Department of Business Studies at the University of Technology and Applied Sciences, Ibra. With a robust academic background and more than 18 years of teaching experience. She holds an MBA in Finance, an M.Com, an M.Phil., and has completed her Ph.D. in management.. She has an extensive teaching background, and a well-established research portfolio in the field of business studies. Her specialization in accounting and finance, coupled with her research in corporate finance, international investment, and blended learning, positions her as a respected and influential figure in academia. She is deeply interested in the role of artificial intelligence in management. Her passion for education, combined with her hard work and dedication, drives her ongoing pursuit of excellence in the academic and business communities.

***

Santosh Reddy Addula, a Senior Member of the IEEE, holds a Master of Science in Information Technology from the University of the Cumberlands in Kentucky, USA. With extensive experience in the IT industry, he has demonstrated expertise across multiple domains. Santosh is an innovator with a strong portfolio of patents and has significantly contributed to academic research through his articles as an author and co-author. Additionally, he serves as a reviewer for esteemed journals, reflecting his dedication to advancing knowledge and ensuring the quality of scholarly publications in his field.

Senthil Kumar Arumugam is a Professor in the School of Commerce at Presidency University, Bengaluru, India. His areas of specialization include Finance, Accounting, Marketing, Computer Applications in Business, and Research Methodology. He earned a PhD in Commerce from Bharathiar University, India, in 2014, and holds an M.Phil in Commerce, an M.Phil in Computer Science, a Master of Computer Applications, and a Master of Commerce. He has 23 years of experience in teaching, research, and administration in the fields of Commerce and Computer Applications. He is the author of 65 research articles, 11 edited books, and 18 book chapters. In 2021, he received the "International Excellence Award for Research Publications in Digital and Finance Domain" from CIMA.

Amit Kumar Tyagi is an Assistant Professor at the National Institute of Fashion Technology, New Delhi, India. Previously, he has worked as Assistant Professor (Senior Grade 2), and Senior Researcher at Vellore Institute of Technology (VIT), Chennai Campus, 600127, Chennai, Tamilnadu, India (for the period of 2019-2022). He received his Ph.D. Degree (Full-Time) in 2018 from Pondicherry Central University, 605014, Puducherry, India. About his academic experience, he joined as assistant professor at Lord Krishna College of Engineering, Ghaziabad (LKCE) (for the periods of 2009-2010, and 2012-2013. He was an Assistant Professor and Head- Research, Lingaya's Vidyapeeth (formerly known as Lingaya's University), Faridabad, Haryana, India (for the period of 2018-2019).

Sharmila Chidaravalli is currently working as Assistant Professor, Department of Information Science and Engineering at Global Academy of Technology Bengaluru; also research scholar pursuing my PhD at Visveswaraya Technological University, Belgaum.I have 16 years of Teaching Experience.Topic of interest includes Computer Vision, Artificial Intelligence,Machine Learning,Deep Learning.

Annie Isaac is a distinguished academic and researcher with a robust background in finance and education. She earned her Master of Commerce (M.Com) degree with a specialization in Accounting and Taxation from Kristu Jayanti College, Bengaluru, from 2016-2018. Further advancing her expertise in education, she completed her Bachelor of Education (B.Ed) from Christ College, Bhopal. Annie has significant experience in academia, having worked as an Assistant Professor, where she contributed to her students' academic growth and professional development. Her commitment to education and research has been evident throughout her career. Annie Isaac is pursuing her Ph.D. in Finance at Christ (Deemed to be University), Bengaluru. Her research focuses on various facets of finance, aiming to contribute new insights and advancements. Her academic journey and professional experiences highlight her dedication to finance and education, making her a valuable member of the educational community.

Revenio C. Jalagat, Jr. is presently employed in Al-Zahra College for Women in the Sultanate of Oman since 2013 and as Associate Professor in 2023. He had a total accumulated experience of 20 years in both the industry serving as Accountant, Chief Accountant, Finance Manager, and in the Academe as Lecturer, Assistant Professor and Dean in the Philippines. Dr. Jalagat was also a lecturer at Gulf College in Oman for almost two and a half years. He is a Certified Public Accountant (CPA) in the Philippines and graduated Doctor of Management at Capitol University, Philippines. He has received various awards such as Best Researcher, Outstanding Philippine Awardee, and has published research in international reputed journals, including Scopus and Web of Science indexed journals, and served as Reviewer and Editorial Member in various international journals.

K. R. Pundareeka Vittala, Professor at ICFAI Business School Bengaluru,, has a prolific research portfolio with over two decades in academia. He has published 40 research papers in journals indexed in WOS, ABDC, Scopus, and UGC Care. His research focuses on AI solutions to Finance Sector, risk management, currency derivatives, data localization's impact on GDP, and econometrics. He has supervised numerous Ph.D. scholars and is involved in funded projects. Dr. Vittala has served as a resource person for workshops, FDPs, and academic conferences, delivering keynote speeches and chairing sessions.

Yashodhan Karulkar is a seasoned marketing professional with a robust career spanning over two decades in both the academic and corporate sectors. Since September 2016, he has been serving as a full-time faculty member at NMIMS University, where he plays a pivotal role in shaping the future of MBA Tech students. As the Area Chair for Marketing, Dr. Karulkar also mentors the Marketing Club, named 4C, actively engaging students in real-world marketing challenges. His corporate experience includes nearly 20 years in leadership roles with some of the most prominent companies in India, such as Birla Sun Life, Max New York Life, Standard Chartered Bank, Airtel and Wipro. Dr. Karulkar's expertise spans the entire marketing spectrum, including Product Management, Sales and Distribution, Relationship Management, Customer Service, and Business Development. He has managed large Pan-India sales teams, leading over 300 employees to successfully achieve critical business and profitability goals.

Kiran Kumar M is an Assistant Professor-Faculty of Finance at CMS Business School, Jain (Deemed-to-be university). He holds a Ph.D. from Annamalai University, Chidambaram, with a thesis titled "A Study on Tourist Awareness and Perception towards Eco-tourism in Karnataka." Additionally, he has completed a certification course-Diploma in Personal Counselling from Banjara Academy,

Bengaluru. With 8 years of teaching experience and 4 years of research experience, Dr. Kiran Kumar M has actively contributed to various aspects of education. He has been involved in areas such as placements, cultural activities, and has served as a coordinator for organizing Faculty Development Programs (FDP), Faculty Improvement Programs (FIP), and Management Development Programs (MDP). Dr. Kiran Kumar M has presented and published papers in numerous national and international conferences and seminars. His works have been featured in Scopus and UGC A Care listed publications. Additionally, he has co-authored three textbooks for undergraduate programs. Apart from his dedication to teaching, Dr. Kiran Kumar M has a keen interest in social activities, volunteering services, and career and personal counseling.

Shabnam Kumari is working as a Ph.D scholar in the Department of Computer Science, SRM Institute of Science and Technology, Chennai, Tamilnadu, India. She has more than 3 years of experience including teaching, research and other areas. She has completed her MCA from YMCA University of Science and Technology, Faridabad. She has filled more than five National and International patent in the area of IoTs, Machine Learning, Deep Learning and Wireless Network. She had published 03 research articles in International Conferences and Journals. Her areas of interests are Machine Learning, Deep Learning, etc. She is a life time member of ACM- Women, SCRS.

Chidambaram N, Professor, Department of BBA, School of Business and Management, CHRIST (Deemed to be University), Lavasa, Pune. His area of specialization is Finance and Higher Control. He has 25 years of teaching experience including domestic as well as international. At present heading the Office of Strategic Planning, CUL. He is the author of several research articles and presented research papers in various platforms. His research interest lies on Behavioral Finance, Stock Market Operations, Investments, Banking and Insurance. Further he is a Member, Board of Studies for several academic institutions.

Rishab Naik is a dedicated professional currently pursuing an MBA Tech program at SVKM NMIMS Mukesh Patel School of Technology Management and Engineering, Mumbai. He specializes in Mechanical Engineering, with a focus on Finance and Business Intelligence & Analytics for his MBA Tech. Additionally, he has earned Honours in Data Analytics and Machine Learning. With a strong foundation in both technology and business, Rishab brings a unique blend of expertise to the fields of finance and technology. He has a keen interest in financial markets and technological advancements.

V M Nisha has a vast experience in Theoretical computer science and has about 12 years of teaching and research experience. She is currently working as Associate Professor at VIT University, Chennai. She has published many quality research papers in SCI indexed journals based on the field of Theoretical computer science and AI and also published papers in in various SCOPUS indexed journals. Her major areas of research is Theoretical computer science, Machine Learning, AI and Data Science.

Seranmadevi R. has a Doctorate in Management and 24 years of rich experience in both industry and Academia, presently working for Christ University, Bangalore, qualified with MBA., M.Com., MCA., M.Phil., Ph.D., and UGC-NET for Management and UGC-NET/JRF – Commerce, recognized with 3 remarkable patents, having the citation index of 176, H index of 7, and publication track of 16 Scopus Indexed journals, 2 WoS journals, 21 UGC Care listed, 7 edited volume Research Books and 10 international and 11 peer-reviewed national journals, and granted the NPTEL Discipline Star Award, 2020, NPTEL Believer Award, 2021, NPTEL Enthusiast Award, 2021, and NPTEL Marketing Domain Star Award, 2022 as a recognition of a continuous learning and upskilling the recent trends like Business Modelling, Business Analytics and AI, ML, BCT and IoT in Business. She has presented papers in 46 international and 35 national level seminars and booked many Best Paper awards, and is trusted as a promising Resource person in different disciplines like exploring knowledge in Research framework, Statistical tools applications in Social Science Research, Digital Marketing, Emerging Technology Trends, etc attended 30 FDP to enrich knowledge and adjudicated four Ph.D. thesis for Bharathiyar University, Coimbatore. Currently working on the internal project work entitled "Civics view on Synergy and Trade-off effect of Sustainable Development Goals in Bangalore". Extending academic services as a Board of Study member, Chairing the international conference, Editorial committee member of a few journals, and resource person for the DEP program of Anna University for both MBA and MCA and other regional universities.

Vimuktha E Salis currently working has Professor, Department of Information Science and Engineering at Global Academy of Technology Bengaluru, also research guide at Visveswaraya Technological University, Belgaum.Has total 14 years of Experience in both Industry and Academics. Topic of interest includes Computer Vision, Artificial Intelligence,Machine Learning,Deep Learning.

Arshi Shah is a dedicated professional who is pursuing her MBA Tech program at SVKM's NMIMS Mukesh Patel School of Technology Management and Engineering, Mumbai, specializing in Electronics and Telecommunication for her B.Tech as well as Finance and Business Intelligence and Analytics for her MBA Tech. With a strong foundation in both technology and business, she brings a unique blend of expertise to the fields of finance and technology. Arshi has a keen interest in research and analytics, demonstrated through her work on research projects.

Pushpa Singh is an Associate Professor of CSE Department at the GL Bajaj Institute of Technology & Management, Greater Noida, India. She has more than 18+ years of experience teaching B.Tech and MCA students. Dr. Singh has acquired MCA, M.Tech (CSE), and Ph.D. (CSE) in Wireless Networks from AKTU Lucknow. Her current areas of research include performance evaluation of heterogeneous wireless networks, machine learning, Blockchain and cryptography. She has published 55 research publications in reputed international journals, conference and edited book. She has published four books and contributed six book chapters in international publication. She is one of active reviewers of IGI, Springer, and other conference proceedings and journals. She has been invited to serve on various technical program committees.

Shrikant Tiwari (Senior Member, IEEE) received his Ph.D. in the Department of Computer Science & Engineering (CSE) from the Indian Institute of Technology (Banaras Hindu University), Varanasi (India) in 2012 and M. Tech. in Computer Science and Technology from University of Mysore (India) in 2009. Currently, he is working as an Associate Professor in the Department of Computer Science & Engineering (CSE) School of Computing Science and Engineering (SCSE) at Galgotias University, Greater Noida, Uttar Pradesh (India). He has authored or co-authored more than 75 national and international journal publications, book chapters, and conference articles. He has five patents filed to his credit. His research interests include machine learning, deep learning, computer vision, medical image analysis, pattern recognition, and biometrics. Dr. Tiwari is a member of ACM, IET. He is also a guest editorial board member and a reviewer for many international journals of repute.

Deepshika Vijayanand is a Computer Science Engineering graduate from Vellore Institute of Technology, Chennai. She has conducted significant research, with publications and presentations on Data Analytics, Artificial Intelligence, Natural Language Processing and Machine Learning. Deepshika has completed several internships, gaining expertise in Artificial Intelligence and Data Analytics, and holds multiple certifications from institutions such as AWS, Google and Cisco. She has also actively contributed to society through volunteering and held various leadership roles in student organizations.

Index

102, 103, 104, 105, 106, 108, 110,
111, 113, 143, 155, 168, 169, 205,
209, 211, 215, 219, 220, 221, 222,
259, 261, 270, 280, 281, 287, 288, 303

S

Scalability 9, 10, 44, 63, 75, 85, 88, 120,
261, 301, 302, 304, 306, 308, 309,
311, 326, 328
Scatter Plots 304, 306, 307, 310, 311
Smart Era 24, 210, 212
Smart Financial services 203, 204, 205,
206, 214, 215, 216, 217, 223
stacking ensemble 314, 315, 329, 330,
332, 333
Sustainable Banking 73, 74, 91, 92, 93, 224
Sustainable environment 247, 272

T

Technology 1, 4, 6, 8, 9, 12, 13, 14, 15,
16, 20, 23, 24, 25, 30, 31, 34, 35, 39,
40, 43, 44, 45, 46, 47, 48, 50, 54, 56,
59, 62, 63, 65, 69, 71, 73, 75, 77, 80,
82, 84, 85, 87, 88, 90, 91, 95, 96, 97,
100, 101, 103, 104, 105, 106, 109,
111, 114, 115, 117, 119, 120, 121,
129, 131, 132, 133, 137, 138, 139,
140, 141, 143, 144, 146, 147, 148,
149, 150, 151, 152, 153, 154, 155,
156, 160, 161, 162, 163, 168, 169,
170, 172, 173, 174, 178, 179, 180,
181, 182, 183, 184, 185, 187, 189,
193, 198, 199, 200, 203, 204, 205,
207, 208, 209, 213, 214, 215, 216,
217, 219, 221, 222, 223, 224, 228,
229, 230, 231, 232, 244, 247, 250,
251, 252, 254, 256, 257, 259, 260,
261, 262, 265, 267, 270, 271, 273,
274, 275, 276, 277, 278, 280, 282, 285,
291, 293, 294, 300, 301, 305, 312, 313
transformation 6, 10, 14, 44, 45, 46, 53,
54, 63, 68, 69, 70, 71, 72, 73, 76, 88,
89, 90, 91, 99, 100, 107, 108, 113,
114, 132, 137, 138, 139, 141, 142,
143, 144, 145, 146, 147, 148, 149,
150, 151, 153, 154, 155, 156, 157,
158, 187, 189, 200, 207, 216, 217,
244, 271, 277, 278, 292

W

Workforce Dynamics 277, 278, 279
work-life balance 313, 314, 315, 316, 317,
325, 329, 330, 331, 332, 333, 334,
335, 336

Printed in the United States
by Baker & Taylor Publisher Services

Printed in the United States
by Baker & Taylor Publisher Services